Brigham Young The Colonizer

Brigham Young The Colonizer

By Milton R. Hunter, Ph.D.

➜ Peregrine Smith, Inc.

SANTA BARBARA AND SALT LAKE CITY 1973

The courtesy of the following sources in supplying photographs is greatly appreciated.

THE UTAH STATE HISTORICAL SOCIETY — 78, 88, 186, 187, 211, 302, 356, inside back cover

ARCHIVES, CHURCH OF JESUS CHRIST OF LATTER-DAY SAINTS — 148, 149, 232, 289, 372, 375, inside front cover

INDEX OF AMERICAN DESIGN, NATIONAL GALLERY OF ART, WASHINGTON, D.C. — 176 (3)

UNION PACIFIC RAILROAD — 223, 303

SALT LAKE CITY CHAMBER OF COMMERCE — 222

Fourth Edition, Revised

Manufactured in the United States of America

ISBN: 0-87905-017-9
Library of Congress Catalog Card Number: 73-85421

Cover and Jacket Design: Keith Eddington & Associates

PREFACE TO 1973 EDITION

While I was working at the University of California under Dr. Herbert E. Bolton, chairman of the history department and one of the world's outstanding historians, he suggested that one of the great fields in Western History that had hardly been touched by historians was the story of Mormon colonization of the West. He pointed out that if I would go through the massive collection of manuscript materials in the archives of the L.D.S. Church and those in the Bancroft Library, I could write a doctoral dissertation which when published could be of inestimable value to historians and those interested in American expansion westward. I suggested that since Brigham Young was the leader of the Mormon movement the study might be called *Brigham Young the Colonizer.*

Shortly thereafter in conversation with Dr. Frederic L. Paxson he told me that Dr. Bolton had informed him that I was going to write my doctor's thesis on Mormon colonization. He suggested that if I desired to make a name for myself among historians I should select some big national problem.

I contacted Dr. Bolton and reported Dr. Paxson's opinion. Dr. Bolton replied that Dr. Paxson was one of the world's great historians but he hadn't worked very extensively in the field of Mormon history. He suggested that I continue with that subject, and by the time my study was published Dr. Paxson and other historians would come to realize the great part played by the Mormons in the opening of the western part of our country to land settlement.

After I gave my first two-hour seminar report on Mormon colonization in Dr. Paxson's class, he inquired where I got so much material on Mormon history in the Great Basin. He suggested that he now realized that I had a very important subject in American history and I should continue my research in that field.

Two or three years after completing my doctor's thesis on *Brigham Young the Colonizer* I took it to Salt Lake City and asked Dr. John A. Widtsoe, the L.D.S. Church Commissioner of Education and past president of two major universities, what should be done with it. After reading the manuscript Dr. Widtsoe reported to me that *Brigham Young the Colonizer* should definitely be published. Thus in 1940, 1941, and 1945 editions came from the press.

Since the book has been out of print for some time, there have been numerous requests from universities, historians, librarians, church members, and others for a new printing. Dr. Ray Allen Billington, today's outstanding authority in the field of Western History, has graciously written the foreword for the revised 1973 edition of *Brigham Young the Colonizer.*

MILTON R. HUNTER
Salt Lake City, Utah
1973

PREFACE TO 1940 EDITION

Although Brigham Young is looked upon by historians as one of the greatest American colonizers, no one, as far as the writer knows, has heretofore published an extended account of his colonizing methods. The present study discusses these methods and the achievements of his people in the settlement of an expansive territory in the Great West. The material is presented in topic form. In order to insure accuracy and thoroughness, manuscript material has been used almost exclusively in the preparation of this book.

The first half of the study stresses the personnel of Mormon colonization, methods of land settlement, and industries founded, and the latter portion gives an account of the actual settling of the various valleys in the Far West. Comparatively little space has been given to such valleys as Salt Lake and Weber, as numerous accounts of their colonization have been published heretofore. More particular attention has been paid to the land settlement of Utah Valley and some of the valleys inhabited by the Saints shortly thereafter, which furnished excellent type examples of directed Mormon colonization. Valleys settled between 1847 and 1857 are discussed rather fully, with special emphasis on the original colony. Those settled between 1857 and 1877 are briefly summarized.

At various places in the book, mention is made of the motivating force back of Mormon colonization—the sincere and impelling faith in the Church of Jesus Christ of Latter-day Saints.

The writer expresses gratitude to Dr. Herbert E. Bolton, chairman of the history department of the University of California, for the many suggestions given during the preparation of the manuscript. Also, appreciation is expressed to Dr. John A. Widtsoe for the encouragement and kindly suggestions given the writer and for helping to make possible the publication of this volume. Special acknowledgment is also made to the staff of the Bancroft Library and to Apostle Joseph Fielding Smith, Andrew Jenson, A. William Lund, and Alvin Smith, who have been so courteous and gracious in allowing the writer unlimited access to the manuscript material in the Church archives in Salt Lake City. Deep appreciation is also expressed to Ferne G. Hunter who has given very valuable help throughout the entire preparation of the book.

MILTON R. HUNTER.

Logan, Utah
November 16, 1940.

FOREWORD TO 1973 EDITION

When a publisher elects to reprint a standard work that has been so long unavailable that its price has soared beyond the reach of students and libraries (as much as $40 for this book), he deserves the plaudits of the entire historical profession. When the monograph that he restores to circulation is a classic that cannot only be still read with profit but remains the last word on its subject, the profession is even more grateful. These are the reasons that make the re-issue of Dr. Milton R. Hunter's definitive study of Utah colonization under Brigham Young an event of major importance in Mormon historiography. For here is a book as essential to the study of the Great Basin as it was when it first saw the light of day in 1940.

That the volume has endured the test of time for nearly thirty-five years is tribute to Dr. Hunter's meticulous scholarship. Prepared originally as a doctoral dissertation at the University of California under the able direction of Professor Herbert Eugene Bolton, and carefully revised before publication, it was based on a reading of manuscript collections so terrifyingly voluminous as to repel the usual researcher: the Latter-day Saint Journal History, files of letters and journals in the priceless collections of the Church Historian's Office, unpublished records of Stakes and Wards, mission transcript histories, documents in Berkeley's Bancroft Library of Western Americana, others wherever they could be found. Every scrap of evidence bearing on the early colonization of Utah, seemingly, was unearthed and used effectively.

The result was a book that said the last word on the subject so authoritatively that scholars since that time have made almost no attempt to investigate the spread of population in the Great Basin. This is the more remarkable in that Mormonism has become, during the past dozen years, a fruitful field for research by both Mormon and non-Mormon historians. Their findings have shed new light on any number of topics. Thomas F. O'Dea and Lowry Nelson have contributed invaluable sociological studies of the Mormon community and the Mormon village. Leonard Arrington.has opened a whole new field for investigation in his studies of economic institutions. Wallace Stegner has retold the story of migration to the Great Basin in works that are both readable and scholarly. Philip A. M. Taylor and William Mulder have explored the gathering of Saints from beyond the seas. Objective studies of the conflict between Mormons and outsiders have been written by Robert B. Flanders, Juanita Brooks, and Norman F. Furniss, while Gustive O.

Larson has dealt understandingly with the later stages of that confrontation. These works—and others like them—have revised whole pages in the history of Mormonism, but one page has needed no revision. Milton R. Hunter's book stands today as authoritative and useful as it was on the day of publication.

Its author has not been content to rest on this one triumph. His lifetime purpose was clear when he left Berkeley with his doctoral degree in 1935; he would dedicate himself to the people of Utah who had endowed him with his ideals and his faith. His University of California master, Professor Bolton, might sputter that such a well-trained young historian could better spend his time in a university than wasting his skills on young Mormon people in an obscure Utah village, but Dr. Hunter was to prove him wrong. The scholarly career that Professor Bolton envisaged for him has been magnificently achieved; over the years he has produced a parade of well-read books: *The Mormons and the American Frontier* (1940), *Utah in Her Western Setting* (1944), *Utah: The Story of Her People* (1946), *Utah: A Centennial History* (1949), *The Utah Story* (1960), and many more in both history and religion. He has also contributed significantly to the educational development of the Mormon people, first as teacher and administrator, then after 1945 as a member of the First Council of Seventy of the Church of Jesus Christ of Latter-day Saints where he has helped administer the religious, social, and educational programs of 625 regional church organizations in the United States and more than 107 missions.

The republication of this book pays tribute, in part, to Dr. Hunter's selfless service to his people and his faith. No less important, it is a recognition of the fact that sound scholarship, admirably presented, is never outdated. *Brigham Young the Colonizer* will benefit the next generation of American historians as much as it did the last.

RAY ALLEN BILLINGTON
The Huntington Library
1973

FOREWORD

The acquisition and settlement of the Trans-Mississippi West was a major phase of the development of the United States in the nineteenth century. In the historic achievement two men stand head and shoulders above all the rest as colonizers. They are, of course, Stephen F. Austin, the guiding hand in the making of Anglo-American Texas, and Brigham Young, the founder of Utah and the moulder of Mormon institutions.

One common feature in the experience of these two Giants of the West is conspicuous. Each led a colony of emigrants from the United States into Mexican territory, and each thereby unintentionally contributed to the conquest of large portions of Mexico's patrimony. Austin settled his people in Texas in a spirit of complete loyalty to his adopted fatherland, and then through the force of events he reluctantly became a factor in the revolution that separated Texas from the parent nation. Brigham Young, driven with his people from the United States by an intolerance that is now a cause for deep mortification, prepared to seek asylum beyond the Rocky Mountains, in a wilderness which then belonged to the Republic of Mexico. But before the Mormon exodus was well under way, the migration became, through the force of circumstances, part of a movement by which the area chosen as a refuge was, like Texas, incorporated into the United States.

Much has been written about Brigham Young as head of the Church of Jesus Christ of Latter-day Saints, and to the general public he is best known in that capacity. But he is equally deserving of fame as colonizer of the West. Without his dauntless spirit, his genius for organization, his flair for practical affairs, and his dominating personality he could not have held his people together, attracted new thousands of converts from Europe, inspired them with the courage necessary to undergo the hardships of pioneer life, and provided the economic basis necessary to sustain them in a most difficult and remote frontier.

To show how Brother Brigham accomplished this Herculean feat was the task which Dr. Hunter set for himself and has admirably accomplished in the writing of this book. Through access to boundless historical materials, long and painstaking research, and affectionate care, he has turned a flood of light on the process by which President Young supervised the recruiting of Mormon adherents in the Old World, assisted them in their migration to the New, personally directed the founding of cooperative settlements throughout the Inter-Mountain Basin, and in the process shaped a set of political, social, and economic institutions which were and to a great extent still are peculiar to the Mormons. Joseph Smith founded the Mormon Church. Brigham Young made it a notably successful working organization.

Among the most interesting chapters of this book is the one which tells how Brigham Young opened a Mormon Corridor to the Pacific Ocean by founding a line of colonies all the way from Salt Lake City to Southern California, as a means of providing an all-sea route from the outside world to the New Zion.

HERBERT E. BOLTON.

University of California,
Berkeley, California.

FOREWORD

The colonization of the Great Basin of North America and adjacent country has become an American historical epic. Students, investigators and writers, in almost every field, have borrowed material from this gripping story of man's conquest over nature. Many lands have used lessons from the Mormon pioneers in their own economic and social ventures. In the midst of our present chaos, thinking Americans are turning to the experiences of Brigham Young and his pioneers for light and help.

It was indeed an epoch-making adventure to invade the inhospitable Great American Desert, and to tame it to man's needs. The pioneers—men, women and children—toiled and suffered, but they won! They made no compromise with ease or luxury. The soil was stubborn and dry; the streams ran in age-old courses; but the pioneers knew that mastery lay with them if they would only persist with courage in the use of their intelligence and knowledge. And should they, themselves, fail to enjoy victory, they knew that generations to come would call them blessed. They sang with a will, "And should we die, before our journey's through, all is well."

As the work progressed, men from afar stood by: "So, it can be done!" they said, and took courage for their own tasks. Thus it happens that out of the colonization experiment of the Latter-day Saints, in the heart of the arid and semi-arid country, have come many of the principles and practices, social, economic and spiritual, that have reclaimed for human welfare the two-fifths of continental United States that lie under a low rainfall. Well may we praise these pioneers of pioneers.

But, how did they do the work? What principles guided their practices? These are the constant questions of all who thrill to see the ancient desert "blossom as the rose," and who enjoy a mighty civilization where sober men declared that man could not live. The answer has never been given quite so well and fully as in this volume. A glance at the table of contents is enlightening. Dr. Hunter has brought together a huge collection of facts, organized and placed in such historical sequence as to emphasize the dominant principles employed by the pioneers. The faith that their cause was of God, and that man had been given sufficient power over the elements to subdue the earth, gave life to their every project and enterprise. It was in the spirit of faith, a living faith, that the different principles that appear in these chapters were called into action. Faith always conquers.

While the book is called *Brigham Young the Colonizer*, it is really the story of the brave people who, under Brigham Young, built an empire in the dreary sagebrush valleys. The mantle of leadership was upon many of the pioneers, perhaps all of them— but they toiled together and supported one another and sustained their chief leader. Such leaders, willing to be led, are great leaders; their works live after them; they are needed today.

This book is entertaining, instructive and inspiring. It is particularly a book for the times. We have become just a little soft, and fearful and complaining. Forbidding deserts lie about us, in almost every human activity. Do we have the courage to conquer them? Are we willing to toil together? The reading of the colonizing of the Great Basin will in every way be a good tonic for striving humanity.

JOHN A. WIDTSOE.

CONTENTS

CHAPTER I: A PROPHET AND A NEW RELIGION ON
THE AMERICAN FRONTIER 1

Establishing of the Church of Jesus Christ of Latter-day Saints—
Early Persecutions—The Saints in Kirtland, Ohio, and in Missouri—
Coming of Brigham Young into the Church—Persecution and Ex-
pulsion of the Mormons from Missouri—Building of Nauvoo—
Persecution of Joseph Smith—The Martyrdom.

CHAPTER II: BRIGHAM YOUNG, THE GREAT
AMERICAN COLONIZER 8

Brigham Young a Great Colonizer—Brigham Young Assumes the
Leadership—Trouble in Nauvoo in 1845—Decision to Move the
Saints to the Far West—Preparing to Migrate West—Exodus from
Nauvoo—Trekking across Iowa—Crossing the Great Plains in
1847—Arrival in the Great Basin—Determination to Keep the
Saints in the Basin—General Colonizing Plan—Missionary Cam-
paign, 1849-1850—Perpetual Emigrating Fund Company—Methods
of Land Settlement—Description of Brigham Young.

CHAPTER III: THE GREAT BASIN BEFORE THE ARRIVAL
OF THE SAINTS 18

Description of the Great Basin—Visit of Spaniards to the Basin—
The Dominguez-Escalante Expedition, 1776-1777—Spanish Trap-
pers and Traders—American-Mexican Trade—Trappers, Scouts and
Mountaineers—Astorians, the First to Trap in the Basin, 1811-1812
—British Trappers Penetrate the Basin, 1819-1824—Activities of
the American Trappers—Official Explorations—Captain Bonneville's
Expedition, 1832-1836—John C. Fremont, the Government Explor-
er, 1843-46—Immigration to California before 1847.

CHAPTER IV: EXPLORING FOR NEW HOMES............................ 30

Trekking of the Pioneer Party Across the Plains, 1847—Gathering
Information Regarding the Great Basin—Orson Pratt's Vanguard
Company—"This is the Place"—Exploring the Salt Lake Valley—
Exploring Cache Valley—Exploring Utah Valley—James Brown's
Trip to San Francisco—Jefferson Hunt Exploring the Southern Route
to California in 1847-1848—Hunt's Second Trip to California—
Addison Pratt's Description of the Southern Route.

CHAPTER V: THE SOUTHERN EXPLORING COMPANY.............. 41

Chief Walker's Request—Exploring Sanpete Valley—Southern Ex-
ploring Company—Route to Sanpete Valley—Visit to Chief Walker
—Description of Mary's Vale—Difficult Trip Over the Mountains
—The Camp at Red Creek—Exploring Dixie Country on Horseback
—Return Trip Via Pauvan Valley—Winter Camp at Chalk Creek—
Pratt and Others Pushing Forward to Provo—Results of Southern
Exploring Company.

CHAPTER VI: FURTHER EXPLORATIONS FOR COLONY SITES.. 52

Exploring for Colony Sites—Description of Pauvan, Beaver, and Little Salt Lake Valleys—Brigham Young's Annual Trip to the South—Exploring the Rio Virgin and Dixie Regions—Exploring Pauvan and Beaver Valleys—Exploring the "Upper Sevier and South Country"—Exploring the Weber and Provo Rivers.

CHAPTER VII: THE PERSONNEL OF MORMON COLONIZATION 59

The Leadership of Brigham Young—Leadership of Brigham Young's Counselors—Leadership of the Twelve Apostles—Bishops and Stake Presidents as Colonizers—Racial Origin of Personnel of Mormon Colonization—Almost Equal Proportions of Sexes—Methods of Mormon Colonization.

CHAPTER VIII: THE MORMON CORRIDOR.................................. 68

A Mormon Empire in the Great West—Mormon Corridor Idea— Exploring the Corridor Route, 1847—Wagon Brought over Corridor Route, 1848—Jefferson Hunt, a Party of Gold Seekers, and the Mormon Corridor, 1849—Howard Egan's Traveller's Guide—Plans for Development of Corridor Route—Colonies Along the Corridor— European Saints to Migrate to the Basin Via San Diego, San Bernardino, and Mormon Corridor—Transportation and Communication over Corridor Route—The Utah War and the Mormon Corridor— Mormons and Colorado River Transportation—Summary of Achievements of Mormon Corridor Project.

CHAPTER IX: PROSELYTING AND EMIGRATION......................... 92

Doctrine of Gathering—European Immigration to Utah—World-Wide Missionary Campaign—Perpetual Emigrating Fund Company —Description of Emigration from Europe—Immigration to Utah —Ten Pound Plan—Handcart Migration——Church Teams and Immigration to Utah from 1861 to 1877—Accomplishments of Perpetual Emigrating Fund Company—Dissolving of the Company.

CHAPTER X: MORMON THEO-DEMOCRACY...............................118

Latter-day Saint System of Church Government—Theo-Democracy in the Great Basin in 1847 and 1848—Re-organization under Brigham Young in 1848—Functioning and Effectiveness of Mormon Theo-Democracy, 1848 to 1851—The State of Deseret—The Territory of Utah.

CHAPTER XI: THE MORMONS AND THE FEDERAL
GOVERNMENT 134

Causes of Friction Between Mormons and Federal Government— The Leaving of Territory of Utah by the First Federal Appointees— Corruption and False Accusations of Judges Drummond and Stiles— The Mormon Doctrine of Plural Marriage—A Political Issue in Campaign of 1856—The Utah War—Mediation of Colonel Thomas L. Kane—Sending of a Peace Commission to Utah by President Buchanan—Johnston's Army in Utah—"Anti-Bigamy Law" of 1862 —George Reynold's Test Case—Edmunds Law of 1882 and Poly-

gamy Persecutions—Edmunds-Tucker Law of 1887—The Manifesto
—Proclamation of Amnesty—Reconciliation—Statehood of Utah.

CHAPTER XII: The Land Problem in Mormon
   Colonization 142
   Free Land and the American Frontier—Selecting Sites for Colonies
   —Methods of Mormon Land Settlement—Dream of a Mormon
   Empire—Factors Determining Choice of the Location of Mormon
   Settlements—Water a Limiting Factor in Land Utilization—The
   Mormon Land Policy—Laying Out of Salt Lake City—Portioning
   Out of City Lots and Farming Lands to the Saints—The Big Field—
   Mormon Cooperation—Small Farms—Mormon Farm-Village System
   —Acquiring of Titles to the Land.

CHAPTER XIII: Utilization of Water by the Saints........164
   The Main Features of the Mormon Water Policy—Brief History of
   Irrigation—Mormon Cooperation in Water Utilization—Doctrine
   of Riparian Rights and Doctrine of Appropriation—Early Utah Irrigation Laws.

CHAPTER XIV: Brigham Young and Home Industry..........173
   Brigham Young and a Self-Supporting Economy—Need to Develop
   Numerous Industries—Drew Industries from the Entire World to
   Build Zion—Value of Hard Work—Domestic Industries—Deseret
   Agricultural Manufacturing Society—Trouble between the Mor-
   mons and Gentiles, and Establishing of Cooperative Stores.

CHAPTER XV: Early Industries in Utah...............................183
   First Sawmills and Gristmills in Utah—Domestic Industries—Sugar
   Industry—Cotton Industry—Flax Industry—Silk and Woolen In-
   dustries——Domestic Manufacturing of Other Articles—Agriculture,
   Stock Raising and Horticulture.

CHAPTER XVI: The Leather Industry...................................190
   Brigham Young and the Leather Industry—Beginning of the Leather
   Industry in Utah—Development of the Industry—Effect of Coming
   of the Union Pacific Railroad—Founding of Zion's Cooperative Mercantile Institution.

CHAPTER XVII: Utah Forty-Niners...................................194
   Brigham Young's Ideas Relative to Mining—Samuel Brannan, Gold,
   and California—Desire of Some of the Saints to go to California—
   Brigham's Attitude—The Utah Forty-Niners—Settlement of Parowan and Cedar City—Early Development of Iron Industry.

CHAPTER XVIII: The Deseret Iron Company.....................203
   Founding of Deseret Iron Company—Iron Works in Cedar City
   Taken Over by the Company—Development of Iron Industry—
   Reverses, 1853—Incorporating Deseret Iron Company—Its Officers
   —Activities of Company in 1854—Major Events in Iron Industry
   from 1855 to 1857—Dissolving of Deseret Iron Company—Appraisal
   of Achievements.

CHAPTER XIX: The Settlement of Salt Lake Valley....212

Objective—Salt Lake City—Utah Colonial Laboratory—Founding
of Bountiful, Farmington, Kaysville, Centerville, Big Cottonwood,
Mill Creek, South Cottonwood, Sugar House, and Draper—A Description of Salt Lake Valley, Its Settlements and Settlers, by a Gentile
in 1849.

CHAPTER XX: The Colonization of Weber Valley........218

The Miles Goodyear Claim—Purchase of Goodyear's Property—
Founding of Ogden by Mormons—Assistance of James Brown to
People of Salt Lake City in 1848—Scarcity and High Price of Food
—Plague of Crickets—Brigham Young and Party at Ogden 1849—
Activities of Lorin Farr in Weber Valley—Summary: Land Settle-
ment of Weber Valley to Fall of 1854.

CHAPTER XXI: Fort Utah 228

Description of Utah Valley—The Establishing of Fort Utah—Mormon Methods of Colonization—Erecting the Fort—Brigham Young,
Selecting a Site for a Settlement, and Establishing an Ecclesiastical
Government in Utah Valley—Indian Policy—Skirmish with the Indians at Fort Utah.

CHAPTER XXII: Directed Colonization into
Utah Valley 238

Settlement of Provo—Chief Sowiette—A Threatened Indian Attack—Surveying, Incorporating, and Growth of Provo—Industries
—Founding of American Fork, Lehi, Pleasant Grove, Alpine, Springville, Payson, Palmyra, and Spanish Fork.

CHAPTER XXIII: Settlement of Tooele and
Rush Valleys 251

Founding of Tooele—Difficulties with the Natives—Growth of
Tooele—Founding of Grantsville—Founding of E. T. City and of
Milton—Settlement of Rush Valley.

CHAPTER XXIV: Sanpete Valley 260

Chief Walker's Request—Calling of Missionaries to Settle Sanpete
Valley—Founding of Manti—Suffering of Chief Walker and the
Sanpitch Indians During Winter of 1849-1850—Difficulties En-
countered in Bringing Food Supplies from Salt Lake City to Manti
—Suffering at Manti During First Year—Brigham Young's Party
at Manti—Development of Industries—President's Party Again at
Manti—Founding of Spring City and Mount Pleasant—Indian
Troubles—Founding of Ephraim—Settlement of Sanpete Valley,
an Example of Directed Colonization.

CHAPTER XXV: The Mormon Station...272

Passing of Battalion Members through Carson Valley—Murder of
Captain Brovitt by Indians—Founding of Mormon Station (Genoa)
—Lucrative Trade at Mormon Station—John Reese: Purchase of

Mormon Station; Trading Activities—Creation of Carson County
—Supervising of Church Activities by Orson Hyde—Carson Valley,
an Outpost Gathering Place for Mormon Proselytes—The Mormons'
Abandonment of Carson Valley.

CHAPTER XXVI: FILLMORE THE CAPITOL OF UTAH............281
Location and Description of Pauvan Valley—Mormons' Early Con-
tact with and Opinions of Pauvan Valley—Selecting a Site for the
Capital City of Utah—The Arrival of Anson Call and Company on
Selected Site to Establish Fillmore—Chief Kanosh and His Pah-
van-te Tribe—Founding and Growth of Fillmore—The State House
—Holding of the Utah Legislature at Fillmore in 1855—Seat of
Government Moved to Salt Lake City.

CHAPTER XXVII: THE NORTHWARD ADVANCE OF

MORMON SETTLEMENTS 290
Establishing of Colonies South of Salt Lake City, then Northward
—Founding of Willard and Brigham City—Molested by Shoshone
Indians—Growth of Brigham City—The "Move South"—Founding
of Harper, Wellsville, Mendon, and Logan.

CHAPTER XXVIII: FORT BRIDGER AND FORT SUPPLY............299
Green River Valley—James Bridger's Property—Reasons Why Brig-
ham Young Desired Mormon Control Over Bridger's Property—
The Mormons and the Mountaineers—Trade on the Overland Trail
—Attempt to Arrest James Bridger—Surveying Bridger's Property—
Founding of Fort Supply—Building Blockhouse—Missionaries to
the Indians—Additional Colonists—Sending Assistance to the Hand-
cart Companies—Supply City—Purchase of Fort Bridger—The Utah
War—Burning of Fort Bridger, Fort Supply and Supply City—
—Mormon Losses—Federal Army at Fort Bridger.

CHAPTER XXIX: BRIGHAM YOUNG'S INDIAN POLICY............311
Origin of the American Indians—God's Promises to Them—Basis
of Mormon Indian Policy—Brigham Young's Attitude and Indian
Policy—To Feed, Teach, Educate, Civilize, and Christianize the Red
Men—Indian Slavery—To Prevent Bloodshed—To Build Forts—
Trading Agents—Indian Missions—Delaware, Cherokee, and Creek
Indian Missions—Skull Valley Indian Mission.

CHAPTER XXX: THE SANTA CLARA INDIAN MISSION............322
Calling of the Missionaries—Locating at Harmony, Utah—Presi-
dent Allen's First Missionary Tour among Indians—The Santa
Clara Indians—Jacob Hamblin's Work among Santa Clara Indians
—Establishing a Mission in the Santa Clara Valley—Missionaries and
Indians Farming Cooperatively—Description of Jacob Hamblin—
Narrow Escape from Navajos—Hamblin and a Company of Gentiles
En Route to California—Escape of Hatch and Leavitt from the
Mojave Indians—Arrival of Saints from San Bernardino and Las
Vegas—The Muddy River Mission—Murder of George A. Smith,

Jr.—Hamblin's Trip Around Grand Canyon of Colorado—Growth and Success of Santa Clara Indian Mission.

CHAPTER XXXI: THE ELK MOUNTAIN MISSION 337

Missionaries Called—Difficulties Encountered En Route—Site Selected—Teaching Indians the Gospel—Indian Policy—Account of Battle with Indians—Abandonment of the Mission.

CHAPTER XXXII: LAS VEGAS MISSION 344

Descriptions of Las Vegas and the Surrounding Country—Difficulties Encountered En Route—Founding Las Vegas Mission—Treaty of Peace with the Natives—Description of the Piutes at Las Vegas—Teaching the Natives—Exploration of Nathaniel V. Jones for Lead Deposits—Quarrel with President William Bringhurst—Efforts to Mine Lead—Building a Church House—Thompson Replacing Bringhurst as President of Mission—Lead Mining Project Discontinued—Abandonment of Las Vegas Mission.

CHAPTER XXXIII: THE SALMON RIVER MISSION 357

Calling of the Missionaries—Purpose of the Mission—En Route to Salmon River—Site Selected—Mission Founded—Supplies Secured from Salt Lake City—Missionaries Learning the Shoshone's Language —Fishing—Brigham Young and Company Visiting the Salmon River Mission—Attack of Fort Lemhi by the Shoshones—Sending of Messengers to Salt Lake City—Abandonment of the Salmon River Mission—Attack by Indians while En Route to Salt Lake.

CHAPTER XXXIV: BIRD'S-EYE VIEW OF MORMON
    COLONIZATION 365

Summary of Eastern Period of Mormon Frontier History—Dr. Thomas Nixon Carver Quoted—Effect of the Desert and Religion on Mormons—Land Settlement in Salt Lake, Weber, Utah, Tooele, Sanpete, Carson, Little Salt Lake, Juab, Pauvan, Box Elder, and Cache Valleys—Mormon Outpost Settlements—Mormon Colonization from 1847 to 1857—Land Settlement from 1858 to 1867—Colonization from 1868 to 1877—Summary of Mormon Colonization of the Great West—A Comparison—Mormon Colonization in Mexico and Canada—Summary of the Outstanding Achievements of Brigham Young the Colonizer.

BIBLIOGRAPHY 384

INDEX 390

ILLUSTRATIONS

IMMIGRANTS AND BRIGHAM YOUNG xx

BRIGHAM YOUNG DURING THE EARLY UTAH PERIOD 16
OX SKULL WRITTEN ON BY BRIGHAM YOUNG 17

MORMON EXPLORATIONS — MAP 32

FIRST PRESIDENCY AND TWELVE APOSTLES IN 1853 60
SALT LAKE CITY IN 1853 61

MORMON CORRIDOR; STATE OF DESERET — MAP 69

FORT SAN BERNARDINO 78
OLD COVE FORT ON MORMON CORRIDOR 79

BRIGHAM YOUNG AND PARTY VISITING SETTLEMENTS...... 88
IMMIGRATION TRAIN CAMPED AT INDEPENDENCE ROCK 89

HANDCART MONUMENT ON TEMPLE SQUARE 117

EAGLE GATE AND BEEHIVE HOUSE................... 148
THE BRIGHAM YOUNG MONUMENT AND THE SALT
    LAKE TEMPLE................................ 149

MORMON HANDICRAFTS — FRIENDSHIP QUILT,
    WINDING REEL, RAG CARPET 176
DESERET STORE AND TITHING OFFICE 177

SUGAR FACTORY AT SUGAR HOUSE 186
COTTON MILL AT WASHINGTON 187

COKE OVENS USED IN EARLY MINING OPERATIONS 211

SEAGULL MONUMENT ON TEMPLE SQUARE 222
COALVILLE, UTAH, 1869 223

FORT UTAH 232
CHIEF KANOSH, CHIEF WALKER AND ARAPENE 233

STATE HOUSE AT FILLMORE, UTAH 289

FORT SUPPLY.................................. 302
MAIN STREET, SALT LAKE CITY, 1865 303

LAS VEGAS, NEVADA 356

BRIGHAM YOUNG ABOUT 1875 372
REDUCTIONS IN UTAH'S TERRITORY 1849-1868 — MAP 373

SALT LAKE TEMPLE 374
SALT LAKE THEATER 375

MORMON COLONIZATION 1847-1857 — MAP 379

MORMON COLONIZATION 1858-1867 — MAP 381

MORMON COLONIZATION 1868-1877 — MAP 383

BRIGHAM YOUNG AND PARTY INVESTIGATING
    NAVIGABILITY OF RIO COLORADO ..... inside front cover
MORMON WAGON TRAIN NEARING SALT LAKE
    CITY .... inside back cover

Brigham Young The Colonizer

BRIGHAM YOUNG
THE COLONIZER

CHAPTER I

A PROPHET AND A NEW RELIGION ON THE
AMERICAN FRONTIER

ESTABLISHING OF THE CHURCH OF JESUS CHRIST

The colonization of the Great Basin and the founding of an extensive commonwealth took place in the westward movement of the nineteenth century,[1] as a direct result of the founding of a new religion. The quest for gold and glory, the opportunity to establish *encomiendas*, cheap and fertile lands, are some of the usual purposes for colonization, but "there is only one example in the annals of America of the organization of a commonwealth upon principles of pure theocracy. There is here one example where the founding of a state grew out of the founding of a new religion."[2] That state is Utah.

Only seventeen years before Brigham Young entered the Great Salt Lake Valley in 1847, seeking a place of permanent residence for his exiled followers, the Church of Jesus Christ of Latter-day Saints—generally known as the Mormon Church—was established. On April 6, 1830, at Fayette, New York, Joseph Smith, a young man of frontier training and experiences, formally organized this new religion. It was based primarily upon revelations and visions, a new holy scripture, and a modern prophet. Previous to the founding of the Church of Jesus Christ, this Prophet—Joseph Smith— claimed having experienced upon several occasions visitations of heavenly personages. The first of these unusual experiences occurred in the spring of 1820 in answer to his prayer as to which church to join. According to Joseph's account, two celestial personages appeared to him. In the Prophet's own words:

I was answered that I must join none of them, for they were all wrong, and the Personage who addressed me said that all their creeds were an abomination in his sight; that those professors were all corrupt, that: "they draw near to me with their lips, but their hearts are far from me; they teach for

---

[1]Fredrick Jackson Turner, *Rise of the New West*, 67.
[2]Hubert Howe Bancroft, *History of Utah*, 1540-1886, Preface, V.

doctrines the commandments of men, having the form of godliness, but they deny the power thereof."³

Three and a half years later young Smith experienced a second heavenly visitation in the personage of the angel Moroni. While living in mortality this heavenly being was the last historian of an ancient race of people called Nephites who inhabited the Americas from 600 B.C. to 400 A.D. Moroni completed the Nephite record, which was recorded on gold plates, and hid it in a hill. After visiting the youthful Prophet several times between 1823 and 1827, the angel gave to Joseph the gold plates with definite instructions regarding their worth and purpose. Through the power of the Lord the Prophet succeeded in translating the engravings which were on the plates from which he published the Book of Mormon. In this way the historical and religious record of the ancient inhabitants of America—including the ancestors of the American Indians—was given to our generation.

While engaged in translating this ancient Nephite record, the Prophet and Oliver Cowdery, his scribe, received the Holy Priesthood of God from heavenly personages. None other than John the Baptist, Peter, James and John—the Savior's choice Apostles— were the heavenly messengers. Thus Joseph and Oliver proclaimed that the power of the Lord of heaven and earth was again delegated to mortal man.

EARLY PERSECUTIONS

After organizing a church on such unusual claims of divine authority and openly declaring all other sects to be wrong— especially their creeds as fostered by Christian ministers—Brother Joseph and his followers, one is not surprised to learn, soon found themselves out of harmony with other Christian denominations. Because the religious beliefs held by Mormons differed so radically from those of their neighbors, the members of the new organization found themselves in difficulties which resulted in acts of violence. The American frontier upon which Mormonism had its birth and early growth lent itself perfectly, not only to the expansion of this new and unusual religion, but also to excessive mob violence.

"The story of the American frontier is a story of adventurous people; people seeking a change, fostering new and radical plans, throwing old ideas overboard. . . . The vast empty west encouraged the liberal thinker."⁴ Restless souls who were difficult to control

³Joseph Smith, *History of the Church*, I, 4-6; *Pearl of Great Price*, 48.
⁴William E. Berrett, *The Restored Church*, 18-27.

in more populous centers were attracted to the frontier. New and liberal religions were born and nurtured there. Lawlessness was always more or less common on the frontier as the restless people moved to the sparsely settled districts when land settlement became too thick and oppressive about them.

Governor Ford's impression of the early settlers of Illinois was rather typical of American frontiers. In his own words: "I had a good opportunity to know the settlers of Hancock county. I had attended the circuit courts there as state's attorney, from 1830, when the county was first organized, up to 1834; and to my certain knowledge the early settlers, with some honorable exceptions, were in popular language, hard cases."[5] After certain distasteful experiences in Missouri, Oliver Cowdery, who was eastern bred, came to the conclusion that "all the demons of the infernal pit" had collected in that part of the country.

It is true that in the frontier district—the land which lay between the home of the red men and the cultural centers—many people became their own law and their own judge. Ofttimes violence met violence. Many atrocious acts not complimentary to American civilization were committed. Religious fever supplied one of the strongest stimuli. These conditions were especially existent during the nineteenth century while Mormonism and the Prophet Joseph were trying to survive on the American frontier.

The Saints in Kirtland, Ohio

Joseph Smith organized the Church of Jesus Christ and found his first supporters in the frontier district of western New York. Within less than a year after the Church was organized (in the early spring of 1831) the Prophet and his small group of followers moved from the state of New York westward to Ohio, making Kirtland the headquarters. This move was accomplished because of the opposition that the Saints had encountered in New York, because of the missionary success of Parley P. Pratt and his companions in Ohio,[6] and because of the revelation the Prophet received in December, 1830.[7]

Saturated with the spirit of the frontier, Joseph and his associates lived in this atmosphere of liberal thought until the financial panic of 1837, coupled with other internal causes, forced the Prophet and those who remained true to the Church to flee to Missouri where another group of Saints resided. Many exciting

---

[5]Cited in John Henry Evans, *Joseph Smith an American Prophet*, 192-193.
[6]Parley P. Pratt, *Autobiography*, 50.
[7]Joseph Smith, *Doctrine and Covenants*, Section 37:1-4.

events and noteworthy accomplishments had taken place during those seven years in Ohio. They ranged from that of vile and cruel miscreants dragging Joseph at midnight from a bed on which his adopted twins were lying critically ill, stripping him of his clothes, beating, scratching and covering his body with a coat of tar, to that of leading an army of untrained men one thousand miles to Missouri to "redeem Zion," or, again, to that of building a temple to the Most High God. Herein Joseph and Oliver were visited by Moses, Elijah and Elias and also by the Lord and Savior Jesus Christ,[8] an experience comparable to one enjoyed by Joseph and Sidney Rigdon when they were permitted to see the various "Degrees of Glory."[9]

Coming of Brigham Young into the Church

About the time the Saints left New York, Brigham Young, a New England painter and glazier then residing at Mendon, New York, received from a friend a copy of The Book of Mormon. Becoming convinced that this book was true, he went to Kirtland the following year and was baptized a member of the Mormon Church. From that time forward he was a close associate of the Prophet and one of the leading characters in the vital movements of the Church. When the quorum of twelve apostles was organized in 1835, Brigham Young was selected as one of the group. He became president of the Twelve in 1838 and retained that position until he was appointed president of the Church in 1847.

Persecution and Expulsion of the Mormons from Missouri

Simultaneously with the establishing of Mormon communities in Ohio, Joseph Smith projected land settlement with his Mormon proselytes into Jackson County, Missouri, a country which lay on the furthermost bounds of the American frontier a thousand miles westward from Kirtland. Here the Prophet proposed to build "Zion," a "New Jerusalem," where the "seed of Israel" from all corners of the earth should assemble. But the project finally met with disaster. There were several reasons why Joseph's plans were unsuccessful.

The religious beliefs of the Mormons were obnoxious to the older inhabitants of the state. Thomas C. Romney stated: "An analysis of the various reports of both friend and foe leads to the inevitable conclusion that the fundamental and basic cause of

---

[8]*Ibid.*, Section 110.
[9]*Ibid.*, Section 76.

trouble in Missouri was a suspicion, dislike, and fear of the religious claims and pretentions of the Saints."[10] "Additional fuel poured upon the conflict was the jealousy and enmity of Protestant ministers in Jackson County. Furthermore, the economic and social phases of Joseph's new society aroused the suspicions of the Missourians. They feared that the Mormons would secure their lands by 'irregular methods' and subordinate them to the Mormon theocracy, because they had heard the claim made by the Saints that Missouri was the 'land of Zion'— the land for an everlasting inheritance."[11] According to B. H. Roberts, some of the "over-zealous and ignorant" of the Mormons helped to bring the Missourian persecutions upon the whole religious body by unwisely "boasting as to what the Lord would do in the immediate future in giving them possession of western Missouri as an inheritance. Perhaps some unwise allusions to the supposed part the Lamanites would take in the establishment and redemption of Zion; and the vehement threats of retaliation in the event of their being further assailed" contributed to the arousal of greater antagonism.[12] Another cause for trouble lay in the fact that the great majority of Joseph's followers were Yankees, naturally antagonistic to the Southerners. As a net result of all these conditions the Mormons were expelled from Jackson County in 1833 and from the state of Missouri in 1838. Regrettable chapters of American history occurred during these persecutions and expulsions of the Saints.

Forced to leave Missouri (1838-1839) and all their earthly belongings, the Mormons sought refuge in Illinois. Since the Prophet and several other leading officials of the Church were in jail in Missouri at the time of the expulsion, the task of moving the refugees across the border to a spot of safety fell upon Brigham Young. This experience furnished a splendid training for his greater task of leading the Saints to the Rocky Mountains.

BUILDING OF NAUVOO

About fifty miles up the Mississippi River from Quincy, Illinois, was located a small town called Commerce. The surrounding land was covered with trees and bushes and, being near the river, was so wet that travel there by team was impossible. Following his release from the Missouri jail, Joseph selected this as the site to

---

[10]Thomas C. Romney, The State of Deseret, 13, Ms.
[11]Doctrine and Covenants, Section 57.
[12]History of the Church, III, 45-46; Andrew L. Neff, The Mormon Migration to Utah, 1837-1847, 21, Ms.

build a city. Taking up residence there on May 10, 1839, he and his devoted followers busied themselves in draining the swamps and building a city dedicated to righteousness and to their God.

Through wise planning, thrift and hard work they wrought such a transformation of the little town of Commerce—which they named Nauvoo—that within three years after their arrival they had made of it "not only the most pretentious city of the state, but one of the best of the entire West"—"a city thrice the size of Chicago of that day." It became known as "Nauvoo the Beautiful," "The City of the Saints," having a population numbering over twenty thousand—the largest city at that time in Illinois.

Here the Prophet had opportunity to put into effect ideas which he had long before conceived. Nauvoo was laid out with broad, straight streets running at right angles to each other—a model which was carefully followed later by Brigham Young in laying out the cities of the Great Basin. The Nauvoo Charter—the work of Joseph Smith—"was the most liberal ever granted to any American city. It provided complete independence educationally, judicially, and militarily." Working under this charter and the guidance of the Prophet, the people of Nauvoo could boast of a University, of a "Legion of Soldiers, the finest trained militia in America," and of a million-dollar structure upon whose massive doors was written "Holiness to the Lord." No such building could be found at that date in any of the frontier districts west of the Allegheny Mountains. All of these marvels existed on the very edge of the wilderness, and even more unusual, they were born and matured within only four years after Nauvoo was no more than an uninhabited swamp.

Joseph Smith, the American Prophet, was responsible for all of these accomplishments, not to mention such other achievements as translating two volumes of holy scripture, receiving by revelation another volume of scripture, and writing his autobiography in six large books under the title of *History of the Church.* And his life was limited on this earth to the short span of only thirty-eight and one-half years.

At Nauvoo the Prophet arose to the pinnacle of his career—to a position of such power and prominence that, in the early summer of 1844, Josiah Quincy, "the sophisticated mayor of Boston," concluded:

It is by no means improbable that some future text-book for the use of generations yet unborn will contain a question something like this: "What historical American of the nineteenth century has exerted the most powerful influence upon the destinies of his countrymen?" And it is by no means impossible that the answer to that interrogatory may be thus written: "Joseph Smith, the Mormon prophet." And the reply, absurd as it doubtless seems to most men now living, may be an obvious commonplace to their descendants. History deals in surprises and paradoxes quite as startling as this."[13]

PERSECUTION OF JOSEPH SMITH—THE MARTYRDOM

The Prophet's life encountered also a darker and more distressing side. From childhood on, he—like the Master—"was despised and rejected of men; a man of sorrows, and acquainted with grief."

Thirty-eight times in his thirty-eight years he was arrested on complaints charging him with offenses ranging from murder and treason down. And in every case, although witnesses perjured themselves, lawyers raked the country for evidence against him, and judges over-reached themselves in an effort to convict him, he was acquitted. . . . Six months in all he spent in Missouri jails. The food was always unsanitary, often putrid. There were no beds to sleep on. The guards were foul-mouthed and abusive. In Illinois he spent months underground, hiding from Missouri ruffians who sought to take him across the line. And in the end the assassin's bullet found its deadly place in his body.[14]

Throughout all these persecutions and troubles, his God was forever with him. When Brother Joseph was in the lowest depth of despair, having been confined in Liberty Jail throughout the long winter months of 1838-39 while his beloved followers were mercilessly driven from their homes in Missouri and while many weaker ones had turned to the ranks of the enemy, God heard the beseeching prayer of this Prophet. Expressive of the love of a true Father, the Lord replied:

My son, peace be unto thy soul; thine adversity and thine afflictions shall be but a small moment. And then, if thou endure it well, God shall exalt thee on high; thou shalt triumph over all thy foes.[15]

Five eventful years elapsed. Joseph "endured" his afflictions "well." He and his beloved brother Hyrum were murdered in Carthage jail, June 27, 1844. Then, according to Mormon belief, he ascended to dwell with the Savior and the Prophets of Old to plan for his beloved devotees who remained on earth. This was his "triumph over all" his "foes." Church members sing:

Hail to the Prophet, ascended to heaven!
Traitors and tyrants fight him in vain;
Mingling with Gods, he can plan for his brethren;
Death cannot conquer the hero again.

[13]Josiah Quincy, Figures of the Past, 376.
[14]John Henry Evans, The Heart of Mormonism, 278-279.
[15]Doctrine and Covenants, Section 121:7-8.

Chapter II

BRIGHAM YOUNG, THE GREAT AMERICAN COLONIZER

Brigham Young a Great Colonizer

The story of the colonization of the Great Basin is inseparably connected with the life and activities of Brigham Young. In following the hopes, the activities, and the accomplishments of this man from 1846 to 1877, one is studying the history of a sturdy group of pioneers in their westward advance and establishment of a great commonwealth. So completely and so thoroughly did President Young dominate the economic, social, political, and religious life of his Mormon followers that even today the institutions in the towns he established bear the stamp of their founder. In the words of Herbert E. Bolton:

Brigham Young was a devout believer, but more especially he was a lion-hearted man of iron will, an organizer, and the founder of a commonwealth. Few if any other examples in Anglo-American history can be found of a man who so thoroughly dominated a great colonization movement as Brigham Young dominated the founding of Utah.

Outstanding in the list of Anglo-American colony builders are the names of Calvert, Penn, Oglethorpe, Stephen F. Austin, and Brigham Young. Calvert founded Maryland on the principle of religious toleration; Penn established his thrifty, peace-loving colony of Pennsylvania; Oglethorpe made a home for English paupers in order to build the buffer colony of Georgia across the Spanish front; Austin founded the republic of Texas and won a "contest of civilization," but it is doubtful if any of these men so completely molded his people and their institutions as Brigham Young molded the Mormons, and certainly none of them had a harder struggle with nature and with neighbors.[1]

Edward W. Tullidge, a Utah historian and a contemporary of President Young, expressed the sentiments of historians in his estimate of Brigham as a successful colonizer. He concluded:

That magnificent system of Mormon colonization which Brigham Young so wonderfully represented in his life and character (was molded by him); for he was perhaps the greatest colonizer that the world has ever seen. The Mormon founders of Utah were in this respect, truly fashioned in his [Brigham's] own likeness and image, by the very genius of their colonizing, state-founding religion. In their lifetime they had built up between three and four hundred cities and settlements.[2]

---

[1]Herbert E. Bolton, "The Mormons in the Opening of the Great West," *The Utah Genealogical and Historical Magazine*, XVII (Salt Lake City, January, 1926), 64.

[2]Edward W. Tullidge, *Quarterly Magazine*, III, 233.

Brigham Young Assumes the Leadership

Since Brigham Young was the chief apostle at the time of the death of the Prophet Joseph, it was but natural that he should assume the leadership of the Church. The martyrdom of Joseph and Hyrum did not end the bitter strife between the Saints and their enemies. Those who hated Mormonism believed that if the Prophet were killed the Church would automatically fall to pieces; but they soon learned that Brigham Young was just as formidable an opponent to them and their designs to destroy Mormonism as Joseph Smith had been. He was a man of broad vision, astute business sense, and natural leadership.

During the summer and fall of 1845 the anti-Mormons of Illinois mobbed the Saints in the outlying settlements, burned their homes, and threatened those living at Nauvoo. Mass meetings were held at Carthage and other towns and resolutions were passed which demanded that the Mormons leave the State and move to the West, as it was generally known before the Prophet's death that he contemplated such a move. The Twelve Apostles and other Church leaders considered the matter and decided to seek freedom from all oppression in the Far West.

Decision to Move the Saints to the Far West

A large portion of the Saints had had trouble with their neighbors in New York, Ohio, Missouri, and Illinois, and had been driven by force from Missouri. They now realized that their religious practices and institutions were such that isolation was the only solution to their fervent hopes for homes and security. Brigham Young knew that extending the frontier a little farther west, as the Saints had previously done, would not suffice. He saw that his people could not exist among other denominations and maintain their religious beliefs, but must have territory of their own far beyond the existing frontier of Gentile settlements, to avoid conflict and persecution. The Saints sought safety, security, and protection from their enemies, and those things Brigham and his associates were determined to provide.

Expressive of the feelings of his people, Brigham Young wrote to the Mormons throughout the world as follows: "The Saints in this vicinity are bearing their privations in meekness and patience, and making all their exertions tend to their removal westward. Their hearts and all their labors are toward the setting sun, for they desire to be so far removed from those who have been their oppressors, that there shall be an everlasting barrier between them and future persecutions."[3]

Oregon, California, Sonora, Texas, Vancouver Island, and the Great Basin were all open for consideration as possible locations for the Mormons' new homes. The last, offering the most seclusion and protection from Gentiles, was chosen. Just when Young definitely selected the Basin as the haven for the Saints is not known, but one of Brigham Young's associates recorded in his daily journal that God showed their leader in a vision the valley of the Great Salt Lake and told him that there was the place where the Mormons should locate.[4] As Bolton has said:

> For the main seat of the Saints the forbidding desert of the Basin best fitted Young's grim purpose. There, Brigham wrote Polk, "a good living will require hard labor and consequently [the land] will be coveted by no other people, while it is surrounded by so unpopulous but fertile country". In the Basin, of all places, the Mormons would be unmolested and would have elbow room in which to expand.[5]

PREPARING TO MIGRATE WEST

During the winter of 1845-1846 Nauvoo was a busy work-shop of fifteen thousand people preparing to migrate West. The great task of transferring them to a new and far distant country could be accomplished successfully, Brigham knew, only by the most carefully arranged and masterfully executed program. Even then the risks were great. The Saints knew that they would have to build a complete new commonwealth hundreds of miles beyond the last American frontier with such tools, farming implements, seeds, clothing, and foodstuff as they could carry with them. But Brigham Young, with his exceptional administrative faculties, was equal to the task. By thoroughly planning the major project with careful attention to details, by organizing the Saints into a semi-military and rigidly disciplined ecclesiastical order, the Mormon leader was able to move his followers to their new home with a minimum of loss.

Young did not lack vision. Realizing that he and his people were departing from civilization to establish themselves in an unsettled country, he wished to make the Mormons self-supporting in all respects. This he intended to do by fostering the development of many industries. In 1847 he wrote from Winter Quarters the following instructions to the Saints:

---

[3]Brigham Young, "General Epistle . . . to the Saints," *Latter-day Saints Journal History,* December 23, 1847. Ms.
[4]Wilford Woodruff, *Journal,* July 24, 1847. Ms.
[5]Bolton, *op. cit.*

Come immediately and prepare to go West, bringing with you all kinds of choice seeds, grains, vegetables, fruits, shrubbery, trees, and vines—everything that will please the eye, gladden the heart or cheer the soul of man, that grow upon the face of the earth; also the best stock of birds, beasts or fowl of every kind; also the best tools of every description; machinery for spinning and weaving, and dressing of wool, cotton, flax, and silk; or models or descriptions of the same by which we can construct them; and the same in relation to all kinds of farming utensils and husbandry, such as corn shellers, grain threshers and cleaners, smut machines, mills and every implement and article within your knowledge that shall tend to promote the comfort, health, happiness, or prosperity of any people.[6]

Exodus from Nauvoo—Trekking Across Iowa

Early in 1846 thousands of Latter-day Saints left Nauvoo and began the long and difficult journey which was to lead eventually to a new birth of freedom in the mighty solitudes of Utah. That spring and summer some 15,000 of them crossed Iowa but were forced to make temporary camp on the banks of the Missouri River where Omaha and Council Bluffs now stand. They called their new towns Winter Quarters (later Florence) and Council Bluffs. This detention in the westward trek until the following year was brought about as the result of the United States Government calling a battalion of 500 Mormons to participate in the war with Mexico.

Crossing the Plains in 1847—Arrival in the Great Basin

On April 14, 1847, Brigham with a small company left Winter Quarters to search out a route to the Great Basin and there to select a home for his followers. This vanguard company was composed of 148 individuals, most of whom were sturdy frontiersmen who had received their training by previously establishing colonies on several American frontiers. There were only three women and two children in the group.

The first view of the Great Salt Lake Valley did not appear inviting to some of the exiled Saints. Mrs. Harriet Young exclaimed, "Weak and weary as I am I would rather go a thousand miles farther than remain in such a forsaken place as this." Yet, when their leader said, "This is the place,"[7] his followers adjusted themselves to their new surroundings and cooperated with him in carrying out his colonizing project. After establishing this first company in the new home, Brigham with a firm but kindly hand directed the thousands who followed.

[6]Brigham Young, "General Epistle . . . to the Saints," *Latter-day Saints Journal History,* December 23, 1847. Ms., Latter-day Saints Archives.
[7]Wilford Woodruff. *op. cit.*

Determination to Keep the Saints in the Basin

But when the crops of 1848—first attacked by frost, then by crickets, then by drought, and finally by more frost—proved to be almost a total failure, a few of the Saints were not quite sure that their leader had selected the right place. Some of them said:

Why the wheat we grew here last year was so short that we had to pull it; the heads were no more than two inches long. Frost falls here every month in the year—enough to cut down all tender vegetation. More, James Bridger and Gudger, who have been in this country ten years or more, say that corn cannot be raised anywhere in these mountains. In fact, Bridger has told President Young that he would give a thousand dollars for the first bushel of corn raised in the open air here, for he says it cannot be done.[8]

Added to the discouragement of having a crop failure during the first harvest season in the Salt Lake Valley was the lure of the newly discovered gold fields in California. President Young heard early in 1849 that some of the discouraged Saints were remarking that he was "too smart a man to try to establish a civilized colony . . . in such a dry, worthless locality, and would be going on to California, Oregon, or Vancouver's Island."[9] The Mormon colonizer decided to kill this small wave of discontent by making a public announcement of what the plans for the future were. He said:

We have been kicked out of the frying-pan into the fire, out of the fire into the middle of the floor, and here we are and here we will stay. God has shown me that this is the spot to locate his people, and here is where they will prosper. . . .

As the Saints gather here and get strong enough to possess the land, God will temper the climate and we shall build a city and a temple to the Most High God in this place. We will extend our settlements to the east and west, to the north and to the south, and we will build towns and cities by the hundreds, and thousands of Saints will gather in from the nations of the earth. This will become the great highway of nations. . . .

Take courage, brethren. . . . Plow your land and sow wheat, plant your potatoes. . . . It is our duty to preach the gospel, gather Israel, pay our tithing and build temples. The worst fear that I have about this people is that they will get rich in this country, forget God and his people, wax fat, and kick themselves out of the Church and go to hell. This people will stand mobbing, robbing, poverty, and all manner of persecution, and be true. But my greatest fear for them is that they cannot stand wealth.[10]

Almost one hundred per cent of the Saints responded to Brig-

[8]James Brown, *Autobiography*, 121.
[9]*Ibid.*, 119.
[10]*Ibid.*, 119-123.

ham's request by remaining in the Basin. The hope of the Mormons at that time was "to secure the merest necessities of life. If ever a dream of anything like comforts or luxuries came to them, they made a grave in their hearts for that dream and buried it, that it might not longer vex them."[11] The secret of this submissiveness to ecclesiastical discipline did not lie entirely in the personality of Brigham Young. Religion—that potent force which has worked miracles in the lives of millions of people—was the dynamic controller that held the Saints in the Great Basin. The Mormon President expressed this idea, which was believed in just as strongly by the laity as by the leaders of the Church:

> I did not embrace Mormonism because I hoped it was true, but because I knew it was that principle that would save all the human family that would obey it, and it would make them righteous. Joseph Smith lived and died a prophet, and sealed his testimony with his blood. He lived a good man, and died a good man, and he was as good a man as ever lived.[12]

It is of importance for historians to understand that the force back of the Mormon migration to the Basin was religion. Brigham Young had the characteristic of humility and faith in the overruling power of Deity. He did not take credit for bringing the Saints to Utah but gave it to the God whom he worshiped. He stated: "I do not want people to understand that I had anything to do with our being moved here; that was the providence of the Almighty; it was the power of God that wrought out salvation for his people. I never could have devised such a plan."[13]

GENERAL COLONIZING PLAN

After the Saints had located in the Basin, Mormonism assumed the character of a great colonizing enterprise. As the days passed by, Brigham's knowledge of the resources and possibilities of the Great West continued to increase. He realized the impossibility of fully developing them with the 25,000 Saints then (1847) available in the United States and Canada.[14] His object was to increase missionary activities and then to expedite the immigration of the converts to Utah. He must gain control over an extensive territory and gather converts as rapidly as possible in order to hold that territory by establishing and developing numerous towns and cities. This vast Basin was an ideal place in which to gather the "seed of

[11]Levi Edgar Young, *Founding of Utah*, 360.
[12]Brigham Young, *Latter-day Saint Journal History*, April 6, 1850, Ms.
[13]Brigham Young, *Journal of Discourses*, VI. 41.
[14]Joseph Fielding Smith, *Origin of the Reorganized Church*, 13, 17.

Israel," so he immediately sent out word for all the Saints throughout the world to hasten to the Mormon Mecca.[15]

MISSIONARY CAMPAIGN, 1849-1850

In order to help fulfill his dreams of an expansive empire, the
Mormon Colonizer in 1849-1850 greatly increased proselyting work
both in numbers of missionaries and in countries to which they
were sent. He continued this active proselyting campaign throughout the rest of his life. Heretofore missionary work outside of
America had been confined to the British Isles, but by the close
of 1851 Mormonism had been preached in Hispanic America, in
the Sandwich and Society Islands, in Australia, India, Italy, Switzerland, France, and in the Scandinavian countries. Thus within
four years after reaching the Basin, President Young had directed
the opening of proselyting activities throughout most of the world.
As Hubert Howe Bancroft wrote:

> In their missionary adventures no sect was ever more devoted, more self-
> sacrificing, or more successful. The Catholic friars in their new-world excursions
> were not more indifferent to life, wealth, health, and comfort, not more in-
> different to scorn and insult, nor more filled with high courage and lofty
> enthusiasm, than were the Mormon elders in their old-world enterprises.[16]

Some countries proved to be more fruitful fields for missionary
work than others. Relatively few proselytes were made in India,
Hispanic America, and Italy, while Scandinavia furnished more
converts than any other of the new missions. However, the
British Isles continued to supply more Saints for Zion than did
any of the other foreign missions. In fact, at the close of 1851 that
mission boasted of a Church membership of 32,894.

PERPETUAL EMIGRATING FUND COMPANY

Since many of the converts were too poor to pay their fare to
Utah, Brigham proposed the creation of a revolving fund for the
purpose of helping them. The other Church officials concurred
with his suggestion. On October 6, 1849, at a general conference
of the Church, the project received the unanimous vote of the
Saints. The company was named "The Perpetual Emigrating Fund
Company." Its purpose was to make possible loans to foreign
converts as well as to the poor in various parts of the United States
who wished to come to Utah. Those who borrowed returned the

[15]Brigham Young, "General epistle . . . to the Saints," *Latter-day Saints Journal History*,
March, 1848. Ms.
[16]Hubert Howe Bancroft, *History of Utah*, 1540-1886, 398.

money with interest after establishing themselves in the Basin. The fund was created by contribution from the Saints. Brigham Young stood at the head of this company and controlled it until his death in 1877. During that period the Perpetual Fund Company assisted in bringing thousands upon thousands of immigrants to Salt Lake City; thus its contributions and influence in colonizing the West were immense.

METHODS OF LAND SETTLEMENT

The Colonizer planned to establish settlements in a vast expanse of country with his Mormon followers. In 1850 he remarked, "I look forward to the day when scores of thousands will join us in our secluded retreat."[17] An epistle issued to the Saints in March, 1849, gives the essential ideas back of his colonizing policy: "We hope soon to explore the valleys three hundred miles south and also the country as far as the Gulf of California with a view to settlement and to acquiring a seaport."[18]

The fact that Brigham Young and his assistants had sent five hundred colonists to San Bernardino, California, had founded Genoa in Carson Valley, Nevada, and Lemhi on the Salmon River in Idaho, had built Forts Bridger and Supply at the east entrance of the Basin, and had small but flourishing communities in most of the fertile valleys of the Great Basin within eight years after the arrival of the pioneers is evidence that they intended to colonize as expansive a country as human resources and safety would permit. It should be remembered that in carrying on his land settlement project, the Mormon leader had a number of very capable helpers. A more detailed discussion of his assistants and the great work he and they accomplished in making "the desert blossom as the rose" will be given later.

The program of land settlement of the Great West was carefully supervised by Brother Brigham. He sent out exploring parties to select favorable sites for new colonies or it may be that he chose the site himself. On many occasions he personally supervised the laying out of towns into definitely surveyed square blocks with wide streets and the allotting of farming lands and city lots to the settlers. Men representing various crafts with their families were called directly by the "Lion of the Lord" to settle these new towns, to till the soil and build industries that would make the people self-sustaining. Brother Brigham was a very practical man, losing

---

[17]Brigham Young, *Latter-day Saint Journal History*, April 6, 1850, Ms. Latter-day Saint archives.
[18]*Ibid.*, March 9, 1849.

no opportunity to apply hard labor and good sense to the multitude of problems encountered in this new arid region. On his annual trips through the settlements, he took advantage of the opportunity to see that his followers did likewise. John Henry Evans described how the President's trips worked "wonders for everybody along the way."

> For one thing, there is a general clean-up of the towns. Things must look at their best for the presidential party. The great leader has a keen eye for broken down fences, machinery out in the weather, rubbish heaps, or any lack of sanitary necessities in the settlements. Nor is he at all backward in telling the people what to do to remedy any situation he sees needs looking into. "Put your machinery under the shed, Brother Blank," he says to a careless farmer, "when you are not using it." And to a housewife who needed the advice, "Sister Blank, don't you know that whitewash is good for bedbugs." The next time he comes down he will see whether his advice has been followed or not.[19]

Description of Brigham Young

An intimate view of Brigham Young the Colonizer was given by Richard F. Burton, a non-Mormon from England who spent a few weeks visiting in Salt Lake in 1860. In the words of Burton we picture the head of the Mormon Church thus:

> I had expected to see a venerable-looking old man. Scarcely a grey thread appears in his hair. . . . His manner is at once affable and impressive, simple and courteous. . . . He shows no sign of dogmatism, bigotry, or fanaticism. . . . He impresses a stranger with a certain sense of power: his followers are, of course, wholly fascinated by his superior strength of brain. It is commonly said that there is one chief in Great Salt Lake City, and that is 'Brigham.' His temper is even and placid . . . and when occasion requires he can use the weapons of ridicule to direful effect, and 'speak a bit of his mind' in a style which no one forgets. He often reproves his erring followers in purposely violent language, making the terrors of a scolding the punishment in lieu of hanging for a stolen horse or cow. His powers of observation are intuitively strong, and his friends declare him to be gifted with an excellent memory and a perfect judgment of character. If he dislikes a stranger at the first interview, he never sees him again. . . . He assumes no airs of sanctimoniousness, and had the plain, simple manner of honesty. His followers deem him an angel of light, his foes, a goblin damned; he is, I presume, neither one nor the other. . . . He has been called hypocrite, swindler, forger, murderer— no one looks it less. . . . Finally, there is a total absence of pretension in his manner, and he has been so long used to power that he cares nothing for its display. The arts by which he rules the heterogeneous mass of conflicting elements are indomitable will, profound secrecy, and uncommon astuteness.
>
> Such is His Excellency President Brigham Young, "painter and glazier"— his earliest craft—prophet, revelator, translator, and seer; the man who is revered

---

[19]John Henry Evans, *The Heart of Mormonism*, 425.

BRIGHAM YOUNG DURING THE EARLY UTAH PERIOD

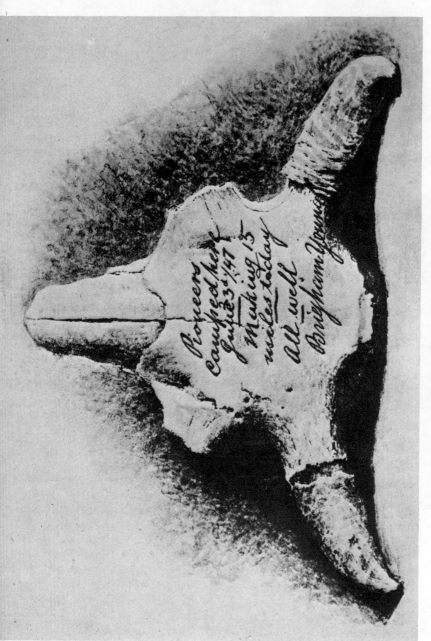

OX SKULL WRITTEN ON BY BRIGHAM YOUNG IN 1847

as king or kaiser, pope or pontiff never was; who, like the Old Man of the Mountain, by holding up his hand could cause the death of anyone within his reach; who, governing as well as reigning, long stood up to fight with the sword of the Lord, and with his few hundred guerillas, against the then mighty power of the United States; who has outwitted all diplomacy opposed to him; and, finally, who made a treaty of peace with the President of the Great Republic as though he had wielded the combined power of France, Russia, and England.[20]

A careful study and comparison of the colonizing activities of various races and peoples throughout history reveals the fact that Brigham Young as a colonizer has no superior.

---

[20]Richard Francis Burton, *The City of the Saints,* and *Across the Rocky Mountains to California* (Liverpool, 1860), 263-266.

CHAPTER III

THE GREAT BASIN BEFORE THE ARRIVAL OF THE SAINTS

DESCRIPTION OF THE GREAT BASIN

Between the Rocky Mountains on the east, the Rio Colorado on the south, the Sierras to the west, and the water shed of the Columbia River at the north, there lies an extensive country, known since John C. Fremont's survey in 1843 as the Great Basin.[1] It represents distances from the extreme points north and south, and east and west of about 900 and 600 miles respectively, and contains an area of 210,000 square miles.

Fremont named it the Great Basin because of the fact that the whole area has no outlet to the sea. The many streams that flow into it make lakes of various sizes, Great Salt Lake being the largest. The most important rivers are the Humboldt, the Bear, the Weber, the Jordan, and the Sevier; and its most important lakes are the Great Salt Lake, Utah, Bear, and Sevier lakes.

This vast Basin region remained the "Dark Continent" of America until late in the eighteenth century. From the time of its discovery until after the advent of the Mormons it was regarded as an obstacle in the path of the traveler who was headed for California or Oregon. Its topography presented miles of desert wilderness and ranges of rugged mountains which threatened the complete destruction by thirst and starvation of him who was forced to traverse its vast solitudes in order to reach his desired goal beyond.

The howl of the lurking coyotes and wolves, the rattle of the snakes, the cunning of the Indians, the weirdness of the canyons, and the scorching mid-summer heat of the open desert made of the Great Basin an area dreaded and, when possible, avoided by the majority of the travelers.

But among the human race there were fearless frontiersmen who were willing when necessary to brave the hazards of the desolate West in order to achieve their desired goals. A succession of them came to the Great Basin. The first to come were the Spanish missionaries and scouts, in search of a route from Santa Fe to the Pacific Coast. Then came the trappers and traders—Spaniards and Mexicans from the south, Americans and Englishmen from

----

[1]The writer is indebted for most of the material in this chapter to Dr. William J. Snow's excellent thesis, *The Great Basin Before the Coming of the Mormons* (University of California. 1923), Ms.

the north and the east. As "Manifest Destiny" pushed the home-seekers westward to the Pacific Coast, official government explorers made accurate surveys of the country, tabulating the geography, topography, climate and flora of the Great Basin. Finally came the home builders. They were Mormons—because the persecuted, unpopular refugees following Brigham Young were the only people at that time who even thought of considering the inland Basin to be a desirable place in which to establish homes; and, strangely enough, Brother Brigham purposely chose this arid country as the haven for the Saints.

Visit of Spaniards to the Basin—The Dominguez-Escalante Expedition, 1776-1777

In presenting briefly the succession of scouts and pathfinders who traversed the vast Basin region of the Far West prior to the coming of the Mormons, we turn first to the Spaniards.

Following the discovery of the New World, Spain laid claim on the western half of North America and upon most of South America. The country was too vast for her to make good all her claims through exploration and colonization; nevertheless she did a very commendable job in colonizing most of the western hemisphere south of the Great Basin.

However, the vast Basin remained unexplored until pressure was brought upon Spain by Russia and England, in the latter part of the 18th Century. Russia was advancing down the Pacific Coast from the northwest, and English trappers, explorers, and seamen were also threatening Spanish claims to the western part of North America. This international rivalry forced upon Charles III vigorous action, if he was to save California from falling into the hands of other powers.

Thereupon José de Gàlvez, the able and energetic Visitador General of New Spain, King Charles' representative in America, promoted and directed from the City of Mexico the colonizing of Alta California between 1769 and 1774. San Diego, Monterey, San Francisco, and other important sites were settled and garrisoned.

Monterey was a long way from the Spanish base in Mexico, and the overland route connecting them was very unsatisfactory. Santa Fe, New Mexico, furnished a much nearer base, but the intervening country via the Great Basin was unexplored. Thereupon the Dominguez-Escalante expedition was organized at Santa Fe for the purpose of exploring the intervening country and locating, if possible, the much needed route. The company consisted of ten men, including the two Franciscan friars, Francisco Dominguez and Silvestre Valez de Escalante.

July 29, 1776, only three weeks after our American forefathers signed the Declaration of Independence, the little Spanish band left Santa Fe. Father Escalante kept a journal of their travels. It is so vivid, detailed, and accurate that the route they took can be followed today with much precision. They traveled in a north and northwestern direction through Colorado to a point directly east of Utah Lake, then veered westward into Utah. On September 21, they crossed the divide at the head of Spanish Fork Canyon and caught their first view of the valley lying below. Two days later they camped on the east shore of Utah Lake. "They were thus the first white men known to have entered the heart of the Basin."

Escalante was greatly impressed with the Yuta Valley and thought it a desirable site for an Indian mission. He concluded that the region could support as many pueblos as there were then in New Mexico. On September 25, while camped on the American Fork River near the lake, Father "Escalante talked to the Indians on Christianity, and explained to them the meaning of the cross. A large number of natives gathered, and this meeting is the first incident recorded in our State's history of Christian missionaries teaching Christ to the red men."[2]

The Spaniards learned of the existence of the Great Salt Lake farther north, but they did not visit it. Instead, after a sojourn of three days with the Indians east of Utah Lake, they continued their journey, traveling now in a southerly direction toward their goal, Monterey. When they arrived in Beaver Valley, their Indian guide left them, the weather grew cold, and snow covered all the surrounding mountains. By October 8 winter had set in with vigor. A scouting party was sent out toward the west to find if possible an opening through the Sierras, but they returned with an unfavorable report. Meanwhile, the company had been detained for several days by a snowstorm.

Having been hampered by these adverse conditions, the Spaniards decided to determine by drawing lots the will of the Lord as to whether they should endeavor to reach Monterey or return to Santa Fe. The lot said return, which decision the Padres accepted as satisfactory.

Continuing their journey, they passed through Cedar Valley and down the Rio Virgin to the high Colorado Plateau. After more than twenty days wandering over the rugged country eastward, they

2Levi Edgar Young, *The Foundings of Utah,* 48-53.

crossed the Rio Colorado. On November 23 they reached the Moqui villages in northern Arizona, weak and exhausted. Eight days later, January 2, 1777, the party arrived at Santa Fe, having been gone five months on their expedition through the Great Basin.

SPANISH TRAPPERS AND TRADERS

The Spanish government did not immediately follow up the work of the Dominguez-Escalante expedition with further efforts to open a route from Santa Fe to Monterey. With the war on in Europe, its attention was diverted to other problems. Further exploration was left to the individual "free trappers and traders, who were more concerned with their own affairs than with world politics." However, these men left very meager data regarding their activities. But a letter written by the governor of New Mexico in 1805 indicated that there had been rather intimate connections between the Yutas and the Spaniards from the days of Escalante. In the words of Dr. William J. Snow:

Alencaster [Governor of New Mexico], in commenting on the virtues and remarkable exploits of one Manuel Mestas, a Genizaro, who had served some fifty years as a Yuta interpreter, refers to him as one who had reduced the Yutas to peace, and who has recovered horses stolen by the Comanches and retaken by the Yutas in a subsequent war between the two tribes.[3]

Further evidence of Spanish contact with the Great Basin Indians is contained in "a recently discovered document in the Spanish archives of New Mexico." It tells of a trading expedition conducted by Mauricio Arze and Legoa Garcia in 1813. They and five companions went to Timpanogos (Utah) Lake, remained three days among the Yutas, and then returned to New Mexico.

Continually after the Arze-Garcia expedition into the Great Basin, Spaniards and Mexicans carried on trade with the Yuta Indians. In 1821 the Basin passed from Spanish to Mexican ownership, and after that date trade increased. Principal articles of exchange were the Indian women and children who were taken southward to the Mexican settlements for slaves. After the Mormons arrived in Utah, Brigham Young stopped that traffic in human beings by legislating against it and fixing severe punishment for the offenders.

AMERICAN-MEXICAN TRADE

During the period of Mexican ownership, another industry brought traders through the Great Basin. The opening of the Santa

---

[3]Snow, op. cit., 13.

Fe road in 1822 from New Mexico to Saint Louis, Missouri, created a new field for trade which had heretofore been restricted by Spanish law.⁴ The prairie schooners—large wagons drawn by several spans of mules—came into existence. Each year caravans traveled from Santa Fe to Saint Louis, bringing large profits to American traders. This new industry created a great demand for mules. California was the main source of supply, and Santa Fe was the central base of exchange.

This new-born commerce of the prairies again compelled attention to the western Basin as a possible shorter route to California. In 1829 two expeditions succeeded in crossing from Santa Fe to California. The first was a Mexican expedition and the second was directed by Ewing Young of Tennessee. They passed along the southern rim of the Basin into the Mojave region but south of what was later termed the Old Spanish Trail.

The first company to go completely through the Basin and on to California over that route was William Wolfskill. In 1830 he led a company of fur traders to California, via Sevier River, southern Utah, across the desert, through Cajon Pass, and on into Los Angeles. Upon arriving they found more profit in purchasing mules and taking them back to Santa Fe than in the fur industry. The mule traffic continued to be a profitable business until displaced by the railroads.

TRAPPERS, SCOUTS, AND MOUNTAINEERS—ASTORIANS, THE FIRST TO TRAP IN THE BASIN, 1811-1812

But the activities of the Americans in the Far West were not limited to the mule traffic. Even while the Spaniards and Mexicans were becoming acquainted with the southern portion of the Great Basin, American and British mountaineers were penetrating the northern area and enriching themselves through the lucrative fur industry. The first Americans to visit any portion of the Great Basin were members of the Astorian company, who detached themselves from the main party in the fall of 1811 and trapped in the Bear River region during the winter. They were picked up the following spring by the group of returning Astorians. This was one year earlier than the Arze-Garcia expedition in the south.

BRITISH TRAPPERS PENETRATE THE BASIN, 1819-1824

After selling Astoria (1813) to a British company, the American fur traders left the rich regions of the Rocky Mountains and

---

⁴Frederic L. Paxon, *History of the American Frontier.* 321-330.

the Pacific Coast entirely to the British companies for nearly ten years.[5] Therefore, the next trappers to visit the Great Basin were members of the British Northwest Company. Donald McKenzie and his party of forty-nine members set out in September, 1818, from Walla Walla on the first Snake River expedition. In 1819-1820 they trapped with considerable profits along what McKenzie termed the "Spanish Waters." The foregoing statement indicates that they were in the Great Basin, which was claimed at that time by Spain. In September, 1819, they were on the shores of Bear Lake and trapped in its vicinity for five months. The following spring they returned to Walla Walla with peltries sufficient to load 154 horses. This party had reaped as much profit as the remainder of the British company who had spent their time in the Columbia River region.

In June, 1824, three years after the Northwest Company had been taken over by the Hudson Bay Company, a group of Iroquois Indians, led by a trapper named Pierre, left the main group of trappers on the Snake River and passed "over the Spanish border and penetrated the interior." For two months they trapped along the Bear River and its branches, catching over 900 beaver.[6]

Activities of the American Trappers

Meanwhile Americans had again entered the fur trading enterprise in competition with the British companies. The British had been without competition in the Far West since their purchase of Astoria in 1813 until William Henry Ashley and Major Andrew Henry organized a large American company with headquarters located at St. Louis, Missouri. In the spring of 1822 they enlisted in the first group 100 young men, many of whom became the pathfinders and explorers of the Great Basin. The names of Jedediah S. Smith, James Bridger, Etienne Provot, Ashley, Henry, Thomas Fitzpatrick, the Sublette brothers, and many others "should become household words in the homes of the Rockies and the inland Basin."[7] They were the first explorers and pathfinders of the vast area. Peter Skene Ogden of the Hudson Bay Company should be added to this list of American trappers. He was a true frontiersman who left his imprint on Utah history. Ogden City and Ogden River were named after him. He camped on the river in 1838, following a hazardous trip from California, across the desert and around the north end of Great Salt Lake. On this journey he discovered

[5]Cardinal Goodwin, *The Trans-Mississippi West*, 1803-1853, 114-149.
[6]Snow, *op. cit.*, 38-46.
[7]*Ibid.*, 50.

the Humboldt River and explored the country from San Francisco to Ogden, Utah.

From 1822 to 1824 the Ashley-Henry company trapped in the Yellowstone Park region, meeting several disastrous reverses, such as Indian attacks. But an event occurred early in 1824 (probably February) which had a far-reaching effect upon determining the future American ownership of the Great Basin and the country westward to the Pacific Ocean. This event was the discovery of the famous South Pass by some of the Ashley-Henry trappers under the leadership of Thomas Fitzpatrick. The South Pass supplied the much needed opening through the almost impassable Rocky Mountains over which passed the trappers, government explorers, and later, the stream of emigrant trains, including Mormons.

In the spring of 1824 the Ashley-Henry trappers had remarkable success in the Green River region, Wyoming. That fall they divided into three groups. The largest party was under William L. Sublette. He and his men wintered in Cache Valley, northern Utah. A small company of only six men, under Jedediah S. Smith, trapped farther north and came in contact with Peter Skeen Ogden and company on their Snake River expedition of 1824-1825. The third group was under Etienne Provot. That winter (1824-1825) he and his companions probably followed Black's Fork from Green River to its head and then down the Weber River to the Great Salt Lake. There most of his men were massacred by Indians, but Provot managed to escape. Later he joined Ashley's men in Cache Valley.

Leaving Saint Louis in November, 1824, Ashley came to Utah to join his trappers and take the peltries back East the following spring. His trip is of unusual importance, because he pursued a new pathway from the Missouri River westward over which the overland trail and the Union Pacific Railroad and the Mormons later followed. He came westward via Platte River, Sweetwater, South Pass, and southwestward to the Green River and Fort Bridger country, and then on northwestward into Cache Valley.

In the spring of 1825, Ashley and his men were led by Provot into the Salt Lake Valley and they explored the country as far south as Ashley (Sevier) Lake.[8] Then Ashley returned to Saint Louis with a fortune which had been collected by his trappers.

Historians have not agreed on whom to give credit for the discovery of the Great Salt Lake. The names Ogden, Provot, Vasquez, and James Bridger have all been suggested for the honor.

----

[8]Young, *op. cit.*, 58.

Before the winter of 1824-1825 had closed, probably several trappers had gazed upon the inland sea, but with the scant records available, it is impossible to state definitely which one saw its waters first. But after weighing all the available evidence, Dr. William J. Snow concluded that Jim Bridger was the first white man that we "positively know to have seen the Great Salt Lake."[9]

Briefly, the story of Jim Bridger's discovery is as follows: In the fall of 1824, William L. Sublette and his party were camped on the bank of the Bear River in Cache Valley. Curiosity caused them to speculate as to where the stream flowed. Characteristic of western fashion, they satisfied their curiosity by making a wager and then sending Bridger to find out who won. In a small boat, he descended the Bear River from Cache Valley until it flowed into the Great Salt Lake. After tasting its brackish waters, he returned to Sublette's camp to inform the trappers that he had discovered "an arm of the Pacific Ocean."

During the spring and the summer of 1825 the trappers were on the Bear, Green and Salt rivers, and when fall came they gathered at their rendezvous in Cache Valley. Before winter set in, however, they moved to the Salt Lake Valley and established a typical trappers' rendezvous at the mouth of the Weber River, near the present site of Ogden. Their camp was in reality a pioneer village. It contained over 600 persons, including the squaws, which some of the trappers had married, and their children.

Of course Ashley's men were curious to learn all they could regarding the Great Salt Lake. Therefore, during the winter they circumnavigated it in canoes, requiring twenty-four days for the trip. They estimated it to be one hundred miles long and sixty to eighty miles wide, a rather close approximation.

In July, 1826, Ashley sold the fur business to Jedediah S. Smith, David E. Jackson and William L. Sublette. American trappers under the new managers continued their industry until every stream of the Great Basin became well known to them. Through their explorations an abundance of information was accumulated which had its influence in determining national thought and policies toward the Far West. In the words of H. M. Chittenden:

They were the pathfinders of the West, and not those later official explorers whom posterity so recognizes. No feature of western geography was ever discovered by government explorers after 1840. Everything was already known and had been for a decade. It is true that many features, like the Yellowstone wonderland, with which these restless rovers were familiar, were afterward forgotten and rediscovered in later years; but there has never been a time until

---

[9] Snow, op. cit., 77-96.

very recently when the geography of the West was so thoroughly understood as it was by the trader and trapper of 1830 to 1840.[10]

The trapper who contributed most to the history of the Great Basin was Jedediah S. Smith. He "is looked upon by historians as one of the foremost frontiersmen of American history. His achievements entitled him to rank with Lewis and Clark in the group of foremost American explorers."[11]

The new managers of the fur company decided that Smith was to explore the extensive country lying south and west of the Great Salt Lake. Thereupon, he and fifteen companions departed southward on August 22, 1826. They struck the Colorado River where the Virgin flows into it. Upon reaching the Mojave village, they rested a few days before resuming their journey to the Spanish Mission at San Gabriel, California. From there they traveled northward about 300 miles through California. Then Smith with only two companions left the main party and struck boldly across the Sierra Nevada, which was covered with snow from four to eight feet deep. Between the Sierras and the Salt Lake region lay 600 miles of barren desert country, but the pathfinder plunged into it unhesitatingly. The trip consumed twenty-eight days, during which time both men and animals almost died from thirst and lack of food.

Smith's trip had taken him almost completely around the southern end and back through the heart of the Basin. He had explored the routes later followed by highways and by railroads.

He had no sooner arrived at the rendezvous on Bear Lake and reported to his partners before he departed (July 13, 1827) on a second exploring expedition through the Basin to California. While traveling he not only suffered from hunger, thirst, and fatigue, but lost most of his men through an Indian attack. On the return trip he became familiar with the country near the north rim of the Basin and north of the Great Salt Lake.

On August 4, 1830, Smith and his partners sold their business to Jim Bridger and others, and the next spring Smith was killed by the Comanche Indians while accompanying a wagon caravan of merchandise from Saint Louis to Sante Fe. Levi Edgar Young wrote in regard to Jedediah S. Smith: "He is interesting to us as a frontiersman in that he was the first white man after Escalante to explore what is now Utah. In fact, he was the first American to write about Utah."[12]

[10]H. M. Chittenden. *The History of the American Fur Trade in the Far West*, I, 9.
[11]H. C. Dale, *Journal of Sublette* (1842).
[12]Young, *op. cit.*, 61.

During the thirties the trappers depleted the streams of beaver, and the fur business waned. Thereupon some of them returned to the East, but others built themselves cabins and settled down in the great West with their Indian wives and children. They were the mountaineers that were still here when the pioneers arrived in 1847. James Bridger and Miles Goodyear came into the story of colonial Utah history rather prominently.

Official Explorations—Captain Bonneville's Expedition, 1832-1836

Following the trappers and traders into the Far West came the government explorers. Captain Bonneville has usually been listed as one of them and given a more important place in Great Basin history than he probably deserved. In fact, his activities in the West cannot really be regarded as an official government expedition, but they will be presented here briefly because he received his orders from the War Department. Those instructions were for Bonneville to examine the soil, mineral resources, climate, geography and topography of the Rocky Mountain section. He followed none of the instructions but tried to enrich himself in the fur industry.

His contribution to the history of the Great Basin was to send forty men in July, 1833, under J. R. Walker, on a trip to California. They traveled from the Green River across the Basin over country which had been explored years earlier by the trappers. And, before leaving the West, he gathered what information he could from trappers relative to the geography of the Great Basin, and from it drew a map. From that map and his journal and from other source materials on the fur industry, Washington Irving published a book in 1837, which had excellent results in stimulating the adventurous people in the East to look towards the Far West as a possible place in which to build homes.

John C. Fremont, the Government Explorer, 1843-1846

However, John C. Fremont's explorations of the Great Basin between 1843 and 1846 are of paramount significance. Their value did not rest on new discoveries, but upon the thorough and scientific observation which he made and published. He was a great explorer who made accurate observations of the entire geography and topography of the Great West. Although the trappers had discovered every important spot in the Basin before Fremont arrived, they had not delineated those discoveries and published them. That Fremont did.

In May, 1843, John C. Fremont, with a company of thirty-nine men, left Kansas City. He followed the Oregon Trail to southern Idaho, then turned south through northern Cache Valley and on to the shores of the Great Salt Lake, arriving there in September. From his camp near the present site of Ogden, he explored the island in the Great Salt Lake, made mathematical calculations relative to the altitude of its highest point, tested the waters of the lake to discover their constituent elements, and made other observations which appeared later in his map and official reports. Fremont spent five days in this activity and then resumed his journey toward Fort Hall and into Oregon.

Soon after arriving at Vancouver, Fremont returned to the Great Basin and made "further explorations and surveys of considerable note." He traveled southward through central Nevada, then westward over the mountains to Sutter's Fort, arriving there in January, 1844. He and his men rested a few days and then resumed the journey southward through California, and across the south end of the Basin via the Old Spanish Trail to Utah Lake, thence eastward up Spanish Fork Canyon and on out of Utah.

The following year, 1845, Fremont was again in the Basin. He spent two weeks making careful topographical observations in the vicinity of the Great Salt Lake, and then struck out directly westward. Reaching the Ogden River in Nevada, he named it Humboldt, and that name has remained attached to the stream to the present time. Thus the trapper Peter Skene Ogden, the discoverer of the river, was robbed of his honor. Fremont's party divided. Part of the company crossed the mountains over Donner's Pass and the rest over Walker's Pass.

Thus Fremont had almost completely circled the Great Basin and had crossed through its center, making careful observation of all he saw. The explorations of the trappers were culminated in Fremont's official reports, and the people of America and Europe learned of the Great Basin.

IMMIGRATION TO CALIFORNIA BEFORE 1847

Fremont's reports combined with other vital forces caused many of the Americans who were endowed with the spirit of the frontier to migrate to the Far West. During the years immediately preceding the coming of the Mormons to the Basin, American home-seekers were finding their way to Oregon and California.

The first to immigrate to California arrived there in 1841. Between that date and the coming of the Donner Party (1846), several companies traveled through the Basin. Their route was usually via southern Idaho and the Humboldt, but the Donner Party passed over the same route from Fort Bridger to Salt Lake that the Mormons followed the succeeding year. The story of their disastrous misfortune in the Sierra Nevada is well known.

None of those earlier home-seekers who migrated to the Far West prior to 1847 thought that the dry, hard, barren, forbidding Basin of the Great Salt Lake was a fit place for a home. In the words of Herbert E. Bolton:

> As the emigrants saw it, it was a country that God forgot. Oregon and California were the only goals of the travel-worn throng who braved perils of the Basin. To change this situation would require a miracle, and a hardier, more determined, more desperate people than any who had so far appeared in the Far West.
>
> Suddenly a new actor stepped out upon the gigantic stage and for a quarter of a century occupied its center. It was Brigham Young, at the head of the Latter-day Saints. . . . For the main seat of the Saints the forbidding desert of the Basin best fitted Young's grim purpose.[13]

[13]Herbert E. Bolton, "The Mormons in the Opening of the Great West," *The Utah Genealogical and Historical Magazine*, XVII (Salt Lake City, January, 1926), 52-53.

CHAPTER IV

EXPLORING FOR NEW HOMES

TREKKING OF THE PIONEER PARTY ACROSS THE PLAINS, 1847, AND THE GATHERING OF INFORMATION REGARDING THE GREAT BASIN

The Great Basin, which was comparatively well known to the trappers, traders, and scouts before 1847, was an entirely new country to the Mormon Pioneers. Their most important task, then, was to make a careful and complete exploration of this land in which they were to build their homes. The directing force and guiding hand in these numerous exploration feats was President Brigham Young. Even before arriving in the Great Basin, the Mormon Leader took advantage of every opportunity to acquaint himself with all of the country lying within and west of the Rocky Mountains.

The exiled Saints had paused (1846), 15,000 strong, on the banks of the Missouri River where Omaha and Council Bluffs now stand. While they built temporary homes they gleaned all the information they could about the Great West and put their future entirely into the hands of God and their prophet and leader— Brigham Young. The Mormons had implicit faith that they would be guided to the safest and best sanctuary.

In the fall of 1846 a man of great prophetic vision, Father Pierre Jean De Smet, a Jesuit priest, visited the Mormon refugees. They listened with attentive eagerness to the Catholic Father's account of his explorations of the Great West and to his impressions of that country. Concerning the incident Father De Smet wrote to his nephew in March, 1851, as follows:

> In the fall of 1846, as I drew near to the frontiers of the State of Missouri, I found the advance guard of the Mormons, numbering about ten thousand, camped upon the territory of the Omahas not far from old Council Bluffs. They had just been driven out for a second time from a State of the Union. . . . They asked me a thousand questions about the regions I had explored, and the valley which I have just described to you pleased them greatly from the account I gave them of it.[1]

Father De Smet and Brigham Young entertained, without doubt, the same dreams about the western wilderness. Brigham, through his wise leadership and position as head of the Church of

---
[1]Cited in Levi Edgar Young, *The Founding of Utah*, 86.

Jesus Christ of Latter-day Saints, made these dreams come true.
Father De Smet wrote prophetically of the Great Basin:

> In my visits to the Indian tribes I have several times traversed the immense plains of the West. Every time I have found myself amid a painful void. Europe's thousands of poor, who cry for bread and water without shelter or hope, often occur to my thoughts. "Unhappy poor!" I often cry, "why are ye not here? Your industry and toil would end your sorrows. Here you might rear a smiling home and reap in plenty the fruit of your toil." The sound of the axe and hammer will echo in this wilderness; broad farms with orchards and vineyards, alive with domestic animals and poultry, will cover these desert plains to provide for thick-coming cities, which will rise as if by enchantment with dome and tower, church and college, school and house, hospitals and asylums.[2]

The story will be told in later chapters how the Mormon missionaries, under the direction of President Brigham Young, gathered thousands of the poor from Europe as well as from other parts of the earth and established them in the midst of the Rocky Mountains. These emigrants from many lands did cover these desert valleys with cities, churches, colleges, hospitals and asylums.

The pioneer company while trekking westward from Council Bluffs occasionally met groups of traders, trappers and mountaineers from whom they secured information relative to the Great Basin. Near South Pass they met Major Harris who had spent most of twenty years in the country between the Rocky Mountains and the Pacific. Orson Pratt reported the conversation with Harris as follows:

> We obtained much information from him in relation to the great interior Basin of the Salt Lake, the country of our destination. His report like that of Captain Fremont's is rather unfavorable to the formation of a colony in this basin, principally on account of the scarcity of timber. He said that he had traveled the whole circumference of the lake, and there was no outlet to it.[3]

Two or three days later, June 28, 1847, the Pioneers met James Bridger and two companies en route for Fort Laramie. Pratt stated that Mr. Bridger "Being a man of extensive acquaintance with this interior country, we made many inquiries of him in relation to the 'Great Basin' and the country south. His information was rather more favorable than that of Major Harris."[4]

ORSON PRATT'S VANGUARD COMPANY

As the sun was nearing the western horizon July 19, 1847,

---

[2] *Ibid.*, 85.
[3] Orson Pratt, *Journal*, June 27, 1847. Ms.
[4] *Ibid.*

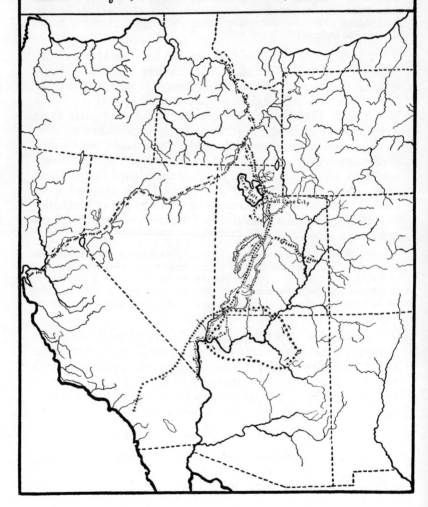

MORMON EXPLORATIONS

Jesse C. Little, August, 1847 >···>···>··
Parley P. Pratt, December, 1847 >>>>>>>
James Brown, fall of 1847 ++ ++ ++ ++++
Jefferson Hunt, 1847-1848 ++++++++···
Parley P. Pratt, 1849-1850 ─···─···─···
Albert Carrington, 1852 ᴨᴨᴨᴨᴨᴨᴨᴨᴨ

John C.L.Smith, June,1852 ─ ─ ─ ─ ─ ─
William Gardner, September,1853 ···+···+···
Salmon River Mission, 1855 ···*···*···*·
Elk Mountain Mission, 1855 ᐊᐊᐊᐊᐊᐊᐊᐊᐊ
Jacob Hamblin, 1858 ∾∾1862 *·*·*·*·*
Anson Call, 1864 ···ᐊ···ᐊ···ᐊ···ᐊ···

Orson Pratt and John Brown climbed a mountain peak near East Canyon and beheld for the first time the valley of the Great Salt Lake.[5] Orson Pratt was the leader of the vanguard commissioned by Brigham Young on July 12 to go ahead of the main company in order to make a road and locate the valley. This advance company consisted of twenty-five wagons and forty-two men. Brigham Young and the main body of the Pioneer company were delayed somewhat due to many of the members, including Brother Brigham, being taken ill with mountain fever.

Erastus Snow on July 21 overtook Orson Pratt with a message from Brigham Young to bear northward after leaving the canyon and to select a convenient place for plowing and planting seed. That afternoon Pratt and Snow, with one horse between them, came to the mouth of Emigration Canyon. After experiencing much difficulty in traveling, they finally reached the summit of a little hill from whence they viewed "a broad, open valley about twenty miles wide and thirty long, at the north end of which the water of the Great Salt Lake glistened in the sunbeams." Snow reported his experience of viewing for the first time the Salt Lake Valley:

> The thicket down the narrows, at the mouth of the canyon, was so dense that one could not penetrate through it. I crawled for some distance on my hands and knees through the thickets, until I was compelled to return, admonished to by the rattle of a snake, which lay coiled up under my nose, having almost put my hand on him; but as he gave me the friendly warning, I thanked him and retreated. We raised on to a high point south of the narrows, where we got a view of the Great Salt Lake and this valley, and each of us, without saying a word to the other, instinctively, as if by inspiration, raised our hats from our heads, and then, swinging our hats, shouted.[6]

Pratt and Snow entered the valley and went south to Mill Creek to examine what had appeared from the distance to be fields of waving grain but upon inspection proved to be merely canes growing near the bank of a stream. Recalling Brother Brigham's instructions, they retraced their steps to the mouth of Emigration Canyon. Pratt continued the journey alone to the present site of Salt Lake City while his companion went in search of his coat which had fallen from their saddle. After standing on the spot where the temple was later erected, Pratt joined his companion, Snow, where they had parted earlier in the day. Together they returned to their other companions in Emigration Canyon, arriving there late in the evening.

----

[5]Levi Edgar Young, *op. cit.*, 118.
[6]Erastus Snow, "Address to the Pioneers," *Latter-day Saint Journal History*, July 24, 1880, Ms.

Early in the morning of July 22, Orson Pratt, George A. Smith, and seven others entered the valley and encamped on the bank of Canyon Creek. From here they explored the valley to the north and to the west, going as far north as Hot Springs and west across the Jordan River.[7] In the words of Orson Pratt:

> After going down into the valley about five miles, we turned our course to the north, down towards the Salt Lake. For three or four miles north we found the soil of a most excellent quality. Streams from the mountains and springs were very abundant, the water excellent, and generally with gravel bottoms. A great variety of green grass, and very luxuriant, covered the bottoms for miles where the soil was good, yet the grass had nearly dried up for want of moisture. We found the drier places swarming with very large crickets, about the size of a man's thumb. This valley is surrounded with mountains, except on the north, the tops of some of the highest being covered with snow. Every one or two miles streams were emptying into it from the mountains on the east, many of which were sufficiently large to carry mills and other machinery. As we proceeded toward the Salt Lake the soil began to assume a more sterile appearance, being probably at some seasons of the year over-flowed with water. We found as we proceeded on, great numbers of hot springs issuing from near the base of the mountains. These springs were highly impregnated with salt and sulphur; the temperature of some was nearly raised to the boiling point. We traveled for about fifteen miles down after coming into the valley, the latter parts of the distance the soil being unfit for agricultural purposes.[8]

The following day, July 23, the camp was moved northward to what was subsequently known as the Eighth Ward square in the section now occupied by the Salt Lake City and County Building. The site selected was on the bank of a stream of pure water which they named City Creek.

"THIS IS THE PLACE"

Saturday, about noon of July 24, 1847, President Brigham Young with the main portion of the pioneer company emerged upon the narrow plateau near the mouth of Emigration Canyon. Wilford Woodruff wrote: "We gazed in wonder and admiration upon the vast valley before us, with the waters of the Great Salt Lake glistening in the sun. . . . Many things of the future, concerning the valley, were shown him (Brigham Young) in vision."[9] The President remarked, "This is the place. Drive on."

By the time Brigham arrived in the Great Basin, he had made definite plans in regard to exploration. He stated that "he intended to have every hole and corner from the Bay of San Francisco

---

[7]Hubert Howe Bancroft, *History of Utah*, 260-261.
[8]*Millennial Star*, XII, 178.
[9]Wilford Woodruff, *Journal*, July 24, 1847, Ms.

known to us (the Mormons)."[10] He immediately began to put
this plan into operation.

Exploring parties were dispatched into the mountains to determine the amount of timber, water supply, grazing possibilities
and altitude of the mountain peaks. This process was repeated
in every valley of the Great Basin as the pioneers pushed the line
of exploration and colonization farther along the frontier. Some
of the instruments used in their computations they brought with
them; others, they devised. The accounts of such exploring expeditions are too numerous to be given here, but one should bear
in mind that a systematic and thorough exploration of each valley
and each mountain and canyon took place as the years passed.

Exploring Salt Lake and Tooele Valleys

Two days after his arrival, Brigham Young organized an
exploring party for the purpose of visiting various points in Salt
Lake and Tooele valleys. The camp historian, Wilford Woodruff,
gave this description:

> On Monday ten men were chosen for an exploring expedition. I took
> President Young in my carriage, and, traveling two miles toward the mountain,
> made choice of a spot for our garden.
>
> We then returned to camp, and went north about five miles, and we all
> went on to the top of a high peak, on the edge of the mountain, which we
> considered a good place to raise an ensign. So we named it "Ensign Peak."
> I was the first person to ascend this hill, which we had thus named.
> Brigham Young was very weary, in climbing to the peak, from his recent fever.
>
> We descended to the valley, and started north to the Hot Sulphur Springs,
> but we returned two miles to get a drink of cold water, and then went back
> four miles to the Springs. We returned to camp quite weary with our day's
> explorations. Brothers Mathew and Brown had crossed the valley in its nar-
> rowest part, opposite the camp, to the west mountain, and found it about
> fifteen miles.
>
> Next day . . . we again started on our exploring expedition. All of the
> members of the Quorum of the Twelve belonging to the pioneers, eight in
> number, were of the company. Six others of the brethren, including Brannan
> of San Francisco, were with us.
>
> We started for the purpose of visiting the Great Salt Lake and mountains
> on the west of the valley. We traveled two miles west from Temple Block
> and came to the outlet of Utah Lake; thence fourteen miles to the west moun-
> tain, and found that the land was not so fertile as on the east side.
>
> We took our dinner at the fresh water pool, and then rode six miles to
> a large rock on the shore of Salt Lake which we named Black Rock, where
> we all halted and bathed in the salt water. No person could sink in it, but
> would roll and float on the surface like a dry log. We concluded that the
> Salt Lake was one of the wonders of the world.

[10]*Ibid.*, July 28, 1847.

After spending an hour here, we went west along the lake shore, and then returned ten miles to our place of nooning making forty miles that day.[11]

Apostle Orson Pratt recorded:

We continued about four miles (Tooele Valley) putting up to the southward from the lake. This valley we judged to be about twelve miles in diameter. On the south there was a small opening into a plain beyond. It was nearly dark and we concluded to return to the place of our noon halt, where we encamped for the night.[12]

The exploring party observed that the land in Tooele Valley was level and the texture of the soil good. But there was very little water, and water was the most important item to the explorers in their efforts to locate sites for prospective communities. The following day Brigham Young and his associates returned to the pioneer camp in the Salt Lake Valley.

EXPLORING CACHE VALLEY

Twelve days later, August 9, 1847, Brother Brigham sent a small exploring party to Cache Valley. Upon returning Jesse C. Little and his three companions made their report to the President, part of which appears here:

On Monday, August 9, 1847, I started north with a little exploring company. . . . At Weber River we found a fort of Mr. Goodyear which consists of some log buildings and corrals stockaded in with pickets. This man had a herd of cattle, horses and goats. He had a small garden of vegetables, also a few stalks of corn, and although it had been neglected, it looks well, which proved to us that with proper cultivation it would do well. We continued north to Bear River. Here we parted with the captain's [James Brown] camp and turned east into Cache Valley, which looked beautiful from the summit of the mountains. We entered the valley and passed up to the southeast, thence returned through the mountains to Box Elder Creek. We then passed down this stream into the valley (Salt Lake) and followed our outward trek to the city, having been gone a week and traveled about two hundred miles.[13]

EXPLORING UTAH VALLEY

Before arriving in the Great Basin, Brigham and his associates had heard not only of the Cache Valley in the northern part of the present state of Utah, but also of the Timpanogos or Utah Valley lying south of the Salt Lake Valley. Naturally these frontiersmen were anxious to see that region also. Accordingly, only three days after the exploring party was sent to Cache Valley,

[11]Ibid. July 26-27.
[12]Toole Stake Manuscript History, July 27, 1847.
[13]Jesse C. Little, Journal, 47, Ms.

Albert Carrington, with two companions, started south. They took with them a boat on wheels. Proceeding as far as the top of the low spur that divides Utah and Salt Lake valleys, they viewed Utah Valley with its beautiful blue lake and its fertile region on the north and east sides varying from two to seven miles in width. After gazing upon that scene, the explorers descended into the canyon where the Jordan River passes from the Utah into the Salt Lake Valley. Here they launched their boat. Albert Carrington piloted it down the river while one of his companions drove the team. Upon returning to Salt Lake, they reported that they had discovered some hot springs close to the trail toward the south end of Salt Lake Valley; also that they had caught a number of fish ranging in length from a foot to eighteen inches in the Jordan River.

Merely seeing Utah Valley from the top of a mountain ridge was not sufficient for these frontiersmen. The fall crops had scarcely been planted before one of the pioneer leaders, Parley P. Pratt, made a rather complete and thorough exploring tour through Utah and adjacent valleys. In the words of Pratt:

Sometime in December, having finished sowing wheat and rye, I started, in company with a Brother Higbee and others, for Utah Lake with a boat and fish-net. We traveled some thirty miles with our boats, etc., on an ox wagon, while some of us rode on horseback. This distance brought us to the foot of Utah Lake, a beautiful sheet of fresh water, some thirty-six miles long by fifteen broad. Here we launched our boat and tried our net, being probably the first boat and net ever used on this sheet of water in modern times.

We sailed up and down the lake shore on its western side for many miles, but had only poor success in fishing. We, however, caught a few samples of mountain trout and other fish.

After exploring the lake and valley for a day or two, the company returned home, and a Brother Summers and myself struck westward from the foot of the Lake on horseback, on an exploring tour. On this tour we discovered and partly explored Cedar Valley, and there crossed over the west mountain range and discovered a valley beyond; passing through which we crossed a range of hills northward, and entered Tooele Valley. Passing still northward, we camped one night on a cold mountain stream and the next day we came to the southern extreme of Great Salt Lake, and passing around between it and the west mountains we journeyed in an eastern course, and crossing the Jordan, arrived in Salt Lake City—having devoted nearly one week to our fishing, hunting and exploring expedition.[14]

JAMES BROWN'S TRIP TO SAN FRANCISCO

When the expedition was sent to Cache Valley in the summer of 1847, it traveled as far as Bear River in company with Samuel

---

[14]Parley P. Pratt, *Autobiography of Parley P. Pratt,* 401-403.

Brannan, Captain James Brown and others, who were on their way to San Francisco. Brannan had already informed Brigham on the general conditions of the country between Salt Lake and San Francisco in his earnest plea for the Mormon Colonizer to bring his people on to the Pacific Coast. Captain James Brown returned from California that same fall with additional geographical data. Also, that autumn, many of the Mormon Battalion group came to Salt Lake from California. By then the pioneers in the Great Basin were rather well-informed on the characteristics of the country to the coast on the northern immigrants' route.

Jefferson Hunt Exploring the Southern Route to California in 1847-1848

Having received first-hand information on the northern route the little pioneer band in the Salt Lake Valley had to wait only a few months before a member of the battalion group, Jefferson Hunt, and eighteen companions, made their way to southern California by the Old Spanish Trail. They were the first Mormons to explore the "southern route" to the sea.

Jefferson Hunt, a captain in the Mormon Battalion, after having been discharged from military services at Los Angeles in July, 1847, obtained prices on cows and seed from Colonel Williams at the Williams' or Santa Ana del Chino Rancho, situated about thirty miles southwest of San Bernardino and about thirty-five miles east of the center of Los Angeles. November 13, 1847, Captain Hunt reported to the High Council of Great Salt Lake City the possibility of securing seed and livestock from that section of the country. The Church officials acted upon Hunt's suggestion, granted him leave to go to California, and called eighteen other men to accompany him. Asahel A. Lathrop, Orrin P. Rockwell, and Elijah K. Fuller were put in charge of the company.

Traveling through a country entirely new to them, and over a difficult trail which was not distinguishable throughout much of its course, greatly hampered their progress. Forty-five days passed before they reached their destination, while their food supply had been planned only for a thirty-day journey. Therefore, they consumed all of their provisions before reaching the vicinity of Las Vegas and thereafter were forced to eat their horses to save themselves from starvation. When they reached a point where Barstow station on the Salt Lake route is now located, they were forced to camp. Two of their strongest men—Shaw and Cornogg —rode ahead to Williams' Rancho del Chino to get provisions.

Mexicans were immediately dispatched with beef and fresh horses for the destitute explorers who then continued their journey to the destination.

Colonel Williams, who had made the acquaintance of Jefferson Hunt before Hunt's release from the Mormon Battalion, was very generous to this exhausted group of Saints. Plenty of food, including wild cows to be milked, was furnished them. After spending five or six weeks in resting, in exploring southern California and in preparing for the return trip, they left the Rancho del Chino (February 15, 1848) for Salt Lake with their supply of grains, seeds of various kinds and livestock.[15]

Thus within a very few months after the first pioneer group had arrived in the Great Basin, their scouts had crossed the desert to California both by the northern and southern routes and had brought back to the Church leaders much valuable information to be utilized in the colonization program. Several of the streams camped on and noted by Hunt and his associates became the sites for thriving Mormon communities within the next ten years.

ADDISON PRATT'S DESCRIPTION OF THE SOUTHERN ROUTE

October 9, 1849, Jefferson Hunt left Salt Creek (Nephi) on a second trip to California via the southern route. This time he was hired to guide a company of emigrants bound for California. Elders Addison Pratt and Hiram H. Blacknell, Mormon missionaries, were traveling with Hunt. By this time President Brigham Young had his associates looking in every direction for sites for settlements. The Journal kept by Addison Pratt on his trip was no doubt of value to the leader of the Mormon colonial movement in helping him to determine where to send colonists. A few extracts from Pratt's journal will illustrate the point. He stated:

Saturday, October 13, we traveled six miles and camped on a fine stream (Chalk Creek). This stream would sustain a small settlement; the bottoms consist of rich soil covered with an abundance of grass; dwarf cedars also abound in the neighborhood. On the head waters of this stream is a tribe of Indians called Pauvans. . . .[16]

October 18. We traveled five miles and camped on Beaver Creek. This is a fine stream flowing through wide bottoms, covered with an abundance of good grass. We remained here two days. The wagons had now all come up, and our company consisted of about 125 wagons and 1,000 head of cattle. . . .

----

[15]Asahel A. Lathrop to Brigham Young, in *Latter-day Saint Journal History*, May 18, 1848. Ms.
[16]Addison Pratt. *Journal*. October 13, 1849. Ms.

I think this creek would support a settlement of some thousands. This creek discharges its water into Sevier Lake, and a range of mountains separate it from little Salt Lake Valley. October 27. We traveled twenty-seven miles and camped on the first creek in Little Salt Lake Valley. This is a large valley with good grass, but it is poorly watered; it ought to sustain a large settlement. October 31. We traveled thirteen miles and camped on a stream called Little Muddy. . . . Near this spring are immense quantities of rich iron ore. . . ."[17]

More detail will be given in the chapter on the "Mormon Corridor" relative to the significance of Hunt's trips to California and also in regard to other Mormon groups who traveled over the southern route to the Pacific Coast at that time and contributed their part to the opening of the Great West to civilization.

[17]*Ibid.,* October 18, 27, 31, 1849. Within a few years colonies were placed on all of the above-mentioned streams.

Chapter V

THE SOUTHERN EXPLORING COMPANY

Chief Walker's Request—Exploring Sanpete Valley

The route to California traveled by the Mormon scouts, explorers and traders from 1847 to 1849 was through Utah, Juab, Pauvan, Beaver, Little Salt Lake, and Dixie valleys, and then across the desert to the Pacific coast. It was the same trail as highway No. 91 follows today. The Saints had learned very little yet regarding the adjacent country lying on either side of the route previously described.

Lying just east and separated by a range of the Wasatch Mountains from the above-mentioned valleys, lies another line— Sanpete, Sevier, and Panguitch being the principal ones there. In June of 1849, Walker, the Ute Indian war chief, visited Brigham Young in Salt Lake City and asked that he send colonists to Sanpete Valley to teach the natives how to live like the white men. The president assured the Indian chief that it should be done according to his desires. Consequently, about two months later, Brigham sent an exploring party to Sanpete Valley to select a site for a colony. They returned to the Mormon Mecca and made a favorable report on the feasibility of sending colonists to that part of the Great Basin.

Southern Exploring Company

A little more than two years had now passed since the first Mormon pioneer company arrived in the Great West. Colonies had spread to various points in the Salt Lake Valley. Ogden had been established on the Weber River thirty-eight miles to the north. Fort Utah (Provo), forty-four miles south of the parent colony was now six months old. Isaac Morley with a group of 224 colonists was arriving in Sanpete Valley, 135 miles south of Salt Lake at that time for the purpose of establishing a settlement. Brother Brigham's dream of an empire was beginning to be a reality. But in order to more systematically colonize the Great Basin, a more scientific and thorough exploration than had heretofore been made was necessary.

Therefore, in the fall of 1849, President Brigham Young was planning and preparing to send out an exploring party which proved

to be the most important expedition of this kind engaged in by
the Latter-day Saints. Apostle Parley P. Pratt was selected to lead
the expedition, with William W. Phelps and David Fullmer as
his counselors. The company was organized at the home of John
Brown on South Cottonwood Creek on November 23, 1849, and
received the name of the Southern Exploring Company. The same
military organization that had worked so effectively in bringing
the Saints across the plains was again utilized. The plan consisted
of a captain over fifty and a captain over ten.

The company consisted of fifty men; and they took the following supplies: twelve wagons, one carriage, twenty-four yoke of cattle,
thirty-eight horses and mules, an odometer to measure distance, a
brass field piece, small arms, seven beeves; also there were one
hundred fifty pounds of flour to each man besides crackers, bread
and meal.[1]

The purpose of this exploring expedition was to observe the
natural resources of the country and to choose sites for other settlements of the Mormons. Isaac C. Haight wrote in his journal:
"On the 9th of November, President Brigham Young desired me
to postpone my intentions of going to the mines, and instead,
accompany Brother Parley P. Pratt to explore the valleys southward . . . to find a valley for another settlement of the Saints in
the south part of the mountains of Israel."[2]

Route to Sanpete Valley

On November 25, the company of explorers passed the summit where they obtained a fine view of Salt Lake and Utah valleys
and the two lakes. Then they traveled down into Utah Valley,
arriving at Fort Utah (Provo) on the Provo River on the 27th.
The camp historian wrote: "The river, twenty-four yards wide,
eighteen inches deep, timber plentiful. . . . The fort was composed
of fifty-seven log houses on seventeen acres of ground, one hundred
rods from the Provo River."[3]

Throughout their journey, a careful and complete record was
kept of the soil conditions, vegetation, streams of water, timber,
pasturage, and any other items which might prove to be important
factors in assisting Brigham Young in determining where to establish colonies. For example, the camp journal reads as follows:

The company camped for the night (at) Hobble Creek . . . a good place

---

[1]*Latter-day Saint Journal History*, November 23, 1849, Ms.
[2]Isaac C. Haight, *Journal*, November 9, 1849, Ms.
[3]*Latter-day Saint Journal History*, November 27, 1849, Ms.

to settle with good soil and plenty of water.[4] November 29, 1849. . . . Sage and greasewood abundant. Sandy soil. Plenty dry feed. No snow. Crossed up creek (68 m.) six yards wide, one foot deep, bad descent, gravelly bottom. Beautiful fine food. The range of mountains on the east of Utah Valley curves from north to south around east. Traveled the west foot of east range round two thirds of a circle. Mountains studded with cedar and fir. Crossed branch of Summit Creek (70¾ m.) three feet wide, ten inches deep, fine rushing stream, and two hundred yards farther Summit Creek, thirty feet wide, one foot deep, beautiful clear water, cottonwood on banks, steep ascent from creek. Crossing seventeen miles from mouth of the canyon. Beautiful fine feed. The stream flows on the summit or ridge between Utah and Juab valleys. Land gently undulating from foot of mountains four or five miles down. . . . This is a pleasant situation overlooking Utah Lake and valley on the north and Juab Valley on the south. Passed a rocky spot (73¾ m.) and then began to descend into Juab Valley.[5]

Pratt's exploring company traveled through Juab Valley as far as Salt Creek (Nephi). Then they left the main road and followed up Salt Creek Canyon and over a range of the Wasatch Mountains into Sanpete Valley, reaching there only twelve days after Isaac Morley had arrived with his colonists.

The following day they left the Sanpete settlement and traveled toward the Sevier Valley. From then on until they reached the Little Salt Lake Valley, the explorers had to make a new trail most of the way. They reached the Sevier River on December 6. The camp historian stated that this place was 149½ miles from Salt Lake City. He described the stream as follows:

The Sevier is a noble river several feet deep with a sluggish current, having much the appearance of the Jordan, but considerably larger. It is apparently navigable for small steamers, but its valley and the country since the company left Sanpitch is mostly a desert, with the exception of small bottoms with grass and willows.[6]

VISIT TO CHIEF WALKER

Here on the Sevier five Utes came into camp and reported that Walker was up the river hunting. The following day Pratt read a letter to the Indian chief from President Young, and Dimick B. Huntington interpreted it. The letter told of the sack of flour that the "big Mormon chief" had sent to the Ute chief. Walker refused to make an answer to Apostle Pratt until he had seen his brother Arapeen, but he did advise the explorers not to pass over the mountains southeast, as there was no good country over there.

---

[4] A few months later Springville was established there.
[5] *Ibid.*, November 28, 29, 1849.
[6] *Ibid.*, December 6, 1849.

Most of Walker's tribe of Sanpitch Indians were ill. So at the request of the Indian chief, Parley P. Pratt, Dan Jones and Dimick B. Huntington, "went and prayed for the Indians . . . laying hands on them in the name of Jesus." The sick were given a supply of tea, coffee, sugar, bread and meat, and some good medical advice. Then the sack of flour sent by Brother Brigham was divided between Walker and Arapeen. Walker was now highly pleased, saying that he would have gone with the company had his people not been sick; however, he would send his brother Ammornah to act as guide in his stead.

DESCRIPTION OF MARY'S VALE

The exploring company continued up the Sevier River. By December 10 the weather became extremely cold, the river having frozen hard and the thermometer ranging around twenty degrees below zero. The following day their Indian guide deserted them. They continued their journey, however, noting each place suitable for a colony. The camp journalist stated:

We crossed the summit (200½ m.), and thence had a beautiful descent, still through the forest, to the foot of the mountain and entered Mary's Vale, a beautiful rich valley, densely covered with luxuriant high grass, mixed with fine rushes, and interspersed with willows. There was scarcely a sage brush to be seen. The valley which is from a quarter to one and a half miles wide contains perhaps two hundred acres of excellent land and is connected with more a few miles further up. . . . Parley P. Pratt appeared delighted with the place and remarked that he had not felt so much at home since he left Juab Valley. He had no doubt that this cozy little nook in the mountains would be settled. . . . Entering the Valley, the company put up a board marked "two hundred miles from Great Salt Lake City," though actually two hundred four miles by the company's travel.[7]

DIFFICULT TRIP OVER THE MOUNTAINS

Continuing their journey up the Sevier to a point two hundred thirty-two miles from Salt Lake City, the explorers found that the Sevier Valley terminated in an impassable canyon, with "an abrupt chain of mountains sweeping before and on each hand, and the river rushing like a torrent between perpendicular rocks."[8] They were forced to turn back and camp while scouts were sent out to find a pass. William W. Phelps and others reported that the road ahead was impassable. Pratt and Driggs rode about eight miles in search of a pass to the left about which Walker had in-

---

[7]*Ibid.,* December 12, 1849.
[8]*Ibid.,* December 15, 1849.

formed them. But they found the country too rough, "marred by huge piles of stones washed down from the mountains, and filled with gulleys, or the dry beds of torrents from the mountains." The snow lay two feet deep, and the hills were too abrupt for a passage with wagons.

Captain Brown and a portion of the exploring company spent most of the following day (December 16) searching a passage way to the right, over the Wasatch Mountains and on into the Little Salt Lake Valley. Toward evening they returned to camp and "reported a route difficult but not impassable, winding over a succession of canyons with steep ascents and descents, nearly perpendicular in places, with rocks and cobblestones all the way."[9] The record continued:

> The camp struck out from the Sevier and ascended a canyon, a rock road. About two and one-half miles up, came to a perpendicular descent. The road was fixed, the hind wheels of the wagons were locked, and the brethren held back with ropes and so passed the descent. . . . One-half of the wagons stopped at the foot of a steep long hill in Deer Canyon (237½ m.). Doubled teams with the other half and ascended to a creek. . . . Ascended a steep rocky long hill, and then descended twelve miles, holding back with ropes, both wheels being locked. Winding to the right, ascended another long hill, sidling and rocky, but the rocks covered with snow, which drifted on the lee side of the hill, one to two and one-half feet deep. Descended sidling steep rocky hollow, the brethren holding back with ropes. . . . Ascended nearly perpendicularly, snow drifted very deep, the wind blowing so strongly from the south on the ridges, as to nearly tear off the wagon covers. Descended to second canyon. . . . Ascended nearly perpendicularly, the snow being shoveled away as high as the oxen, ropes were hitched round the yokes, and the oxen pulled up by the brethren standing on the summit. The oxen then pulled up the wagons. . . . Some of the company ahead, breaking roads and shoveling the snow out of the way. Others held back their wagons. Moved down sidling into hollow and camped (241 m.).[10]

THE CAMP AT RED CREEK

On December 20, Pratt and Brown, who had ridden several miles ahead to explore the road, came into camp toward evening and reported that a pass had been discovered. The following evening the explorers camped on the northern extremity of Little Salt Lake Valley. They continued their journey southward, camping on Red Creek on December 23, two hundred seventy-eight miles from home. The camp historian wrote of this location:

> This was judged a suitable place for a settlement of from fifty to one

⁹*Ibid.*, December 16, 1849.
¹⁰*Ibid.*, December 17-20, 1849.

hundred families. The land is beautifully undulating, with a fall to the westward, well-calculated for watering. Willows, weeds and grasses are exceedingly
dense for thousands of acres. The pasture lands extend for miles north and
south of the farming lands. The foothills, one or two miles distant, black
with inexhaustible supplies of cedar and scrub pine, about twelve feet high
and easy of access.[11]

The cattle of the company had become so reduced by the
rough traveling and lack of sufficient feed that it was considered
absolutely necessary for them to rest. Accordingly the decision
was reached for a portion of the explorers to continue the expeditions to the Rio Virgin by pack animals, while the rest of the
company remained encamped with the cattle and wagons. David
Fullmer was appointed head over the camp which remained, with
Isaac C. Haight captain and clerk. Pratt instructed patrols of
the brethren to guard the camp incessantly. Exploring parties
were to be sent out for ten-day trips, but no more than one-half
of the camp were to be gone at one time.

Exploring Dixie Country on Horseback

Under the personal direction of Parley P. Pratt, twenty men
on horseback with pack animals left the camp on Red Creek,
December 26, for the purpose of continuing their exploration to
the Rio Virgin. Not many miles distant they passed Big Creek
(Center Creek, the present site of Parowan). They were highly
pleased with the natural resources of this particular part of the
valley, noting in some detail the "rich meadows and black soil . . .
the inexhaustible stores of lofty pine, of any desirable size . . .
quarries of free sand and limestone (which) abound in the neighborhood. All these streams afford excellent mill sites." Two or
three miles beyond that, they came to the south outlet of Little
Salt Lake Valley and entered into a more extensive one, running
to the southwest. They spent two days exploring it. Part of the
detailed description which they wrote appears here:

Left the road and camped on Muddy Creek [present site of Cedar City].
On the banks of which for several miles down, is a considerable quantity of
scattering cottonwoods, some large ones. Traveled twelve miles, good feed.
Below is a handsome expansive plain of very rich land, consisting partly of
overflowed wire grass meadows, all of which it was judged might be drained
and cultivated, using the water on the higher levels. Other portions of this
plain are dry and level, delightful for the plough and clothed with rich meadow
grass, rabbit weed, etc. The soil was mostly a rich black loam. These meadows

----

[11]*Ibid.,* December 23, 1849.

are two or three miles wide and appeared to extend from ten to twenty miles in length. . . .

On the southwestern borders of this valley are thousands of acres of cedar, constituting an almost inexhaustible supply of fuel, which makes excellent coal. In the center of these forests rises a hill of the richest iron ore. The water, soil, fuel, timber and mineral wealth of this and Little Salt Lake valleys, it was judged, were capable of sustaining and employing from 50,000 to 100,000 inhabitants, all of which would have these resources more conveniently situated than any other settlements the company had seen west of the States.[12]

Continuing their journey southward, the explorers crossed a summit and then descended into a country where the climate was distinctly changed. They had crossed the rim of the Great Basin. Within a distance of less than fifty miles, from the rim of the Basin to the junction of the Santa Clara and Rio Virgin, the elevation dropped over three thousand feet. There was no snow, for the climate was warm and springlike. They were in what was later named "Utah Dixie." The country exhibited an extremely barren appearance, but where there was vegetation, the grass was green and six inches high. "Prickly pears, mastqual, cactus, and tamimump, a wood used by the Indians as a substitute for tobacco," intermingled with greasewood and sage, were typical of the vegetation. The scouts were not very highly pleased with the appearance of this Dixie country. The camp historian wrote:

December 30. . . . Passed through scattering cedars and over a rugged, stony, sandy, almost indescribable country, thrown together in dreadful confusion and reminding one of the country near the South Pass and the Sandy, only a hundred times worse. The passes were very bad; indeed it seemed impossible for a wagon road to be made through the country. . . .

A wide expanse of chaotic matter presented itself, consisting of huge hills, sandy deserts, cheerless, grassless plains, perpendicular rocks, loose barren clay, dissolving beds of sandstone and various other elements, lying in inconceivable confusion—in short, a country in ruins, dissolved by the pelting of the storms of ages, or turned inside out, upside down, by terrible convulsions in some former age. Eastward, the view was bounded by vast tables of mountains, one rising above another and presenting a level summit at the horizon, as if the whole country had once occupied a certain level several thousand feet higher than its present, and had been washed away, dissolved, or sunk, leaving the monuments of its once exalted level, smooth and fertile surface. Poor and worthless as was the country, it seemed everywhere strewed with broken pottery, well-glazed, and striped with unfading colors.[13]

---

[12]Ibid., December 28-29, 1849. Within less than a year after the exploration of this section of the country, President Brigham Young sent George A. Smith with a group of Saints to establish a colony there. The colonists left Provo on December 15, 1850, and arrived in Little Salt Lake Valley on January 13, 1851. Thus Parowan was a direct outgrowth of the previous year's exploring expedition.

[13]Ibid., December 30, 31, 1849. It is of interest to note that within about four years the Mormon Colonizer began to establish settlements in the unpromising Dixie country, first by sending missionaries to the Indians on the Santa Clara in 1854. A few years later, large groups of colonists were sent to Dixie to develop semi-tropical industries such as cotton.

The company traveled down the Virgin River to where it joins the Santa Clara near the present city of Saint George, arriving there on the first day of 1850. Two days earlier three Indians had joined them and were at this time serving as guides. On the Virgin the explorers passed a small Indian farm where some stalks of corn, squashes, and grape-vines were growing, but the Indians had deserted the place. When they reached the Indian village on the Santa Clara, they found good irrigated crops of corn, pumpkins and squash. The village was composed almost entirely of men, the women and children having been sold to the Spaniards.[14]

Upon learning from the Indians the unpromising character of the country beyond, the explorers decided to travel northward up the Santa Clara and return to the camp in the Little Salt Lake Valley. Four days later they ascended the rim of the Basin and camped in a valley subsequently named Mountain Meadows. January 7 they entered the southern extremity of Little Salt Lake Valley. Parley P. Pratt and Dan Jones proceeded ahead of the company that night to Fullmer's camp, which had moved from Red Creek to Center Creek (Parowan).

A celebration next day welcomed the pack train. At the dinner, Pratt offered the following toast: "May this, the 8th of January be kept as the anniversary of the founding of a city of the Little Salt Lake Valley which will hereafter be built."[15]

While Pratt and his companions were exploring the Dixie country, those left at Fullmer's camp on Center Creek obtained a thorough knowledge of Little Salt Lake Valley and the adjacent canyons and mountains. They discovered large quantities of excellent timber and rich iron ore. They were so pleased with the valley that they regretted to leave it. Isaac C. Haight expressed himself as follows:

We are preparing to start for home tomorrow. I shall leave this place with regret, as it is one of the most lovely places in the Great Basin. On the east there are high towering mountains covered with evergreen forests and one of the most beautiful creeks running from them. On the west and north there is a large valley of the most beautiful land, and beyond a range of hills covered with eternal snow; all of which contribute to beautify the scenery, and while the clouds hang heavily on the mountains and the storms and tempests are raging, the valley enjoys a beautiful serenity.[16]

---

[14]*Ibid.*

[15]John Brown, *Journal,* January 8, 1850. Ms.

[16]Isaac C. Haight, *Journal,* January 9, 1850. Ms.

RETURN VIA PAUVAN VALLEY—WINTER CAMP AT CHALK CREEK

The following day the entire company began the difficult journey toward home, this time traveling through the valleys parallel to those by which they had come. They pronounced the country surrounding Beaver Creek an excellent place for a settlement. On January 15, snow began to fall and continued falling for three or four days. At Meadow Creek in Pauvan Valley on the 18th a foot of snow fell during one night, making it two feet deep on the level. The following day they were able to travel only ten miles to Chalk Creek (the present site of Fillmore). Because of the depth of the snow, it was impossible to continue farther with the wagons; the company was forced to go into winter camp on Chalk Creek. Apostle Pratt's journal states:

Snowing severely. . . . We held a council, and finding that our provisions would only sustain half of our company till spring, and traveling with the wagons was impossible, we decided upon leaving half the company to winter there with the wagons and cattle, and the other half, with some of the strongest mules and horses, should attempt to reach Provo—the southen frontier— distance upwards of one hundred miles. The company that remained were mostly young men without families. My counselor David Fullmer, being placed in command.[17]

PRATT AND OTHERS PUSHING FORWARD TO PROVO

January 22, Pratt with a company of about twenty men and animals left the main camp on Chalk Creek and started for Provo. That day they made nine miles, camping at night on the spot where Holden was subsequently built. The following day they pushed forward through snow three to four feet deep on the level. It was necessary for men to go ahead on foot and break the trail, while the entire company followed in one track. As it snowed all day, the travelers could see the course only at intervals so they set their course by a gap in the mountain which they took to be the pass.[18] They made only nine or ten miles under those extremely difficult conditions. They camped at night on a mountain pass (Scipio Ridge) on almost the exact spot where Father Escalante had camped in 1776. The next two days they traveled from Scipio Ridge to the ridge about four miles south of the Sevier River. Several of the animals gave out because of the lack of feed and were left in Round Valley (now Scipio). Snow was still falling. On the

---

[17]Parley P. Pratt, *Journal*, January 31, 1850, Ms.
[18]Brown, *op. cit.*, January 22, 1850.

morning of January 26, while encamped four miles south of the Sevier, Parley P. Pratt wrote in his journal:

> In the morning we found ourselves so completely buried in snow that no one could distinguish the place where we lay. Someone rising, began shoveling the others out. This being found too tedious a business, I raised my voice like a trumpet, and commanded them to arise; when all at once there was a shaking among the snow piles, the graves were opened, and all came forth! We called this Resurrection Camp.
>
> January 27. Our provisions being nearly exhausted, Chauncey West and myself volunteered to take some of the strongest animals and try to penetrate to Provo, which was still some fifty miles distant, in order to send back provisions to the remainder, who were to follow slowly.
>
> We started at daylight, breaking the way on foot, leading the mules in our track, and sometimes riding them. Traveled all day, averaging about knee-deep in snow. Camped at eleven at night on Summit Creek, extremely hungry and feet badly frozen. We built a small fire, it being the coldest night we had ever experienced,[19] and after trying in vain to thaw out our frozen shoes, stockings and the bottoms of our drawers and pants, we rolled ourselves in our blankets and lay trembling with cold a few hours.
>
> January 28. Arose long before day; bit a few mouthfulls off the last frozen biscuit remaining. Saddled up our animals, and after another laborious day, living on a piece of biscuit not so large as our fist, we entered Provo at dark; raised a posse of men and animals, with provisions, and set back the same night.[20]

The posse sent out with Pratt found one of the exploring party, a man named Taylor, who had wandered off ahead of the rest, about eight miles south of Provo. He was lying in the snow in a helpless condition with his horse standing by him. He lived, but lost the use of his limbs. The remainder of the company left behind were found in the southern end of Utah Valley about twenty miles south of Provo. They were entirely without food.

Results of Southern Exploring Company

The exploring party arrived at Fort Utah on January 31, and at Salt Lake City, February 2, 1850, without the loss of any life. They had traveled seven hundred miles and all of the trip had been during severe winter weather. The members of the company who were left at Chalk Creek with the wagons and oxen wintered themselves and cattle very well. They arrived at Salt Lake safely the following March.

The reports of the Southern Exploring Company under the

----

[19]Isaac C. Haight's journal states that the weather was thirty degrees below zero on the morning of January 28.

[20]Pratt, op. cit., January 26-28, 1850.

direction of Parley P. Pratt were of the most vital significance in helping to determine where colonies should be established. Within the next ten years President Young had sent out colonists to practically every site recommended by the report of the expedition. Latter-day Saints were building their homes on several of the best sites within the next two or three years. Only six months had passed after the return of Pratt's company before Brother Brigham and his counselors had made definite arrangements to establish a colony in Little Salt Lake Valley on Center Creek (Parowan). A year later the place where Pratt's wagon group wintered on Chalk Creek in Pauvan Valley was selected as the site upon which to build Fillmore, the first capital city of the Territory of Utah.

Chapter VI

FURTHER EXPLORATIONS FOR COLONY SITES

Exploring for Colony Sites

As Brigham's followers left the Mormon Mecca to establish new homes in various parts of the Great Basin, they were always eager to find other sites feasible for land settlement. It may be that en route to their new settlement they would observe desirable sites and report their findings to Brother Brigham; or it may be that after establishing a town far distant from the parent colony further explorations were made at even a greater distance.

Description of Pauvan and Beaver Valleys

A good example of Mormon colonists locating sites for other settlements while en route to establish a colony can be found in a letter written by Apostle George A. Smith. After arriving at Center Creek (Parowan) with his colonists only a year after Pratt's company had camped there, he wrote to President Young as follows:

Center Creek, Iron County,
January 17, 1851.

To His Excellency, Brigham Young:

. . . After crossing two ridges south of the Sevier, we found ourselves in an extensive valley, called the Pauvan Valley; as large, if not larger than Utah. There were several small creeks in this valley, about the size of Canyon Creek. Corn Creek sinks and forms a large meadow. The grazing is extensive; the range very good; plenty of cedar at hand, and the appearance of timber in the canyons, and the mountains. The soil had the appearance of being very good; it seemed to suit many farmers of our camp, who would have been perfectly satisfied to have remained at that point.

The Pioneers last season could make no report, on account of its being deeply covered with snow; but it truly is a prospect for a colony not to be slighted. If the legislature should organize Silver County, and send out a colony, it would succeed better than Iron County. Though this is the place where the pioneers were blocked with snow, they found, seven miles below, plenty of food for their animals, and found but little snow; not enough to obstruct the cattle grazing. Upon Corn Creek, we found about two acres which had been farmed by the Indians—corn stalks which would have been creditable in Ohio; and cobs, showing that the crop had ripened; also some wheat-heads, of this year's growth.

Beaver Valley is a pleasant valley, and finely located; the soil had the appearance of being fine; at a glance there are about six thousand acres, and plenty of water, plenty of wood, and from appearance (as we did not explore it), there is plenty of timber. Some of our camp think this valley far preferable to Little Salt Lake.[1]

There is no doubt that Smith's report had much influence in determining the selection of a site on Chalk Creek in Pauvan Valley the following year as the place to build the capital city of the Territory of Utah. However, before Fillmore was thoroughly established a rather extensive exploration was made of the entire valley, resulting in an enthusiastic feeling held by the officials as to colonizing possibilities there. President Young believed that hundreds of thousands of people could be supported in Pauvan Valley. Down to our time the lack of water has prevented this dream from coming true.

Brigham Young's Annual Trip to the South

Although Parley P. Pratt led the chief exploring party in the Utah colonial period, President Young himself went on many minor expeditions. Every year, accompanied by some of the other Church officials, he made frequent tours of the settlements. Throughout the course of these trips—which extended from the southern to the northern end of the Great Basin—the Mormon Colonizer was always alert for suitable sites to which he could send settlers.

A typical journey began on April 22, 1851, when President Young left Salt Lake to visit the southern settlements and especially "to explore the valley of the Sevier and other places."[2] His counselor Heber C. Kimball, his clerk Thomas Bullock, and at least four apostles were in the company. Bishop Anson Call and several families who had been called to strengthen the settlement recently established in the Little Salt Lake Valley also constituted a part of the president's party. Governor Young was elected president of the company.

They traveled into Utah Valley and then on into Juab Valley. Here careful observations of the streams, springs, vegetation, timber, and mountains were recorded. Ascending along Salt Creek through the canyon below Mount Nebo, the party crossed over the ridge into Sanpete Valley on April 28. But while passing through the canyon, they investigated a salt cave and salt springs from which they took along a half bushel of pure salt.

After Brigham had been accorded an enthusiastic reception

---

[1]George A. Smith, to Brigham Young, in *Latter-day Saint Journal History*, January 17, 1851, Ms.
[2]Thomas Bullock, *Deseret News*, June 28, 1851.

from the settlers in Manti, the party continued across an arid region to the Sevier River with which they were much impressed. Their route through the Sevier Valley approximated that taken by the Pratt expedition, and they met the same difficulties, having to descend ravines by doubling teams, and with the help of ropes. After they had been received by the colony in Little Salt Lake Valley, which Brigham named Parowan, they spent four days examining that region, paying special attention to its natural resources. On the return trip they followed Pratt's route to Salt Lake.

EXPLORING THE RIO VIRGIN AND DIXIE REGIONS

An exploring trip of somewhat less importance than Pratt's was begun in January, 1852, by John D. Lee, under the direction of Governor Young. Lee, who had just been sent to found a colony somewhere south of Parowan, received a letter from the President instructing him to form a party to explore the Virgin River. Although the project was at first distasteful to Lee, he remarked, "The policy was doubtless good, however revolting the disappointment may have been to my feelings; and past experience taught me that to hearken was better than to sacrifice."[3]

His company was composed of twelve men, four wagons, thirteen horses, and fifteen days' provisions. Lee stated, "The brethren and they that had joined our company in Iron County sold out their improvements in full faith of helping to form another settlement south of the waters of the Santa Clara and the Rio Virgin."[4] This attitude was typical of the willingness of the Saints to sell their property and assist in new projects when Brother Brigham called them to do so.

The company left Parowan, January 27, 1852. Upon reaching the Rio Virgin, Lee left half of the company with the wagons and ten of the animals, while he with six men and three horses explored the rough Dixie country. Lee's report suggested sites for settlement.

Otter Creek . . . affords land and other facilities sufficient, in many places, to warrant small settlements; one of which contained about three hundred acres of splendid land, and completely enclosed on three sides with a low range of mountains. . . . At the distance of fifteen miles from camp, we found ourselves in one of the most pleasant, lovely valleys that the mountains afford; it is about five miles in diameter. The soil is of a lovely, alluvial nature; and of dark chocolate color, and easily irrigated; banks of the stream low.

----

[3]John D. Lee, "Report," *Saint George Stake Manuscript History, 1847-1873,* 9.
[4]*Ibid.*

Two miles over a small range of mountains brought us in full view of the Santa Clara country and valley. This valley is about the same magnitude of the one already described. The soil is equally as good, and climate as pleasant; the beautiful springs, grapevines and meadows not excepted.[5]

While passing down the Santa Clara Valley, Lee and his companions observed about one hundred acres of squash and corn that had been cultivated by the Pinto Indians. Judging from the size of the stalks, the explorers concluded that this valley could raise crops as abundant as those raised in any part of the Great Basin.

The Santa Clara Indians were very friendly to the explorers and expressed the desire to have the Mormons settle among them. The establishing of an Indian mission there only two or three years later came about partly as a result of this expedition.

The explorers passed down the Santa Clara River and up the Rio Virgin, following a route similar to that followed by Pratt's company, only in the opposite direction. Traveling up the Rio Virgin some distance, they struck the California road and returned to Parowan.

Exploring Pauvan and Beaver Valleys

In the spring of 1852, while at Fillmore on another tour of the southern settlements, President Young took occasion to have Pauvan and Beaver valleys thoroughly explored. Heretofore the exploring parties had merely passed through these valleys, skirting the eastern mountain range. A portion of a letter of May 29, 1852, from Brigham Young to Colonel Thomas L. Kane described this excursion:

At Fillmore City . . . we sent out a small party under the direction of Colonel Albert Carrington to explore for lead, some indication of which had been reported and moreover being an article very much needed. He proceeded in a northwesterly direction skirting the mountain ranges on his right through the passes of which we had made our way from Salt Lake City until he reached the Sevier River, some forty miles distant, which having now taken a southerly course makes its way to Sevier Lake. In this direction from Fillmore the country is open, no mountain intervening between it and the great western desert, and the river can be brought around to supply any deficiency of water in the Pauvan Valley.[6]

Following down the devious windings of this stream the Colonel found an opening into another valley lying west of Pauvan in which the aforesaid city is located and tributary thereto, which passing on his left continued down

---

[5] *Ibid.*

[6] Only about twenty years ago the canal that Brigham mentioned was built from the Sevier River across the Pauvan Valley, striking just west of Fillmore. Brigham Young's engineering ability was remarkable.

to the mouth of the river and along the eastern shore of the lake from its head about twenty miles, passed over a low range into it. The lake is about twenty-five or thirty miles long and ten to twelve broad and salt water with hard gravelly shores, steep slopes from low mountain ranges on eastern and western sides. The valley which he now entered laying as before shown westerly and southerly from Fillmore city is one of exceeding beauty and fertility, having a large stream called the Beaver running through the entire length of it in a northerly direction entirely past the lake, west of the range spoken of, and in high water empties into the Sevier in a contrary direction of that river about five miles above its mouth. For fifty miles he traveled up this stream, the valley sloping smoothly from the bank on either side to the mountain benches from fifteen to twenty miles apart. How many inhabitants, think you, will such a valley sustain? An abundance of cedar groves grow on the benches and mountain slopes. The Colonel remarked that he never saw a more beautiful valley, nor one that could be so extensively and easily irrigated, no ravines nor ridges to intervene the gentle flow of the waters on either side. This valley taken in connection with Pauvan furnishes a greater extent of country lying in a body susceptible of cultivation than any that has hitherto been explored, as the Pauvan itself is from fifty to sixty miles long, by thirty to fifty broad.[7]

Exploring the "Upper Sevier and South Country"

Further exploration was begun in June, 1852, when John C. L. Smith, who was then presiding over the Saints in Iron County at Parowan, received word that the old Indian chief Awannap, or as Walker called him, Quinarrah, wished to see him. He requested Smith to visit him at the Panguitch Lake where he had his tribe collected. Smith consented. Taking John D. Lee along as an interpreter, he and five companions traveled up Center Creek, took the left fork, passed over the divide and came to Panguitch Lake where they were given a friendly welcome by the natives. They returned by the same route, the first explorers to travel over it.

Smith and three companions then made arrangements to explore the "upper Sevier and south country." On June 12, 1852, they left Parowan and passed Red Creek where a settlement named Paragonah had already been established. The party traveled up Little Creek Canyon and over the pass into Sevier Valley. On the Sevier side of the mountain, John C. L. Smith suggested that "there is a good chance for a small colony to settle there, of some fifty to one hundred families, who might wish to go into the lumber trade."[8]

Upon striking the Sevier River, the company proceeded along

7Brigham Young, to Colonel Thomas L. Kane, in *Latter-day Saint Journal History*, May 29, 1852. Ms.
8John C. L. Smith, *Deseret News*, August 7, 1852.

its course for two days, finding only one place which they regarded as a suitable site for a colony. This was near the headwaters of the stream where the present town of Hatch is located. They continued their journey southward, passing along the main divides and down into Pleasant Valley. Smith stated: "There can be a good wagon road got from the Sevier country, to this point. There are plenty of hops and timber, and some handsome places for settlements in the narrow but fertile bottom of the stream."[9]

Shortly, they reached the headwaters of the Virgin and advanced along its course to the forks of the Virgin, LaVerkin and Ash Creek. Here Indians were farming. They were well pleased when John D. Lee told them that the Mormon chief, Brigham Young, was going to send missionaries among them to "teach them to work and raise breadstuff, make clothing, etc." It was not many years before colonizing activities were extended over this country newly explored by Smith and his companions.

The explorers crossed Ash Creek, took the Old Spanish Trail, and soon arrived at Parowan. They had been gone twelve days and had traveled three hundred thirty-six miles.

Exploring the Weber and Provo Rivers

Exploration was being carried on simultaneously in the northern as well as the southern part of the Great Basin. On September 2, 1853, William Gardner, accompanied by several others, left Salt Lake City for an exploring expedition along the Weber River and back down the Provo River. Gardner recorded the careful observations that were made for favorable sites for settlements, for grazing lands, for timber supply, for accessibility for floating lumber down the two rivers, and the possibility of building a road through the district. The party observed a few good valleys which were recommended to the Mormon Colonizer for settlement; for example, a valley on the Weber River was described:

> Here we struck into a beautiful valley at the mouth of the West Branch (of the Weber River), which runs along the back of the second mountain. The valley seemed to be from two to three miles wide, extending to the mountains on each side of the river, and about five or six miles long and running up the west branch some two or three miles. We named this valley Gardner's Valley. It affords fine facilities for a settlement. The surface of the valley is smooth, the soil excellent and grass good.[10]

Special mention was made throughout the whole report of the

---

[9]*Ibid.*
[10]William Gardner. *Latter-day Saint Journal History,* September 13, 1853, Ms.

excellent pasturage in the section of the country explored. Upon arriving at the head of the Weber River, the party discovered and described a large number of lakes. The group of explorers then followed the Provo River to Utah Valley. Gardner's journal account of September 13 stated:

> The Provo River is as handsome a stream for floating purposes as could be desired; it is not so rapid as the Weber River and the channel is deeper, but it is pretty rough at the mouth of the canyon, which is the best canyon for a road that I have ever seen, having fine narrow valleys with rich soil and good pastures. At the present time I think that there is more water in this river than in the Weber River. A continuation of settlements from the mouth of the Weber around to the mouth of the Provo, a distance of about one hundred twenty miles could easily be made. From the mouth of the Weber to the headwaters of the same the distance must be about one hundred miles; good roads could be made without much expense except the last ten miles and the streams can also be utilized pretty well for floating down timber. We arrived home Monday night September 13 in good health having had a pleasant journey.[11]

The Saints continued to explore the country in various directions from the Mormon Mecca, as they extended the frontier. Only the earlier explorations of the Great Basin have been narrated in this chapter. A few other noteworthy scouting trips are given in later pages as they fit into the story. Organized companies of explorers, scouts, traders, and missionaries to the Indians penetrated the districts unknown to the Saints and brought back to Brigham Young an abundance of information in regard to mountain streams and fertile valleys affording suitable localities for colonization. This information was utilized to the best advantage by the Mormon Colonizer in building his empire.

----

[11]*Ibid.*

Chapter VII

THE PERSONNEL OF MORMON COLONIZATION

The Leadership of Brigham Young

The Mormon settlers were characterized by leadership as well as a remarkable willingness to follow those in authority. Their system of colonization developed a group of strong executives, aided by a people who with intense fervor attempted to carry out the advice of their superiors. The cooperation of these groups was a factor which helped to make Mormon colonial history one of the most successful, thoroughly organized, and systematically executed colonial projects in the story of the American frontier.

The dominating personality in the first group, or indeed in all the personnel of Mormon colonization, was President Brigham Young. "The lines of authority led from his hands, through the hands of divisional leaders, to the most remote settlement."[1] Brigham Young by any name and in any place would have been one of the great captains of industry in American history. He was a man of true vision and sound organizing sense. One might picture him as usurping the place of Hill, McCormick or any other great man of his period had he not been a Mormon.

It would hardly be possible to over-estimate the influence he had over his co-religionists. The settlement of the Basin was achieved "under the direction of Brigham Young, who, throughout his lifetime, was the 'all in all' in the colonization of Utah."[2] His followers obeyed him, they respected him, they admired him, and —greatest tribute of all—they loved him. Mormon literature is replete with expressions of how their beloved President inspired and stimulated these persevering frontiersmen whenever he paid a visit to their most remote hamlet or to their most thriving settlement. The esteem in which he was held is comparable to that accorded kings or emperors. A typical reception for President Young is described by Thomas Bullock when the Mormon leader visited Parowan only four months after its establishment:

At noon they gathered up their teams to resume their journey and were soon met by George A. Smith and his carriage and the eight horse company who received the President and his company with martial honors and escorted the company to their fort on Center Creek, amid the roaring of cannon, and

---

[1]Feramorz Young Fox, *The Mormon Land System*, 124, Ms.
[2]Edward Tullidge, *History of Salt Lake City*, 57.

saluted by the "Stars and Stripes" from their liberty pole and received the joyous welcome of the inhabitants.[3]

An article in the *Deseret News* shows Brigham's influence over his followers, as expressed after his visit to Provo, September 27, 1868:

President Young holds no government appointment. Man has had no share in elevating him to the position which he fills; but God who chose him to lead His people has filled them with a deep abiding and increasing love for him. He reigns in their hearts, and it is their highest delight to render him all the honor in their power. The most exacting ruler could not fail to receive gratification from such honor as is paid President Young. But the question arises, are the people as willing to receive and obey his counsels as they are to honor him? . . . In every quarter of this land we see the fruits which it [obedience] has produced. We feel assured that such visits as this, from which President Young and company have returned, will contribute to increase these fruits, and to bring the people into a condition of greater unity than at present—a consummation so desirable that to effect it every true Saint will unceasingly pray.[4]

Mark Twain (Samuel L. Clemens) wrote, in his humorous style, of a visit he made to Salt Lake City.

The second day we made the acquaintance of Mr. Street (since deceased) and put on white shirts and went and paid a state visit to the king (Brigham Young). He seemed a quiet, kindly, easy-mannered, dignified, self-possessed old gentleman of fifty-five or sixty, and had a gentle craft in his eye that probably belonged there. He was very simply dressed and was just taking off a straw hat as we entered. He talked about Utah, and the Indians, and Nevada, and general American matters and questions, with our secretary and certain government officials who came with us. But he never paid any attention to me notwithstanding I made several attempts to "draw him out" on federal politics and his high-handed attitude toward Congress. I thought some of the things I said were rather fine. But he merely looked around at me, at distant intervals, something as I have seen a benignant old cat look around to see which kitten was meddling with her tail. By and by I subsided into an indignant silence, and sat until the end, hot and flushed, and execrating him in my heart for an ignorant savage. But he was calm. His conversation with those gentlemen flowed on as sweetly and peacefully and musically as any summer brook. When the audience was ended and we were retiring from the presence, he put his hand on my head, beamed down on me in an admiring way and said to my brother: "Ah—your child, I presume? Boy, or girl?"[5]

LEADERSHIP OF BRIGHAM YOUNG'S COUNSELORS AND OF THE TWELVE APOSTLES

Closely associated with the President were his two counselors,

[3]Thomas Bullock, *Deseret News*, June 28, 1851.
[4]*Deseret News*, September 27, 1868.
[5]Samuel L. Clemens, *Roughing It*, 112-113.

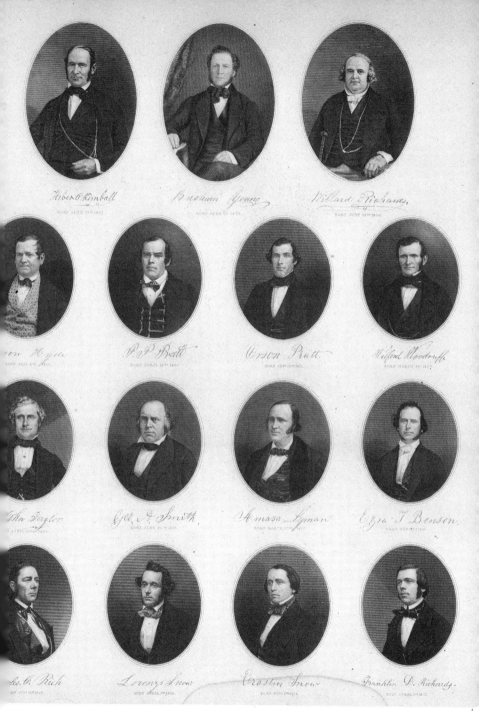

FIRST PRESIDENCY AND TWELVE APOSTLES IN 1853

SALT LAKE CITY, 1853

Heber C. Kimball and Willard Richards, men of no mean ability as colonizers. With them worked the twelve apostles as leaders of important projects. The following men composed that quorum during the early Utah colonial period: Parley P. Pratt, Orson Pratt, Orson Hyde, John Taylor, Wilford Woodruff, George A. Smith, Amasa M. Lyman, Ezra T. Benson, Franklin D. Richards, Charles C. Rich, Lorenzo Snow and Erastus Snow. These men developed exceptional powers of leadership, rising to every responsibility that was placed upon them. Surely "there were giants in the earth in those days" just as truly as there were at the time of Noah. These giants were indispensable aids to Brother Brigham in building the Mormon empire.

During the early and most active period of Mormon colonization, Young divided the areas selected for settlement into large divisions territorially speaking and placed the responsibility of settlement in the hands of apostles.[6] For example, Apostles Amasa M. Lyman and Charles C. Rich were sent "to Southern California in 1851 to preside over the affairs of the Church in that land and to establish a stronghold for the gathering of the Saints."[7] George A. Smith was sent to the Little Salt Lake Valley (Iron County) in 1851 and from that time forward was actively engaged in helping establish numerous settlements south of Salt Lake City. Whenever there was a colonial project of great importance, Apostle George A. Smith was sure to be at its center. Apostle Lorenzo Snow was appointed in the fall of 1853 to manage the affairs in Brigham City, where for a number of years he experimented in the "United Order." Ezra T. Benson was called to gather colonists for Tooele Valley Apostle Orson Hyde directed the establishment of colonies at Fort Supply and Fort Bridger, Wyoming, in 1853, and two years later was sent as overseer of the Saints in Carson Valley. After returning from Nevada in 1858, Hyde was put in charge of the founding of settlements in Sanpete and Sevier counties. Charles C. Rich and Marriner W. Merrill supervised the Saints in northern Utah and southern Idaho after the Johnston Army episode.[8]

In 1861 Apostle Erastus Snow and George A. Smith were appointed by Brigham Young to lead a group to "Dixie,"[9] where he wished a city to be located on the slope north of the junction

---

[6]Brigham Young, "Tenth General Epistle," *Millennial Star,* XVI, 19.
[7]*Latter-day Saint Journal History,* February 23, 1831, Ms.
[8]Trouble developed between the Mormons in the Territory of Utah and the United States government which resulted in President Buchanan sending an army to Utah in 1857.
[9]The elevation drops very rapidly in the southwest corner of Utah which results in a much milder climate around Saint George than elsewhere in the state. That portion of Utah is called "Dixie."

of the Santa Clara and the Rio Virgin. The city, he said, was to
be named St. George in honor of George A. Smith.[10] From this
time Erastus Snow came forward as the most prominent figure in
the southern part of the Great Basin. In fact, he ranks in importance as a Mormon colonizer next to Brigham Young himself.
As actual founder of colonies, his achievements are unsurpassed in
Utah history.

When called by President Young to direct the colonization
of Utah Dixie, Erastus Snow expressed to his associates the attitude
and feelings of the Mormon pioneers in their submissiveness to
authority in the building of an empire—the frontier spirit of the
Saints which resulted in the conquering of the desert. He said:

> I feel to speak encouragingly to my brethren, so far as our removal from
> this to the southern part of the Territory is concerned. I feel to go body and
> spirit, with my heart and soul, and I sincerely hope that my brethren will
> endeavor to do the same; for so long as we strive to promote the interests of
> Zion at home and abroad, we shall be happy and prosperous; and what seems
> to be a temporary leaving and losing of present comforts that we have gath-
> ered around us, will be like bread cast upon the waters, which after many
> days shall be gathered like seed that brings forth much fruit . . . will accom-
> plish more good for the Territory and enjoy much more happiness than we
> could by staying here. To you that think you cannot bring your feelings to
> go upon this mission like men, so far as I am concerned I will vote to release
> you.[11]

Erastus Snow was a natural-born leader of men. His great
success as a colonizer lay in "his ability to make a friend of every
person he met. People loved to be with him no matter where he
was, or what he was doing."[12] Like the great Nazarene, he worked
with and for his followers—not as one who domineered them. His
method was " 'How many will come with me? He never sent men;
as a rule—it was 'Come.' And according to reports he had all the
men he wanted, pay or no pay.'"[13]

Apostle Snow made his annual trips throughout southern Utah,
Nevada, and northern Arizona, to the various settlements under
his direction, just as Brigham Young made his annual tours throughout the Great Basin. Both used the same methods in directing
settlement. "Suggestions would generally be made for improvement in one form or another. The campsite may need moving to
safer quarters or to a healthier place; the damsite had been located
too near the settlement for needed expansion; or the site chosen

[10]*Saint George Stake*, 1847-1875, 73, Ms.
[11]James G. Bleak, *Annals*, 100, Ms.
[12]Joseph William Olsen, *Erastus Snow, Missionary and Pioneer*, 118, Ms.
[13]*Ibid.*, 118.

was too limited to warrant sufficient numbers to locate permanently and safely against Indians."[14] At least two or three months of each year Erastus spent in traveling. He would go from town to town and from ranch to ranch in his old carriage. Joseph William Olsen made the following observation of Apostle Snow:

The slowness of transportation making his visits to various communities rare, people sometimes marveled at President Snow's ability, when traveling through isolated ranches, to know the particular needs of the individual. He was so methodical in his affairs that every farmer, by request, had acquired the habit of placing a red rag on top of a very high pole which was the signal for Apostle Snow to drive in.[15]

Bishops and Stake Presidents as Colonizers

Other important leaders in Mormon colonization were the bishops of wards and the presidents of stakes. Frontier conditions gave the former an opportunity to develop direct control over their wards. They were the leaders of the pioneer bands which went in various directions from Salt Lake City to found settlements. Usually before the nucleus groups left the Mormon Mecca for the purpose of establishing colonies, Brigham selected a man of good common sense and a marked degree of leadership to ordain as a bishop. If the appointment was not made before the colonists left Salt Lake, the President or one of the Twelve visited the infant colony for the purpose of ordaining one and completing an organization. The bishops actually pioneered the settlements, directed their activities, and nourished their growth; and after struggling villages became self-sufficient, they kept them so. In the words of Edward W. Tullidge:

In Utah, they [the bishops] soon became the veritable founders of our settlements and cities; and, having founded them, they have also governed them and directed the people in their social organization and material growth. . . .

Under the government of the bishops, Utah grew up. . . . Brigham Young was their director, for he formulated and constructed everything in those days. . . . Under their temporal administration all over Utah, as well as in Salt Lake, cities were built, lands divided off to the people, roads and bridges made, water ditches cut, the land irrigated, and society governed.[16]

As the colonies multiplied about the hub city of a particular district, an outstanding character was chosen as president over a stake consisting of several towns. He and his two counselors, acting under the direction of the Church Presidency, ministered to the

---

[14]*Ibid.*, 176.
[15]*Ibid.*, 189.
[16]Edward W. Tullidge, *History of Salt Lake City*, 75.

spiritual as well as to the material needs of the Saints in their territorial district.

RACIAL ORIGIN OF PERSONNEL OF MORMON COLONIZATION

The personnel of the laity of the Church varied slightly as to characteristics. The question as to racial origin is of interest. During Brigham Young's period, the Church was proselyting very intensively in Europe and the United States, but only one-third of the population of Utah during that period was of foreign birth. The majority of the foreign converts were from Scandinavian and English speaking countries, two-thirds being converts from the British Isles.

Of the Mormon colonizers of the Great Basin, then, two-thirds were born in the United States. By far the greater portion originally lived in states north of the Ohio River—New York, Pennsylvania, Illinois, and Ohio furnishing from fifty to sixty per cent of the group. Missouri, Kentucky, and Tennessee made up the majority of the remaining forty per cent of native-born Mormons during Brigham Young's period. Most of the Missourians who immigrated to Utah were children of northern stock who had come south during the thirties when the Mormons first established themselves there. So if the sources were traced back, one would find that the original home of a large percentage of the Mormon pioneers was the eastern states. Many of the leaders of the colonial movement, including Brigham himself, were originally from New England, which fact helps to account for so many similarities between the institutions established in Utah and those in the New England states.

ALMOST EQUAL PROPORTIONS OF SEXES

The one motive which dominated the migration of the Latter-day Saints to the Great Basin—that of finding a place to establish permanent homes in which to worship God according to the precepts of their creeds—resulted in the settlers coming in family units. Each member had certain duties to perform as his share of the work. Mormon group life was characterized by many children. Early marriages and large families were the rule. Church doctrine urged that the Saints obey these precepts, and the economic system made obedience to such teachings profitable to all concerned. Cheap land was another factor in the system of large families. These conditions favored the doctrine of polygamy, and the practice furthered the rapid growth of the Mormon empire.

Another significant characteristic of the personnel of Mormon colonization was the almost equal proportion of sexes. Adventure and quest of fortune attracted thousands of men to most of the other far western states, with the result that in many of the non-Mormon settlements the male population far out-numbered the females and children. For example, in 1855 when the Mormon families first began to settle in Carson Valley, Nevada, the population was about two hundred. There were only two women. The same number of women were living at Gold Canyon where the male population was near two hundred. At that time there were approximately fifteen white females in the whole of what is now Nevada.

The Mormon empire, however, from the advent of the second group of pioneers, contained as many female as male colonists. Religion appealed to women and that appeal brought many of them into the wilds of the Great West with their husbands in search of a home in Zion. They were willing to brave the hazards of pioneer life in order that they might serve God according to their religious convictions. Because of the force of religion, family units pioneered the Great Basin.

Methods of Mormon Colonization

When a new colony was to be founded, its membership was selected by Brigham Young. Families and groups of families were called as missionaries to leave their homes for the purpose of establishing new towns. A few of them he told to remain in the new place until called to go elsewhere and assist in establishing other colonies. But the majority of the settlers sent to various sites in the Great Basin went with the understanding that their mission was to remain and build up that part of the Basin. No matter how isolated or unpromising the district, the Saints accepted the call as coming from God.

Sometimes Brigham named each family which was to assist in establishing a certain colony, and at other times he merely appointed a leader and gave him authority to select a given number of families. Isaac Morley was appointed to establish Manti and told to choose his colonists. On the other hand, in the founding of Saint George each family received a specific call from Young. The following quotation is illustrative of the President's method of calling missionaries:

At the general conference of the Church, held in Great Salt Lake City, April 6, 1855, a large number of missionaries were called to different parts of the world, some to preach the Gospel in the United States and foreign

lands, and others to locate new settlements in the valleys of the Rocky Mountains, or in the Great West. Among these were the following brethren called
to locate a settlement at Las Vegas, which at that time belonged to New
Mexico:[17]

In selecting the Las Vegas group, as well as on other occasions,
Governor Young was careful to provide a balanced company of
industrial and agricultural workers. His policy was to see that each
colony was supplied with the various craftsmen needed. In establishing new settlements like Saint George, men were usually selected
from nearly every older community in Utah. Then the group was
augmented by immigrants who had recently arrived at Salt Lake.
This resulted in a mixture of the experienced frontiersmen and a
certain number of novices in pioneer life. In this way Brigham
was able to take care of the stream of immigrants flowing continuously into Salt Lake and at the same time to assure the success of
the colonial projects.

Many of the Mormons, especially those who came after the
first pioneer migration from the States, were completely lacking in
the two essentials which would assure their agricultural success—
they had neither farming skill nor capital. It is quite true that
many had had considerable experience as mid-western farmers, but
that experience had all been in a humid country. But added to that
smaller group with experience were thousands who were entirely
ignorant of the science of agriculture. Especially was this true of
the emigrants from England, who numbered about one-fourth of
the group arriving in the Basin during the early colonial period.
A large majority of them before joining the Church were either
miners or factory workers. From figures given by James Linforth,
out of 2,282 emigrants from the British Isles only 173, or less than
eight per cent, were farmers, gardeners, and shepherds. There were
mechanics, blacksmiths, weavers, along with a few professional
men.[18]

From this heterogeneous group Brigham had to select men
who could be valuable in some capacity in a new community. Those
who did not fit in were taught new trades, but an effort was made
to let each man keep his former occupation if he was in any way
outstanding in it.

As a whole the personnel of the early Mormon colonies was
much like that of other frontiers. Through their experiences in
trying to open a new country and make a living, the men devel-

--- ---

[17]*Record of the Las Vegas Mission*, April 6, 1855, Ms.
[18]James Linforth, *Liverpool to Salt Lake*, 16-17.

oped ingenuity, fortitude and a certain ruggedness of personality; the women were hard working and persevering, as in any other new country. The greatest difference in the makeup of the groups was that the Mormons were the type of people to whom the chief appeal had been religion rather than material gain. But those valiant pioneers successfully planted towns and cities over a broad expanse of country and made for themselves of the desert a paradise.

Chapter VIII

THE MORMON CORRIDOR*

The Mormon Empire in the Great West—Mormon Corridor Idea

The first Saints to reach the Basin arrived in July, 1847. As Brigham Young and his vanguard of 148 pioneers emerged from the mouth of Emigration Canyon, he gazed "in wonder and admiration" for a few moments upon the Salt Lake Valley lying below him; then, turning to Apostle Wilford Woodruff he remarked: "This is the place. Drive on."[1] Dry, barren, and desolate the valley appeared to the majority of his followers, but this man of vision realized that here was the place—and probably the only place in the Great West—that would furnish the Mormons the desired seclusion and protection from their enemies. Lofty mountain ranges and saline deserts hemmed in a number of valleys which Brigham believed could be made productive if his people were willing to work.

The pioneers established themselves in Salt Lake Valley and for two years devoted themselves to making the soil productive to provide for their own needs and for the many immigrants who would join them later. Then Brigham began to expand his colonizing activities to other valleys.

During this formative period President Young sent party after party of explorers in every direction to search out the possibilities of the Basin. Within six months explorations had been made to the Pacific Coast—westward to San Francisco and southwestward to Los Angeles.

Each month in the Great Basin brought more vividly to Brigham's mind a broader conception of its resources and with this his dream of a vast ecclesiastical commonwealth came closer to realization. Yet he knew he could not fulfill his hopes with only the 25,000 devotees affiliated with the Church at that time in the United States and Canada. His immediate object, then, was an increase of missionary activities and the immigration of the converts to the Mormons' headquarters. He, therefore (1849-50), increased

---

*This chapter is reprinted from *The Pacific Historical Review*, VIII (June, 1939), 179-200, by special permission.

[1]Wilford Woodruff, *Journal*, July 24, 1847, Ms.

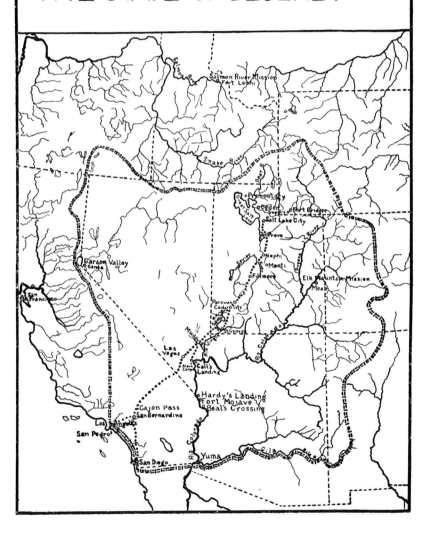

THE MORMON CORRIDOR⋯⋯⋯
THE STATE OF DESERET

the missionary activities and expanded the field for proselyting work. This active missionary program continued throughout the remainder of his life. Proselyting was begun in France, Switzerland, Italy, Scandinavia, Hispanic America, India, Australia, the Sandwich Islands and the Society Islands, while heretofore missionary activities had been confined to America and the British Isles.

In order to expedite immigration the Presidency of the Church devised a plan to assist the converts financially. On October 6, 1849, the "Perpetual Emigrating Fund Company" came into existence with Brigham at its head. This fund company assisted in bringing over 70,000 European proselytes to the Mormon empire before the death of Brigham Young in 1877. In the words of Katherine Coman, "It was, taken all in all, the most successful example of regulated immigration in United States history."[2]

The Latter-day Saints' missionary activities throughout the world and the bringing of the converts to Utah proved to be two of the determining factors in assisting Brigham in molding his commonwealth and in developing the "Mormon Corridor," i.e., the "southern route" to the sea. Before the State of California was created and as converts multiplied, the desirability of establishing a definite corridor—that is, the founding of a contiguous line of Mormon settlements from a good seaport to Salt Lake City and also the connecting of those towns by a highway over which immigrants could be conveyed with ease and safety—became more pronounced.

One of the principal teachings of the Church of Jesus Christ of Latter-day Saints was that its members were required by God to spread its tenets throughout the world and to gather the "seed of Israel to Zion," i.e., to gather to the central meeting place. Church members believed that the Lord required them to convert as many people as they could to Mormonism and do so as rapidly as possible in order that God's children might be brought into his kingdom. Thus the religious motive dominated Brigham's empire building aspirations. He planned to gain control over a vast territory and to hold that territory by right of colonization. His dream of a commonwealth was one wherein the Saints were the original settlers and remained in the majority after the colonies matured.

Within less than two years after his arrival in the Basin, President Young's ideas on the extent of his desired empire had definitely crystalized. He remarked, "I look forward to the day when scores

----

[2]Katherine Coman. *Economic Beginnings of the Far West.* II, 184.

of thousands will join us in our secluded retreat."[3] In the spring of 1849, "true to the character of typical frontiersmen, independent of Congress,"[4] the Mormons set about to establish a government. President Young issued a call to the people east of the Sierra and north of Mexico to send delegates to a convention at Salt Lake for the purpose of writing a constitution and applying for admission into the Union. The result was the adoption of a constitution and the inauguration of a temporary government known as the "State of Deseret" (March, 1849).

The boundary lines of Deseret as outlined by its constitution enclosed an exceedingly extensive territory.[5] On March 9, 1849, President Young wrote to Orson Pratt and the Saints in England as follows: "We have petitioned the Congress of United States for organization of a territorial government here, embracing a territory of about seven hundred miles square, bounded north by Oregon, latitude 42 degrees, east by the Rio Grande del Norte, south by the late line between United States and Mexico, near the latitude 32 degrees, and west by the sea coast and California mountains."[6]

Brigham was careful to include a substantial strip of sea coast in his new Mormon commonwealth, with at least two good seaports —San Pedro and San Diego.[7] It appears that the Mormon Colonizer had extensive ambitions. The fact that the constitution designated the governor of "Deseret" as the "commander in chief of the militia, navy, and all armies"[8] of the state is evidence that those who wrote and adopted that document had concluded that as far as they were concerned the Mormon empire should include the territory to the sea. Thus the western boundary line of "Deseret" followed the Pacific coast northward from Mexico to Los Angeles.

Nature provided a perfect geographic outline for an immense commonwealth in the heart of the West; Brigham Young supplied the empire building genius to define and set claim to the land within those natural boundaries. "Deseret" was bounded on the east by the Rocky Mountains, on the south by Mexico, and on the west by the Sierra Nevada. Deserts, mountains, and rivers provided a fairly secure barricade—one with few pregnable spots. Here was the maximum of seclusion and protection.

[3]Brigham Young, Latter-day Saint Journal History, April 6, 1850, Ms.

[4]Leland Hargrove Creer, Utah and the Nation, 66; Frederic L. Paxson, History of the American Frontier, 27-31, 350.

[5]Laws and Ordinances of the State of Deseret, Compilation of 1851 (reprint, Salt Lake City, 1919), 78-79.

[6]Brigham Young, "Epistle . . . to Orson Pratt and the Saints in England," Latter-day Saint Journal History, March 9, 1849, Ms.

[7]Laws and Ordinances . . . op. cit.

[8]Ibid., 82.

After establishing "Deseret," Brigham Young strengthened the weak spots in its geographic outline by building Fort Supply and Fort Bridger in Wyoming as controls over the eastern entrance to the Basin and as stations on the Mormon trail where the immigrating Saints could replenish their exhausted supplies preparatory to the last 125 miles of difficult mountain and canyon traveling. Carson Valley, Nevada, at the foot of the passes over the Sierra, was settled by Mormons. It served as a midway station between Salt Lake City and San Francisco on the northern route to the sea. Colonists were also sent to Moab, Grand Valley, at an opening in the southeastern boundary; others were dispatched far northward of the Mormon empire to the Salmon River in what was then Oregon and is now Idaho; and over 500 Saints settled at San Bernardino, California, in 1851. Thus within eight years after arriving in the Great Basin, Brigham Young had his commonwealth surrounded with control settlements.

The fact that Governor Young established San Bernardino, California, in 1851, Las Vegas, Nevada (Territory of New Mexico), in 1855, and Lemhi on the Salmon River in Idaho (Oregon Territory), in 1855—all founded outside Utah after Congress had reduced the size of the "State of Deseret"—is evidence that he intended not to be thwarted in his plans to control by colonization as expansive a country as possible in the Great West. But this control he intended to achieve through a legitimate, peaceable method of land settlement.

Meanwhile President Young determined to provide, if possible, a cheaper and surer means of transporting both immigrants and goods to the stronghold of the Saints. From the time of their arrival in the Basin, Mormons had recognized an almost indispensable need for such a route. During early Utah history the route generally followed by immigrants was via Omaha, North Platte River, South Pass, Fort Bridger, and on into Salt Lake City. The winter snows on the Rocky Mountains effectually shut the Saints off from commerce with the people of the East for nearly half of the year. Furthermore, transportation across the plains from Omaha by ox teams was very expensive and difficult. Through exploration, the Mormons had already ascertained that the route from Salt Lake to southern California, because of the mildness of the climate, was always open, and the Pacific settlements were much closer to the Mormon Mecca than was the American frontier to the east.

EXPLORING THE CORRIDOR ROUTE, 1847

Jefferson Hunt and eighteen companions were the first of Brigham's followers to explore the "southern route" to California. In November, 1847, only four months after the first pioneer group landed in the Great Basin, Hunt and his party left Salt Lake City for the purpose of purchasing seed grains and cattle from the ranchers near Los Angeles and, incidentally, to explore the region between the Mormon Mecca and the Pacific. They followed what is known as the Old Spanish Trail a portion of the way. The trail was so indistinct and so difficult that the travelers made slow progress. In fact the Old Spanish Trail was mainly a name and not a trail. The company spent forty-five days in making the trip to Williams' Rancho del Chino, thirty miles southwest of San Bernardino. As they took provisions enough for only thirty days, they nearly starved to death before reaching their destination. Hunt's son, who was a member of the party, stated that after their food supply was exhausted "we did what I think no other party of Mormon emigrants ever had to do—we killed and ate our horses. Three horses in all were consumed."[9]

After spending five or six weeks in reconnoitering southern California and in securing forty bulls, two hundred cows, a few pack animals and mares, grains, and seeds of various kinds, the trail builders left the Rancho del Chino on February 15, 1848, for Salt Lake Valley. They arrived in May. All of the bulls and half of the cows died from thirst en route. However, flattering reports of the agricultural possibilities of the San Bernardino country were given to the Church officials, resulting in centering the Mormons' attention on developing the Mormon Corridor to the sea and in establishing an outpost in southern California.

WAGON BROUGHT OVER THE CORRIDOR ROUTE, 1848

Following the trail made distinct by the livestock that Hunt's party brought from California, a company of twenty-five battalion members who had been mustered out of service at Los Angeles arrived in Salt Lake, June 5, 1848. They brought with them one wagon and 135 mules. "The wagon of this battalion company was the first to make the journey over the pack trail."

JEFFERSON HUNT, A PARTY OF GOLD SEEKERS, AND THE MORMON CORRIDOR, 1849

Early in October, 1849, Jefferson Hunt left Salt Lake on a

---

[9]John Hunt. *Latter-day Saint Journal History*, November 16, 1847, Ms.

second trip to California via the southern route. This time he was hired to guide a company of fortune seekers bound for the gold mines. Hunt had already demonstrated that the southern route to the sea could be used successfully as a trail for pack train parties. This trip gave him opportunity to demonstrate its feasibility for a wagon road. In fact, in the words of John Walton Caughey, "The conviction later became general among those who set out with Hunt that they were being utilized by Brigham Young to open a road to southern California for the benefit of the Mormons."[10]

Many of these forty-niners thought that Hunt's trail was taking them too far southward, so by the time they had traveled 250 miles southwest from Salt Lake they were urging their guide to attempt a shorter route. Having previously had experience traveling over the desert from the Basin to southern California, Hunt wisely refused to lead the party over an untried course. But one of the emigrants named O. K. Smith persuaded most of the travelers to follow him on a new route directly west to the Pacific Coast which he called "Walker's Cut-off." He asserted that by going in that direction they would miss the desert and be saved 500 miles of travel en route to the gold fields. Captain Hunt insisted that it was very unsafe to travel directly west as Smith advocated. Regardless of Hunt's forcible suggestions, all but seven wagons, eleven men, two women, and three children, decided to follow Smith on the cut-off. Hunt and those who remained with him arrived at Williams' rancho, thirty-five miles east of Los Angeles, December 22, 1849, having lost only one ox. This pioneer group demonstrated the feasibility for a wagon road over the Corridor, a road which became the main thoroughfare between Salt Lake and Los Angeles, route 91.

Those who took the cut-off did not fare so well as Hunt's party. After wandering for twenty days in the desert and mountains, the majority of the emigrants turned and traveled southward until they struck Hunt's trail. This they followed to California. But a number of them continued to struggle westward. Of the latter only two arrived in California to tell a horrible story to the residents of that state. The others died of hunger and thirst en route. None of the adventurers who left the southern route in search of a better one succeeded in establishing a wagon road through Death Valley for future travelers to follow as Hunt did on his trail.

––––

[10]John Walton Caughey, "Southwest from Salt Lake in 1849," *Pacific Historical Review*, VI (June, 1937), 146.

HOWARD EGAN'S TRAVELLER'S GUIDE

On November 18, 1849, another Mormon party led by Howard Egan left Fort Utah (Provo) for southern California. Its forty-nine members followed Hunt's road. Egan kept a detailed account of the distance, watering places, feed and suitable camp grounds, numbered from one to eighty-nine, from Fort Utah to California. His journal was published and made available for a future traveler's guide. President Young and his associates thereby came into possession of a detailed account of every possible site for a town on the southern route to the sea. Even by this time the Mormon Colonizer was contemplating a connected line of settlements along that course to a Pacific seaport. Hunt's work in exploring and establishing his trail and his reports to the church officials, augmented by the journal of Howard Egan and the report of Parley P. Pratt's "Southern Exploring Company," were paramount factors in determining the great amount of attention that Brigham Young paid to the development of the "Mormon Corridor."

PLANS FOR DEVELOPMENT OF CORRIDOR ROUTE

Throughout the next twenty years (1849-69) Hunt's route (the corridor) was the only road from Salt Lake to the coast that was open during the winter. The Mormons were greatly responsible for its development into the most important road from the Basin to the Pacific Coast during that period. Although some of the early season travelers to California went via Fort Hall and the Humboldt, yet later in the season the southern route was the one always used. Sheep drivers also repeatedly traversed this road. "Consequently it was the most important route for freighters as well as emigrants until the completion of the Central Pacific and Union Pacific railroads in 1869 restored the preference for the old western route" (northern route) from Salt Lake City.[11]

In 1849 the southern route lay entirely within the confines of the Mormons' contemplated empire—within the "State of Deseret." Naturally, Brigham Young directed his attention toward the Pacific Ocean. A continuous line of Mormon settlements from the seaport of San Diego or from San Pedro to Salt Lake City would, Brigham concluded, be an important factor in developing the best route over which merchandise and Mormon proselytes could be conveyed to the heart of the Basin. In 1850 he definitely stated that "we want to plant colonies from here [Salt Lake City]

----

[11]*Ibid.*, 164.

to the Pacific Ocean; a few will go into the neighborhood of Cajon Pass and make a settlement there."[12] As early as March 9, 1849, he had pointed out some of the benefits to be derived from such a plan:

> If, on a more thorough knowledge of the country, we can find a practical wagon route up the Arkansas or up the Rio Grande, it will avoid the winter and a contact with the corrupt apostates and Gentiles that swarm at New Orleans, Saint Louis and upper Missouri; or if we find a practical seaport at the head of the Gulf of California, or elsewhere on the Pacific, and can find a practical route across some of the Isthmuses of Central America it will, perhaps, facilitate the emigration from Europe to these valleys.[13]

In a general epistle to the Saints, he gave definite shape to his plans:

> We are about to establish a colony of about thirty families in the Utah Valley, about fifty miles south. We hope soon to explore the valleys three hundred miles south, and also the country as far as the Gulf of California, with a view of settlement and a seaport.[14]

Attached to the same letter but dated a month later is a statement which indicates that the Church officials took almost immediate action in establishing themselves in California. The statement reads, "Since the above was written, Elder Charles C. Rich, of the Twelve, is appointed to take his stand in western California, with a view of giving guidance to the affairs of the Church and kingdom in that region."[15]

COLONIES ALONG THE CORRIDOR

Within three weeks after Brigham Young wrote the foregoing epistle, 150 colonists had settled in Utah Valley on the Provo River. The beginning of the Mormon Corridor—that is, a line of Mormon settlements along the southern route to the sea—had been made. Before the year closed a large exploring party of over fifty members under the direction of Parley P. Pratt was on its way to "explore the valleys three hundred miles south" of Salt Lake City for the purpose of locating suitable places for settlement.[16] Pratt's report was a big factor in determining the sites for the establishment of twenty-five towns in a continuous line southwest toward the Pacific.

In the autumn of 1850 a large company settled in the Little Salt Lake Valley about 250 miles south of the parent colony on

---

[12]Brigham Young, *Latter-day Saint Journal History*, October 27, 1850, Ms.

[13]*Ibid.*, March 9, 1849.

[14]*Ibid.*

[15]*Ibid.*, April 12, 1849.

[16]Parley P. Pratt, "A report of the Southern Exploring Company," *Ibid.*, November 23, 1849 to February 2, 1850, Ms. A presentation of the accomplishments of the "Southern Exploring Company" was given in Chapter V.

the route to the sea. Apostle George A. Smith was appointed to be the founder of that community (Parowan). Young instructed Smith that if winter overtook his company before it reached Iron County he was to plant colonies on one or more of the intermediary streams, as the church officials were planning on establishing a line of such colonies from Salt Lake southwestward.[17]

Plans were progressing rapidly for the immediate projection of land settlement near a good seaport. Brigham's intention was to build a station near the Pacific Ocean that could be used as an outfitting post for immigrants bound for Utah and as a shipping point. It was to be the gateway settlement from the Pacific into the Mormon commonwealth—an outpost of the greatest importance. On February 23, 1851, President Young selected two apostles "to take a company to southern California to preside over the affairs of the Church in that land and to establish a stronghold for the gathering of the Saints."[18] This company totaled 520 persons. Early in April Brigham wrote:

Amasa M. Lyman and Charles C. Rich left this place . . . with others . . . for the purpose of establishing a settlement in the southern part of California, at no great distance from San Diego, and near Williams' ranch and the Cajon Pass, between which and Iron County we design to establish settlements as speedily as possible, which Elder Lyman will commence on his route, if practicable, so as to have a continued line of stations and places of refreshment between this point and the Pacific, which route is passable during the winter months.[19]

Their objective, Williams' or a neighboring ranch, was chosen because the Saints had become acquainted with that region through reports of the Mormon Battalion and through Hunt's trips to southern California. Nearly five years before Brigham sent the colonists to California, while the Saints were on their trek westward, 500 Mormons had been recruited in the United States Army for one year's service during the war with Mexico. They had marched from Fort Leavenworth, Kansas, over the Old Santa Fé Trail to New Mexico, and then on to San Diego. Fighting had ceased in California before their arrival, and so they were given some degree of freedom from military duties to obtain employment in the surrounding settlements and ranches. After receiving their discharge from the army on July 16, 1847, Captain Jefferson Hunt and some of the other members of the Battalion had joined their families at

---

[17]Brigham Young to George A. Smith., in *ibid.*, December 16, 1850.
[18]*History of San Bernardino*, February 22, 23, 1851, Ms.
[19]Brigham Young, "Fifth general Epistle . . . to the Saints," *Millennial Star*, XIII (Liverpool, April, 1851), 213.

Salt Lake City that fall. They arrived in the Basin only three months after the first Mormons had entered that district.

Southern California, especially the country adjacent to Williams' ranch, was sparsely settled and the farming land was excellent. The fact that it was far enough from the seaport to escape the immediate influx of "gentiles" enhanced its value for the Mormons. It furnished the possibilities of isolation and security with the advantage of easy access to the sea—two important requirements.

Lyman and his company arrived in southern California on June 1, 1851. They were not able to obtain the tract of land which they had intended to buy. But the Rancho de San Bernardino, thirty miles northeast of Williams' Rancho and "about one hundred miles from San Diego, seventy miles from the seaport of San Pedro, and fifty miles from Pueblo de los Angelos,"[20] was finally selected and purchased for $77,500.[21] It contained 35,509 acres. A typical Mormon settlement named San Bernardino was established there.

EUROPEAN SAINTS TO MIGRATE TO THE BASIN VIA SAN DIEGO, SAN BERNARDINO, AND MORMON CORRIDOR

After President Young had sent the colonists to California in the spring of 1851, he instructed Franklin D. Richards, president of the European Mission, to "open every desirable correspondence in relation to the various routes, and rates, and conveniences, from Liverpool to San Diego, and make an early report so that if possible the necessary preparations may be made for next fall's emigration."[22]

The Saints in the countries bordering the Pacific were instructed to travel directly to San Diego and then to San Bernardino, from which place they could, if they wished, go to the Basin. Brigham also advised:

> It is wisdom for the English Saints to cease emigration by the usual route through the States, and up the Missouri River, and remain where they are till they shall hear from us again, as it is our design to open up a way across the interior of the continent, by Panama, Tehuantepec, or some of the interior routes, and land them at San Diego, and thus save three thousand miles of inland navigation through a most sickly climate and country.[23]

Lyman and Rich were informed of Brigham's plan. December 10, 1851, they wrote Richards in England that their location at

---

[20]Amasa Lyman to Franklin D. Richards, in *ibid.*, XIV (December, 1851), 75-76.
[21]*History of San Bernardino*, September 22, 1851. Ms.
[22]Brigham Young, "Fifth general Epistle . . . to the Saints," *Millennial Star*, XII (February, 1851), 214.
[23]*Ibid.*

Fort San Bernardino.
From the North East.
Oct. 1852.
W.R.N. del.

FORT SAN BERNARDINO

OLD COVE FORT ON MORMON CORRIDOR
EXAMPLE OF FORTS MORMON PIONEERS BUILT

San Bernardino had been made "in view of forwarding the emigration of the Saints from abroad, and from Europe in particular, to the valley of the Great Salt Lake."[24] They also asked Richards to inform them "in relation to the practicability and probable expense of transporting the Saints from Liverpool to San Diego, by any of the present routes across the Isthmus."

While waiting for a reply from Richards, Rich and four companions made an exploring trip to San Diego "to examine the road between that place and San Bernardino, and to inspect the practicability of bringing the Saints to San Bernardino by that route.[25] Their report was favorable. The Mormons had now completely explored and practically developed the corridor route from Salt Lake to San Diego, but the water route from England to San Diego at that time proved impracticable. In a general epistle early in 1852, Brigham wrote:

> By recent communication of President Franklin D. Richards, of England, we learn that the prospect of immediate emigration of European brethren to San Diego, as we had anticipated, is in no wise flattering, there being no regular shipping from England to that port; therefore Elder Richards will continue to ship the Saints by way of New Orleans to Kanesville, as hitherto.[26]

When the State of California came into existence, Young's interest in the southern route changed from one of Mormon ownership to one of making a route over which immigrants and merchandise could be brought safely and peaceably into the Basin. The establishment of Mormon settlements the full length of the route would, Brigham felt, assure the success of this purpose.

Transportation had developed to the extent that in making preparations for immigration to Utah in 1853, devotees in Europe and throughout the whole world were instructed by President Young to come either by way of San Diego or via New Orleans, choosing the route that best suited their convenience and desires. Those who were accustomed to a warm climate could settle in southern California while those who preferred a cooler weather could come on to the Basin.[27]

At this time Young intended to make San Bernardino a second Salt Lake City—that is, a gathering place for thousands of his followers who could best live under southern California condi-

[24]Amasa Lyman to Franklin D. Richards, op. cit.; Howard Stansbury, *An Expedition to the Valley of the Great Salt Lake,* 139.
[25]*History of San Bernardino,* January 29, 1852.
[26]Brigham Young, "Sixth general Epistle . . . to the Saints," *Millennial Star,* XIV (January, 1852), 23-24.
[27]Brigham Young, "Eighth general Epistle . . . to the Saints," *Millennial Star,* XV (January, 1853), 116.

tions.[28] The seaport of San Diego was looked upon by Brigham Young as the logical ending of the Mormon Corridor, but further investigation would probably have revealed to the Colonizer's keen mind that San Pedro would be a better terminus. This seaport was nearer to San Bernardino than San Diego. Furthermore, the coastal region southward from San Bernardino and extending past San Diego was hemmed in by lofty mountains, which have lost for San Diego much of its natural advantage as a seaport.

TRANSPORTATION AND COMMUNICATION OVER THE CORRIDOR ROUTE

Simultaneously with the preceding events, Brigham Young and his associates had been exerting every effort to connect the Mormon Mecca with the outside world, desiring to employ all available means of transportation and communication. Their first activities began at Salt Lake and extended outward. During the first two or three years in the Basin, they built roads and bridges through cooperative effort to connect the new settlements with Salt Lake City. In fact, the very first law enacted by the Legislative Assembly of the State of Deseret provided for a state road commission, whose duty it was to survey the roads "on the most feasible and practical routes."[29] The law also granted to each county the right to elect a county road commission vested with power to collect taxes and spend the money in constructing roads and building bridges. As the Mormon settlements were being established south of Salt Lake in greater numbers than in other directions during the early Utah period, the main improved highway was in that direction. It followed Hunt's route—the Mormon Corridor—southwestward toward California.

On March 5, 1850, the General Assembly of Deseret enacted a provision to establish a stage route south from Salt Lake City with the ultimate aim of having it extend the full length of the Corridor, terminating at the seaport of San Diego. The ordinance, signed by Governor Young, read as follows:

> Section 1. Be it ordained by the General Assembly of the State of Deseret that James A. Little [and others] . . . have the entire control and management of the state route from Ogden City and the settlements north through Great Salt Lake City, Provo, and Manti to the county seat of Iron County, and as soon as practicable continuously to intersect a stage route from Cajon Pass and San Diego and southern California.[30]

----

[28]Brigham Young, "Ninth general Epistle . . . to the Saints," *Millennial Star*, XV (July, 1853), 441.
[29]"Enactments of the State of Deseret," *History of Brigham Young, 1849-1851*, Ms.
[30]*Latter-day Saint Journal History*, March 5, 1850, Ms.

Brigham Young and his associates were extremely anxious to develop all the facilities of communication and transportation on the southern route to the sea, yet they did not cast aside any opportunity for the improvement of the routes from Salt Lake to other colonized portions of America. Having located in a new territory far distant from the frontier to the East and the settlements on the Pacific Coast, the Saints had little opportunity for intercourse with the outside world. Therefore, among the early acts passed by the first session of the Legislative Assembly of the Territory of Utah (1850-52) were several petitions to the federal government asking for assistance in developing all of the main routes leading from the Mormon Mecca.[31] Congress was asked to connect Salt Lake City with the frontier settlements in the East and with a seaport on the Pacific Coast by an overland telegraph line, by a transcontinental highway, by a "national central railroad," and by a semi-monthly mail.

One of the memorials, dated March 3, 1852, asked Congress to construct a "telegraph line from some convenient point on the Mississippi or Missouri, via Great Salt Lake City, to San Diego, San Francisco, Astoria, or such other eligible port on the Pacific Coast as your wisdom may direct."[32] The Saints continued to support this project. Later when Edward Creighton was constructing the telegraph line, Young became a contractor, supplying poles, subsistence, and transportation for the workers out in Wyoming. The line was completed in 1861. Soon thereafter Brigham organized the Deseret Telegraph Company for the purpose of connecting all of the Mormon settlements with the parent colony. By 1867 telegrams could be sent from towns in southern Idaho to Saint George in southern Utah. Later the telegraph line was continued along Hunt's route to Los Angeles, thereby taking another step in the development of the Mormon Corridor.

Brigham was anxious to improve the facilities for communication and transportation along every route from the Mormon Mecca to the sea; yet the contents of three other memorials sent to Congress in 1852 show that the Mormon leaders were directing their main efforts to the development of the southern route via San Bernardino to San Diego. Part of one of the petitions, approved March 9, stated:

Whereas, the locality of Utah Territory is such as to render it inaccessible to the mail from Missouri during four months in the year; . . . and also,

---

[31]*Utah Legislative Enactments, Session of* 1851-1852 (Salt Lake City, 1852), 219-28.
[32]*Ibid.,* 226-27.

for a period of six months in the year, it is inaccessible to the mail from
Sacramento and Oregon by the way of Fort Hall, and, . . .

Whereas, natural facilities do exist for establishing a mail route from
Great Salt Lake City to San Diego, or some other eligible position on the
coast of the Pacific near that place; which route can be traversed without any
serious obstacles, during every month in the year; and, . . .

Whereas, cities and settlements are already formed on this route. . . .
Therefore, we, your memorialists, do humbly pray Congress to establish a
semi-monthly mail route from Great Salt Lake City to San Diego, and make
appropriations suitable to effect the same.[33]

In order to improve the route over which to carry the mail,
the Mormons also petitioned Congress (March 6, 1852) for an
appropriation of $60,000 to be used in the construction of a "terri-
torial road, beginning at some convenient point in the northern
settlements of the Territory, and extending in a southerly direction
through Fillmore City . . . to the extreme settlements near the
southern boundary of the Territory."[34] The arguments presented
were all in favor of the superiority of the southern over the northern
route from Salt Lake to California. Quoting from the document:

The construction of a territorial road . . . would be of incalculable
benefit to the country, and greatly add to the comfort and convenience of
emigrants, and other travelers as they pass through the rough and mountainous
portion of the continent. . . . The difficulties attending the northern routes
across the Sierra Nevada to California are very great, arising chiefly from the
more hostile conduct of the Indians, in that direction, and from the mountain
snows which effectually blockade the path of the traveler for several months
in the year; and which expose both men and animals to innumerable hardships, if even not to death itself. To avoid these difficulties and hardships,
a more southern route has been explored, where the climate is more congenial, and where grass, in luxuriant abundance can be obtained during the
whole year.[35]

Another memorial asked Congress "for the establishment of
a national central railroad from some eligible point on the Mississippi or Missouri rivers, to San Diego, San Francisco, Sacramento
or Astoria, or such other point on or near the Pacific Coast."[36] But
from the contents of the petition, it is evident that the Mormons
preferred having the iron road run from Salt Lake City along the
Mormon Corridor via Fillmore, Parowan, San Bernardino, to San
Diego. In the words of the petition:

That an eligible route can be obtained your memorialists have no doubt,
being extensively acquainted with the country. We know that no obstruction

----

[33]*Ibid..* 219-20.
[34]*Ibid..* 221-22.
[35]*Ibid.*
[36]*Ibid..* 225-26.

exists between this point and San Diego; and that iron, coal, timber, stone, and other materials exist in various places on the route; and that the settlements of this Territory are so situated, as to amply supply the builders of said road with materials and provisions for a considerable portion of the route, and to carry on an extensive trade after the road is completed.[87]

COLONIES ALONG THE CORRIDOR

But to ask for federal assistance was only one of the minor details connected with the establishment of good facilities for communication with the frontiers to the East and the Pacific Coast and to improve the routes for travel. Far more important was the establishing of a line of towns and the building of a highway along the Corridor southwestward from the Mormon Mecca to San Bernardino. By the spring of 1855 twenty communities running in a direct line from Salt Lake to Cedar City, a distance of 265 miles, were connected by a good wagon road, and the road had been extended on to the Pacific Coast.

Brigham was now ready to project a colony into the heart of the desert about midway between Cedar City and San Bernardino. The site selected was Las Vegas Springs located in what is now southern Nevada. Since the stream of water from the springs made the only oasis for miles in that arid region, Las Vegas was a spot of great importance on the southern route. Early in 1855 William Bringhurst was sent with a group of missionary-colonists to establish the settlement. He was instructed to exert every effort to civilize and Christianize the desert Indians, which would result in making the Corridor safe for travel.

THE UTAH WAR AND THE MORMON CORRIDOR

Within ten years after the arrival of the Mormons in the Great Basin, Brigham Young's dream of an extensive commonwealth was nearing the point of established reality when, unfortunately, trouble developed between the Saints and the United States Government. This trouble really had its beginning when the first federal appointees arrived in the Basin in 1851 after Congress had rejected Deseret for statehood but instead had created the Territory of Utah. Some of the federal appointees—including Brigham Young as governor—were Mormons, while others were Gentiles from the East. Trouble inevitably developed between those groups, whose viewpoints were so radically different. A number of the Gentile officials left Utah at various times and upon resigning from office

----

[87]Ibid.

made lengthy reports to the government making various accusations —some true and some false—against the Mormons.[38]

From these reports President Buchanan's administration was "led to believe, or feigned to believe" that the Mormons were in "substantial rebellion against the laws and authority of the United States."[39] Also, the United States government maintained that in order to uphold the supremacy of federal authority in the Territory of Utah, an "Expedition" must be sent to the Great Basin. Incidentally the agitation at Washington, D. C., against the Saints before the sending of the "Expedition" reached its peak during the political campaign of 1856, and the Mormon problem became one of the issues of that campaign. Both the Republican and Democratic parties allied themselves against the Mormons' doctrine and practice of plural marriage.[40]

Albert Sidney Johnston, one of the most capable generals in America at that time, was selected to lead the troops to Utah. Accompanied by 2500 well-seasoned soldiers—some of the very best of the federal army—General Johnston was sent to the Basin in 1857 by President Buchanan.

Naturally, the Latter-day Saints, then constituting practically the whole population of the Great Basin, were anxious to defend for themselves the American principle of the right of local self-government and to preserve conditions under which they could practice their religious beliefs unhampered. Therefore, they decided to resist the United States' soldiers. They prepared to prevent, if possible, the entrance of the federal troops into the Salt Lake Valley.

Writers have referred to the Johnston army episode as "The Utah War," "The Army for Utah," "The Expedition," or "Buchanan's Blunder." Opinions vary as to the basic motives which resulted in the sending of the "Expedition"; but all writers on the subject agree that the costs of the Utah Was were excessive.

The coming of Johnston's army to Utah resulted in greatly upsetting the Corridor plans. Not knowing what the outcome would be and thinking that the Saints might again be exiled from their homes, the Mormon leader called all of the settlers at the outposts to return to Utah. Fort Bridger, Fort Supply, Salmon River Mission, Las Vegas, Carson Valley and San Bernardino were

[38]Brigham H. Roberts, A Comprehensive History of the Church (6 Vols., Salt Lake City, 1930), IV, 203-4.
    [39]Instructions to General Harney, signed by George W. Lay, Aide de Camp to General Scott, Commander in Chief of the United States Army, House Executive Documents, 35 Cong. 1 Sess., X, 71, p. 7; also given in Edward W. Tullidge, History of Salt Lake City, 122.
    [40]Thomas V. Cooper, American Politics (book 2, Washington, D. C., 1884), 39.

all abandoned. Brigham desired to have the concentrated strength of his followers while they awaited the outcome of the trouble.

The Saints at San Bernardino, on October 30, 1857, received a letter from President Young stating that under existing circumstances "the valleys of the mountains was the place for the Saints, that they should leave California for the Basin as soon as possible."[41] The colonists at San Bernardino did not hesitate in making their decision, although it meant that over 3,000 people must either leave their beautiful homes and farms for non-Mormons to take possession of, or, if possible, sell them for very little. Within three days after they had received instructions from Governor Young, the San Bernardino historian wrote that the president of the settlement "thought it wisdom to forward a few immediately and then in a short time . . . send the remainder."[42] The last entry made by the local historian stated: "Tuesday, December 15, 1857, left San Bernardino for Utah."[43] Brigham Young never sent colonists back to any of those abandoned outposts. After the "Utah War" he advanced his frontier settlements more gradually from the parent colony.

Mormons and Colorado River Transportation

The withdrawal of the colonists from San Bernardino and Las Vegas left Santa Clara, in the extreme southern part of the Territory of Utah, as the outpost settlement of the Saints on the southern route. Having given up those two towns, Young immediately focused his attention on another outlet to the ocean over which Mormons could enter the Basin without coming into contact with Gentiles.

He was anxious to develop a cheaper mode of transportation in order to reduce the heavy expense involved in bringing immigrants and merchandise into the Utah Territory.[44] With the steady growth of Mormon colonization southwestward toward the Pacific Coast, he conceived the idea of utilizing the Colorado River as a possible solution of the expensive transportation problem. In 1855 he began investigating this route. Little was known at that time of the navigability of the Colorado. In order to "get the soundings of the river and see if it were navigable for boats," Governor Young sent Rufus Allen with four companions to explore it.[45] They

- - - - -
[41]*History of San Bernardino,* October 30, 1857, Ms.
[42]*Ibid.,* November 2, 1857.
[43]*Ibid.,* December 15, 1857.
[44]By special permission the following material is a reprint of "The Mormons and the Colorado River," *American Historical Review,* XLIV (April, 1939), 549-55.
[45]*Record of Las Vegas Mission,* June 17, 1855, Ms.

traveled as far as Las Vegas springs with William Bringhurst and a group of missionary-colonists who had been sent there by Governor Young to establish a Mormon settlement. They reached Las Vegas springs on June 15, 1855. Bringhurst assigned two of his company, Sylvester Hulet and George W. Bean, to accompany Allen's exploring expedition.

Four days after arriving at Las Vegas, Allen and his companions started off for the Colorado. After traveling twenty-eight miles they reached the river and followed its course. They remained on the trip only five days and then returned to Vegas and reported that on account of the extreme heat and desert country it was impracticable to proceed farther at that season of the year. Although they had traveled down the river for two days, they had found nothing but barren deserts, high mountains, and deep canyons. It was impossible for them to decide with certainty on the feasibility of navigating the Colorado to its mouth.[46]

Two years more passed before the interest of the Saints was again awakened in regard to the navigation of the Colorado. In the fall of 1857 the United States Department of War sent Lieutenant Joseph C. Ives "to explore the Colorado River for the purpose . . . of learning whether it could be used to advantage in the transportation of soldiers and munitions of war on the way to the valley of Salt Lake."[47] Lieutenant Ives brought to the Pacific Coast a small steamer having "powerful machinery adapted for steaming currents." It had been tried on the Delaware River, found to meet expectations, and taken to pieces and transported seventy-five miles up the Colorado River, where its parts were landed and reassembled. Then the ship, christened the *Explorer*, was launched, and Ives sailed up the river from Fort Yuma, where the Gila River flows into the Colorado.[48] The course of the stream above the mouth of the Gila was found to be crooked and the channel obstructed by numerous shifting sand bars. For miles the river flowed through a desert where at certain times high winds filled the air with fine sand almost to the point of obstructing vision. Upon reaching a point 272 miles above Fort Yuma, Lieutenant Ives was able to get his ship over a troublesome rapid only by fastening a line to the shore and helping the ship up. He reported to the United States government as follows: "It appeared, therefore, that the foot of Black Cañon should be considered the

[46]George W. Bean to George A. Smith, *ibid.,* June 24, 1855.
[47]*Los Angeles Star,* December 5, 1857; *Alta Californian,* May 20, 1858.
[48]"On January 13, Lieutenant Ives started with the Explorer from Fort Yuma upon the unknown waters of the Colorado." *Deseret News,* July 21, 1858.

practical head of navigation, and I concluded to have a reconnaissance made to connect that point with the Mormon road, and to let this finish the exploration of the navigable portion of the Colorado."[49]

An editorial appeared in the *Alta Californian* on May 20, 1858, which helped to heighten the interest of the Mormons in the transportation possibilities of the Colorado River. The editorial stated: "At a distance of 325 miles above Fort Yuma is the great kanyon of the Colorado. . . . The mouth of this kanyon is the head of navigation, at least for boats on the lower part of the river. The body of water is large at the kanyon, and perhaps the river may be navigable above it. . . . From the mouth of the kanyon to Las Vegas is fifty miles."[50]

When the report reached Salt Lake City that "examination of the Colorado River for navigation was being conducted by the United States Government with some success," the hope of using the river as an outlet to the sea was revived in Brigham's mind. He waited hardly long enough for Lieutenant Ives' expedition to sail down stream before he dispatched George A. Smith with a company of twenty men "to explore the Rio Colorado and the country adjacent to it for suitable locations for settlements of the Saints."[51] Smith and his companions left Cedar City on March 31, 1858, and made their way to the Colorado by following the courses of the Santa Clara and the Rio Virgin. After traveling down the Colorado as far as Beal's Crossing and searching in vain for desirable sites for settlements, they returned to Cedar City. Probably Smith's report was instrumental in the postponement of plans for developing shipping via the Colorado. During the next few years, however, the leaders exerted their energies in strengthening the colonies south of the rim of the Basin and in planting new towns on the Mormon Corridor route at important points on the Virgin, Santa Clara, and Muddy rivers.

When President Young and company visited the colonies in Utah Dixie[52] in May, 1861, they found that, notwithstanding the efforts during the past to colonize that region, the number of inhabitants was still very small—only seventy-nine families, living in eight small towns. The Mormon leaders, therefore, decided to exert

---

[49]Ives, *Report upon the Colorado River of the West* (Washington, 1861), 87.
[50]*Alta Californian*, May 20, 1858.
[51]*History of Saint George Stake*, 1847-73, f. 37, Ms.
[52]The elevation drops very rapidly in the southwest corner of Utah, which results in a much milder climate around Saint George than in other parts of the state. On account of this mild climate that part of Utah is called Dixie.

special efforts in colonizing and developing the natural resources of the south part of Utah. Accordingly, at the October conference of 1861 held in Salt Lake City, President Young called 309 families to establish a city at the junction of the Santa Clara and Rio Virgin. A total of 748 persons responded to the call, and President Young named the new city "Saint George" in honor of George A. Smith. At the same time a company of thirty families of Swiss converts settled at Santa Clara, five miles from Saint George. In the fall of 1864 a number of missionaries were sent to form colonies on the Muddy River, a tributary of the Virgin.

Brigham Young was now ready to test the practicability of directing immigration traffic and the transportation of goods from Europe and New York to the Caribbean Sea, overland across the Isthmus of Panama, and thence, via the Gulf of California, up the Colorado to the head of navigation. He announced to his followers: "We shall shortly want another path to bring home the Saints, and we want to prepare for it. . . . The Colorado is not far from our southern settlements, only one hundred twenty-five miles from Saint George."[53] He also stated that if he went to live in Dixie, "he would soon have steamboats passing up the Colorado." Saint George was to serve as an inland supply station for the other communities in the Dixie country and as an outpost to furnish supplies to immigrants bound for Salt Lake City.

Shortly after making the foregoing statements, on November 1, 1864, Brigham appointed Bishop Anson Call to establish a colony directly on the Colorado. Call received the following instructions: "Take a suitable company, locate a road to the Colorado, explore the river, find a suitable place for a warehouse, build it, and form a settlement at or near the landing."[54] In that same month the leading merchants of Salt Lake City formed "The Deseret Mercantile Association," the controlling interest in this organization being held by the Church. Call was appointed the official agent for the association and immigration agent for the Mormon Church. It was the purpose of the association to ship merchandise from New York and other eastern cities by water to Panama. From there the goods were to be shipped up the west coast of Mexico, through the Gulf of California, and up the Colorado River to the uppermost point that could be successfully navigated.

Call and his companions left Salt Lake on November 15, 1864. At Santa Clara, Jacob Hamblin, the most famous Mormon explorer

----

[53]*Deseret News,* March 2, 1864.
[54]Brigham Young on Call's Landing, "Saint George Stake." Nov. 1, 1864.

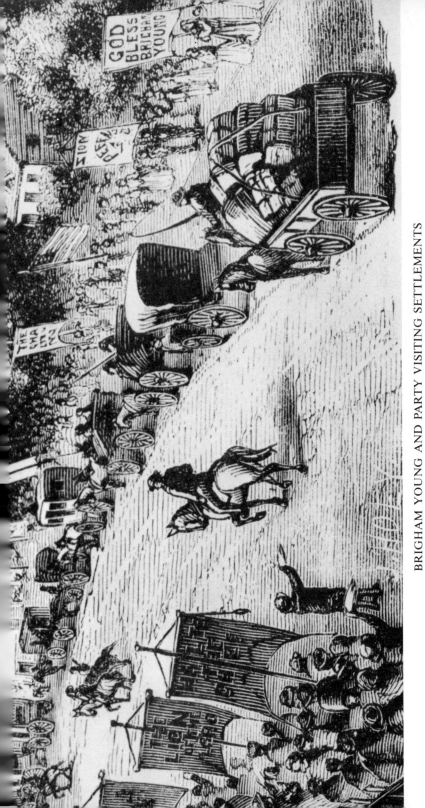

BRIGHAM YOUNG AND PARTY VISITING SETTLEMENTS

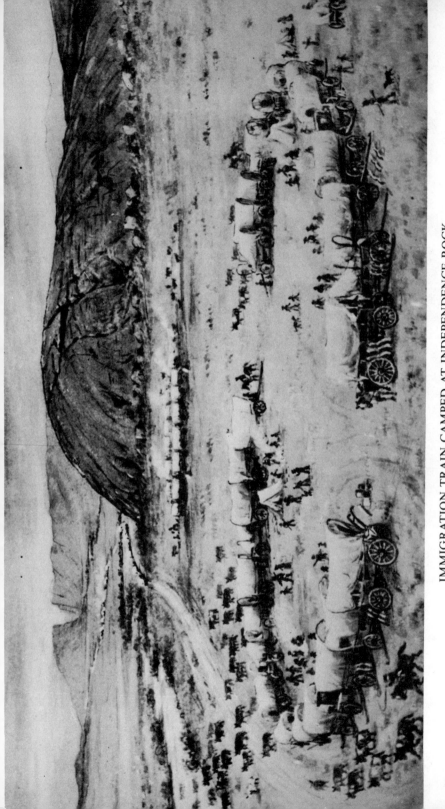

IMMIGRATION TRAIN CAMPED AT INDEPENDENCE ROCK
BY W. H. JACKSON

and Indian missionary, joined the party to act as guide and interpreter. Call's report of December 2 stated:

We came to the Colorado River a mile below the narrows and several
miles above the mouth of Black Canyon. About one-half of a mile below
the mouth of the wash [Callville Wash], we found a black rocky point, which
we considered a suitable locality for the erection of a warehouse above high
water marks; here we considered the best landing could be established. We
found the river . . . one hundred fifty yards wide, or about as wide as the
Illinois River—the selected site can be made as good a landing as the Peoria
landing.[55]

The location chosen for the warehouse was on the north bank
of the Colorado about fifteen miles upstream from the site of the
present Boulder Dam. The place was given the name of Call's
Landing, known also as Call's Fort and Old Callville. After selecting the site for the warehouse, the explorers continued down
the Colorado 150 miles to Hardy's Landing, near the extreme
southern tip of Nevada, and thence to Fort Mojave. They then
returned to the site previously chosen with a conviction that the
best place had been selected. "Laborers, mechanics, supplies, tools,
and every necessary thing to facilitate the erection of the warehouse
without delay" were secured at Saint George. In February, 1865,
the building was completed. Portions of the old warehouse were
still standing when Boulder Dam was constructed. At the present
time the remains of Old Callville are submerged in the waters of
the Colorado.

When the warehouse was first completed, the Saints were
rather optimistic as to the advantages they expected that steam
navigation and the establishing of Call's Landing would bring to
the inhabitants of the Great Basin. Several editorials and articles
appeared in the Deseret News in the spring of 1865. One article
definitely pointed out that a church warehouse had been built
"one hundred twenty-five miles from Saint George, it being contemplated to have the church immigration from Europe come to
Utah via Panama and the Gulf of California, and up the Colorado
to this landing as the highest practicable head of navigation on the
river."[56] In the words of an editorial:

We are satisfied that the Colorado route will receive a fair and thorough
trial, with flattering prospects of becoming, sooner or later, commercially
beneficial. . . . [Goods] can be brought by water to within some five hundred
miles of this city [Salt Lake], and from there by land transportation on a road

[55]Call to George A. Smith, Ibid., December 25. 1864.
[56]"Report on Call's Landing," Deseret News, January 20, 1865.

free from desert and alkali water, and affording markets at short intervals along its entire length.[57]

There was very little shipping, however, either to or from Call's Landing. On January 2, 1865, William H. Hardy left Hardy's Landing in a flat bottomed barge, and by means of poles and oars propelled it to Call's Landing, arriving there in twelve days. He believed that with a little work upon the stream bed the Colorado could be made safe for steam navigation. At least three trips per month could be made from the mouth of the river to Call's Landing. Hardy was also of the opinion that goods could be shipped up and down the river most successfully during the month of April and from July to October. The high water and driftwood would make navigation unsafe from the middle of May to early in July.[58]

Thomas E. Trueworthy attempted to bring one hundred tons of freight to Call's Landing in the spring of 1865. He arrived at his destination with only part of his load, having had to leave some of it at La Paz. Learning that Bishop Call had returned to the Great Basin, Trueworthy left his steamboat and cargo at the landing and made a trip overland to Salt Lake City, where he gave a discouraging report on Colorado River transportation."[59]

Whether or not the Mormons could have made the Colorado a practicable shipping route was never determined, for hardly had Call's Landing been built when their attention was turned from it to the transcontinental railway then under construction. Thus conditions beyond Brigham Young's control put an end to his plan of making the Colorado the main route of entrance into the Territory of Utah and altered his Corridor project. Realizing that a railroad would supply cheaper and safer transportation, Brigham and his people abandoned the Colorado River project and gave their full support to the construction of the newer agent—the railway—in which they had for years been interested.

SUMMARY OF THE ACHIEVEMENTS OF MORMON CORRIDOR PROJECT

When the Los Angeles and Salt Lake City Railroad was constructed later on, it adhered closely to Hunt's trail of 1849 which Brigham and his followers had worked so assiduously in helping to develop. Although Young was not directly connected with its construction, there is no doubt his earlier activities as a pioneer, planner, and colonizer in that section of the country did much to

[57]"The Colorado Route," *ibid.*, March 8, 1865.
[58]*Latter-day Saints Journal History*, January 14, 1865, Ms.
[59]*Ibid.*, March 25, 1865.

influence the route. The twentieth century Salt Lake City-Los Angeles air line also follows the same route.

The efforts of the great Mormon pioneer, statesman, and empire builder and his co-workers to connect the Mormon Mecca with the sea were not in vain. They contributed a generous share to the establishment of a highway along the southern route which today is the main thoroughfare between Salt Lake and Los Angeles, Highway 91. Besides exploring and developing this route through a 750-mile country which was almost impassable in certain places, Brigham Young had supervised the building of some forty towns and cities along this road before his death in 1877. Every mountain stream along the Mormon Corridor had been utilized to refresh the thirsty soil in order to produce the bounties of life. Also, over 325 other towns and cities in the Great West had been founded by the Mormon colonizer—a commonwealth indeed had been established in thirty years' time. The Saints gave their valuable contribution to the building of the West by exploring and assisting in the development of several good routes from the heart of the Basin to the sea. Brigham's dream came true. Utah was connected with the East, with the West, and with the Southwest by highways, telegraphs, and railroads.

CHAPTER IX

PROSELYTING AND IMMIGRATION

DOCTRINE OF GATHERING

The doctrines of the Church of Jesus Christ of Latter-day Saints included the teaching that missionaries were to be sent to "every kindred, nation, tongue and people" for the purpose of gathering unto Zion all the seed of Israel, i. e., all people who would affiliate themselves with Mormonism. Joseph Smith expresses Mormon belief as follows: "We believe in the literal gathering of Israel and in the restoration of the ten tribes; that Zion will be built upon this [the American] continent."[1]

The main efforts in missionary work outside the United States before the Mormons left the East in 1846 were carried on in the British Isles. The mission was opened in 1837 under the direction of the Prophet Joseph, but the elders were at first instructed to "remain silent concerning gathering . . . until such time that the work was fully established."[2]

EUROPEAN IMMIGRATION TO UTAH

Emigration from Britain to the United States did not commence until 1840. In April at Preston, England, the twelve apostles, with Brigham Young at their head, announced the doctrine of gathering.[3] From that time forward during the life of Brother Brigham, gathering to Zion was urged by the missionaries and practiced by the Saints, even under adverse conditions.[4]

Immediately upon the announcement of the doctrine of gathering, the Church officials in England began preparations for an organized and directed system to facilitate emigration. From 1814 to 1846, the president of the British Mission acted as shipping agent for the Church. He supervised the fitting out of companies of converts at Liverpool and arranged for their transportation.

Brigham Young, being president of the British Mission in 1840, chartered the first ship and served as the first emigration agent in Europe for the Church. He continued in this capacity until April 15, 1841, at which time he left England for America.[5]

---

[1]Joseph Smith, *Articles of Faith,* Article ten; *Doctrine and Covenants,* Section 29:7-8.
[2]Joseph Smith, *History of the Church,* II, 492.
[3]Orson F. Whitney, *Life of Heber C. Kimball,* 288.
[4]Joseph Smith, *History of the Church,* IV, 185-187.
[5]Andrew Jenson, *Contributor,* XII, 402-405.

The first organized company of British converts to immigrate to Utah left Liverpool on June 6, 1840, only one month following the announcement of the doctrine of gathering. Between that date and 1846, when the exiled Mormons left Ohio, thirty-one organized companies of proselytes had sailed from England, increasing the Church population at and around Nauvoo by nearly five thousand members.[6]

Missionary work in the British Isles was carried on very successfully. About the time the first emigrants left for America, 6,614 converts had been made in the British Mission. Ten years later the Church membership in that mission had increased to 32,747,[7] although during that period only 10,319 had migrated to America.[8]

But after the Mormons had located in the Great West, Governor Young began immediately to extend land settlement in every direction. Each month spent there brought more vividly to Brigham's mind a broader conception of the resources of the Great Basin and the hopelessness of fully developing them with the 25,000 Saints then (1847) available in the United States and Canada.[9]

In accordance with the Mormon principle of gathering, he decided to increase missionary activities and then to expedite the immigration of proselytes to the Mormon empire of the West. If he was to gain control over an expansive territory, he must gather converts rapidly to their mountain rendezvous. This vast Basin was an ideal place in which to establish Zion, so Brother Brigham immediately sent out word for all the Saints of God throughout the world to hasten to the Mormon Mecca.[10]

Immediately upon receipt of President Young's letter, Orson Spencer, President of the European Mission, issued instructions on February 1, 1848, as follows:

The channel of Saints' emigration to the land of Zion is now open. The long looked for time for gathering has come. . . . The resting place for Israel for the last days has been discovered. . . . Let all who can gather up their effects, and set their faces as a flint to go Zionward in due time and order. . . . It is now designed to fit out a ship's company of emigrants as soon as practicable. The first company this winter ought to be embarked from Liverpool, as early as the 9th of February. The presidents of conferences are requested to forward to us the number of those who are prepared to emigrate by the

———
[6]*Ibid.,* 405, 441-450.
[7]*Millennial Star,* XIII, 15.
[8]James Linforth, *Route from Liverpool to Great Salt Lake City,* 15.
[9]Joseph Fielding Smith, *Origin of the Reorganized Church,* 13, 17.
[10]Brigham Young, "General Epistle . . . to the Saints," *Latter-day Saint Journal History,* March, 1848, Ms.

9th of February, and also the number that will be ready by the 23rd of February.[11]

In March of 1848 the Mormon Colonizer issued from Winter Quarters further instructions to the Saints scattered throughout the world. The building of a Mormon commonwealth in the Great Basin was the central idea.

Gather yourselves together speedily near this place on the east side of the Missouri River, and, if possible, be ready to start from hence by the first of May next, or as soon as grass is sufficiently grown, and go to the Great Salt Lake City. . . . To all the Saints in the United States and Canada, gather to the same place. . . . To the Saints in England, Scotland, Ireland, Wales, and adjacent islands and countries, we say, emigrate as speedily as possible to this vicinity, looking to and following the counsel of the Presidency at Liverpool, shipping to New Orleans, and from thence to Council Bluffs, which will save much expense.[12]

World-Wide Missionary Campaign

After establishing the Saints securely in the Great Basin, Brigham Young devoted his attention to the establishment of missions throughout the world. While thousands of people in America were gold crazed in 1849 and were madly rushing to the gold fields of California, Brigham and his followers turned their backs upon the yellow metal and their hearts toward the meek of the earth. Young inaugurated in 1849-50 an active and extensive proselyting campaign, both by increasing the number of missionaries and the countries to which they were sent. This dynamic missionary work continued throughout the remainder of his life and even to the present time.

Heretofore Mormon proselyting work outside of America had been confined to the British Isles. At the October conference of 1849 the Church leaders decided to expand the missionary field to the entire world. Addison Pratt, James Brown and Hiram H. Blackwell were sent to the Society Islands, in the southern Pacific, to extend proselyting work there. From that date to the present time Mormon elders have been in those islands and have converted thousands to the Church of Jesus Christ.

Also in October, 1849, Lorenzo Snow and Joseph Toronto were assigned to open the door of the Gospel in Switzerland and Italy. Having been reinforced by Elders T. B. H. Stenhouse and Jabez Woodward, the four elders succeeded in making enough converts in Italy to organize a branch of the Church in the vicinity

---

[11]*Millennial Star,* X, 40-41.
[12]Brigham Young, "General Epistle . . . to the Saints."

of La Tour. Elder Snow supervised the translation of the Book of Mormon into Italian and had it published before he left the mission. Joseph Toronto, a native of Sicily, visited his relatives but had no success in converting them. Italy and Sicily have never been very fertile fields for Mormonism, they being Catholic countries.

Lorenzo Snow sent Elder Stenhouse to Switzerland to open proselyting work in that country. His labors met with much success, and the mission he founded remained, until the withdrawal of the elders in 1940, one of the most fruitful missions in the Church.

In June, 1852, Elders Snow, Woodward, and Thomas Obray from England introduced the Gospel into the Island of Malta. Success was met with, and Apostle Snow felt that from this point the Gospel should be taken to Russia, Turkey and Spain.

Shortly thereafter Lorenzo Snow made a trip to England. He met William Willis, a Mormon convert who had spent several years in India. Snow and the other apostles who were in England decided to send Willis to Calcutta. Soon after Willis arrived in India, he baptized nine natives of the East Indies. Later he organized a branch of the Church consisting of 300 natives and over forty Europeans. Elder Hugh Findlay was sent to Bombay, and Joseph Richards was sent to assist Elder Willis. Thus the doors of the Gospel were opened in far off India. However, after three years of proselyting, the mission was closed in 1855 by order from Brigham Young because of adverse conditions there. All the missionaries were instructed to return from that land and bring with them all the converts that could conveniently come.

Apostle John Taylor was also appointed at the October Conference, 1849, to open missionary work in France and Germany. He took with him Curtis C. Bolton and John Pack. By December, 1851, five branches of the Church had been established in France, including the Jersey Island branch. A conference was held in Paris and more than 400 members of the French Mission were in attendance.

While in France, Elder Taylor published the Book of Mormon in French and arranged for its publication in German. He also introduced the Gospel into Germany by organizing a branch of the Church at Hamburg in the summer of 1851. Orson Spencer and Jacob Horitz were refused admittance in Germany in 1853. Later, however, the German Mission was reopened, and at times it has been a fruitful field.

The October conference of 1849 sent the newly ordained apostle Erastus Snow to preach the Gospel in the Scandinavian countries. Accompanied by several other missionaries, Elder Snow and his companions opened the door of the Gospel to Denmark, Norway, Sweden, Jutland, and Iceland.

During Elder Snow's stay of twenty-two months in Denmark about six hundred persons were baptized. The Book of Mormon and Doctrine and Covenants were translated and published in the Danish language, as also a number of pamphlets in Swedish and Danish, and the Scandinavian Stjerne founded, which continues the organ of the Church in that country to this day.[13]

From the day that Erastus Snow opened the Scandinavian countries to proselyting work, thousands and thousands of converts to Mormonism have been made there. That mission furnished Brigham Young with a sturdy, dependable group of colonists to assist in establishing a commonwealth in the Great West.

In April, 1849, Amasa M. Lyman was appointed president of the Californian Mission. The following October he was joined by Apostle Charles C. Rich. The main result of the mission of these two Apostles was the purchase of the Rancho San Bernardino about two years after their appointment to the presidency of the mission in California. Under their direction about 500 Saints from Utah moved to the ranch and established the city of San Bernardino. The importance of that outpost has been discussed in the Mormon Corridor chapter.

The following year (1850), Parley P. Pratt and companions began preaching the Gospel in Hispanic America. They went as far south as Valparaiso, Chile, but a civil war was on in South America which prevented them from making many converts. Thus they returned to California.

The Hawaiian Mission was opened in 1850-51. George Q. Cannon and nine companions were sent there to labor among the whites. They at first met with little or no success. All the missionaries except Elder Cannon, a youth of twenty-three years, were determined to return to Utah. But George Q. Cannon felt that they should remain in Hawaii and labor among the natives. One day he went into a banyan grove to pray over the matter. "There the Lord talked to him as one man talks to another." He was instructed to remain on the island, for there were many natives who would join the Church. Four of Cannon's companions con-

----

[13]Millennial Star, XII.

sented to remain with him. They did a marvelous work. George Q. Cannon translated the Book of Mormon into the Hawaiian language, and after he returned to San Francisco, in 1855, he published it. March 1, 1852, F. A. Hammond reported the success of the Hawaiian Mission as follows:

> The missionaries (that is, other denominations) succeeded in putting a stop to our labors, but the government gave their full consent to our laboring here, and the United States Consul took an active part in getting to us the same rights as the other denominations, since which time the work has been increasing rapidly and we now number about six hundred members upon all the islands, four hundred and fifty of them upon this island (i.e. Maui). We baptized about two hundred and fifty since Christmas and the work is still going ahead.[14]

In 1851 Elders John Murdock and Charles Wendell began teaching Mormonism in Australia. A year later they were joined by nine other missionaries. Some of them went to New Zealand and Tasmania. Branches of the Church were established in all of these lands and the missions have been continuous there since that time.

A successful proselyting activity was carried on in South Africa in 1853. Jesse Haven, William Walker, and Leonard I. Smith succeeded in establishing several small branches of the Church.

But there were also missionary endeavors during this period which were completely unsuccessful. Mormon elders were rejected in China and Burma, while Elder Luddingham was stoned out of Bankok. Elders Edward Stevenson and Nathan T. Porter were not permitted by the authorities to preach the Gospel at Gibraltar nor in Spain. Neither would the authorities permit the Mormons to preach in the West Indies and British Guiana.

Thus within five years after inaugurating his comprehensive missionary campaign in 1849, President Brigham Young had directed the opening of proselyting activities throughout much of the world. A heroic attempt had really been made to carry the Gospel to every "kindred, nation, tongue, and people." The remarkable thing is, this missionary work was done by a people who were trying to open a frontier country to colonization, 1000 miles from civilization, and the colonizers had just been driven from their homes with the loss of their property in Illinois.

The missionaries in the different countries met with varying degrees of success. Scandinavia furnished more converts than any other of the new missions while the British Isles continued to

---

[14]*Deseret News,* July 24, 1852.

supply thousands of emigrants for Zion. Toward the close of 1851 the records of the British Mission showed a Church membership in England of 32,894, the greatest number of Saints ever reported there.[15] Orson Pratt had been the president of the British Mission since 1848, replacing Orson Spencer. He did some of the most vigorous and successful work of his life during this period, especially in writing articles. In Pratt's own words:

It is now one year and a half since our arrival in this country; during this period, the kingdom of God has rolled forth with unparalleled success; its numbers have increased in Great Britain alone, from about fifteen thousand to twenty-nine thousand souls (increase of 11,000). Two thousand of this number have emigrated to America. The circulation of the Star, during the same period, has increased from thirty-seven hundred to fifty-seven hundred.[16]

Orson Pratt ranks as one of the greatest of Mormon missionaries. He crossed the Atlantic sixteen times for his Church. Quoting John Henry Evans:

When everything is said and done, it will be found that Orson Pratt traveled more miles on land and sea delivering the Word; that he brought more people into the Fold through his spoken and written message; that, with the exception of Joseph Smith and Brigham Young, he was in the vanguard of more undertakings; and that he was more prolific in his written defense of the Faith—than any other Mormon that can be mentioned.[17]

Perpetual Emigrating Fund Company

Almost immediately after arriving in the Salt Lake Valley in 1847, President Young had issued orders to the Saints throughout the world to migrate to the Mormon Mecca. After two years of continuously urging them to migrate he saw that the gathering was not progressing fast enough to satisfy his empire building aspirations. But the mission presidents explained that many of the converts were too poor to buy the expensive equipment required in crossing the plains.

Therefore, in September, 1849, the Mormon leader proposed the creation of a revolving fund for the purpose of helping those proselytes who possessed insufficient money to migrate to the Basin. The other officials concurred to his suggestion. Less than a month later, at a general Church conference held at Salt Lake on October 6, the subject received the unanimous vote of the Saints. The proposed organization was named "The Perpetual Emigrating Fund Company."

[15]Andrew Jenson, Church Chronology. 38-44.
[16]Millennial Star. XII, 89.
[17]John Henry Evans, The Heart of Mormonism, 411-412.

A committee was appointed to collect money by contributions for beginning the fund.[18] Several thousand dollars were voluntarily subscribed during that conference.[19] Brigham Young appointed Bishop Edward Hunter to take the funds back to the States, "buy cattle, take the oversight of the property, and bring the poor to this place."[20] On October 16, 1849, President Young wrote the following letter to Orson Hyde, the presiding officer in the Pottawatamie country, which explains the functioning of the company:

Great Salt Lake City,
October 16, 1849.

President Orson Hyde:

We write you more particularly this time concerning the gathering and the mission of our general agent for the Perpetual Emigrating Fund for the coming year, Bishop Edward Hunter, who will soon be with you, bearing the funds already raised in this place, and we will here state our instructions to Brother Hunter, so that you may the more fully comprehend our designs.

In the first place this fund has been raised by voluntary donations, and is to be continued by the same process and by so managing as to preserve the same and then to multiply.

Bishop Hunter is instructed to go direct to Kanesville and confer with the general authorities at that place and, by all means within his reach, procure every information so as to make the most judicious application of the funds in the purchase of young oxen and cows that can be worked effectively to the valley, and that will be capable of improving and selling after their arrival so as to continue the fund the following year. . . .

The poor can live without the luxuries of life upon the road and in the valley as well as in Pottawatamie and other places, and those who have means to purchase luxuries, have money to procure an outfit of their own and need no help. Therefore, let such as are helped receive as little in food, clothing, wagons, etc., as can possibly make them comfortable to this place, and when they arrive they can get to work and get their outfit of all things necessary for comfort and convenience better than where they are, and even luxuries.

As early in the spring as it will possibly do, on account of feed for the cattle, Brother Hunter will gather all of his company, organize them in the usual order, and preside over the camp, traveling with the same to this place, having previously procured the best teamsters possible, such as are accustomed to driving, and be gentle, kind and attentive to their teams. When the Saints thus helped arrive here they will give their obligation to the Church to refund to the amount of what they received, as soon as circumstances will permit, and labor will be furnished to such as wish on the public works, and good pay; and as fast as they can procure the necessaries of life, and a surplus, that surplus will be applied to liquidating their debt and thereby increasing the Perpetual Fund.

By this it will rapidly be discovered that the funds are to be appropriated in the form of a loan rather than a gift; and this will make the honest in heart rejoice, for they love to labor and be independent by their labor, and

---

[18]*Latter-day Saint Journal History*, October 6, 1849, Ms.
[19]*Millennial Star*, XIII, 53.
[20]*Journal History, op. cit.*

not live on the charity of friends, while the lazy idlers, if such there be, will find fault and want every luxury furnished them on their journey and in the end pay nothing.

Brother Hunter will return all the funds to this place next season, when the most judicious course will be pursued to convert all the cattle and means into cash, that the same may be sent abroad as speedily as possible on another mission, together with all that we can raise in the States will increase the fund by all possible means the coming winter so that our agent may return with a large company.

The few thousand that we send out by our agent at this time is like a grain of mustard seed in the earth; we send it forth into the world and among the Saints, a good soil, and we expect it will grow and flourish, and spread abroad in a few years so it will cover England, cast its shadow in Europe and in process of time compass the whole earth. That is to say these funds are designated to increase until Israel is gathered from all nations, and the poor can sit under their own vines, and inhabit their own houses, and worship God in Zion.[21]

The immediate purpose of the fund was to bring the exiles from Iowa to Utah, as Brigham Young and others had pledged themselves to use all their influence and property, if necessary, to bring all the Saints expelled from Nauvoo to the Great West.[22] Another object was to assist the needy converts throughout the world defray their expenses to Zion. So almost the same day (October 14, 1849) that President Young wrote to Orson Hyde in Iowa, he also wrote to Orson Pratt, president of the British Mission, informing him in regards to the purpose and contemplated workings of the Perpetual Emigrating Fund Company.

He explained to Pratt that the fund was to remain perpetual, as the name implied. In order to keep it so, all the poor who were benefited by its operations were to reimburse as soon as possible the amount they had borrowed. Donations were to be accepted from all parts of the world, as the plan was devised to assist Saints from every country. Orson Pratt's office in Liverpool was designated as a place of deposit for funds received in Europe, but the money could be used only upon the order of the First Presidency.[23]

Brigham and his associates had great hopes as to the immense assistance the Perpetual Emigrating Fund was going to be in helping toward a rapid establishment of a populous Mormon empire in the West. But their hopes were not entirely realized. The following quotation from Brigham Young expresses at least their desires:

----

[21]James A. Little, *From Kirtland to Salt Lake City*, 215-218.
[22]*Millennial Star*, XII, 120; Brigham H. Roberts, *A Comprehensive History of the Church*, III, 407-410.
[23]Linforth, *Route from Liverpool to Great Salt Lake Valley*, 8.

The estimated population of 15,000 inhabitants in Deseret the past year, having raised grain sufficient to sustain the 30,000 for the coming year, inspires us confidently to believe that the 30,000 the coming year can raise sufficient for 60,000 the succeeding year, and to this object and end our energies will be exerted to double our population annually by the assistance of the Perpetual Emigrating Poor Fund, and otherwise provide for the sustenance of that population.

Viewing the gathering of Israel, which produces our increased population in the valleys of the mountains, an important part of the gospel of Jesus Christ . . . we say, arise! to your wagons and your tents, O scattered Israel! Ye Saints of the Most High! rich and poor, and gather to the State of Deseret. . . . We will soon send the Elders abroad by hundreds and thousands to a harvest of souls among the nations, and the inhabitants of the earth shall speedily hear of the salvation prepared by Israel's God for His people.[24]

Throughout the first year of operation of the Perpetual Emigrating Fund Company, President Young and his associates were working out plans for its perfection. The enterprise, such as the ambition of those leaders visualized, certainly was of sufficient proportions to demand special planning and administering. Large sums of money would have to be collected and spent in order to handle the enterprise. Ships must be chartered and buying agencies for migration equipment must be maintained.

In order to transact business with other corporations, the First Presidency had the Perpetual Emigrating Fund Company legally organized and chartered by the Provisional State Government. The act of incorporation was signed by Governor Brigham Young on September 14, 1850.[25] The following March (1851), the act was made legal by the Territorial Legislature and confirmed by the same body January 12, 1856.[26] The ordinance of incorporation gave a number of reasons for establishing the Emigrating Company and listed in detail its duties. Section fourteen stated that "the members of the company shall hold their office at the pleasure of the conference herein before mentioned; but the First Presidency of the Church shall have full power to fill all vacancies that may occur by death, removal, or otherwise."[27]

Officers were elected for the new company shortly after the act of incorporation was signed by the Governor. Brigham Young was elected president; Willard Richards, secretary; Newel K. Whitney, treasurer; Thomas Bullock, recorder; Orson Hyde, Orson Pratt, John Brown, and Franklin D. Richards, traveling agents;

---

[24]Brigham Young, "General Epistle . . . to the Saints," cited in Little, op. cit., 229-230.
[25]Deseret News, September 14, 1850.
[26]Hubert Howe Bancroft. History of Utah, 415.
[27]Deseret News, September 14, 1851.

and several others, principally apostles, were chosen to assist in the work.

Although the Mormon leaders intended to give the direct assistance of the Emigrating Fund only those who could not afford to come otherwise, yet in its actual workings the company assisted all classes of emigrants. Directly, it supplied definite means of transportation for the poor; indirectly, its organized methods benefited those who were able to pay their own transportation. An announcement in the *Millennial Star* stated:

A prompt observance of these instructions, concerning deposits and remittances of funds is as necessary on the part of those who intend to go through independent of the P. E. F. Company, but who wish our agents to have their outfit in readiness for them on the frontiers, as it is for the P. E. Fund passengers.[28]

DESCRIPTION OF EMIGRATION FROM EUROPE

Under the direction of the company, a group of officials in England arranged for the chartering of ships, the assembling of prospective emigrants, and the organizing of converts for the contemplated migration.

Previous to the date of sailing, the shipping agent announced in the *Millennial Star* the complete plan with instructions to the emigrants. A Saint who wished to sail with a particular company gave one pound deposit and filed an application, stating his age, occupation, and nativity.[29] Usually the day before that set for sailing, the emigrants assembled and boarded the ship in the most orderly manner, all arrangements and details having been previously taken care of by the shipping agents.

A captain was appointed to take charge and be responsible for every member of the Church on board. Throughout the course of their journey, the Saints held regular religious preaching services daily and attended to morning and evening prayers. This was carried on under the direction of an ecclesiastical organization effected to provide for the spiritual needs of the Saints en route to Zion. The companies were always divided into wards, over which a bishop and two counselors presided. Social activities, such as dances and concerts, were occasionally provided for the entertainment of the travelers.[30]

The regular route followed by the emigrants was from Europe

---

[28]*Millennial Star.* XVIII. 713.
[29]*Ibid.,* XV. 618.
[30]Edward W. Tullidge. *History of Salt Lake City,* 100.

via New Orleans to Kanesville until 1853. In 1854 the landing place was changed to Kansas City near which the Saints built a camp known as Mormon Grove.

IMMIGRATION TO UTAH

At the landing place the emigrants were received by another group of agents who organized them for travel and provided them with proper equipment for the journey to Salt Lake Valley.[31] The general procedure can be learned from the following instructions of one of the frontier agents, Erastus Snow:

It is intended that the remainder of our European emigration destined for Utah the present year will sail during the months of February and March from Liverpool via Philadelphia, Cincinnati, and St. Louis to a point on the Missouri River, hereafter to be determined as a point of outfit for the plains. . . . All others from the eastern states or provinces, who intend crossing the plains this season, will do well to concentrate at St. Louis, and report themselves at this office during the month of April or early in May and embark hence under my personal arrangements.

Those of northern Illinois, Iowa, and Wisconsin who choose to travel by land across the country should also rendezvous at the same place on the Missouri. . . . There I will meet them personally, or by my agent, to organize them into companies, and give them such instructions, and adopt such regulations, as will be necessary for their security in crossing the plains. My assent will not be given to any Saint to leave the Missouri River unless so organized in a company of at least fifty effectual well-armed men, and that too, under the command of a man appointed by me; one who would carry out my instructions. . . .

I will furnish at this point an outfit, for such as desire it, wagons, oxen, cows, guns, flour, bacon, etc.

Choice wagons, made to order and delivered at the point of outfit with bows, projectors, etc., will be about $78, without projectors, $75. Oxen with yokes and chains from $70 to $85 per yoke; cows from $16 to $25 cash.

My experience derived from six journeys over the plains, enables me to know what kind of teams and outfits are wanted for the plains. Those wishing me to supply them in part or in whole, should lose no time in sending in their orders. . . .

One wagon, two yoke oxen, and two cows will be sufficient (if that is the extent of their means) for a family of eight or ten persons, with the addition of a tent for every two or three families. Of course, with that amount of teams, only the necessary baggage, provisions and utensils can be taken, and then the person ride but little. Those who have a surplus of means, after paying their tithing and making provisions for their own outfit, should contribute to the "Perpetual Emigrating Fund," according to their means and faith, so that other long tried and faithful Saints who lack means, may receive aid through that channel.[32]

---

[31]Linforth, op. cit., 6.
[32]Erastus Snow, The Luminary, February 16, 1835, cited in William E. Berrett, The Restored Church, 401-402.

The first Saints directly aided by the Perpetual Emigrating Fund were those who had been temporarily camped in Iowa. The records indicate that there were 7,828 Mormons there in 1850. As too few of them had responded to the aid offered, President Young on September 21, 1851, issued a sharp order to them to come to Utah the following spring.[33] Early in 1852, Ezra T. Benson and Jedediah M. Grant accompanied Bishop Edward Hunter to Iowa to aid in moving the refugees to the Great Basin, so that the Pottawatamie lands were practically evacuated by the Mormons. The population of Utah in 1850 was 11,380. This number was increased to between 25,000 and 30,000 by the close of 1852.[34]

The last of the Saints exiled from Nauvoo arrived in Salt Lake by the aid of the Fund Company almost exactly at the time of the arrival of the first European proselytes assisted by the fund. This European company, consisting of 250 people, left Liverpool on January 16, 1852. Franklin D. Richards, president of the European Mission, directed the outfitting of the travelers. There were also 726 other emigrants from Europe that year which included twenty-eight from Scandinavia, the first emigrants from that mission, which had recently been opened by Erastus Snow. In the words of Andrew Jenson:

> This was the first company of Saints emigrating from any country where the English language is not spoken. Soon afterwards, the missions which had been established in Germany, France, Switzerland and Italy by Apostles John Taylor and Lorenzo Snow and other Elders, began to ship converts to the gathering places of the Saints in America.[35]

President Young was now determined to move the Saints from Europe to Utah as rapidly as possible, so he sent them the following instructions on April 18, 1852:

> Prepare against another season, to come by tens of thousands. . . . We have been willing to live on bread and water, and many times very little bread too, for years, that we might search out and plant the Saints in a goodly land. This we have accomplished, . . . therefore, let all who can procure a bit of bread, and one garment on their back, be assured there is water plenty and pure by the way, and doubt no longer, but come next year to the place of gathering, even in flocks, as doves fly to their windows before a storm.[36]

Ten Pound Plan

So responsive were the Saints to the President's request that

[33]Andrew Jenson, "Church Emigration," *Contributor*, XIII, 131-138.
[34]Hubert H. Bancroft, *History of Utah*, 397; William E. Berrett, *The Restored Church*, 399.
[35]Jenson, *op. cit.*, 134.
[36]Brigham Young, "Seventh General Epistle . . . to the Saints," *Millennial Star*, XIV, 325.

the Perpetual Emigrating Fund was not able to meet the needs of all the converts who wished to emigrate in 1853. This necessitated the adoption by the Fund Company of a new plan known as the ten pound plan. Under it each adult was charged ten pounds and each child under one year of age five pounds, the money to be paid in advance. By buying equipment carefully and in large quantities, Brigham thought that the company could bring emigrants to Utah for these low prices. Although 957 from Great Britain alone were brought to the Basin that year under the ten pound plan, the Fund Company underestimated the cost of transportation and had to borrow money to help complete the journey.[37]

The Mormon emigration system had now developed three distinctive classes of emigrants: those who paid their own way; those who came under the ten pound plan; and those whose transportation was financed by friends at Salt Lake. From 1853 to 1856 the cost of transportation and outfitting companies of Saints for the journey across the plains continuously increased, so that the ten pound plan had to be modified to meet the increase in costs. In 1854 thirteen pounds per person was the rate while in 1855 it was raised to fifteen pounds.

IMMIGRATION TO UTAH, 1840-1855

Notwithstanding the increase in cost of transportation, the number of proselytes migrating also increased. In 1853 the total emigration from Europe was 2,606, all but 314 of them being from the British Isles.[38] Seventeen were from Germany and 297 from the Scandinavian Mission. Of the 2,312 British emigrants, 955 paid their own way either by arranging for their own outfits or by sending money ahead to the emigrating agents, 957 traveled under the ten pound plan, and 400 were directly assisted by the Fund. The following year out of the total British emigration of 2,034, all but 875 were fund emigrants.[39] In 1855 of the 4,225 European emigrants, 1,161 persons came under the Fund.[40]

Andrew Jenson estimated that the cost of the Fund Company for emigrating the Saints in 1853 and 1854 was 70,000 pounds, while the cost in 1855 was 30,000, a total of 100,000 pounds.[41] In the words of Gustive O. Larson:

It is probable that for the four years from 1852 to 1855 over 125,000

---

[37]Jenson, op. cit., 134.
[38]Ibid., 134-135, 458-467.
[39]James Linforth, Route From Liverpool to Great Salt Lake Valley, 120.
[40]Jenson, op. cit., XIII, 135-137.
[41]Ibid., 136.

pounds were expended by the company in emigrating poor converts. A total of 9,753 emigrants sailed during that period, 2,885 of whom were aided entirely by the Perpetual Fund Company. One thousand forty-three came under the special rate arrangements and the remaining 2,825 were aided through the services of the purchasing agencies and general organization of the company.[42]

"From 1848 to the close of 1855, fifty-nine vessels sailed from Liverpool, England, with organized companies of Latter-day Saints on board." Sixteen thousand, five hundred and ninety-two souls registered with the emigrating agents, while 319 converts came to America during that period without registering. Between 1840 and 1855, 21,911 Mormons migrated to the United States, and practically all of them gathered with the Saints in the Rocky Mountains. From Andrew Jenson's article on "Church Emigration" is quoted the following grouping of the companies and the years of emigration:

> "1840,   3 companies, or 291 souls.
> 1841,   7 companies, or 1,056 souls.
> 1842,   8 companies, or 1,614 souls.
> 1843,   5 companies, or 772 souls.
> 1844,   5 companies, or 644 souls.
> 1845,   3 companies, or 411 souls.
> 1846,   1 company, or 45 souls.
> Miscellaneous in 1840-1846, 137 souls.
>
> 1848,   4 companies, or 754 souls.
> 1849,   9 companies, or 2,078 souls.
> 1850,   6 companies, or 1,612 souls.
> 1851,   4 companies, or 1,370 souls.
> 1852,   4 companies, or 760 souls.
> 1853,   9 companies, or 2,626 souls.
> 1854, 10 companies, or 3,167 souls.
> 1855, 13 companies, or 4,225 souls.
> Miscellaneous in 1848-1855, 319 souls.
>
> Total, 21,911 souls."[43]

HANDCART MIGRATION

The year 1856 marks a new experiment in Mormon emigration —the handcart transportation. The increased cost of travel threatened a decrease in the number of immigrants to Utah and placed the finances of the company in a precarious position. If the Mormon Colonizer were to maintain a large and even flow of converts to his commonwealth, some way to increase the funds

---

[42]Gustive O. Larson. *History of the Perpetual Emigrating Fund Company,* 91-92, Ms.
[43]Jenson, *op. cit.,* 137-138.

or to provide a cheaper mode of transportation had to be devised.
During the six years of the operation of the company, a plan
had been evolving in Brigham's mind. By following it, he believed
firmly that Saints could cross the plains and Rocky Mountains at
much less expense and with greater rapidity and freedom than by
ox teams. The handcart was the center of the plan. It could be
easily pushed or pulled, and if each person was restricted as to the
number of pounds he could take, the load would be comparatively
light. That mode of travel had been tried by a few people and
had succeeded. President Young thought that, by wise and careful
supervision, transportation with handcarts could be made not only
an equal but a far superior method of bringing poor converts to
the Basin. On September 22, 1851, he gave public expression to
his ideas in the sixth general epistle to the Saints. Quoting:

> The voice of the "Good Shepherd" is to all Saints, even to the ends of
> the earth; gather yourselves together, come home. . . . O ye Saints in the United
> States will you listen to the voice of the "Good Shepherd"? Will you gather?
> Will you be obedient to the heavenly commandment?
> Some of the children of the world have crossed the mountains and plains,
> from Missouri to California, with a pack on their backs to worship their god
> —gold! Some have performed the same journey with wheel-barrow, some have
> accomplished the same with a pack or a cow.
> Some of the Saints now in our midst came here with wagons or carts
> made of wood, without a particle of iron, hooping their wheels with hickory,
> or rawhide, or ropes, and had as good and safe a journey as any in the camps
> with their wrought iron wagons, and can you not do the same? Yes, if you
> have the same desire, the same faith. Families might start from the Missouri
> river with cows, handcarts, wheelbarrows, with little flour, and no unneces-
> saries, and come to this place quicker, and with less fatigue, than by following
> the heavy trains, with their cumbrous herds, which they are often obliged to
> drive miles to feed. Do you like this way of traveling? Do you think salvation
> costs too much? If so it is not worth having.[44]

Only six months later, April, 1852, Brigham Young presented
"the subject of the Saints walking over the prairies with handcarts
and wheelbarrows" to the general conference at Salt Lake. Ninety-
three men immediately volunteered to go East with teams, wagons
and provisions to meet handcart emigrants and assist those who
traveled by that method to Utah.[45] But no direct action was
taken on that project until three and one-half years later.

On September 30, 1855, Brigham Young, as president of the
Emigrating Company, announced to the president of the European
Mission, Franklin D. Richards, the emigrating plans for the

---

[44]Brigham Young, "Sixth General Epistle . . ." *Millennial Star*, XIV, 23.
[45]*Ibid.*, XIV, 324.

coming year. The following decision had been reached only after the most careful study and experience in directing the immigration of the Saints to the Great Basin during the past nine years:

Great Salt Lake City,
September 30, 1855.

We have not much of interest to communicate more than you are aware of—such as meeting our heavy liabilities constantly falling due here and in St. Louis for this year's emigration. If I had about one hundred thousand pounds a year to expend for the purpose there would be some satisfaction to gather the Lord's poor, although in so doing we might also gather some of the devil's poor, and poor devils as well. . . .

I have been thinking how we should operate another year. We cannot afford to purchase wagons and teams as in times past, I am consequently thrown back upon my old plan—to make handcarts and let the emigration foot it, and draw upon them the necessary supplies, having a cow or two for every ten. They can come just as quick if not quicker, and much cheaper— can start earlier and escape the prevailing sickness which annually lays so many of our brethren in the dust. A great majority of them walk now even with the teams which are provided, and have a great deal more care and perplexity than they would have if they came without them. They will only need ninety days ration from the time of their leaving the Missouri River and as the settlements extend up the Platte, not that much. The carts can be made without a particle of iron, with wheels hooped, made strong and light, and one, or if the family be large, two of them will bring all that they will need upon the plains.

If it is once tried you will find that it will become the favorite mode of crossing the plains; they will have nothing to do but come along, and I should not be surprised if a company of this kind should make the trip in sixty or seventy days. I do know that they can beat any ox train crossing the plains. I want to see it fairly tried and tested, at all events and I think we might as well begin another year as any time and save this enormous expense of purchasing wagons and teams—indeed we will be obliged to pursue this course or suspend operations, for aught that I can see at the present. . . . Advise Brothers Taylor and Spencer that they may make arrangements accordingly. . . .[46]

No doubt the President's plan met the approval of the other Church authorities, as only a month after writing to Richards, Brigham announced the plan to the European proselytes. The following is part of his letter of October 29th:

Let all the Saints who can, gather up for Zion, and come while the way is open before them; let the poor also come, whether they receive aid or not from the (P. E.) Fund; let them come on foot, with handcarts, or wheelbarrows; let them gird up their loins and walk through, and nothing shall hinder or stay them.

In regard to the foreign emigration another year, let them pursue the

----

[46]Brigham Young to Franklin D. Richards, in *ibid.*, XVII, 813-814.

northern route from Boston, New York, or Philadelphia, and land at Iowa City or the then terminus of the railroad; there let them be provided with handcarts on which to draw their provisions and clothing; then walk and draw them, thereby saving the immense expense every year for teams and outfit for crossing the plains.

We are sanguine that such a train will out-travel any ox train that can be started. They should have a few good cows to furnish milk, and a few beef cattle to drive and butcher as they may need. . . .

We propose sending men of faith and experience with some suitable instructions to some proper outfitting point, to carry into effect the above suggestions; let the Saints therefore, who intend to emigrate the ensuing year, understand that they are expected to walk, and draw their luggage across the plains, and that they will be assisted by the Fund in no other way.[47]

In his instructions to the emigration agents, President Young emphasized very strongly the necessity of an early start in order that the converts might reach the Basin in safety. Carts were to be completed at Iowa City in time to supply the emigrants at their arrival so they would not be delayed.

Immediately upon being informed of the emigrating plans for 1856, the agents, both in Europe and on the American out-fitting frontier, began operations. February 23, 1856, President Franklin D. Richards announced to the Saints in Europe that John Taylor, the agent in America, had informed him that Iowa City had been selected as the outfitting frontier-post for that year, that the transportation cost had been placed at nine pounds for each adult, and that "the P. E. F. Emigrants will use handcarts in crossing the plains, in which they will convey their provisions, tent, and luggage, according to instructions . . . from Brigham Young. . . . There will of course be means provided for the convenience of the aged, infirm, and those unable for any cause to walk."[48]

Hundreds of the European proselytes were anxious to avail themselves of this opportunity to come to Zion. There were 3,756 Saints who migrated to America in 1856.[49] Of these, 3,543 were from the British Isles, 178 from the Scandinavian Mission, 19 from Switzerland, 9 from Channel Islands; 2 from East Indies, 1 from Germany and 4 from South Africa. Almost half, or 1,978, of the 3,756 Saints who emigrated to the United States in 1856 came under the direction of the Emigrating Fund Company and were listed to travel by handcarts. Only 385 had arranged to travel on their own means while the remaining 1,393 anticipated staying

---

[47]Brigham Young, "Thirteenth General Epistle . . . to the Saints," *ibid.*, XVIII, 54; *Deseret News*, October 31, 1855.

[48]Franklin D. Richards, *Millennial Star*, XVIII, 122.

[49]Andrew Jenson, *Contributor*, XIV, 18, listed the total emigration of 1856 at 3,756, while B. H. Roberts, *A Comprehensive History of the Church*, IV, 85, puts the figure at 4,326 souls.

in the states for that season.[50]   Under this method of travel the
entire cost to each person was about forty-five dollars to make the
trip from Liverpool, England to Salt Lake City.

The handcart emigrants of 1856 crossed the plains in five
companies. They traveled from Iowa City to Florence, Nebraska,
by handcarts, then on to the Basin. The first company left Florence
on July 20, the second on July 24, the third on July 30, the fourth
on August 14, and the last on August 26. The first three companies fared very well.   On September 15, 1856, Erastus Snow
reported that "the advance companies were in the region of Fort
Laramie and all were in excellent health and spirits, moving on
finely and far outstripping the ox teams."[51]

On September 26, the first two companies reached their destination and the third company arrived six days later. President Young
and his counselors, with a military escort and band, met them near
the mouth of Emigration Canyon. The populace turned out en
masse to receive and welcome them in their new home in the West.
One of the observers, Charles M. Tresedor, recorded the following
picture of their arrival:

> As they came down the bench you could scarcely see them for dust. When
> they entered the city the folks came running from every quarter to get a
> glimpse of the long looked for handcarts. I shall never forget the feeling that
> ran through my whole system as I caught the first sight of them. The first
> handcart was drawn by a man and his wife. They had a little flag on it, on
> which were the words, "Our President, may the unity of the Saints ever show
> the wisdom of his counsels." The next handcart was drawn by three young
> women. . . . The tears ran down the checks of many a man who you would
> have thought would not, could not, shed a tear.[52]

If those three companies had been all which endeavored to cross
the plains by handcarts in 1856, that method of travel might have
passed without serious objections. In fact, these companies demonstrated that such a method of migration was quite satisfactory,
as is evident from a report in the *Deseret News* of their successful
trek of 1300 miles:

> The journey has been performed with less than the average amount of
> mortality attending ox trains; and, although somewhat fatigued, stepped out
> with alacrity to the last, and appeared buoyant and cheerful. They had often
> traveled 25 or 30 miles in a day, and would have come through in a much
> shorter time, had they not been obliged to wait upon the slower motion of
> the oxen attached to the few wagons containing the tents and the groceries.[53]

[50]Jenson, "Church Emigration," *Contributor*, XIV, 16-23.
　　[51]Erastus Snow, to John Taylor, in *Latter-day Saint Journal History*, September 15, 1856,
Ms.
　　[52]Charles M. Tresedor, *ibid.*, September 29, 1856, cited in Larson, *op. cit.*, 106.
　　[53]Cited in Roberts, *op. cit.*, 87.

But unfortunately the two last handcart companies to cross the plains in 1856 resulted in tragedy, "making one of the saddest pages in Latter-day Saint history."

There were delays at Iowa City and at Florence while members of those companies waited for carts, as well as yokes, tents, and other equipment to be constructed.[54] They therefore began their westward journey much later in the season than Brother Brigham had instructed them to do. Those delays were largely responsible for the later disasters.

The fourth company was under the direction of Captain James G. Willie and the fifth under Captain Edward Martin. Some of the members of those groups suggested remaining at Florence until the following spring, as winter was so near at hand.[55] However, they were overruled by enthusiasm and the desire of many of the proselytes to reach the stronghold of the Saints. The fifth company was even more handicapped than the fourth, as it started later and had a larger number of feeble emigrants.

It is probable that even these two last companies could have reached Salt Lake safely if circumstances had favored them. As it was, however, difficulties soon confronted those Zion-bound home seekers. The chief hardships of the early part of the journey were the mid-summer heat and the dust; and when the rains converted the latter into mud, the heavy roads.

The emigrants were not long en route before many of their handcarts needed repairs. They had been hastily constructed of green timber which readily dried and fell apart under the burning August sun.

Almost from the very start the handcart companies had been put on rations. Suffering became intensified because the emigrants were not able to replenish their food supplies at Fort Laramie as they had planned to do.

But the biggest factor which made tragedy inevitable was the fact that heavy snows and extremely cold weather set in much earlier than had been the case for many years previously. By the middle of September, heavy frosts made the nights uncomfortable. It was impossible for the members of those unfortunate companies to keep warm with their scant supply of clothing, as their load had been reduced to seventeen pounds each. Snow storms came every few days, accompanied by fierce winds, piling the snow a foot and a half deep on the level.

---

[54]*Latter-day Saint Journal History*, October 2, 1856.
[55]T. B. Stenhouse, *Rocky Mountain Saints*, 314; William A. Linn, *Story of the Mormons*, 420.

Improperly clad and weakened by the rations, the more delicate ones died and were hastily buried by the wayside. Fear that winter would exterminate the entire company if they did not hasten onward "prevented even proper ceremonies for the departed, but they wrapped their loved ones in sheets, lowered them into hastily dug graves, and covered them with rocks to keep away the wolves which hovered constantly along their trail."[56] Food supplies rapidly vanished and there was no chance to have them replenished. Unable to continue their journey farther because of sheer exhaustion, the destitute sufferers established camp. They sought shelter in hollows and in willow thickets and awaited whatever fate was theirs.

Anticipating an early and hard winter, Brigham Young organized relief parties early in October to send out to meet the immigrants, although no word had as yet been brought to Utah of their plight.[57] At a general conference the President made the following announcement:

It is this day on the 5th of October, 1856, many of our brethren and sisters are on the plains with handcarts and probably many are now several hundred miles from this place and they must be brought here; we must send assistance to them. The text will be "To get them here." This is the salvation I am now seeking for, to save our brethren that would be apt to perish, or suffer extremely if we did not send them assistance.

I do not want to send oxen, I want good horses and mules. They are in the territory and we must have them; also twelve tons of flour and forty good teamsters besides those that drive the teams.[58]

The Saints responded willingly to Brother Brigham's call. Only three days later a relief train left Salt Lake. The First Presidency themselves set out on October 13 but were forced to return to the city a few days later because of President Young's having fallen ill. Later in the month messengers returned to the Mormon Mecca and reported that the handcart companies were in a serious condition. Another call for aid was made with the result that before October had passed about 250 teams had been sent to assist the sufferers.

The relief train found the Willie Company encamped two miles below Rocky Ridge on the Sweetwater, and the Martin Company at a point sixteen miles above the Platte bridge, about one hundred miles behind the Willie Company. Both groups had exhausted their food a few days before the rescue party arrived.

When some of the members of the rescue party first appeared

[56]William E. Berrett, *The Restored Church*, 404.
[57]Orson F. Whitney, *History of Utah*, I, 557.
[58]Brigham Young, *Latter-day Saint Journal History*, October 5, 1856, Ms.

on horseback over a distant hill overlooking the Martin Company's camp, some of the emigrant children, who were eating bark off willows to prevent starvation, were badly frightened, thinking the white men were Indians. But upon the approach of the horsemen, the children were happily surprised to be given a few crackers, which kept them alive until the wagons loaded with provisions arrived four days later.

One of the children who was eating bark was the writer's grandmother, Nichalous Gourley Teeples. She was only twelve years old. A handcart containing all the earthly belongings of the Gourley family was pushed and pulled from the Missouri River by Nichalous, assisted by her sister Jenett, eight, and her brother George, seven. Their father pulled another handcart containing his wife, who was ill, and two small children. My grandmother, one of the last survivors of the Martin Company, passed beyond the veil, October 9, 1938, shortly before reaching her ninety-fourth birthday.

The mortality, due to cold and hunger, was terrific in both companies. Captain Willie lost 75 souls out of something over 400, and nearly 150 found wayside graves out of Martin's company of 576 emigrants. Fifteen died in one night in the latter company. The survivors were so cold and destitute that they huddled together and sat on and around the bodies of the deceased until the heat had left them. In the words of William E. Berrett:

> The two young men [Joseph A. Young and Stephen Taylor] found the Martin Company encamped in a ravine between the Platte and the Sweetwater, now called "Martin's ravine." Their food was gone, and the newly dug graves gave the place the aspect of a cemetery. The company had about given up hope and were waiting for the inevitable end when the word of relief arrived.[59]

Mr. Chislett, a member of the Willie Company, gave a graphic account of the meeting of the handcart company and the relief train. In his own words:

> On the evening of the third day after Captain Willie's departure, just as the sun was sinking beautifully behind the distant hills, on an eminence, immediately west of our camp, several covered wagons, each drawn by four horses, were seen coming toward us. The news ran through the camp like wildfire, and all who were able to leave their beds turned out en masse to see them. A few minutes brought them sufficiently near to reveal our faithful captain slightly in advance of the train. Shouts of joy rent the air; strong men wept until tears ran freely down their furrowed and sunburnt cheeks, and little children partook of the joy which some of them hardly understood,

[59]Berrett, op. cit., 405.

and fairly danced around with gladness. Restraint was set aside in the general rejoicing, and, as the brethren entered our camp the sisters fell upon them and deluged them with kisses. The brethren were so overcome that they could not for some time utter a word, but in choking silence repressed all demonstration of those emotions that evidently mastered them.[60]

The suffering emigrants of both the Martin and Willie companies were conducted to Salt Lake by the rescue party, arriving there late in November. Brother Brigham had instructed Bishop Edward Hunter to provide care for the survivors upon their arrival. The Mormon President told the Saints that "When those persons arrive . . . I want them distributed in this city among the families that have good, comfortable homes; and I wish the sisters now before me, and all who know how and can, to nurse and wait upon the newcomers, and prudently administer medicine and food to them."[61]

There were several causes for this unhappy disaster. The emigrants themselves were somewhat fool-hardy in their over-enthusiasm to reach Zion. Much of the blame is due those officials who permitted them to start on their journey so late in the year, contrary to the instructions of President Young, which were so emphatic on this subject. Bancroft stated that, "Even the worst enemies of Brigham Young admit that he was in no way to blame for the disaster and that he spared no effort to relieve."[62]

Moreover, the successful trip made by the first three handcart companies of 1856 demonstrated this mode of travel to be a practicable and valuable method of transportation. October 31, 1856, President Young concluded that:

This year's operations have entirely proved the feasibility and success of the handcart enterprise when the business is rightly managed and the companies leave the frontiers in anything like the proper season. Those companies that left Iowa City in the forepart of July arrived in good time and were in excellent condition and spirits.[63]

So successful did the handcarts prove that the authorities had the emigrants travel under the same plan for four more years.

On August 30, 1856, Brigham Young informed the president of the European Mission that during the coming year he did not want the emigrating agent there to borrow money with which to send converts to Utah by Perpetual Emigrating aid, as the operations of that company had been so extensive the past year that its

[60]Cited in Roberts, op. cit., IV. 93-94.
[61]Manuscript History of Brigham Young, November 30, 1856.
[62]Bancroft, op. cit., 429.
[63]Brigham Young, Deseret News, October 31, 1856.

resources were drained. Continuing, the President advised: "We cannot longer stand this constant drain, without reimbursements from those who are owing the Fund. We are, therefore, necessarily obliged to operate exclusively within the resources of the P. E. F. Company, instead of borrowing."[64] Accordingly on December 27, 1856, the agent at Liverpool announced:

> This office will not send any P. E. Fund Emigrants to Utah during the year 1857. All the funds the company can command will be exhausted in discharging the heavy liabilities incurred in sending out over two thousand souls in 1856. . . . It will probably require nearly two years from the present time before the P. E. Fund Company will have discharged the debts contracted by last season's operations.[65]

Naturally, when the Perpetual Emigrating Company temporarily withdrew its aid in 1857, there was a large decrease in emigrants. That year 1,994 Saints sailed from Europe under Mormon arrangements. Of this number 511 furnished their own teams, 567 used handcarts, and the remaining 916 located in the States temporarily.

The coming of Johnston's army to Utah seriously hampered European emigration the following two years. The European agent announced: "In view of the difficulties that are now threatening the Saints, we deem it wisdom to stop all emigration to the United States and to Utah for the present."[66]

Gustive O. Larson summarized the handcart immigration to Utah as follows:

> The foreign emigration for 1858 and 1859 was only 179 and 809 respectively. In 1860, the record lists a total of 1,588 immigrants of whom 268 appear under the headings of handcarts. Thus in the period from 1856 to 1860, approximately 8,000 immigrants arrived in the United States bound for Utah and of these 3,000 came with the intention of walking the full distance from the frontier outfitting post to Salt Lake City pushing or pulling a handcart.[67]

CHURCH TEAMS AND IMMIGRATION TO UTAH FROM 1861-1877

In 1861 Brigham Young adopted a new method of bringing the proselytes to the Great Basin. From that date until 1869 at the coming of the railway, large numbers of teams were sent from Salt Lake each season to meet the emigrants at the western terminus of

---

[64]Brigham Young, *Millennial Star*, XVIII, 821.
[65]*Ibid.*
[66]*Ibid.*, XIX, 668.
[67]Larson, *op. cit.*, 115.

the railway. As the railroad advanced the overland trip by wagon
was shortened. Funds collected by the Perpetual Emigrating Company were dispersed in paying train fares while teams and teamsters
were supplied gratis in response to calls made by the Mormon Colonizer. The first year of operation of this new plan (1861), 1,959
Saints, of whom 1,283 came by the Church teams, migrated to Utah.

The largest wagon train assisting the Saints to Utah was in
1866. Ten separate companies including 456 teamsters, 3,042 oxen,
397 wagons, 89 horses, 134 mules besides 49 mounted guards are
said to have assisted that year in bringing proselytes to Utah. In the
words of Gustive O. Larson:

> From 1861 to 1868 inclusive, there were in all approximately 1,913
> wagons sent east to receive the emigrants and bring them to Utah. . . . Com-
> puting on a ration basis with the number of wagons, there were 2,389 men
> and 17,543 oxen employed during the sixties in crossing the plains to the
> railway terminal and returning with the emigrants to Utah.[68]

On June 25, 1869, the first Saints to come all the way to Utah
over the Union Pacific arrived at Ogden. From that time forward
the agents of the Emigrating Company directed immigration to Utah
by rail. The coming of the railroad did not increase the number of
immigrants from Europe to the Basin. In fact, in the eight year
period preceding 1869 during which the Church teams were in operation, the number of emigrants exceeded the number for the next
eight year period by 6,644.[69]

ACCOMPLISHMENTS OF THE PERPETUAL EMIGRATING FUND COMPANY —DISSOLVING OF THE COMPANY

When Brigham Young died in 1877, the Mormon Church was
still exerting its best efforts in gathering Israel to Zion in the Great
Basin. The Perpetual Emigrating Fund Company was still in active
operation, directing immigration to the Mecca of the Saints. But
it was not destined to exist many more years. A little over a year
after the President's death, opposition to the Fund Company—
caused mainly by enemies of the Church who thought that Brigham
had used the company to further the practice of polygamy in his
empire—had crystalized to the extent that the matter was called to
the attention of the State Department at Washington, D. C. Finally, on February 15, 1887, a bill known as the Edmunds-Tucker
law, framed for the purpose of disincorporating the Church of Jesus

----

[68]*Ibid.,* 118-119.
[69]*Ibid.,* 123.

Christ of Latter-day Saints and dissolving the Perpetual Emigrating
Fund Company, passed both houses of Congress. On March 3, it
became a law without the signature of President Grover Cleveland.

Although it is impossible to estimate the exact amount of assistance the Perpetual Emigrating Fund Company contributed in
the colonization of the Great West, there is no doubt that its influence was remarkable. Approximately 85,220 proselytes in Europe
migrated to the Mormon commonwealth between 1840 and 1887
under the direction of the Church. While Brigham Young was at
the helm (1847-1877), over 70,000 European emigrants were
brought into the Great Basin.[70] As Katherine Coman has said, "It
was, taken all in all, the most successful example of regulated immigration in United States history."[71]

- - - -
   [70]Robert W. Sloam, *Utah Gazetter and Dictionary*, 1884, stated: "The last forty-three
years the Church immigration has helped to the United States from foreign countries, 78,225."
   [71]Katherine Coman, *Economic Beginnings of the Far West*, II, 184.

HANDCART MONUMENT ON TEMPLE SQUARE
BY F. S. KNAPHUS

CHAPTER X

MORMON THEO-DEMOCRACY

LATTER-DAY SAINT SYSTEM OF CHURCH GOVERNMENT

One of the first vital problems to be solved in founding frontier colonies was that of providing the settlers with a government. It was but natural that the Mormon pioneers, having been driven from their homes three or four times because of their religious beliefs, having endured the hardships of a thousand miles of uninhabited, desolate country, and, finally, having selected the desert wastes of the Great Basin as their home, should choose to establish at first a theocracy or, as Gunnison termed it, a "theo-democracy."[1]

Before discussing the actual operation of the theo-democracy in the valleys of the Rocky Mountains, it would be advantageous to explain briefly the main factors in the Latter-day Saint system of church government. There were two groups of officers in the Mormon Church: the group which had jurisdiction over the affairs of the Church as a whole and those officers whose authority extended over only a small territorial division. The former consisted of such officers as the First Presidency, the Council of the Twelve Apostles, and the Presiding Bishopric; while the latter group comprised the stake presidencies, high councils, ward bishoprics and other similar officials. The first group mentioned were known as general authorities of the Church while the latter were called local authorities.

At the head of the Mormon hierarchy stood the president. He was ordained and sustained as the "Prophet, Seer, and Revelator" of the Church of Jesus Christ of Latter-day Saints. According to Mormon belief, only one person in the world at any given time could hold the keys of the kingdom of God[2]—"the keys . . . of revelations;" and that individual was the only authorized agent of the Lord to receive revelations and commandments for the guidance of the Church.[3]

The president held supreme authority over all church members throughout the world; and his jurisdiction included not only the spiritual affairs, but the temporal as well. He was the chief official in all branches of church government; namely, legislative, executive,

----

[1] John Williams Gunnison. *The Mormons or Latter-day Saints in the Valleys of the Salt Lake.* 23.
[2] *Doctrine and Covenants.* Sec. 81:2; 90:1-8; 112:15.
[3] *Ibid.,* 28:1-7; 43:1-8; Franklin D. Richards. *Narratives* (Bancroft Library). 52, Ms.

and judicial. Those receiving the priesthood and officiating in any official capacity of the Church did so by special commission from the president as he was also the president of the priesthood.

Two high priests served as counselors to the president. Their duty was to advise, counsel and assist the president in general administrative work. Therefore, those three men constituted the First Presidency and the presidency of the High Priesthood. They also constituted the highest court in the Church, a court whose decisions were final.[4]

The fact that such unlimited authority was vested in the president of the Church helps to explain Brigham Young's power over his followers. In him centered law-making, law-determining and executive authority.[5] The Saints looked upon him as God's choice to take the place of the Prophet Joseph. Upon him had descended that same power of God which, they believed, had been bestowed on Joseph Smith by heavenly messengers. The real nature of Brigham's genius was deeper than his personality alone. In the words of Romney:

> After a full measure of credit is allowed for the inventive genius of Brigham Young and the power of his commanding personality to impel men to do his bidding, it is still difficult to account for the great accomplishments of Brigham Young and his followers without taking into consideration a hidden force more potent than those mentioned. That potent force springs from the fervent and almost mystic reverence of the devotees of the Mormon faith for the ecclesiastical organization with which they are affiliated.[6]

Next in authority to the First Presidency was the Council of the Twelve Apostles which was composed of twelve High Priests. The second quorum was slightly inferior in authority to the first; its nearness of equality of authority was merely an emergency provision to be used in case of the disorganization of the First Presidency. When the president of the Church died the Twelve Apostles presided over the Church until they selected a new president. He, in turn, selected his two counselors.[7] One of the major duties of the apostles was to act as presiding officials, both in the colonies of the Great West and in the missions abroad. Another duty was to officiate as a "Traveling High Council." In this capacity they had jurisdiction over special cases that might arise in various parts of the Church.

Another group of general authorities, known as the Presiding

[4]Ibid., 107:1-100; B. H. Roberts, "History of the Mormon Church," Americana, VI, 890.
[5]Ibid.
[6]Thomas C. Romney, The State of Deseret, 71, Ms.
[7]Richards, op. cit., 51.

Bishopric, had as its special work the satisfaction of the temporal rather than the spiritual needs of the people. This quorum was composed of a bishop and two counselors who were directly responsible to Brigham Young—as were all other church authorities. They were of great importance in Utah pioneer days when much effort had to be exerted in order to secure enough food for the colonists. Never has their importance waned. Today they effectively do their share in taking care of the "Church Welfare Program," and the other economic affairs of the Church.

A high ecclesiastical tribunal known as the Presiding Bishopric's court consisted of the bishop, his counselors, "and twelve other high priests. Such a court would sit only in case of serious transgression on the part of some member of the Presidency of the Church."[8]

It was impossible for the general authorities to attend personally to all the spiritual and material needs of the Saints. Therefore, in order to make an effective administrative organization, the Church was divided into territorial units called stakes, which later on corresponded in geographical extent, generally speaking, to the counties. Under the Mormon theo-democracy, the stake officials had about the same relative position to the general church authorities as county officials have to state officials under civil governments.

A stake president and two counselors presided over the stake, concerning themselves with the legislative, executive and judicial affairs of their ecclesiastical territory. Assisting them in this administration was a high council consisting of twelve high priests. These bodies together formed the highest ecclesiastical court within the stake.

Stakes were also divided into territorial divisions called wards. The smaller towns contained but one ward, the larger towns several. At the head of a ward, having very extensive legislative, administrative and judicial powers, stood the bishop and his two counselors. Bishops presided over their wards much as fathers preside over their families. Because of their peculiar duties and their close contact with the people, they became the most effective and most influential portion of the Mormon ecclesiastical machine in shaping the lives of the people and in influencing the growth of the settlements.

The "government of the bishops" was a unique ecclesiastical order. Pioneer conditions gave the bishops an opportunity to develop direct control over their wards. The important part which the bishops took in the land settlement of the Great West was pointed

8Romney, op. cit., 85.

out in the chapter on "The Personnel of Mormon Colonization."
They were the key men of the whole project upon whom Brother
Brigham depended for the execution of his program. They were
the judges who dictated the daily actions of the Saints. Quoting
Edward W. Tullidge:

> In Utah, . . . until the regular incorporation of Great Salt Lake City in
> 1851, they [the bishops] held what is usually considered the secular admin-
> istration over the people. . . . Each of these nineteen wards developed, during
> the first period, before the regular incorporation of the city, like so many
> municipal corporations, over which the bishops were as chief magistrates or
> mayors. Under their temporal administration all over Utah, as well as in Salt
> Lake, . . . society was governed. In fact, under them all the revenue was
> produced and the work done of founding Great Salt Lake City.[9]

Possibly the most important of the tribunals in Mormon theocracy was the bishopric's court made up of a bishop and his two
counselors. To these tribunals were brought all the minor difficulties
of the Saints to be adjudicated. Most of the problems which arose
were settled without any appeal to a higher tribunal. If, however,
the bishop's court failed to solve the difficulty, or, if either one
of the parties involved in the trouble was dissatisfied with the decision of that tribunal, the case was referred to the stake tribunal,
and finally, if need be, to the highest court of appeal—to the First
Presidency of the Church.

Besides the ecclesiastical tribunals already described, there was
the "Temporary High Council Abroad." This court consisted of
twelve high priests "called to adjudicate a matter outside the boundary of an organized stake." The Mormon theo-democracy had
sufficient types of tribunals to meet any emergency that might arise.
With such a system of courts, not even the highest officials of the
Church could escape being brought to justice in case they transgressed.

In general, the only rigorous punishment that the early ecclesiastical tribunals had at their disposal was the excommunication of
the offenders from the Church. No punishment could have been
more severe nor more dreaded by the Saints because they loved their
religion and believed sincerely that to retain good standing in the
Church was essential to future salvation and admittance into the
Celestial degree of glory.

One conspicuous point in the Mormon tribunal system was
that there were no lawyers nor paid court officials. The ecclesiastical appointees rendered their services as religious duties, without

---

[9]Edward W. Tullidge, *History of Salt Lake City*. 75.

charge. It was their desire to bring about a fair and friendly settlement of all difficulties which arose among the Saints with the least
expense and the biggest degree of justice possible to all concerned.
There was no place for lawyers, nor was there a need for civil courts,
juries or judges in the Mormon theo-democracy. Brigham Young
expressed himself very pointedly on this matter when he said:

> Do you think we should want any lawyers in our society?   No, I think
> not. . . . I feel about them as Peter of Russia is said to have felt when he was
> in England.   He saw and heard the lawyers pleading at a great trial there,
> and he was asked his opinion concerning them.   He replied that he had two
> lawyers in his empire, and when he got home he intended to hang one of
> them.   That is about the love I have for some lawyers who are always stirring
> up strife.   Not but lawyers are good in their places; but where is their place?
> I cannot find it.[10]

After the establishment of the civil government in Salt Lake,
Brigham Young and his associates urged the Mormons to bring their
difficulties before the church tribunals rather than before the civil
courts for adjustment. To Brother Brigham the process of administering the law in the state courts was but "amusing sham." In
his own words:

> Some men will go into court and spend five hundred dollars and feel as
> nicely about it as possible, even when their case has not been adjudicated as
> justly as a sensible "Mormon" boy, ten years old, would do it.   And yet, when
> they know this fact full well, they will spend their time, day after day, and
> their means with seeming contentment, saying to themselves, "Oh, if we can
> only go into the court, and address the court, and say, may it please you, gentle-
> men of the jury, O, how joyous we shall be—we shall feel as though we were
> men of some importance, if we can only get up and strut and splutter before
> a court."   Even when merely a judge is sitting there, like a bean on the end
> of a pipe stem, who would be flipped off should a grain of good sense happen
> to strike him, how big he feels while sitting there for days to adjudicate a
> case that should not require five minutes.[11]

In the Mormon theo-democracy the nominations for church
offices were all made by the presiding authorities, yet the selection
did not become effective until voted upon favorably by the Saints.
From the day the Church was established (April 6, 1830) to the
present time, the ecclesiastical officials have been appointed and
sustained in office by the method known as "divine appointment"
and the "law of common consent." This principle was instituted
by the Prophet Joseph in accordance with the word of the Lord
wherein He said: "For all things must be done in order, and by

[10]*Journal of Discourses*, XV, 220-227.
[11]*Ibid.*, III, 326.

common consent in the Church. . . . No person is to be ordained to any office in this Church, where there is a regularly organized branch of the same, without the vote of that Church."[12]

Therefore, no person could hold an office, either as a general or a local authority, except by the consent of those people who were affected by his appointment. At each quarterly conference of the Church, the names of the ecclesiastical officers were read before the congregation of Saints for their acceptance or rejection. Their approval or disapproval was "manifested by a show of hands" rather than by secret ballot. This system of voting, no doubt, had its weaknesses and in many respects did not represent the will of all the people. The fear of social disapproval for casting a contrary vote would have a certain amount of influence. Thus, the vote of approval for the nominees as selected by the presiding authorities was taken more or less for granted by the majority of the Saints, so their voting often became somewhat automatic.

But to be entirely fair to the Mormons it should be pointed out that most of the positions have always been filled by the best talent available. The appointees under the Mormon theo-democracy were men possessing natural abilities and qualities of leadership, well-fitted to the administration of the affairs of frontier communities. They were men who were following the laws of the Gospel, as neither the First Presidency nor the people had confidence in anyone who was not actively engaged in church work. The following extract from one of the Prophet's revelations describes upon what principles the rights of the priesthood operate in the Latter-day Saint Church government:

> The rights of the Priesthood are inseparably connected with the powers of heaven, and the powers of heaven cannot be controlled nor handled only upon the principles of righteousness. That they may be conferred upon us, it is true; but when we undertake to cover our sins, or to gratify our pride, . . . or to exercise control, or dominion, or compulsion, upon the souls of the children of men, in any degree of unrighteousness . . . Amen to the Priesthood, or the authority of that man.[13]

Richard F. Burton expressed himself favorably toward the actual working of the Mormon ecclesiastical government under Brigham Young as he observed it when he visited Salt Lake City in 1860. Quoting from Burton:

> The Mormon policy is, in my humble opinion . . . the perfection of government. . . . At the semi-annual conference . . . all officers from the

---
[12]*Doctrine and Covenants,* Sec. 20:65.
[13]*Ibid.,* 121:36-37.

president to the constable are voted in by direction and counsel: i. e. of the Lord through his Prophet; consequently, re-election is the rule, unless the chief dictator (Brigham Young) determines otherwise. . . . Mormon society is modeled on a civilized regiment; the prophet is the colonel-commanding, and the grades are nicely graduated down to the last neophyte or recruit. I know no form of rule superior to that of Great Salt Lake City.[14]

Other writers since the days of Burton have marveled at the degree of perfection manifested in the Mormon Church government, comparing it in its efficiency to the German army of 1914. There is no doubt that it functioned under President Young just as efficiently as its organization would indicate.

THEO-DEMOCRACY IN THE GREAT BASIN IN 1847 AND 1848

We shall now turn our attention to observing the Mormon theo-democracy as it actually functioned under Brigham Young in the valleys of the Rocky Mountains. Almost immediately after arriving in the Basin in 1847 Brigham established an ecclesiastical government to preside over the two thousand Saints in the Salt Lake Valley. Then he, with several of the apostles, departed for Winter Quarters to prepare the main body of the Saints for the great migration to take place the following year.

The government established was that of a stake of Zion presided over by a stake presidency and a high council. John Smith,[15] the uncle of the Prophet Joseph, was selected to be president, with Charles C. Rich and John Young as his counselors. Three other officials were to act under the stake authorities: namely, Charles C. Rich, chief military commander; John Vancott, marshal; and Albert Carrington, clerk and historian. According to the statement of one of the pioneers, this government was adopted in accordance with the Mormon law of common consent. He said: "The high council, a local ecclesiastical court, consisting of twelve members, presided over by the president of the stake and his two counselors, fifteen in all besides the clerk, assumed provisional municipal powers by the common consent of the community."[16] This was the first government established by the Saints within the confines of the Great Basin.

The duties of the officials were numerous and varied. Besides being the spiritual guides to the people and serving as a court of

---

[14]Richard F. Burton, *The City of the Saints and Across the Rocky Mountains to California,* 366-367.

[15]John Nebeker, *Early Justice* (Bancroft Library), 4, Ms. "Father John Smith was looked upon as president of the camp; but Taylor and Pratt took the lead and in fact were in charge."

[16]*Early Utah Records* (Bancroft Library), 19, Ms.

justice, they had to fulfill all the duties accompanying the establishment of a frontier community such as the assignment of farming lands, the granting of licenses to establish sawmills and to control the mountain streams, the issuing of building permits and the supervision of timber.

Naturally, some cases of disobedience to law occurred which had to be handled by the officials. During the first year in Salt Lake (1847-1848) there were no jails, so offenders had to be punished by other methods. The ordinary penalty for theft was for the offender, after having had a fair trial before the high council and having been declared guilty, to promise to do better and to "make proper confessions and restore fourfold."[17]

John Nebeker related an incident which caused much fun. One man insisted on keeping a dog and feeding him as much food as a person would eat. Food being very scarce, most people could not afford to keep dogs. This dog stole four biscuits from a man who, in return, borrowed a shotgun and killed the thief. The owner of the dog brought the case before Mr. Nebeker for arbitration. In relating what happened, Nebeker said: "I gave the man who had lost the biscuits the full benefit of the law, namely, allowed him fourfold—or sixteen biscuits, which kept the fellow a whole week."[18]

In general, the Saints had no occasion for severe punishment at first, as most difficulties were settled in a friendly manner. However, on one occasion at least, a whipping post was established and used. A culprit was caught in the act of stealing a lariat. The high council decided that he must pay a ten dollar fine or receive ten lashes. The offender, being rather defiant, refused to pay the fine even when Mr. Nebeker offered to help him pay it. Consequently John Nebeker was appointed to do the whipping. The bell post —a pole in the center of town on which was hung a bell to call the people together—was selected as the whipping post. The thief was stripped to the waist and then given ten lashes in the presence of the public.[19]

Re-organization under Brigham Young in 1848

At the close of a year's absence from the Great Basin, Brigham Young returned to the new Mormon Mecca in September, 1848, bringing another large company of immigrants. He immediately reorganized the stake, divided it into nineteen ecclesiastical wards,

[17]Nebeker, op. cit., 4.
[18]Ibid., 6.
[19]Ibid., 5.

and filled the vacancies in the quorum of Twelve Apostles and other church offices. At the October conference the Saints ratified these nominations and also sanctioned the appointment of Brother Brigham as president of the Church with Heber C. Kimball and Willard Richards as his counselors, the nomination having taken place the previous December at Winter Quarters. The Mormon Colonizer had been directing the affairs of the Church from the time of the death of Joseph in June, 1844, until December 5, 1847, as president of the Twelve. Brother Brigham and his associates now established the complete system of Mormon ecclesiastical government, putting every phase of its machinery into good working order.

Functioning and Effectiveness of Theo-Democracy, 1848-1851

The next three years (1848-1851) serve as the best period to study Mormon theo-democracy, because during this period President Young was the directing power over a completely organized and efficient ecclesiastical machine. There were numerous opportunities to test the adaptability and efficiency of church control.

During the first year in the valley governmental control was entirely in the hands of the stake officials. Now, in the fall of 1848, most of the administration of the secular affairs was placed under the direction of the bishops of the nineteen wards. The transfer of control from stake officials to the bishops was made in a meeting of the members of the high council, January 6, 1849, wherein the council decided to relieve themselves of "municipal duties."[20]

The Mormon theo-democracy as it functioned in the West between 1847-1849, as it continued its influence over civil affairs after the inauguration of the provisional State of Deseret, and as it was modified even after the territorial government had been established, was a complete fusion of church and state. This fusion met with the hearty approval of the people because practically all the inhabitants of the Great Basin belonged to the Latter-day Saint Church. They believed that they were building the "Kingdom of God" on earth—that they should submit themselves to the rule of God's authority as exercised through the Priesthood. Franklin D. Richards, writing after Utah had been made a territory, stated: "Theoretically church and state are one. If there were no gentiles and no other government, there would be no civil law."[21]

Mormon theo-democracy had brought the people peace and contentment after many years of persecution. The following extract

----

[20]*Early Utah Records, op. cit.*, 57.
[21]Franklin D. Richards, *Narratives* (Bancroft Library), 87, Ms.

from a letter written at Salt Lake City, September 5, 1848, by Parley
P. Pratt to his brother Orson in England pictures accurately the
feelings of the Saints toward their government and their new home:

I have now resided almost a year in this lonesome retreat, where civilized
man has not made his home for the past thousand years, and where the ripen-
ing harvest has not been enjoyed for ages, until this present season. During
this period, the sound of war, the rise and fall of empires, the revolutions of
states and kingdoms—the news of any kind has scarcely reached my ears. . . .
All is quiet—stillness. No elections, no police reports, no murders, no wars
in our little world. How quiet, how still, how peaceful, how happy, how
lonesome, how free from excitement we live. The legislation of our high
council, the decision of some judge or court of the church, a meeting, a dance,
a visit, an exploring tour . . . is all that break up the monotony of our busy
and peaceful life. Our old firelocks have not been rubbed up, or our swords
unsheathed because of any alarm. No policemen or watchmen of any kind
have been on duty to guard us from external or internal danger. The drum
has beat, to be sure, but it was mingled with merry making, or its martial
sound was rather to remind us that war had once been known among the
nations, than to arouse us to tread the martial and measured step of those
who muster for the war, or march to the battlefield. Oh, what a *life we live!*
It is the dream of the poet actually fulfilled in real life.[22]

Captain Howard Stansbury, of the United States Topographical engineers, and associates arrived in Utah in August, 1849, for
the purpose of exploring parts of the Great Basin and making a
government survey of the lakes. He and his men wintered with the
Saints in Salt Lake City, 1849-1850. Stansbury remarked that
"nothing can exceed the appearance of prosperity, peaceful harmony
and cheerful contentment that pervaded the whole community."[23]

Both he and Lieutenant John W. Gunnison, one of his party,
made studies of Mormon social life and published their accounts.
Each of them testified that Mormon theo-democracy administered
justice equitably. In speaking of the courts of the State of Deseret, Gunnison said that "there was every appearance of impartiality and strict justice done to all parties."[24] In the words of
Stansbury:

The jurisdiction of the State of Deseret had been extended over and was
vigorously enforced upon all who came within its borders, and justice was
equitably administered alike to "saints" and "gentile"—as they term all who
are not of their persuasion. . . . Their courts were constantly appealed to by
companies of passing emigrants, who, having fallen out by the way, could
not agree upon the division of their property. The decisions were remarkable

[22]Parley P. Pratt to Orson Pratt, in *Early Utah Records* (Bancroft Library), 33-35. Ms.
[23]J. Howard Stansbury, *An Exploring Expedition to the Valley of the Great Salt Lake,* 133.
[24]John Williams Gunnison, *The Mormons or Latter-day Saints in the Valley of the Great
Salt Lake,* 65.

for fairness and impartiality, and if not submitted to were sternly enforced
by the whole power of the community.[25]

THE STATE OF DESERET

For the first year and a half in the Great Basin the Saints had
no form of government other than their ecclesiastical organization.
This proved satisfactory as long as practically all of the people were
Mormons. However, as the population increased, non-Mormons
began to settle among the Saints, many coming to Utah as a result
of the California gold rush. Brigham Young and his associates realized that the influx of Gentiles would increase, as the Great
Basin had become a part of the United States by the signing of the
treaty of Guadalupe Hidalgo in 1848.

It seemed necessary, therefore, to provide a government that
would prove satisfactory to both Gentiles and Mormons and, at
the same time, one that would be "acknowledged and recognized
by the Government of the United States."[26] "True to the character
of typical frontiersmen, independent of Congress"[27] and as other
groups of people had done,[28] the people set about to establish such
a government.

On February 1, 1849, President Young issued a call for a convention to meet in Salt Lake to consider the political needs of the
people. The document bore the signature of many of the prominent citizens of the Great Basin. It was addressed to "all the citizens
of that portion of upper California lying east of the Sierra Nevada."

Early in March, 1849, a considerable number of the inhabitants
responded to the call and assembled at Salt Lake. The members
of the convention decided "to petition Congress for a territorial
form of government, and to organize, pending Congressional action
upon the petition, a provisional government,"[29] but later it was decided to ask for statehood. Accordingly a committee, with Albert
Carrington as chairman, was appointed to draft a constitution for
the "temporary State of Deseret." On March 8, 9, and 10, the
convention considered the report of the committee. After careful
deliberation the constitution was adopted without a dissenting vote.
Its preamble stated in a definite and clear manner the reasons for
establishing a provisional government without awaiting for Congress
to sanction this action. Quoting from the preamble:

Whereas, a large number of citizens of the United States, before and

[25]Stansbury, op. cit., 130.
[26]Ibid., 131-132.
[27]Leland Hargrove Creer, Utah and the Nation, 66.
[28]Frederic L. Paxson, History of the American Frontier, 27-31, 350.
[29]Latter-day Saint Journal History, March 8, 1849, Ms.

since the treaty of peace with the Republic of Mexico, emigrated to, and settled in that portion of the territory of the United States, lying west of the Rocky Mountains, and in the great interior Basin of Upper California; . . . Whereas, the Congress of the United States has failed to provide a form of civil government for the territory so acquired, or any portion thereof; and, whereas, civil government and laws are necessary for the security, peace and prosperity of society; . . . Therefore, your Committee beg leave to recommend the adoption of the following *Constitution*, until the Congress of the United States shall otherwise provide for the Government of the Territory, hereinafter named and described, by admitting us into the Union.[30]

An extract from the "First General Epistle of the First Presidency" written to the "Saints scattered through the earth" (April, 1849) and signed by Brigham Young, Heber C. Kimball, and Willard Richards gives additional information as to why it was thought desirable to establish a civil government at that time. It states:

In consequence of Indian depredations on our horses, cattle, and other property, and the wicked conduct of a few base fellows who came among the Saints, the inhabitants of this valley, as is common in new countries generally, have organized a temporary government, to exist during its necessity, or until we can obtain a charter for a Territorial Government, a petition for which is already in progress.[31]

After the adoption of the constitution of the "provisional government of the State of Deseret, . . . a General Assembly was elected by the people (March 12, 1849), consisting of a Senate and a House of Representatives."[32] It convened in its first session July 2, 1849, and remained the governing unit of the Great Basin until April 5, 1851.

The constitution adopted for the provisional State of Deseret resembled, in most respects, the constitution of other states of the Union. It provided for three departments of government—legislative, executive, and judiciary—and for a state militia, mainly for the purpose of protection against the Indians. All white able-bodied male citizens between the ages of eighteen and forty-five were required to belong to the state militia, "except such as are, or may hereafter be exempt, by the laws of the United States, or of this State." The franchise was given to all white male residents of the State over twenty-one years of age.

However, under the Mormon theocratic rule from July, 1847, until the establishment of the provisional State of Deseret in March

---

[30]*Laws and Ordinances of the State of Deseret* (reprint, Salt Lake City, 1919), 78.
[31]Brigham Young, *Early Utah Records* (Bancroft Library), 68-74, Ms.
[32]*Laws and Ordinances, op. cit.,* Prefactory.

1849, woman suffrage was practiced in the Great Basin. According to Leland Hargrove Creer: "For the second time in the history of the United States, women were given the right to vote in all political matters. . . . New Jersey was the first state to allow women to vote. . . . This privilege, extended in 1790, was withdrawn, however in 1807."[33] The rights of women to vote in Utah were also withdrawn in 1849.

The legislative authority was vested in a general assembly which consisted of a senate and a house of representatives, both being elected by the people. The qualifications for a seat in either house were similar to those of most other states. Each member of the assembly was sworn into office by taking an oath "to support the Constitution of the United States, and of this State."[34]

The chief executive of the State of Deseret was a governor elected for four years. He was "commander in chief of the militia, navy, and all armies" of the state and had the executive powers and duties usually attached to such an office. A lieutenant-governor was also provided for in the constitution to officiate mainly as the president of the Senate, or to become governor in case of a vacancy in that position.[35]

The judicial power was composed of a supreme court "and such inferior courts as the General Assembly shall from time to time establish." Judges were "elected by joint vote of both houses of the General Assembly" for a period of four years, as were the rest of the state officers.

In accordance with the provisions of the constitution, elections were held to ratify the constitution and to elect officers, who were as follows: Brigham Young, governor; Willard Richards, secretary; Newel K. Whitney, treasurer; Heber C. Kimball, chief justice; John Taylor and Newel K. Whitney, associate justices; Daniel H. Wells, attorney general; Horace S. Eldredge, marshal; Albert Carrington, assessor and collector of taxes; Joseph L. Heywood, surveyor of highways; and the bishops of the various wards, magistrates.

In considering the list of officials elected to preside over the State of Deseret, one acquainted with Mormon history of pioneer days immediately recognizes two things—that the majority of the officers were selected from among the high church officials and that all of the men elected were among the most capable citizens in the territory. Brigham Young was, without doubt, the best choice for governor. Likewise Richards, Whitney, Kimball, and Taylor

---

[33]Creer, op. cit., 62.
[34]Laws and Ordinances . . . op. cit., 81.
[35]Ibid., 82-85.

were well qualified for civil positions because of their experience as church executives. The others selected were also men of ability.

Although the Mormons had established a civil government, yet in actual practice they were still being governed by a theo-democracy. There was a complete blending of church and state, so intimate that it was difficult to distinguish in which capacity the official was acting—whether in his civil or ecclesiastical office. This was but the natural development under those conditions where another organization was imposed upon an already efficiently working one. It was to be expected that a fusion of church and state would continue as long as most of the people in the Great Basin were of one religious faith. Under those conditions the citizens looked to their ecclesiastical leaders, who had very successfully led them in all other affairs, to guide them in politics. Captain Stansbury was in the Great Basin during the first year of the operation of the provisional state government. As he was an unbiased non-Mormon, his observations picture that government fairly:

> The provisional State Government, with all the machinery of executive, legislative, and judicial functionaries, was in regular and harmonious action, under the constitution recently adopted. . . . While, however, there are all the exterior evidences of a government strictly temporal, it cannot be concealed that it is so intimately blended with spiritual administration of the church, that it would be impossible to separate the one from the other. The first civil governor under the constitution of the new State, elected by the people, was the president of the church, Brigham Young; the lieutenant-governor was his first ecclesiastical counselor, and the secretary of state his second counselor. . . . The bishops of the various wards . . . were appointed under the civil organization to be justices of the peace. . . . The supreme power in both being lodged in the hands of the same individuals, it is difficult to separate their two official characters, and to determine whether in any one instance they act as spiritual or merely temporal officers. . . . In the organization of the civil government, nothing could be more natural than that, the whole people being one faith, they should choose for functionaries to carry it into execution, those to whom they had been in the habit of deferring as their spiritual guides, and by whom they had been led from a land of persecution into this far-off wilderness, which, under their lead, was already beginning to blossom like the rose.[36]

It was but natural, therefore, that the General Assembly, in establishing inferior courts, should select the bishops of the various wards as magistrates. This arrangement, advantageous in efficiency and economy, was very satisfactory to the major portion of the people. Stansbury made the following observation:

---

[36]Stansbury, *op. cit.*, 130-132.

The bishops of the several wards, who, by virtue of their offices in the church, had exercised not only a spiritual but a temporal authority over the several districts assigned to their charge, were appointed, under the civil organization, to be justices of the peace, and were supported in the discharge of their duties, not only by the civil power, but by the whole spiritual authority of the church also. . . . Thus the bishop, in case of a dispute between two members of the church, would interpose his spiritual authority as bishop for its adjustment, while in differences between those not subject to the spiritual jurisdiction, and who could not be made amenable to church discipline, he could act in the magisterial capacity conferred upon him by the constitution and civil laws of the State. Thus the control of the affairs of the colony remained in the same hands, whether under church or state organization; and those hands were, in a double capacity, those into which the constituents had, whether as citizens or as church members, themselves chosen to confide it.[87]

Meanwhile, the Saints were waiting for favorable action of Congress which would admit Deseret into the Union as a state. The Mormons had sent Colonel Almon W. Babbitt to Washington in the latter part of 1849 as their delegate to Congress with a copy of the constitution of the State of Deseret and a memorial asking for admittance into the Union. On December 27, Stephen A. Douglas presented the memorial and constitution to the Senate, making application for admission of the Mormon country as a state "with the alternative of admission as a territory if Congress should direct." After much debating, a resolution was adopted in July, 1850, stating "that it is inexpedient to admit Almon W. Babbitt to a seat in this body as delegate from the alleged State of Deseret."[88]

The Territory of Utah

The problem of what to do with the Mormon empire was solved by Congress in 1850 in connection with several other troublesome matters. The important question which concerned the United States Senate at the close of the war with Mexico was that of slavery in relation to the vast territory recently acquired by the treaty of Guadalupe Hidalgo. Senator Henry Clay was made chairman of a committee to devise a scheme of compromise for all the territory recently acquired from Mexico. The recommendations of this commitee were later incorporated in the Omnibus Bill, which proposed the establishment of the Territory of Utah out of the State of Deseret, with, however, greatly reduced boundaries. September 9, 1850, the Omnibus Bill passed both houses of Congress and was signed the same day by President Millard Fillmore. This law created the Territory of Utah.

---

[87]*Ibid.*, 131-132.
[88]*Congressional Globe* (1849-1850), XXI, 1433.

However, another year elapsed (September 22, 1851) before the territorial government was fully put into effect.[39] During this time the laws of the State of Deseret continued to operate. One of the first acts of the legislature of the Territory of Utah (October 4, 1851) was to legalize and make binding and in full force all the laws of Deseret.

Of the seven officials appointed by President Fillmore for Utah, only four were Mormons. This was a great disappointment to the Saints because they desired to be governed by members of their own church. Brigham Young, however, was appointed governor. He occupied this position until 1858, when he was replaced by Alfred Cumming of Georgia.

With the establishment of the territorial government the Mormon theo-democracy was nominally ended, yet even after Brigham was replaced by Cumming as governor, his influence and authority over his people remained supreme until his death in 1877. He fully realized his power. On one occasion, being asked if he believed himself to be a prophet, he replied, "I am of profit to my people." In the words of Brother Brigham:

Though I may not be Governor here my power will not be diminished. No man they can send here will have much influence with this community, unless he be the man of their choice. Let them send whom they will, and it does not diminish my influence one particle. As I said the first time I spoke on this stand, my Governorship and every other ship under my control, are aided and derive direct advantage from my position in the Priesthood.[40]

Morris Robert Werner in his book on Brigham Young concludes that:

He [Brigham] never betrayed cravings for personal glory, but his vanity was likely to be more than satisfied by the realization that he was the state and the church too; he could afford to merge his own personality in his organization, for his organization was his personality to a greater extent than any organization was ever the expression of one man in the history of the United States.[41]

[39]Orson F. Whitney, *History of Utah*, I, 393.
[40]Cited in Morris Robert Werner, *Brigham Young*, 397.
[41]*Ibid.*, 433.

CHAPTER XI

THE MORMONS AND THE FEDERAL GOVERNMENT

TROUBLE BETWEEN THE MORMON OFFICIALS AND THE FEDERAL APPOINTEES

A troublesome factor throughout the history of Mormon colonization was friction between Mormon leaders and the United States government. This friction began when the first federal appointees arrived in the Basin in 1851, after Congress had rejected Deseret for statehood but instead had created the Territory of Utah.

Four of the federal appointees, which included Brigham Young as governor, were Mormons, and the rest were Gentiles from the East. Trouble was inevitable between those two groups whose viewpoints were so vastly different. "The Mormons were devoted primarily to the Church of which they were members, and were suspicious of a government which had either been unable or unwilling to protect them."[1] On the other hand, the Gentile appointees came to Utah with certain preconceived impressions of the Mormons which were unfavorable, and, no doubt, quite erroneous. Yet, the Gentiles had picked up those impressions from the numerous disreputable stories which had been circulated from the time of the Prophet Joseph's first vision. They, no doubt, accepted in sincerity and honesty on their part many of the things which they had heard, not having had the background to look at the evidence from the Mormon viewpoint. It was but natural, therefore, that Mormon leaders and Gentile officials should misunderstand each other.

Three of the federal officers—Chief Justice Brandebury, associate Justice Brocchus and Territorial Secretary Broughton D. Harris—had scarcely arrived in Utah and taken the oath of office when they refused to stay in the Territory. They returned to the East and reported in Washington that they had been forced to leave Utah "on account of the lawless acts and seditious tendencies of Brigham Young and the majority of the residents"; also that the governor was wasting public funds and the people were immoral and were practicing polygamy.

Governor Brigham Young, September 29, 1851, "wrote to President Fillmore, setting forth the facts which clearly contra-

---

[1]William E. Berrett. *The Restored Church.* 462.

dicted the accusations." His position was sustained by letters from Jedediah M. Grant, mayor of Salt Lake, and Colonel Thomas L. Kane. Upon receipt of the letters, Daniel Webster, Secretary of State, ordered the runaway officials to return to Utah or resign. They immediately resigned.

Thereupon, the federal government filled the vacancies by appointing Lazarus H. Reed, of New York, Leonidas Shaver, and Benjamin G. Ferris, to be chief justice, associate justice and Territorial secretary, respectively. These men had no trouble with the Saints.

But in 1855 two new associate justices came to Utah who aroused the resentment of the people and were the principal factors in causing the United States government to send an army to the Basin at a cost of forty million dollars. Judge George P. Stiles, an apostate Mormon, replaced Judge Shaver who had died, and William W. Drummond took the place of Judge Snow, whose term of office had expired.

Both of these new appointees were immoral and unprincipled in their conduct. Drummond had left his wife and children in Illinois without support and had brought with him to Utah a womanwhom he introduced as his wife. When his corruption was discovered he left the Territory, never to return. He wrote a letter of resignation to Jeremiah S. Black, attorney general of the United States, and also other reports in which he made various scandalous accusations against Brigham Young and the Saints.

In an affidavit to the President, Judge Stiles affirmed many of the charges against the Saints made by Drummond. Furthermore, false charges against the Mormons were made in letters to President Buchanan by Mr. W. F. Magraw, who had been underbid by a Mormon firm for a mail contract, and by Thomas S. Twiss, Indian agent of the upper Platte.

Among the many accusations, the reports alleged that all the male members of the Church were under secret oath to resist the laws of the country. They were bound to obey no law save the laws of the priesthood, and President Brigham Young determined those laws at will. Therefore, the Saints were accused of being in open rebellion against the laws and government of the United States.

Although Governor Young and his people denied the charges, making lengthy reports to the federal government relative to the true state of conditions in Utah, misunderstanding between the United States and the Mormons continued.

PLURAL MARRIAGE AND THE POLITICAL CAMPAIGN OF 1856

Coupled with the reports of Drummond and others in helping determine the future course followed by the President of the United States were the conditions which developed during the political campaign of 1856. By that time the question of the Mormons' doctrine and practice of "plural marriage"—commonly called "polygamy"—had become a political issue. The Republican Party, desirous of throwing upon the Democrats the obligation to defend the right of a people to practice polygamy, had taken a decided stand against the Mormon people and their practices by adopting as a party plank in its platform at Philadelphia, June 17, 1856, the following:

> Resolved, that the Constitution confers on Congress sovereign powers over the territories of the United States for their government, and that in the exercise of his power it is both the right and the imperative duy of Congress to prohibit in the territories those two twin relics of barbarism—polygamy and slavery.[2]

The Democrats, in making their party's platform, claimed that the territories held the right to decide for themselves relative to the domestic problem of slavery, but the members of that party were not willing to defend the doctrine that territories should determine for themselves the domestic problems of marriage. This should be done by federal legislation. Therefore, the two major political parties both took a decided stand against the Mormons' practice of polygamy.

In fact, the whole country was so wrought up over the Mormons' doctrine of "plural marriage" that the Democratic administration decided to answer the Republicans' challenge by sending an "Expedition" against the Mormons; also, it was publicly claimed that Brigham Young and his people were "in substantial rebellion against the laws and authority of the United States," which would furnish a justification for such an "Expedition." An armed force sent to Utah would show to the voters of the nation that the Democratic Party, no less than the Republican party, was definitely opposed to the Mormons and their practice of polygamy.

The pro-slavery group was also in favor of sending an "Expedition" to the Basin, as that would certainly delay the chances of Utah becoming a member of the Union as a "free state."

––––

[2]Thomas V. Cooper, *American Politics* (book 2, Washington, D. C., 1884), 39.

THE "UTAH WAR"

Therefore, without thoroughly investigating the situation to find what the real conditions were, President Buchanan and his associates accepted as facts the charges made by Drummond and others against the Mormons and sent 2,500 soldiers to Utah in 1857. He appointed Alfred Cumming as governor to replace Brigham Young. Cumming accompanied the army to the West.

The first word that the Mormons in the Basin received of the approach of federal troops was on July 24, 1857. Nearly 3,000 people, including Brigham Young and the other Church officials, were at Silver Lake, at the head of Big Cottonwood Canyon, celebrating the tenth anniversary of the arrival of the Saints in the Salt Lake Valley when Abraham O. Smoot, Orrin Porter Rockwell, Judson Goddard and Judge Elias Smith rode into the encampment and privately informed Governor Young and his counselors that a United States army and supply trains were *en route* to Utah.

While on a trip carrying mail to the East, these men happened by chance to discover that the Great Basin was the destination of a federal army which they had met headed westward. They hurried back to the Mormon Mecca to warn the Saints of the impending danger.

When Governor Young was informed of the approach of federal troops, he immediately determined to resist their entrance into the Basin.

Intolerance and land hunger had driven the Mormons to the Ohio and then to the Missouri. Accentuated intolerance hurled them back to Illinois, where they built a new Zion at Nauvoo. Lawless and wicked intolerance turned their thoughts to the Far West, toward which the frontier tide had now begun to flow.[3]

And now that the Saints of God had established another Zion in the heart of a great desert, Brigham Young was determined not to let even the United States government dislodge his people if it could possibly be helped. When news first reached him at Silver Lake he said:

Liars have reported that this people have committed treason, and upon their representations the President has ordered out troops to assist in officering the territory. We have transgressed no law, neither do we intend to do so; but as for any nation coming to destroy this people, God Almighty being my helper, it shall not be.[4]

---

[3]Herbert E. Bolton, "The Mormons in the Opening of the Great West," *The Utah Genealogical and Historical Magazine,* XVII (Salt Lake City, 1926), 53.
[4]Cited in Joseph Fielding Smith, *Essentials in Church History,* 500.

Throughout the whole period of the Johnston Army episode, Brother Brigham maintained that God would protect his people even against the aggression of a nation. But not knowing exactly what the outcome of the "Utah War" would be, the Mormon leaders prepared for the defense of the Saints. The Utah militia, under Daniel H. Wells, was mustered into service; the people at the Mormon outpost settlements were calld back to the Basin; and all the Saints in Salt Lake and neighboring valleys prepared to burn their homes and all their property and "move south."

The Utah militia went eastward of Fort Bridger, Wyoming, along the emigrant road, and harassed the approaching troops by burning their supplies, grass, timber, bridges, and any other objects which might hamper the progress and the success of the federal army. Thereupon, when General Albert Sidney Johnston reached Fort Bridger in November, 1857, with his troops, he found the old trading post in ashes. Fort Supply, twelve miles to the west, had also been burned.

The snow was deep and the weather had turned intensely cold. So General Johnston was forced to make winter quarters with his troops on Black's Fork.

The failure of the army to reach Utah in 1857 gave time during the coming winter to clear away the misunderstanding which existed between the Mormons and the federal government.

Throughout the East the Democratic administration received severe criticism for sending an "Expedition" against the Saints. Senator Sam Houston of Texas strongly condemned the government's action on the floor of the United States Senate.

RESULTS OF THE MEDIATION OF THOMAS L. KANE

On February 25, 1858, Colonel Thomas L. Kane arrived in Salt Lake City. He had made a long and dangerous journey from New York via the Isthmus of Panama to Los Angeles and then to the stronghold of the Saints for the purpose of helping to bring about an amicable agreement between the Mormons and the federal government.

The work of Colonel Kane was effective. Coupled with other forces, he was able to convince Brigham Young and his people that Governor Cumming was an upright man and that the "Expedition" would not make war upon the Saints.

On March 12, 1858, Colonel Kane arrived at Camp Scott with a letter to Governor Cumming from Brigham Young "accrediting him as a negotiator in the existing difficulties." Kane con-

vinced Cumming that he should come to Salt Lake and assured
him a cordial reception. The Governor accepted the invitation and
journeyed to the Mormon Mecca. Upon arriving there, he was
amazed at the hospitality shown him.

"Governor Cumming reported to Washington the true state
of affairs and the deliberate falseness of Drummond's charges."

Several United States senators and some of the leading newspapers of the East took up the cause of the Mormons and strongly
protested the action of President Buchanan in sending the army
to Utah. They demanded an investigation of the whole affair,
resulting in the President's appointing a commission to come
to Utah for the purpose of offering the Mormons peace.

The peace commission reached the stronghold of the Saints on
June 7, 1858. It had a proclamation of pardon from the President
which declared the Mormon leaders to be in a state of "rebellion"
and "treason," but that the government would grant a pardon to all
who were willing to accept the authority of the United States.

Brigham Young definitely maintained that none of the Mormons were guilty of treason nor rebellion but stated that they would
accept the pardon. Shortly thereafter it was agreed that General
Johnston might bring his army into Utah if he would establish
camp at least forty miles from Salt Lake City. Thereupon, on
June 26, 1858, the army passed through the Mormon Mecca, and a
few days later a permanent camp was established in Cedar Valley.

Federal troops were retained in Utah until after the outbreak
of the Civil War in 1861. However, following the secession of the
Southern States, General Albert Sidney Johnston returned to his
native land, the South, and served as a Confederate general in the
rebellion against the Union. He was killed in battle during the
course of the war.

BITTER STRIFE OVER THE PRACTICE OF PLURAL MARRIAGE

Even after the withdrawal of the army, strife continued between the Mormons and the federal government. The Saints'
practice of plural marriage was the primary cause of this friction.

As Utah was a territory of the United States, the chief argu-
ment against its admission into the Union as a state was based
upon "polygamy."

Lobbyists and the press made bitter attacks upon the Mormons
and their practice of plural marriage, which resulted in Congress
passing an "anti-bigamy law" in 1862. This law was not put into ef-

fect immediately, as President Lincoln's policy was to let the Saints alone. However, a long and bitter struggle continued between Gentiles and Mormons in the Utah Territory, and further legislation was enacted against the latter's religious practices.

However, a time came when the "anti-bigamy law" of 1862 was tested for its constitutionality in the George Reynolds case. He was tried before the court of Utah Territory in 1874, declared guilty, sentenced to one year's imprisonment and forced to pay a fine of $500. Reynolds and his people felt that the decision of the court was unjust and that the law against plural marriage was unconstitutional, as the constitution of the United States guaranteed religious freedom to American citizens. Feeling confident of vindication, he appealed to the Supreme Court of the United States. On January 6, 1879, that august body handed down a decision unanimously confirming the sentence of the courts of Utah and also declaring the "anti-bigamy law" of 1862 to be constitutional.

Following this decision agitation against the Mormons continued and resulted in Congress (1882) amending the law of 1862 under the name of the Edmunds Law. It not only stipulated a fine and imprisoment but a disfranchisement to be administered to polygamists, which denied them the right of the traditional trial by jury. Federal officers were immediately sent to Utah to replace all existing officers and to put the new law into operation.

A period of conflict and persecution followed while the federal officials and the agencies which cooperated with them were trying to stamp out the practice of polygamy, and the enemies of the Church were endeavoring to kill Mormonism. This campaign of bitter persecution lasted throughout the entire administration of President John Taylor. Fathers and mothers were sent to prison and hundreds of homes were broken up. The Church leaders— as they were the main ones who practiced plural marriage—were forced to go into hiding, called "the underground." From there they conducted as best they could the affairs of the Church.

Principally because of exposure as a result of the polygamy persecutions, President John Taylor died while in exile at Kaysville, Utah, on July 27, 1887.

As if all these troubles were not enough, Congress passed in March, 1887, a still more rigid law against the Mormons and polygamy known as the "Edmunds-Tucker Law." The main features of this measure were the disincorporation of the Church of Jesus Christ of Latter-day Saints, the dissolving of the Perpetual Emigrating Fund Company, and the taking over of the property of those organizations by the United States government for the benefit of the common schools of Utah.

Not only did the federal government bear down severely upon those practicing plural marriage, but the feeling against polygamy in Idaho and Arizona was intense. Their legislatures passed extremely hostile laws against the polygamists.

But after Grover Cleveland became President of the United States, more tolerance was shown the unfortunate Saints. He pardoned Rudger Clawson, Charles Livingston, and a number of others who had been given extremely long jail sentences.

THE "MANIFESTO" AND RECONCILIATION

Wilford Woodruff became President of the Church in April, 1889. He and his followers found that it was impossible to continue the practice of plural marriage in opposition to the Edmunds-Tucker Law. Thereupon in 1890, after having appealed to the Lord in prayer to determine His will, President Wilford Woodruff issued what is termed the "Manifesto"—a proclamation suspending the practice of plural marriage. At the October conference the Saints voted to sustain the "Manifesto." Thereafter those who continued to enter into plural marriages came under the condemnation not only of the federal government but also of the Church.

After the issuing of the "Manifesto," conditions became such as to make possible reconcilation between the Mormons and the federal government. On January 4, 1893, President Harrison issued a proclamation of amnesty to polygamists who had entered into plural marriage prior to November 1, 1890. Also, the franchise was bestowed upon those who had previously been deprived of it, and the Church property which had been confiscated was returned to the rightful owners.

By 1896 the breach was healed, and Utah took her place as a sister State in the Union. Gradually antagonism, bitterness, and hatred betweeen Mormons and those who had formerly opposed them died out. Today members of the Church of Jesus Christ of Latter-day Saints are regarded with respect throughout the nation.

Chapter XII

THE LAND PROBLEM IN MORMON COLONIZATION

Free Land and the American Frontier

Mormon colonial history in the Great Basin differs in many respects from frontier history in most other sections of the United States. Most new frontiers were only thirty or forty miles from the last frontier. The sons reached maturity, got married, put their young brides with their few possessions in wagons, and after two or three days' journey, establishing themselves on new land. In this way the line of land settlement was gradually extended forward. This frontier process contrasts greatly with that undertaken by the Mormons. Brigham Young brought his followers over a thousand miles from the base of supplies; they located also nearly a thousand miles from the settlements on the Pacific Coast. Then, too, the Mormons moved as a large organized group under strict leadership, rather than as individuals or as small family units.

According to the frontier hypothesis, the most significant factor in American frontier history was easy access to cheap land. The majority of the people who came from the Old to the New World had in mind the abundance of inexpensive or free land in America —a place where they could make a home and own a farm. Likewise, as depressions or hard times were experienced in the East, large groups of people moved west, motivated by the urge of easily acquiring ownership to farms of their own. Those who lived along the line of the frontier early developed a craving for cheap lands. That is really the "manifest destiny" that caused America to expand.

However, this frontier hypothesis does not explain the outstanding cause of Mormon migration to the Great Basin, but it is impossible to determine just how much the material advantage of coming to Zion influenced the European proselytes or what promises some of the Mormon missionaries held out to them. It is a fact that the one major factor which caused the migration of the Saints was religion. Yet when they arrived in the Great Basin they became typical frontiersmen and immediately were confronted with the problem of land—the problem of building for themselves homes. Frederic L. Paxson stated in regard to the typical colonizer:

> The American frontiersman had to erect, in the course of a lifetime, all of the institutions of private or public life that he desired. At the start, he

was forced to sift them over, and decide which duty first. Invariably the earliest of his problems was that of land, since his first need was to find a place that he might call his own, and build a home.[1]

This statement holds true in Mormon colonization. Thus, upon arriving in the Salt Lake Valley, Brigham Young and his associates immediately set about to solve the land problem in order to exist under the most inhospitable frontier conditions.

SELECTING SITES FOR COLONIES

In complete consistency with Brigham Young's declared intention of learning the possibilities for colonization of the western part of North America, he not only encouraged but directed systematic and careful exploration. This was continued until all of the valleys in the Great Basin suitable for settlements were thoroughly known.

The Mormon leader became personally acquainted with much of the Great West through his frequent trips to the various settlements during the early Utah period. At regular intervals, in company with some of the other leading Church officials and usually a few members of his family, Brigham went on an extensive trip throughout the settlements, giving practical as well as spiritual advice to the Saints. While on these trips he carefully noted the territory passed through and personally selected many places which he later designated for colonization.

In this way there gradually accumulated a great fund of information which, added to the knowledge gained by the early explorers and pathfinders, completely determined the location of new settlements. The fact that the Mormon leaders were specially careful in choosing sites for colonies, in taking stock of all agricultural and industrial possibilities before sending out their settlers, and in carefully selecting the personnel of the various companies sent made Brigham Young and his associates extraordinarily successful in land settlement.

DREAM OF A MORMON EMPIRE

They set out to pre-empt all the accessible locations over an area as extensive as available human resources would permit. These people had repeatedly come into conflict with their neighbors in three or four different states in the East. Having been driven from their homes, and having come a long way to escape conflict with Gentile settlers, they wanted every advantage possible connected

---

[1]Frederic L. Paxson, *History of the American Frontier*, 45.

with being the first colonists in a frontier country. Thus, when they became well-rooted in the Great Salt Lake Valley, they pushed out with vigor into a very extensive territory.

At times this great colonization project was broken into or hampered by Indian wars and by trouble with the federal government, and upon some of those occasions the furthermost colonies had to be abandoned. In spite of these difficulties added to the obstacles of a stubborn environment, the Mormon colonization movement was successfully achieved.

As long as there were canyon streams not yet utilized, the constant urge to open new areas dominated. The more inaccessible lands were left to be brought under cultivation only after all of the canyon streams had colonies permanently established upon them. During the period of Brigham's regime, 1847-1877, the spread of settlements continued, and most of the colonies established by the Mormons within the confines of the United States were made at that time. Under the direction of capable leadership, over 365 towns and cities sprang up on man-made oases amid wide stretches of land either wholly waste or suitable only for grazing. Captain Howard Stansbury, who came to Utah in 1849 in the employ of the Federal Government, described the desolate condition of the Great Basin in the following words:

> One of the most unpleasant characteristics of the whole country . . . is the entire absence of trees from the landscape. The weary traveler plods along, day after day, and week after week, his eyes resting on naught but interminable plains, bald and naked hills, or bold and rugged mountains; the shady grove, the babbling brook, the dense and solemn forest, are things unknown here; and should he by chance light upon a solitary cottonwood or pitch his tent among some stunted willows, the opportunity is hailed with joy, as that of unusual good fortune.[2]

Brigham Young had conceived within his mind a Mormon empire—an expansive colonized land in the western desert section of North America, with its people securely knit together by political, economic, and religious bindings. He planned to settle the Mormons where they could never be uprooted again. Feramorz Young Fox aptly stated:

> Brigham Young's dream of empire was inspired by political and economic as well as by religious motives. He did not expect to establish a politically independent commonwealth, but he did hope to bring together a body of people so numerous and so tied by common interest that they could not again be easily dispossessed. He is reported to have said:"If the people of the United

---

[2]Howard Stansbury. *Explorations and Survey of the Valley of the Great Salt Lake* (1852), 129.

States will let us alone for ten years, we'll ask no odds of them." Upon his arrival in the Salt Lake Valley he had said that he intended to know every hole and corner from the Bay of San Francisco to the Hudson Bay. There is no doubt that the Mormons planned to pre-empt as far as possible all the choice lands to prevent occupancy by those who might oppose them. They did not expect to exclude those who were not members of the Church—they brought two or three along in the first pioneer company—but they did hope to keep them in the minority. In the settlement of "Dixie," for example, Erastus Snow sent out men to take and hold certain choice valleys to head off some non-Mormons thought to be intending to settle. In later periods of Mormon history when anti-polygamy raids were being conducted by federal officials, exploration for lands beyond the territorial limits of the United States was stimulated. Apart from political dominance the survival of the Mormon commonwealth depended on economic self-sufficiency. A wide diversity of mineral and agricultural products was needed, and some early colonies were established in places considered favorable to their production.[3]

Factors Determining Choice of Location of Mormon Settlements

An article in the "Deseret News Weekly," June 17, 1885, points out four important factors which determined the choice of the location of Mormon settlements:

1. Accessibility. Easy communication was vital to the Mormon system. Social solidarity was absolutely essential to the realization of Mormon objectives and these could only be possible when there was relatively frequent contact between communities and between the people and their leaders. Settlement spread from the center outward and the maintenance of lines of communication greatly influenced the selection of sites. Costly experience revealed the weakness of extending the lines too far.

2. Favorable climatic conditions, assuring a growing season of sufficient length to mature the crops. The lands of lower elevations were first settled and those southward more rapidly than those to the north of the parent colony.

3. Fertility of soil. This was determined from the texture of the soil and natural vegetation. It is interesting to note, however, that the order of appropriation of land did not depend wholly upon degree of fertility. . . . Not the most fertile, but the most available land—the best under the conditions —was taken up first. Pioneers had to produce a crop the first year or starve. The lands for which water was most readily accessible were earliest brought under cultivation. Those were usually the lands of heavier soils found in the valley bottoms. The bench lands, though frequently superior, were taken up later when water was provided through more extensive and higher canals. In the growth of Salt Lake City the lower northwest portions of the city were selected in preference to the higher lands southeast. In Davis County the bottom lands were first taken up. Bishop Johnson of Redmond, Sevier County, calls attention to a similar procedure in his community where very choice lands were available many years after the establishment of the colony.

4. The presence of water and wood.[4]

[3]Feramorz Young Fox, *The Mormon Land System*, 105, Ms.
[4]*Deseret News Weekly*, June 17, 1855.

WATER A LIMITING FACTOR IN LAND UTILIZATION

Numerous mountain streams flow down through the canyons and out into the valleys during the spring and early summer. These water-courses were the determining factor in the location of the Mormon settlements. Thousands of acres of good land lie in the confines of the Great Basin, most of which would be completely incapable of supporting human life if it were not for the high mountain ranges serving as water sheds for the winter snow. The snow-banks melt during the warmer seasons, furnishing water to irrigate about five per cent of the land in Utah.

The limiting factor in land utilization in this arid belt, then, is water. Thousands of acres of fertile land remain uncultivated because of insufficient moisture. The problem that confronted Brigham Young and his associates was not that of merely finding land to settle upon. There was plenty of unoccupied country in the Great Basin. The problem was to find land to which water could be applied with minimum of effort and cost.

THE MORMON LAND POLICY

July 25, 1847, the first Sabbath that the Saints were in the Salt Lake Valley, and the day following the arrival of Brigham Young, he told the people what principle he would follow in distributing land to them. He said that "no man who came here should buy land, but every man should have his land measured out to him for city and farming purposes, what he could till. He might till it as he pleased, but must be industrious and take care of it."[5] It was to be the policy of the Church, Brigham pointed out, to dictate to whom land should be given and the amount each man should receive. The idler, it was generally understood, should lose his inheritance. In fact, Brother Brigham had definitely announced at Garden Grove a year earlier "that no man should hold more land than he could cultivate; 'and that if a man would not till his land, it should be taken from him.'" Thus Brigham Young established the Mormon land law.[6]

One significant point of President Young's land policy was that no land was to be bought or sold. The Church officials looked upon land as a gift of God—something that belonged to the community and not to the individual. Therefore, social prosperity and good will among the Saints depended upon proper distribution of the land. Each man was to have given to him the amount that he

---

[5] Wilford Woodruff, *Journal*, July 25, 1847, Ms.
[6] Cited in Brigham H. Roberts, *A Comprehensive History of the Church*, III, 269.

could use properly and profitably. But no man was to usurp all of the best land at the expense of the other Saints who had arrived and those who had not yet arrived in the Great Basin.

The Mormon leader realized that the success of his colonial enterprise depended entirely upon the principle of equity and justice in the temporal as well as in the spiritual realm. The very existence of the project was based upon an equitable and successful land economy—a land economy that would be self-sufficing to the group as well as to the individual. Brigham, with his keen power to view the problem in its entirety and at the same time to foresee the most minute detail, immediately realized the importance of a well-controlled land policy. In a letter to the Saints at Salt Lake dated September 9, 1847, he gave further particulars upon the subject:

> We have no land to sell to the Saints in the Great Basin, but you are entitled to as much as you can till, or as you need for your support, provided you pay the surveyor for his services, while he is laboring for you; and at a future day you will receive your inheritance on the farming lands as well as in city lots; and none of you have any land to buy or sell more than ourselves; for the inheritance is of the Lord, and we are his servants, to see that every one has his portion in due season.[7]

In accepting the viewpoint that settlers should receive land without cost, merely for reclaiming it, the Mormon leaders were completely in accord with frontier opinion. In the words of Frederic L. Paxson:

> Between 1820 and the panic of 1837 the frontier crystalized its opinion that any price for the land was an imposition and that the auction was an affront.[8]

In fact, a fundamental belief in America during the early part of the nineteenth century was that agriculture was the basis of wealth. Brigham believed strongly in that doctrine, especially as it applied to his people in the opening of the Great West. Lowry Nelson summarized in a very clear way the attitude regarding land which prevailed in this country at the time the Mormon pioneers migrated to the Basin. Dr. Nelson says:

> The disposal of public lands, however, was the most absorbing economic question of the day. The labor idealist such as Horace Greeley and George Henry Evans were advocating free land as an alternate employment for workers in the overcrowded industrial centers.

---

[7]Brigham Young, "Epistle of Brigham Young and the Twelve," *Latter-day Saint Journal History*, September 9, 1847. Ms.
[8]Frederic L. Paxson, *op. cit.*, 390.

Physiocratic agrarianism of the French school of economists headed by Quesnay, with its emphasis upon the supposed natural superiority of agriculture as a form of wealth, and concomitant depreciation of commerce, having entered this country by way of Virginia, gained a foothold in this period.

Associated with this doctrine of "natural right" of the individual to a portion of the earth's surface, was that of equality. No person was entitled to more land than he could use for himself.[9]

However, the Mormon colonizers differed from many of the pioneers who opened the American frontier to land settlement in putting a religious interpretation on land ownership—i.e., the earth and all that is in it belongs to God, and men are merely His stewards.

If Brother Brigham had permitted the advanced companies of immigrants to seize upon and monopolize the resources of the valleys of the Great West, an act of injustice would have been committed against the other Saints who were to follow. The Mormon land policy was expressed in statesman-like measures, necessary to safeguard the interest of all.

Laying Out of Salt Lake City

One of the first problems to absorb the attention of the apostles after arriving in the Great Salt Lake Valley was that of laying out a city. Brigham Young was thoroughly convinced that the spot on City Creek selected by Orson Pratt and his group on July 22 was the best place to establish their new Mecca. On July 28, the Mormon leader wrote as follows:

Some of the brethren talked about exploring the country farther for a site for a settlement; I replied that I was willing that the country should be explored until all were satisfied, but every time a party went out and returned, I believed firmly, they would agree this is the spot for us to locate.[10]

The pioneer company voted to sustain the Twelve as a supervising committee to direct the laying out of the city. After President Young had selected a spot on which to build the temple between the forks of City Creek, the decision was reached to lay out the city in square blocks of ten acres each with the temple block containing forty acres. Each city block should be divided into eight lots, ten by twenty rods, the streets to be eight rods wide. The plan designated that only one house be built to a lot, each house to be located in the middle of the lot, twenty feet back from the front line. "It was also determined that upon every alternate block four houses were to be built on the east, and four on the west side of the square,

[9]Lowry Nelson, The Mormon Village: A Study in Social Origins, 14.
[10]Latter-day Saint Journal History, July 28, 1847, Ms.

EAGLE GATE, ERECTED IN 1869, AND BEEHIVE HOUSE, ONE OF BRIGHAM YOUNG'S HOMES

THE BRIGHAM YOUNG MONUMENT AND THE SALT LAKE TEMPLE

but none on the north and south sides. But the blocks intervening were to have four houses on the north and four on the south, but none on the east and west sides. In this plan there will be no houses fronting each other on the opposite sides of the streets."[11]

This plan provided ample space for the planting of flower gardens and shrubbery in front of the house and served as a safeguard against fire. The plan was accepted by the entire camp by unanimous vote and was later put into effect, with the exception of reducing the Temple Block to ten acres to make it uniform with the others.

It should be noted that this method of city building is nearly identical with that given by Joseph Smith (1833) for the city of Zion—"the New Jerusalem"—in Jackson, County, Missouri. In the words of Lowry Nelson:

> The plan of the City of Zion sent to Missouri by Joseph Smith . . . in 1833 made provision for the practical needs of a frontier farming community. . . . . The Plat of the City of Zion is in reality the foundation of the Mormon village. . . .
> Several towns were laid out according to this plan in the Middle West, including Kirtland, Ohio, (1834); Far West (1836) and Adam ondi-Ahman, in Missouri, and Nauvoo, Illinois.
> The plan of the City of Zion then became the foundation for the settlements of the Mormons in the Great Basin, Salt Lake City being the first "village" established there in 1847.[12]

On July 31, 1847, Orson Pratt and Henry G. Sherwood began the survey of the city with some instruments brought from abroad by John Taylor in the spring of that year and delivered to President Brigham Young at Winter Quarters.[13] The first survey, comprising 114 blocks, is known as Plat A. It was completed August 20.[14]

While the survey of Plat A was being made, the Church leaders decided upon a plan for selecting the lots or "inheritances." On August 13 the Twelve Apostles agreed that each member of that quorum should choose lots for himself and his friends to settle upon. Wilford Woodruff recorded in his journal the location of the various tiers of blocks selected by the Church officials. Some apportionments were made which were not recorded by Woodruff.[15] This selecting of lots made in 1847 was only a temporary arrangement. The actual general distribution of lots was not made until a year later, after the arrival of Brigham Young and the other

---

[11]Cited in Roberts, op. cit., III, 280.
[12]Lowry Nelson, op. cit., 16-20.
[13]Orson Pratt, Journal, July 31, 1847; Millennial Star, XII, 180.
[14]Howard Egan, Pioneering the West, 125.
[15]Wilford Woodruff, Journal, August 13, 1847, Ms.

Church leaders on their second journey across the plains from Winter Quarters.

In a very comprehensive and detailed letter written while he was in Winter Quarters, Brigham sent specific instructions upon building the fort, preparing the ground, planting crops, fencing, irrigation, and putting up sawmills. Of the land policy that the people were to put into effect, he said:

> The High Council will be furnished with a city plat, on which will be registered the names of those who have had their inheritances assigned them; others may wait our return to receive their inheritances, which will in nowise interfere with their occupying all the land they can cultivate.[16]

The Saints in the Great Basin complied with the instructions given them. Building, planting, fencing, and other activities kept the industrious people busy throughout the following year. Finally, on September 20, 1848, Brigham Young and his company of immigrants arrived at Salt Lake. The fact that the Mormon leader was back with his people was an event of significant importance. A period of vigorous activity ensued. Only four days after his arrival, at a public meeting held in the Bowery, the decision was made to permit building outside the fort.

PORTIONING OUT OF CITY LOTS AND FARMING LANDS TO THE SAINTS

A committee of two, Brigham Young and Heber C. Kimball, were unanimously sustained, September 24, 1848, by the body of the Church to apportion city lots and farming lands to the Saints. The first step taken by this committee was to assign to the Mormon leaders and their friends the lots that had been reserved for them since August 7, 1847. There is no doubt that the faithful Saints were perfectly willing that Brother Brigham and the other leaders, with their friends, should have first choice of lots nearest to the temple block. If there was any dissatisfaction with this distribution, it does not appear in the records.

"To prevent any hardness of feelings that might occur by any other method of dividing land," Young and Kimball conducted the distribution of lots to the rest of the people by the method of lot-drawing instead of assignment, as had been the practice the year before. There are so many allusions in the early Mormon record to lot-drawing as a method of apportioning land that it seems to have been the common method employed by the Saints.

The lots were without cost to the settlers except for a fee of

---

[16]Brigham Young, *op. cit.*

$1.50, one dollar of which was to pay the surveyor and fifty cents to carry the expense of recording each lot. This was exactly in accordance with the previously expressed idea of Brigham Young on what the land policy of the Mormons was going to be. Thus at Salt Lake City the precedent of free land for the Saints was established. The same land policy was followed in the other Mormon colonies established before 1869. In speaking of Provo, Apostle George A. Smith wrote in 1853: "Last week I let the brethren who are newcomers have fifty town lots, which cost them only the expense of recording and surveying—one dollar and a half each."[17]

Having completed the arrangements for the distribution of city lots, President Young and Brother Kimball now devoted their attention to the apportionment of farming lands. After formulating what they considered a practicable and workable plan, they presented it to the high council. The council endorsed the plan and offered it for the approval of the people, on September 30, 1848.

This arrangement proposed that the farming lands be divided into small lots or farms, which were to be assigned to the people by casting lots, and that all of the farming lands be enclosed in one large field under one common fence.[18] Brigham Young, in a letter to Orson Hyde, October 9, 1848, explained the plan that had been devised to equalize the values of the respective holdings so that there should be no room for criticism. He wrote:

> It is our intention to have the five acre lots next to the city accommodate the mechanics and artisans, the ten acres next, then the twenty acres, followed by the forty and eighty acre lots, where farmers can build and reside. All these lots will be enclosed in one common fence, which will be seventeen miles and fifty-three rods long, eight feet high; and to the end that every man will be satisfied with his lot and prevent any hardness that might occur by any other method of dividing the land, we have proposed that it shall all be done by ballot, or casting lots, as Israel did in the days of old.[19]

When the above plans were presented to the people they were asked to file a request with the clerk stating the number of acres they desired. It was President Young's purpose to divide the land in such a way that each family could have the amount that it could take care of properly. The first day that the clerk received applications for land his office was filled with anxious applicants from early morning until late at night. Brother Brigham had a difficult time getting through the crowd to his office. That day 776 applications

---

[17]George A. Smith, *Deseret News*, September 27, 1853.
[18]Roberts, *op. cit.*, III, 282; *Latter-day Saint Journal History*, September 30, 1848.
[19]Brigham Young to Orson Hyde, in *ibid.*, October 9, 1848.

were filed, asking for 9,650 acres of land. A week later the acreage applied for had increased to 11,005.[20]

In the actual distribution of the farm lands, only five and ten acre lots were included in the big field. A committee consisting of Bishops Newel K. Whitney, Edward Hunter, and Tarlton Lewis conducted the drawings for the five-acre fields. The drawings for the ten-acre fields must have taken place, also, by the early part of November because on November 5, Brigham Young suggested that the mechanics, whose full time was needed to do their professional work, should give their five and ten-acre fields to the farmers.[21] Thomas Bullock, Brigham's secretary and clerk, carefully recorded the allotments of the city lots and farming lands.

THE BIG FIELD

It was decided when the allotments were made that each person receiving land should help build a fence around the big field in proportion to his acreage, regardless of the location of his land within the field.[22] The advantages of all of the Saints of a given community working together when the village was first being established and fencing all of their land under one common fence in one big field were clearly set forth by the Mormon leader soon after they arrived in the Great Basin. On August 22, 1847, at a special conference of the Church, President Young urged that the people adopt a plan of enclosing all of the lands to be cultivated within one fence. He pointed out that such a plan would make it possible for the group to have more spare time to devote to raising of grain. No doubt enough crops could be raised the first year, he suggested, to feed all of the people in the valley and thousands of those who had not yet reached the Great Basin. He continued by saying, "I would rather fence a block of ten acres, and have a crop, than plant a hundred acres for the cattle to destroy."[23] The Saints voted favorably in regard to Brigham's plan. About three weeks later, the Mormon leader instructed the Saints at Salt Lake as follows:

A sun-dried brick wall eight feet high is considered the best farming fence in our present situation. It is desirable that the brethren unite their labors so as to enclose their farming lands in large tracts, every one fencing in proportion to the land he agrees to occupy; thus much land may be enclosed with little labor and more time can be had for tillage; every man can plow and sow as much as he pleases, and have his field to himself as though it were

    [20]*Ibid.*, October 2, 1848; Fox, *op. cit.*, 69.
    [21]*History of Brigham Young,* 79, Ms.
    [22]*Latter-day Saint Journal History,* October 17, 1848, Ms.
    [23]Brigham Young, *ibid.*, August 22, 1847.

surrounded by his own fence. If the brethren choose to fence the city, or any portion of the city in large sections for farming purposes, we have no objection. In that case it would be well to lay a sun-dried brick wall eight feet high on the line of the blocks, crossing and enclosing the streets where necessary. Otherwise you may expect that your crops will be removed and trampled upon by the Indians and their horses; the last four feet may be built after planting, provided the time would not admit previously.[24]

In accordance with the President's instructions, a field of 5,133 acres was marked off for plowing during the winter of 1847-1848. Part of the group plowed while others did the fencing. The first winter the pioneers sowed 872 acres of winter wheat and kept the balance of the plowed land for spring and summer crops of various kinds.[25] Fifteen acres of plowed land were allotted to each public official whose entire time was absorbed in the service of the community.[26] An effort was made to enclose the field by a pole instead of an adobe fence. To attempt a fence eleven miles in length was an immense task which was never entirely completed.

The establishment of a large field at Salt Lake served as a precedent for later colonization. As Brigham sent groups out to settle various sections of the Great Basin, the same procedure of joint-enclosure was followed, making it one of the definite land policies of Utah colonial history. Common pasture lands were also jointly enclosed by the founders of Utah in their various settlements.

Mormon Cooperation

One factor which made Mormon land settlement especially successful was the people's ability to organize and to cooperate. President Young united his immigrants into military formation for better discipline, control and efficiency while crossing the plains. They were organized after the order of Moses' "Camps of Israel," the larger companies being divided into hundreds, the hundreds into fifties, and each fifty into tens, with a captain over each division. In compliance with a suggestion made by Apostle Parley P. Pratt, at a general conference, October 24, 1847, this military organization was retained as an agricultural tool.[27] To each unit was apportioned as much land as it could successfully farm—about ten acres per man. Captain Stansbury was greatly impressed by the ability of the Mormons to cooperate and to convert a desert into a paradise. According to Stansbury:

---

[24]*Ibid.*, September 9, 1847.
[25]*Ibid.*, March 6, 1848.
[26]*Ibid.*, October 19. 1847.
[27]*Latter-day Saint Journal History*, October 24, 1847, Ms.

The foundation within the space of three years of a large and flourishing community upon a spot so remote from the abodes of men, so entirely unconnected by water courses with either of the oceans that wash the shores of the continent—a country offering no advantages of inland navigation or of foreign commerce, but on the contrary, isolated by vast uninhabited deserts, and only to be reached by long, painful, and often hazardous journeys by land—presents an anomaly so very peculiar, that it deserves more than a passing word.

In this young and prosperous country of ours, where cities grow up in a day, and states spring up in a year, the successful planting of a colony, where the natural advantages have been such as to hold out the promise of adequate reward to the projectors, would have excited no surprise; but the success of the enterprise under circumstances so much at variance with all our preconceived ideas of its probability, may well be considered one of the most remarkable incidents of the present age.

Their admirable system of combining labor, while each has his own property, in lands and tenements, and the proceeds of his industry, the skill in dividing off the lands, and conducting the irrigation canals to supply the want of rain, which rarely falls between April and October; the cheerful manner in which everyone applies himself industriously, but not laboriously; the complete reign of good neighborhood and quiet houses and fields, form themes of admiration for the stranger coming from the dark and sterile recesses of the mountain gorges into the flourishing valley, and he is struck with wonder at the immense result produced in so short a time, by a handful of individuals.[28]

SMALL FARMS

Another phase of the land system which is distinctly Mormon is that of small farms.[29] President Young and the other Church officials preached the theory of small farms so much that the idea became almost a part of Latter-day Saint doctrine. In the chapters —which will appear later—which deal with the founding of towns, numerous examples of the actual application of the small-farm doctrine will be presented. The following statements are given as examples of the teachings of the leaders relative to the foregoing concept:

In 1860 Brigham Young advised the people of Richmond, Utah: "Do not be anxious to have large farms, more than you can till; but divide your lands with your brethren and make yourselves humble and happy." Judging from the following remark made by one of the early settlers of Richfield, Orson Hyde must have taught the same theory: "We believe in Elder Hyde's doctrine that ten acres of good land well-cultivated is better than twenty or thirty or more acres skimmed over and producing weeds." Henry Lunt wrote from Cedar City to George A. Smith:[30] "A little farm well-

[28]Stansbury, op. cit., cited in Levi Edgar Young, The Founding of Utah, 162-164.
[29]George Thomas, The Development of Institutions Under Irrigation, 33-36.
[30]Henry Lunt to George A. Smith, in Latter-day Saint Journal History, February 5, 1860, Ms.

cultivated near homes, I know, is your doctrine, and it is mine and ever was." The following was reported from the same city in 1854:

> To accommodate the newcomers of the fall of 1853, a new field containing one thousand acres was surveyed west of the former field. The brethren who have lately come in have not taken more than ten or five acres. We are especially instructed to fence it with a good picket fence, that our crops may be secure.[31]

It has already been pointed out that the distribution of the land in Salt Lake was in five and ten-acre fields, each farmer receiving from ten to fifteen acres of irrigated farming land. No provision was made in the decision of February, 1849, for farms larger than ten acres. The precedent established at Salt Lake was adopted by the other settlements and the practice of adhering to small holdings became general. For example, in 1854, Jesse W. Fox surveyed the "Big Field" at Brigham City which was divided principally into five-acre lots.[32] At Las Vegas the plots ranged from two and one-half to five acres each in size. Feramorz Young Fox collected the following important data:

> Mormon practice is seen to be quite unusual when viewed in the light of that of the country as a whole. . . . The average acreage per farm in the whole United States in 1850 was 203 acres. If we take the sections with which the Mormon people were most familiar, the states and territories of their nativity, or those in which they had resided prior to the exodus, we find average farm sizes as follows:

State	Average size of farms, acres
New York	113
Ohio	125
Missouri	179
Illinois	158
Iowa	185

> These averages help us to see how vastly different was the system of land holdings that the Mormons had devised. The average size of Utah farms increased considerably after 1870. This is to be accounted for by the taking up of lands under the Desert Land Acts and not to any great change in the size of irrigated farms.[33]

A number of conditions caused the Church leaders to apportion lands for cultivation into small holdings. The Mormon colonizers were settling a desert country where the presence of water for irrigation was an important factor in helping to assure their existence.

[31]*Deseret News*, XV, 159.
[32]*Ibid.*, February 2, 1854.
[33]Feramorz Young Fox, *The Mormon Land System*, 147-148, Ms.

The distribution of large groups of people upon a limited number of canyon streams with an equally limited source of water made it necessary for Brigham Young and his associates—in fairness to all —to divide the land into small lots.

Just as the scarcity of water helped to determine the size of land holdings so did the economic system of cooperative work in the formative period of Mormon colonization tend to limit the size of farms. A group of colonists would be sent out from the mother colony to establish a settlement on a previously selected site. In the early days of the village the people would work together as one large family, fencing a large field, building irrigation ditches, plowing farm lands, building school houses, churches and private homes.[34] Economy of labor, then, forced them to farm small plots.

The very fact that they settled as a group and that the land had to be divided among so many brought about a system which contrasts greatly with that found in the settlement of many parts of the United States, where the colonists established themselves upon farm lands in single family units or in small groups, with land and water both plentiful. Under the Church system in the desert West, large holdings were not possible.

The Mormon colonization project differed from the usual westward flow of immigration in that it was an organized and controlled religious project, whereas in most sections of the United States the principal urge to "go West" was to better economic conditions. The Saints came to the Great Basin in order that they might worship God as they saw fit.

The fundamental and controlling factor, then, in Mormon colonization, and the basis of their economic system as well, was the belief in the doctrines of the Church of Jesus Christ of Latter-day Saints as established by their Prophet Joseph Smith. The idea that divine authority was exercised by their leaders through the restoration to them of the Holy Priesthood, the doctrine of human brotherhood of man, as well as the belief that the Kingdom of God was upon this earth, with Brigham Young and his associates standing as God's representatives, all contributed to an efficiently organized and thoroughly controlled colonization project. Added to these things was a strong character—a natural born leader—who had inherited the position of "Prophet, Seer, and Revelator" to a young, dynamic Church. In the words of Dr. Lowry Nelson:

While Brigham had demonstrated early that he had spiritual "gifts," and

---

[34]Lowry Nelson, *The Mormon Village: A Study in Social Origins*. 27-28.

was able to give revelations, the people came to look upon him as a little short of a miracle man in directing the group in temporal affairs. . . . He was destined to deal with mundane affairs, the building of empire. . . .
His reputation for wisdom in agricultural affairs went far and wide among his followers. Many are the traditions among the people today which feed the stereotype of the "empire builder. . . ." The fantastic dream "city of Zion" became the corporeal, mundane farm village of Utah [under Brigham Young's leadership]. That he succeeded in doing it, is no small tribute to his leadership.[35]

Brother Brigham and his co-workers were almost as greatly concerned about the members of their organization who had not yet come to Utah and those investigators who were not yet enrolled within the Church as they were about the ones already within the confines of the Great Basin. For this reason ample provisions were made in the distribution of farm lands for the Saints not yet in the valleys of the Rocky Mountains. This, again, limited the size of farm holdings.

MORMON FARM-VILLAGE SYSTEM

Another very important factor in determining the size of farm lands in Utah was the farm-village system under which the Mormons chose to live. Whenever possible Brigham planned to establish settlements every ten miles, which he quite systematically achieved. This fixed the distance of the most remote farms at little farther than seven miles from the village.

The Mormon leaders felt very keenly the advantages gained by settling in compact towns, and impressed the importance of such a system upon their followers. There were recreational, civil, educational and religious opportunities to be found in town life.[36] Brigham Young urged that each new community immediately provide itself with facilities to enjoy those benefits. Also, there was the advantage of protection from the Indian menace. But Dr. Lowry Nelson concluded—in his study of "The Mormon Village" —that the pattern used by Brigham Young in building the communities of the Great West resulted from the following influences:

"1. The plan of the "City of Zion."
2. The development of extraordinary group solidarity.
3. The favorable environment of the Great Basin."[37]

The New England town-meeting was reproduced in early Utah

---

[35]*Ibid.*
[36]Thomas, *op. cit.,* 34.
[37]Nelson, *op. cit.,* ·29.

for the conduct of civil affairs. Often when the Saints assembled in their religious gatherings the presiding officer would devote much of his time talking about the economic affairs of the community. There was continuously a mixture of the temporal and the spiritual in the sermons that were preached. The pioneers were practical frontiersmen who were making a struggle for existence against a barren desert country. There were canals to be dug, bridges to be built, lands to be plowed and planted, insects to be fought and killed. Those urgent matters were closely associated with the religious life of the people and the ecclesiastical leaders saw no incompatibility between the two. "The religion of Jesus Christ is a matter-of-fact religion," Brigham said, "and taketh hold of the everyday duties and realities of this life."[38]

Mormon philosophy, as taught by Joseph Smith and his successors, drew little distinction between the temporal and the spiritual. Men needed both for a proper and complete development of human personality. The natural resources of the earth were put here by God, they believed, to be judiciously used by men. President Young was schooled in this type of thinking. He was naturally a practical man, and the work he was doing as leader of a great colonizing movement in an arid country called forth every ounce of intelligence and wisdom at his command. One is not surprised, then, to find his sermons filled with practical advice to the Saints on how to conduct their economic affairs.

A few years after the death of the Mormon Colonizer, his successors clearly stated the general paternal policy regarding colonization employed by President Brigham Young; and that policy was to be continued. They wrote as follows:

To President William B. Preston and Counselors,
Logan, Utah.
Dear Brethren:

That you may more fully understand our wishes with regard to the organization of new settlements throughout your Stake, more especially in the distant and most thinly settled parts, we address you this communication. . . .

In all cases in making new settlements the Saints should be advised to gather in villages, as has been our custom from the time of our earliest settlement in these mountain valleys. The advantages of this plan, instead of carelessly scattering out over a wide extent of country, are many and obvious to all those who have a desire to serve the Lord. By this means the people can retain ecclesiastical organizations, have regular meetings of the quorums of the Priesthood and establish and maintain day and Sunday schools, Improvement Associations, and Relief Societies. They can also cooperate for the good of all in financial and secular necessary improvements. Further than this they are a mutual protection and source of strength against horse

------

[38]*Discourses of Brigham Young,* 19.

and cattle thieves, land jumpers, and against hostile Indians, should there be any, while their compact organization gives them many advantages of a social and civil character which might be lost, misapplied or frittered away by spreading out so thinly that inter-communication is difficult, dangerous, inconvenient, or expensive.

It would be well, therefore, for you in company with Brother Ricks to visit the country and make such locations of settlements as may be desirable and as the circumstances may require, and have your town lots surveyed by a competent person and such arrangements made for this kind of settlement as you and your counsel and Brother Ricks may deem advisable. In doing this, however, it would be well not to interfere with homestead entries, or to embarrass new settlers too much, but to have it positively understood that this method must be adopted in your settlements.

We know of no reason why the methods that have been pursued in the past on these matters are any less applicable to the Saints in Idaho and Wyoming than they have proved to those in Utah and Arizona. While the families are gathered in settlements there can be no disadvantage in having the farms outside, within easy reach, as the peculiarities of the country may admit, the same as in our older settlements. A spirit to spread far and wide out of sight and reach of the authorities of the Church, must be discountenanced, as all Latter-day Saints must yield obedience to the laws of the Gospel, and the order of the Kingdom of God, and a methodical comprehension and intelligent system be inaugurated that we may gain influence (and not lose strength) by strengthening the cords of the Stakes of Zion. . . .

The Twelve have this matter in hand and will see that things are conducted right. The local presiding Bishop will cooperate with you in all of these affairs, and on matters of importance it would be proper for you to consult us.

We remain, as ever, your brethren in the Gospel.

> JOHN TAYLOR,
> JOSEPH F. SMITH,
> Of the First Presidency.[39]

ACQUIRING OF TITLES TO THE LAND

Another phase of the Mormon land problem was that of the Saints' acquiring titles to their farms. Brigham Young thoroughly understood that sooner or later each of his followers would have to deal with the government for his land and that it would not always be possible for the Church officials to control the distribution of mother earth, both as to place and amount. He rightly guessed, however, that his system would be well-established before any interference from the government would develop. He also believed that when the government took direct jurisdiction over the Great West his followers would experience the same traditional

---

[39]John Taylor and Joseph F. Smith, to William B. Preston, in *Fremont Stake Manuscript History*, December 26, 1882.

leniency of the Federal Government in the enforcement of land laws which other newly developed territories had received.

At the time the Mormons first began to deal with the land problem in the Basin (1847), Utah was nominally a part of Mexico. The transfer of the territory to the United States was not made until the following year at the signing of the treaty of Guadalupe Hidalgo on February 2, 1848.

Even when the United States became the owner of the country the Mormons had located on, it did nothing for a number of years to "satisfy claims and extinguish the rights of the Indians to the land occupied by the whites, or to extend the Federal Land Laws to the territory for the benefit of the settlers."[40] In 1849 the Mormons established a provisional government which they termed the State of Deseret. Its constitution "did not contain a provision giving to the General Assembly any authority over land, water or timber in the new commonwealth." Neither did the act which established the territorial government for Utah, approved by President Fillmore on September 9, 1850, grant the territorial legislature any authority over land. The Mormons had been in the Basin over twenty years before the Federal Government took definite steps toward granting them titles to their farms.

Until 1869 the Saints were merely squatters on the public domain. During that period Brigham and his followers systematically colonized land to which they had no title. They surveyed their farms, devised their own system of allotting, registering, recording, and giving temporary land titles, awaiting the action of the Federal Government to grant them official titles to the land.

During this period (1847-1869) the Mormons devised a procedure for protecting their claims—a procedure which was continued while three successive governments, the ecclesiastical government, 1847-1849, the provisional government of the State of Deseret, 1849-1851, and the territorial government which was finally set up in 1851, ruled over them.

Various land laws were passed during the administration of those governments with the sole purpose of securing the right of possession of the land. The Saints had to wait for a legal title to their farms until the Federal Government was willing to grant it to them. In order to maintain a claim to surveyed lots and farms, the territorial government passed an act in 1853 providing that all such claims must be fenced within one year. All lands not complying with that rule, at the expiration of the year, again became public domain, and thereby open to any person who made application for

---

[40]Thomas, *op. cit.*, 30.

them. The passage of this act affected the ownership of many unfenced lots in Salt Lake, though they had been claimed for more than three years under the original allotment.

The idea back of requiring the owners to fence their claims was to define as clearly as possible their land. This would minimize "land jumping." Also fencing was a practical way of limiting the size of claims in harmony with Brigham's policy of small farms. In addition to their numerous other jobs the labor of cutting poles, hauling them from the mountains, and fencing was too great to permit the pioneers to enclose large areas.

Again, in March, 1852, the Utah Territorial Legislature passed an act which stated that when a piece of surveyed land was disposed of the seller should "make and execute to the purchaser a full and written quit claim, . . . and acknowledge the same before the county recorder where the premises are situated. On January 18, 1855, the legislature provided for the transfer of all land claims whether surveyed or not."[41]

In 1861 a law was passed concerning the ownership and control of land. It gave ownership to anyone who inclosed "a portion or portions of unclaimed government land, or caused it to be done at his expense." Also, he would be declared the lawful owner of all buildings and other improvements that he placed upon said property. Thus the Mormons made their own land laws while they waited for legal titles from the Federal Government.

As soon as the Utah Territorial Government was established in 1851, the officials began to take action preparatory to securing titles to the land in the Basin from the Federal Government. As the Saints were not esteemed very highly by the government, they had to patiently await the slow process of the law.

In order to encourage the settlement of Oregon, Congress had passed a law in 1841 known as the Pre-emption act. Under its terms, each single man who settled in that territory before 1850 received a half section of land. Married men and their wives received a half section each. To all those who settled in that territory between 1850 and 1853, quarter sections of land were to be given. Hoping that the Mormons might receive the same consideration as the settlers of Oregon had received, the Legislature of Utah in its first session asked Congress for similar grants. In 1859 a like memorial was sent to Congress. Neither of these petitions, however, brought favorable action from the Federal Government.

Brigham Young and his associates realized that the Pre-emption Act of 1841 would have to be liberally interpreted to meet the situation as it existed in Utah. According to that act one hundred and sixty acres of land would be granted on condition that the colonizer resided on the farm for fourteen months. Technically, under the Mormon's farm-village system, the people did not live directly upon their farming lands.

That fact would also make it difficult to apply literally the Homestead Act of May 20, 1862, to the Mormon situation because of the required five year's residence upon the land. It also provided for the entry of 80 to 160 acres, which could not fit well with the Mormon small-farm system. The legislature of Utah made repeated appeals to Congress to adjust the federal laws to fit the peculiar Mormon needs in a desert country, but nothing was done to solve the problem for a number of years.[42] The Utah situation was clearly stated in the following memorial to Congress in 1859:

MEMORIAL: To Congress for the preemption of Irrigated lands. To the Honorable, the Senate and House of Representatives, in Congress Assembled:

Your memorialists, the Governor and Legislative Assembly of the Territory of Utah, would respectfully represent, that in the settlement of this wild and desert country, it was found necessary against the savages, and to enable the settlers to irrigate the lands, they were under the necessity of surveying and enclosing small tracts of from one to forty acres each; very few, however, exceed twenty acres. By this means, in locating almost every settlement, from fifty to one hundred farmers cultivate the same section, which is watered by a canal owned by each agriculturist, in proportion to the area of his farm, meadow, or garden; the waters of said canal being distributed to each man in separate water ditch; a hundred or more of these streams water every section cultivated.

Your memorialists would therefore respectfully pray your honorable body, to pass a law enabling the occupants of such portions of land, to appoint one of their number an agent, who shall be authorized to preempt and enter said lands in a body, and distribute the same by giving titles to proper claimants.[43]

Finally, in 1869, a land office, authorized to grant land titles to the Saints, was opened in Salt Lake City. The federal land laws, however, were not modified to meet the peculiar Mormon situation, yet in the actual procedure the suggestions made in the memorial of 1859 were carried out. Their claims were entered in quarter-sections as homesteads by "trustees." Those trustees in turn deeded the soil in small lots to the rightful claimants. The same procedure was applied to Church holdings and to townsite lands. The mayors of the towns entered the townsite claims

---

42*Ibid.*, 29-41.
43*Latter-day Saint Journal History*, January 12, 1859, Ms.

and later issued deeds to the actual residents. Likewise, leading Church officials filed applications and received official titles for Church lands under their names. "It was almost an unheard of thing for the holder of the patent to fail to transfer the land to the occupants."

Of course the above procedure of securing titles to their soil was not in complete harmony with either the Pre-emption Act or the Homestead Act. George Thomas concluded:

> The only thing to be said for the violation of the land laws of the United States was that it was done with the full knowledge and at least the connivance of the United States officials and not with the idea of speculation or fraud against the government but to secure title to the soil that the pioneers had reclaimed and made productive by irrigation.[44]

Over twenty years had now passed since the colonization of the Great Basin was begun. A definite Mormon land policy had been developed, and the Saints had become legal owners of the land which they had for so long been cultivating. Meanwhile the Saints had also developed a water policy—distinctively Mormon —in their efforts to utilize the limited supply of moisture to the best possible advantage.

————

[44]Thomas, op. cit., 41.

Chapter XIII

UTILIZATION OF WATER BY THE SAINTS

The Main Features of Mormon Water Policy

In the utilization of the limited supply of water found in the Great Basin, Brigham Young and his co-religionists developed a definite water policy which was distinctly Mormon. "Colorado and California borrowed their early water laws and customs from the miners; Utah made hers first hand."[1]

Some of the main features of the Mormon water policy included the practice of "appropriation" in opposition to the "common-law doctrine of riparian rights,"[2] which they had been acquainted with in the more humid East, and ecclesiastical control of the water supply with a "water master" appointed to supervise each project. Other distinctive features were the use of many small ditches — cooperatively constructed, the cooperative ownership of the water supply with numerous small water companies, and a very wide distribution in ownership of water which resulted in a thorough utilization of all of the canyon streams. In fact, the "public ownership of natural resources, including water, was one of the foundation principles of the State of Deseret, and later of the Territory of Utah."[3] In the words of Elwood Mead:

> Locating in an unknown desert, . . . they had to begin at the foundation in building a commonwealth. . . . The leaders of these pioneers, with wisdom if not inspiration, made agriculture the foundation industry of the people. In this respect, the beginnings of Utah were different from those of every other arid State. Here, agriculture was from the first the principal industry; in many of the others it was, at the outset, a mere incident.[4]

When the Saints first arrived on the sun-baked grounds of the Basin, they knew nothing of the science of irrigation. But the arid condition of the Great West forced them to apply water to the soil before they could plow and plant their seeds.

Brief History of Irrigation

Up to the time of the advent of the Mormons in Utah in July, 1847, "there had been among Anglo-Saxon peoples no sig-

---

[1]Elwood Mead, *Irrigation Institutions*. 220.
[2]*Ibid.*, 62; George Thomas, *The Development of Institutions under Irrigation*, 42-56.
[3]Mead, *op. cit.*, 221.
[4]*Ibid.*, 220-221.

nificant experience with irrigation;" but it was not new to civilization. For centuries before the Mormon trek to the West irrigation had been carried on in Persia, Syria, Palestine, and the Mesopotamian countries. The Egyptian records state that Menes, the first Egyptian king, "extended greatly the irrigation structures of his day." He lived 5,000 years ago. The monuments of Babylon declare that in Abraham's time king Hammurabi "built a great and wonderful canal by which the desert was made into gardens, and an elaborate system of irrigation covered the Babylonian plain."[5]

Irrigation on the American continent also goes back further than historical records. Early in the sixteenth century when the Spaniards first came to the New World, they found the natives practicing irrigation. Some of the canals which the Indians were using dated back to the first traditions of the native population. In Peru, Chile, and Argentina, remains of ancient irrigation structures existed comparable with the best that we have today. In fact, "in some places stupendous irrigation canals may be traced—400 to 500 miles long—far beyond our modern attempts."[6]

Seventy years before the English colony landed at Jamestown, the Spanish missionaries gained a foothold in the valley of the Rio Grande and continued the practice of the natives of irrigating their farms. In the desert lands of North America, such as Arizona and New Mexico, irrigation was also practiced by the modern successors of the ancient Americans—the Indians, and the Spanish settlers.

But "for the beginning of Anglo-Saxon irrigation in this country, we must go to the Salt Lake Valley of Utah."[7] "The Mormons were the first among the Anglo-Saxon peoples to practice the art of irrigation on an extensive scale." Quoting Dr. John A. Widtsoe:

The Mormon pioneers possess the honor of having founded modern irrigation in America, not because of the initial irrigation on July 24, 1847, but because the Mormon people continued the work, dug extensive canals, brought thousands of acres under irrigation, devised methods of irrigation, established laws, rules and usages for the government of populous settlements living "under the ditch,"—in short, because they developed permanent irrigation on a community scale, under the conditions and with knowledge of modern civilization. Irrigation knowledge and inspiration have been drawn by the whole world from the work of the first American irrigation pioneers.[8]

[5]John A. Widtsoe, *Principles of Irrigation Practice*, 445-446.
[6]*Ibid.*, 447-453.
[7]Mead, *op. cit.*, 42; Widtsoe, *op. cit.*, 454-456; Ray P. Teele, *Irrigation in the United States*, 9-10.
[8]Widtsoe, *op cit.*, 455-456; R. H. Hess, "Irrigation Policies," *Cyclopedia of American Agriculture*, IV, 160.

The Saints had no preconceived ideas on water utilization, but the system that they developed was the natural result of trying to make a livelihood in a stubborn environment. Rainfall in the Great Basin region was very scanty, the major portion of the precipitation coming during the winter months in the form of snow. If it had not been for a wise provision of nature—the mountains —few inhabitants would have been able to live in that desert region.

The vanguard company of pioneers under Orson Pratt, July 24, 1847, completely failed in their early attempt to plow the parched and flinty ground of the Salt Lake Valley. After bending a plow point or two, these resourceful frontiersmen dammed off a near-by stream (City Creek), thereby diverting its waters to the thirsty ground. Thus the Mormons began their experimentation in irrigation. The following instructions given to the Saints six weeks after arriving in the Basin by their leader, Brigham Young, show the complete lack of knowledge of irrigation that he and his people had at that time:

Should irrigation be found necessary, the City Creek will yield an abundance of water for that purpose, and it is wisdom that you should provide for any such contingency. We would therefore recommend that you prepare pools, vats, tubs, reservoirs, and ditches at the highest points of land in your field or fields that may be filled during the night and be drawn off to any point you may find necessary, through a tight and permanent gate prepared for that purpose when it shall have become sufficiently warm, so as not to check vegetation.[9]

The Saints had to learn by the trial-and-error method the whole technique of farming under arid conditions. Through their ingenuity, added to a great deal of practical experience, they soon turned this experimentation into noteworthy achievements. The policies which they developed, the marked success with which they met the new conditions, show the great foresight of those frontiersmen.

Mormon Cooperation in Water Utilization

The early experiments in the Salt Lake Valley brought about a water utilization policy which served as a pattern for subsequent practice in all other Mormon colonies. From the journal of Orson Pratt we learn that the first irrigation dams and canals

----

[9]Brigham Young. "Epistle of Brigham Young and the Twelve." *Latter-day Saint Journal History.* September 9, 1847. **Ms.**

in Utah were the result of cooperative work. Quoting Pratt's journal:

We appointed various committees to attend to different branches of business, preparatory to putting in crops, and in about two hours after our arrival we began to plow, and the same afternoon built a dam to irrigate the soil; which at the spot where we were plowing was exceedingly dry.[10]

In Salt Lake City as well as in the other new communities, the most pressing problem confronting the pioneers was that of providing food quickly. It was certainly wisdom for every colony to establish itself on the lands to which water could be easily and quickly diverted. Only by the method of cooperative work were the colonists able to survive. While some of the group plowed and fenced the farm lands, others threw dams across the streams of water and hastily constructed irrigation ditches, thereby bringing water upon the lands in the quickest and least laborious manner. The first irrigation ditches were, therefore, naturally small and built in the most accessible places.

But as the population increased the old ditches had to be enlarged, lengthened, their courses changed, and in many cases, new ditches had to be constructed. More intricate and expensive water systems such as high-line canals were made later as the population increased and as the economic position of the settlement improved. Thus in many of the Utah communities several small canals at different levels supply water to the many fields.

The method followed in construction of irrigation ditches proved in many cases to be an expensive one, yet it was the only policy that could be pursued under those peculiar frontier conditions. "To have constructed a high line canal, covering all the good land as far as the water would flow, would have been, in the long run, more scientific and economical, but for a body of poverty stricken colonists with the meager quantity of supplies on hand, would have meant starvation."[11]

Under the cooperative plan of building irrigation ditches and canals, each man did the amount of work according to the number of acres of land which he intended to cultivate. The upkeep or maintenance of the water system was governed upon the same basic principle. The amount of water allotted to each individual was determined by the amount of work he had done in helping to construct the ditches, and each farmer receiving benefit under a certain water system was required to do a prescribed amount of

----

[10]Orson Pratt. *Journal.* July 23, 1847, Ms.
[11]Thomas, *op. cit.*, 20.

work each year for the maintenance of the canals according to the number of shares of water he owned. Later settlers were privilged to earn shares in the old water ditch by labor performed, or to join others in a new irrigation project.

By the end of the first year the Mormon leaders saw many of their mistakes and failures in the agricultural trial-and-error experiment, yet they were not discouraged. President Young and his counselors expressed themselves as being well-pleased with that year's achievements, especially in regard to the experiment of raising crops by irrigation. They remarked:

> On our arrival in this valley (September, 1848), we found . . . the brethren had succeeded in sowing and planting an extensive variety of seeds, at all seasons, from January to July, on a farm about twelve miles in length, and from one to six in width, including the city plot. . . . The brethren were not sufficiently numerous to fight the crickets, irrigate the crops, and fence the farm of their extensive planting; consequently they suffered heavy losses; though the experiment of last year is sufficient to prove that valuable crops may be raised in this valley by an attentive and judicious management.[12]

About the time of making the above report, the Church leaders began plans for a more systematic irrigation project. President Young proposed to the high council that a large canal be constructed to carry the water from Big Cottonwood Canyon along the east side of the Big Field. He thought that the canal could be made to serve as a fence on the upper side of the field.[13]

The decision was made that the labor of construction of the canal should be apportioned to each man according to the amount of farm land which he had been allotted. Thus the principle of cooperative construction and cooperative ownership of water systems was begun at Salt Lake. This practice set the pattern for later settlements.

The plan devised at Salt Lake in the fall of 1848, and adopted by the other communities later, placed the management of the irrigation water under the control of the ecclesiastical heads, or bishops.[14] The residents of each ward, under the direction of their bishops, constructed ditches leading the water to each block in their respective wards. The building of the principal canals and ditches carrying water to all of the wards was under the direction of the high council, who allotted the work out to the bishops, making them responsible for its completion. Besides being the spiritual heads of the colonies, the bishops directed the construction of canals, the allotment of farm lands and water rights, as

[12]*Latter-day Saint Journal History*, October 2, 1848, Ms.
[13]*Ibid.*, September 30, 1848.
[14]*Ibid.*, April 5, 1849, Ms.

well as the building of bridges, churches, and forts. Therefore, the bishops in early Utah history were very important factors in the Mormon water system.

In the Utah communities, the small canyon streams were appropriated by individuals or groups of individuals, but the larger streams necessitated the united efforts of a community, and the water was used as the main irrigation project for the entire settlement. Laterals or branch ditches were taken out of the main canal below the mouth of the canyon. These ditches were further divided until it came down to the ditch of the individual farmer. Through cooperative effort, all of these canals and ditches were constructed. Then the water was used in rotation, which gave a rather large stream of water to be used by each farmer once every several days.

Each year, early in the spring before the snow began to melt on the mountains thereby bringing to the valleys streams of water, each community cooperatively cleaned and repaired all of their irrigation ditches. Each man was assessed his portion of labor according to the number of shares of water that he owned. The water-master took charge of this work. A committee estimated the cost of cleaning and repairing the canals. Then each man was notified relative to his portion of the work which he was to do at a stipulated wage per man and team. Practically always the farmers did their own work and very little labor was hired.

From the beginning of Mormon history in the Great Basin, canals, ditches, and water were owned by the water users. Not only the upkeep of the water system was carried on by them, but the management of the irrigation companies was in their hands They in turn elected officers, the most important of whom was the water-master. Every irrigation project had its water-master, who, if the system was large enough, devoted his full time to seeing that the water was fairly distributed. Some of his duties were to see that dams, headgates, and ditches were kept in proper order and to notify each water owner when to take the water. Bolton made the following conclusions:

Irrigation was one of the signal contributions of the Mormons to the upbuilding of the Great West. Without it, starvation was as certain as death in old age. So the Mormons built reservoirs in the mountains, ran ditches and great canals across the valleys, and poured the life giving waters of the Wasatch upon the thirsty soil of the sunbaked desert, causing it to bloom like the rose.[15]

— — — —

[15]Herbert E. Bolton, "The Mormons in the Opening of the Great West," *The Utah Genealogical and Historical Magazine*, XVII, 69.

By 1869, according to a report to the Utah Legislature, the Saints had constructed 215 canals of a total length of about one thousand miles, at an estimated cost of $1,700 per mile. The building of sub-ditches had cost almost as much as the main canals. Most of the water, which irrigated 167,000 acres of land, was cooperatively owned. In the words of George Thomas:

> The farmers supplied the labor themselves to build the canals and reclaim the land. So that the thousands of miles of canals of early Utah were built without bonded indebtedness or indebtedness of any kind. They were built by the farmers, owned by the farmers, and operated by the farmers. In fact they constitute one of the greatest and most successful community or cooperative undertakings in the history of America.[16]

From the foregoing evidence it is certain that cooperative ownership, wide distribution, and thorough utilization of water became an established policy early in Utah colonial history. There was an adequate supply of water for the Saints who arrived in the Great Basin during the early years of Mormon land settlement, but conditions would not remain that way as the inhabitants of the Basin increased. So Brigham Young, anticipating a large and compact population—just as many people as the mountain streams could support, early adopted the policy of prohibiting anyone from taking more water than he had immediate use for. Thus his water policy, as well as his land policy, was formulated to promote the welfare of the community in preference to that of the individual and to insure a productive future for his people. Over thirty years after his death, the policy he inaugurated persisted and it still determines the distribution of water in Utah. Statistics compiled in 1910 show the following condition at that date:

> Out of a total irrigated area of 999,410 acres in Utah, individual and partnership canals irrigated 222,448 acres, and cooperative canals, 687,260 or 91.1 per cent of the entire irrigated area of the State at a cost of $11.22 an acre. The average size of these irrigated farms is 32.9 acres.[17]

DOCTRINE OF RIPARIAN RIGHTS AND DOCTRINE OF APPROPRIATION

Another important feature in the Mormon water policy was the laws which Brigham and his people enacted to control water distribution and ownership. The settlers of Utah came from the East or humid part of the United States. They were familiar with the water laws of that section of the country. Those laws

---

[16]Thomas, op. cit., 27.
[17]Ibid., 27-28.

had originated in England where it was necessary to take water off the land rather than to bring it on. The law of riparian rights governed their use of water.

According to the provisions of that system, the owner of land bordering on a lake or stream had the right to have the stream or lake remain as nature had placed it. But the Mormon colonizers of the Great Basin soon recognized that the law of riparian rights was an unsound principle for an arid country. They absolutely abrogated that doctrine and acted "on the theory that the waters of the streams and the lakes of the territory belong to the public and are subject to appropriation by individuals or to grants by the legislature or subordinate bodies created by it."[18]

The adoption of the doctrine of appropriation was necessary in the arid West if the people were to survive. Water was the least abundant natural element of productivity which made it the most fundamental and most desired object of property. The fact that the Mormon colonizers of an entirely new and untried country abrogated the doctrine of riparian right and substituted for it the doctrine of economical and beneficial use of water is indicative of the wisdom, sagacity and initiative of the founders of Utah.

EARLY UTAH IRRIGATION LAWS

From the time the first pioneer group arrived in the Basin, the Church leaders approved the doctrine of the diversion of waters from streams for beneficial use by the people. Finally, laws were enacted to sustain that doctrine and practice. In the words of Elwood Mead: "The system adopted by the territorial legislature at its first season in 1852 contains some of the best features of the highest development of irrigation law as it is now understood."[19]

The following extract is quoted from Section 38 of a statue of the first Utah territorial Legislature of 1852:

The county court shall have control of all timber, water privileges, or any water course or creek, to grant mill sites, and exercise such powers as in their judgment shall best preserve the timber and subserve the interest of the settlement in the distribution of water for irrigation or other purposes. Grants of rights held under legislative authority shall not be interfered with.

For twenty-eight years the water resources of the Great Basin were controlled under the law of 1852. That act gave to the county court full and complete control over the waters of that county.

[18]*Ibid.*, 44.
[19]Mead, *op. cit.*, 220-221.

Based upon the theory that the waters belonged to the public, the purpose for the court control was to distribute irrigation streams as widely as possible. However, in 1880 a law was passed which shifted the theory of waters belonging to the State to that of private ownership of the stream and lakes. The latter statute was more elaborate than the first but in some respects inferior.

The Mormon colonizers of the Great West showed exceptional ability in the practical use and distribution of water, but they' did not do as well in granting and recording titles to water claims.

But the point of importance in this study is to recognize the empire building ingenuity and wisdom of the founders of Utah in their setting aside the long adhered to doctrine of riparian rights and adopting the doctrine of appropriation of available waters for the economic benefit of the people as a whole. This doctrine of appropriation was sustained in the law of 1852 and served as the basis for the building of a commonwealth in the arid West by Brigham Young and his associates.

Chapter XIV

BRIGHAM YOUNG AND HOME INDUSTRY

Brigham Young and a Self-Supporting Economy—Need to Develop Mormon Industries

Throughout his entire administration, Brigham Young lost no opportunity to help his people to be self-supporting. He maintained that "the bread and butter problem" was a vital part of the Gospel of Jesus Christ. Mormonism "seeks to make people prosperous and happy here and now, not merely to point their eyes skyward. It would make the will of God prevail in this world as well as in heaven."[1] Brigham's preparations before leaving Nauvoo were with the foregoing purpose in mind. He wanted the Saints to be absolutely independent and to develop every available resource.

Even while camped at Winter Quarters on the banks of the Missouri, Brother Brigham advised the building of a flour mill. In announcing, on January 7, 1847, that the mill was ready for operation, the high council stated:

> This would not have been were it not that Brother Brigham had kindly offered the council to superintend the whole work and see that the establishment was put in operation. This he did solely for the benefit of this people, and it has thrown an immense burden upon his shoulders, which in justice ought to have been borne off by other hands, but the greater toil, the greater glory. Our President does not stick at anything that tends to advance the gathering of Israel or promote the cause of Zion in these last days; he sleeps with one eye open and one foot out of bed, and when anything is wanted he is on hand, and his counselors are all of one heart with him in all things.[2]

Selecting as they did an isolated home in the midst of a desert a thousand miles from civilization, President Young and his associates realized that a self-sufficing economy was more than a matter of policy. It meant life or death to the people. Later, distances were so great and freight so expensive that it was imperative for the Mormons to supply all their needs by means of home industry. This new country offered unlimited opportunity for development of old and experimentation in new industries.

Before his return to Winter Quarters and upon leaving the first group of Mormon pioneers in the Great Basin in the fall of

---

[1]John Henry Evans, *The Heart of Mormonism*, 161.
[2]*Latter-day Saint Journal History*, January 7, 1847, Ms.

1847, Brigham made sure that they were amply instructed on providing for themselves in their new home. He gave the Saints the following written order:

We feel that it is necessary to urge upon you the importance of planting and sowing in their appropriate time and season, every kind of grain, fruit and vegetable, that will yield sustenance to man and beast. We have no doubt that your past experience and present necessities will prompt you to the most active exertion on this subject and that you will make this your principal business this year, not forgetting the flax, cotton, or any kind of seed at your command, from which you may raise those commodities that are absolutely indispensible for your future clothing, and there is and will be in your midst means for such abundant manufactures as soon as the new material can be produced. The culture of rice should not be neglected.[3]

In the same letter Brother Brigham advised the Saints to plant their grain and other crops early—even before spring—as an experiment to see if crops could be ripened in the valley before the "summer drought should demand the labor of irrigation." He told them to keep an accurate record of the manner of sowing, planting and cultivating, and of the daily weather, in order that their experiences might teach them the best methods of surviving in this untried country. Brigham's instructions were detailed and, some people feel, rather high-handed; but they were practical, and the Saints always obeyed them to the letter if they were able. Following are further instructions that the Mormon Colonizer gave to his people:

Not neglecting your plowing and sowing, when the rains commence this fall, it is desirable that one or more sawmills should be put in operation as speedily as possible; place should also be provided for the carding machine by the time of sheepshearing, and a grainmill will be indispensable for the comfort and convenience of the city as soon as grain shall ripen; therefore, we shall expect that those who are interested in these things will use all diligence in giving every branch of business its proper attention at its appropriate time. . .

Winter . . . will be a convenient time for the farmers to ditch and fence and enclose and prepare for their spring labor, and the mechanics will not want for occupation until the city is supplied with all the instruments of husbandry, machinery for domestic manufactures, household furniture, mills, etc., sufficient for the accommodation of many thousands.[4]

Drew Industries from the Entire World to Build Zion

In his dreams and plans for the establishment of a Mormon commonwealth in the Great Basin, Brigham considered that the

---

[3]Brigham Young, "First general Epistle . . . to the Saints." *Latter-day Saint Journal History*, September 8, 1847, Ms.
[4]*Ibid.*

whole world was not too large as a storehouse from which to draw the choicest of all seeds, plants, new machinery and inventions. The Mormon missionaries served as excellent collectors of the good things of the world. Although Brigham Young had selected an isolated spot for his followers, he did not intend their culture and civilization to remain one whit behind the very best in the world insofar as he was able to shape it. His ideal included a beautiful city as well as a prosperous one, and eventually a multitude of such cities. Even six weeks after arriving in the Salt Lake Valley, the Mormon leader advised his people:

> While it is your duty to devote the coming year to the raising of such articles as are most necessary for food and clothing, we wish you to bear in mind continually that the valley in which you are located promises in prospect to be fruitful in many things and that it is your duty at every opportunity that presents to stretch forth your hands to the four corners of the earth and gather choice seeds of every kind of grain, of vegetables, of fruits, or flowers or shrubbery, even everything which will tend to nourish or clothe the body, gratify the appetite, gladden the heart, or please the eye of man: so that your city can be so adorned and beautified that it will be a good desirable location for all good men, secure the admiration of angels, even a paradise of the world where Gods will delight to visit.[5]

From this time forward Brigham Young repeatedly addressed letters called "general epistles" to the Saints throughout the world, as well as private letters to presidents of missions and missionaries in foreign lands, urging them to keep watch for anything new or valuable that would be of use to the Saints in the Basin.

These instructions had the desired results. For example: the "Deseret Iron Company" was organized in England; machinery was shipped from Europe for the manufacture of sugar; the silk industry was studied in France, and an effort was made to produce silk in Utah; and cotton seeds were brought from the Southern States to the Great Basin. In fact, choice materials and expert workmen were gathered from various parts of the world and sent to Utah from time to time whenever Brother Brigham informed the mission presidents that he wished a particular industry to be founded. Oceans, therefore, were no barriers to the power and influence of the Mormon Colonizer. The following extracts are taken from some of the general epistles:

> And to all the Saints in any country bordering upon the Atlantic, we would say, come immediately and prepare to go West—bringing with you all kinds of choice seeds, of grains, vegetables, fruits, shrubbery, trees, and

---

[5]*Ibid.*

vines; . . . also, the best stock of beasts, bird and fowl of every kind; also, the best tools of every description, and machinery for spinning, or weaving, dressing cotton, wool, and flax, and silk, etc., or models and descriptions of the same, by which they can construct them; and the same in relation to all kinds of farming utensils and husbandry, such as corn shellers, grain threshers and cleaners, smut machines, mills and every implement and article within their knowledge that shall tend to promote the comfort, health, happiness, or prosperity of the people.[6]

The Saints were also asked to bring their gold, silver, copper, zinc, tin, brass, iron, ivory and precious jewels, and their curiosities of science and art, in order that they might build beautiful cities and adorn the "House of the Lord." The converts and missionaries were exceptionally responsive to the church leader's instructions. Among the numerous articles forwarded to the Mormon Mecca were two shepherd dogs sent by one of the Saints from Europe to be President Young's personal property.

While developing the physical features of his empire, the Mormon leader did not neglect the spiritual and intellectual interests of the people and made little effort to distinguish one from the other. It has already been told how each community built churches and schoolhouses as soon as its members had erected enough shelter for protection from the Indians and from the cold weather. In 1850 Brigham Young made the following request:

We earnestly solicit the cooperation of all the Saints, and particularly the elders in all nations, to gather, as they may have the opportunity, books in all languages, and on every science, apparatus, and rare specimens of art and nature, and everything that may tend to beautify and make useful; and forward or bring the same to the Regents of our University [University of Deseret, founded in 1850], for the benefit of all such as may hereafter seek intelligence at their hands.[7]

Certain public works in the Basin had to be constructed before the church leaders could stress any particular industry. There were bridges, roads, irrigation canals, mills, and public and church buildings to be built. This work was done under the direction of the Church.

"Temple Block Public Works"

Then came the opportunity to provide temporary employment for the stream of proselytes arriving in the Basin each year. By 1850 shops of various kinds on the Temple Block were opened in

⁶Brigham Young, "Second general Epistle . . . to the Saints," Manuscript No. 080-8 No. 7394, December 23, 1847, Ms.
⁷Brigham Young, "Third general Epistle . . . to the Saints," Millennial Star, XII, 246.

MORMON HANDICRAFTS—FRIENDSHIP QUILT

WINDING REEL

RAG CARPET

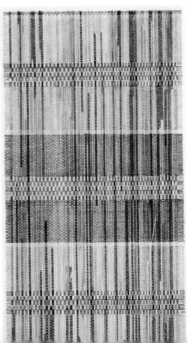

DESERET STORE AND TITHING OFFICE, SALT LAKE CITY

order to take care of many new immigrants who were of the European industrial classes. The "Temple Block Public Works" did much to stimulate the development of industry in Utah.

VALUE OF HARD WORK

President Young was continuously instructing the Saints on the importance of work—an abundance of hard work—in making themselves self-supporting, prosperous and happy. "True charity to a poor family or person consists in placing them in a situation in which they can support themselves " was Brigham's philosophy.[8] He urged:

Deplorable indeed must be the situation of that people whose sons are not trained in the practice of every useful avocation, and whose daughters do not mingle in the hum of industry. . . .

It will become us to give the proper direction to that labor, to that untiring and persevering effort which so happily characterize the history of this people.

The enjoyment of a free and independent people can be accomplished only through this principle. Produce what you consume; draw from the native element the necessities of life; permit no vitiated taste to lead you into the indulgence of expensive luxuries, which can only be obtained by involving yourselves in debt; let home industry produce every article of home consumption. . . .[9]

Fathers, teach your children to practice agriculture, or some useful mechanical trade.

Mothers of Israel, you also are called upon to bring up your daughters to pursue some useful avocation for a sustenance, that when they shall become the wives of the elders of Israel, who are frequently called upon missions, or to devote their time and attention to the things of the kingdom, they may be able to sustain themselves and their offspring.[10]

DOMESTIC INDUSTRIES

It is hardly necessary to state that the pioneer women of the church followed his advice, carrying on every industry which was adapted to the home. They washed and carded the wool, spun the yarn, wove the cloth, and made the wearing apparel for the family, and furthermore performed all necessary household duties under very adverse conditions. Early in February, 1852, President Young wrote in his journal: "We are going in for home manufactures pretty extensively. My own family alone have this season manufactured over five hundred yards of cloth, and the homemade frequently makes its appearance in our streets and in our gather-

8Cited by Preston Nibley, "Brigham Young, the Man and His Work," *Deseret News,* March 30, 1935

9Brigham Young, *Latter-day Saint Journal History,* January 5, 1852, Ms.

10Brigham Young, "Fourteenth general Epistle . . . to the Saints," *ibid.,* December 10, 1856.

ings."[11] He also observed carefully the efforts of his people in domestic manufacturing, as evidenced by the following statement: "Sister Hulda Duncan of Davis county, between August 5, 1854, and January 27, 1855, wove 194 yards of jeans, 508 of linsey and 64 of flannel, besides doing other work. Much cloth of the kinds named, and large quantities of rag carpeting have also been manufactured the past year in Utah. This was done by looms and spinning wheels of a very primitive character."[12] Again, Brigham remarked:

> The Saints of the most high God should sustain themselves by their industry, economy, and sobriety; their health by their virtue, prudence, cleanliness, faith and observances of the holy ordinances. . . . Let us bestow our charity, not so much to feed the hungry and naked, as to cause them to feed and clothe themselves.[13]

The development of domestic manufacturing and other industries was one of his greatest concerns. One might almost call it Brigham's pet hobby. His numerous sermons are replete with words of wisdom on this subject. In January, 1852, he advised:

> The question is, what is most needed now, at the present moment, the present year, by the Saints, to bring about their most desirable of all objects, a celestial salvation or eternal happiness? We answer, without hesitation, *domestic manufactures, homemade goods, implements, materials and useables of all kinds that we cannot do without.* . . .
> "And must we go to work with our own hands to make, and build, and manufacture everything we want for our own use?" Yes, you must do it, and that forthwith, or do a great deal worse! "But may we not go to California and get some gold, and pay off our debts, and then we can buy what we want and be independent again, and go ahead as usual?" No! Saints you cannot go to California, as you have done in years gone by, and retain the fellowship of the Church. . . .
> It is labor that makes a people rich, and our Father knew this when he gave the commandment for all to be *diligent* in business; and required of his Saints that they should wear apparel of their own make, in these last days, and that the beauty of their apparel should be the workmanship of their own hands. . . .
> There is scarce a thing that can be named, which is indispensibly necessary for our growing Territory, but that can be produced by our own industry within one year. Suppose we cannot raise the cotton, we can raise the flax, spin, weave, and wear it, which is a good substitute. Suppose we cannot get wool enough to keep us warm, we can get furs to make up the remainder, and not sell them for a song, suffer them to be wasted; and every family can kill, tan and make their own clothing from wild beasts.[14]

[11]Brigham Young, *History of Brigham Young*, February, 1852, "pp." 15, 16, Ms.
[12]*Ibid.*, 19.
[13]Young, "Fourteenth general Epistle . . .," *op. cit.*
[14]*Latter-day Saint Journal History*, January 24, 1852, Ms.

Brother Brigham not only urged the people to practice home industry but while governor of the territory used his influence to make government appropriations for the establishments of useful industries in the Mormon settlements. January 5, 1852, the Governor's message shows his great concern on this subject:

I have no hesitation in saying that our true interest is and will be most wisely consulted in domestic manufacturing to the exclusion of almost every article of imported goods. Our clothing of every description, sugar, candles, soap, leather, crockery, paper, glass, nails, much of the hardware, castings, steel, and many other articles, for which our merchants continually drain the country of money, might be manufactured just as well at home, within our own limits, thereby furnishing lucrative employment to the many artisans of every description, who are constantly flocking hither, and form the basis of a free and independent State, that can in no other way be accomplished. . . . I do therefore most earnestly and sincerely hope, that all needful and necessary encouragement may be given in protective legislation, as well as in appropriations, as shall be conducive to the accomplishment of such desirable results.[15]

Brigham H. Roberts described President Young's policy on domestic manufacturing in the following words:

The policy of encouraging domestic manufactures adopted by the "State of Deseret" was continued under the regime of the territory of Utah. . . . Both in the general epistles of the Presidency of the Church and in his messages as governor, Brigham Young emphasized the importance of establishing home manufactures; and in these documents notes the advancement made in these industries. . . .

Encouragement of domestic manufactures, then may be written down as the policy of Brigham Young—a policy most willingly accepted and followed by the Latter-day Saints—both as President of the Church and governor of the territory; but always . . . he was opposed to such governmental aid, or such combinations of capital, as would result in monopoly against labor.[16]

Deseret Agricultural Manufacturing Society

Accordingly, in 1856 the "Deseret Agricultural and Manufacturing Society" was organized by a law enacted by the Legislative Assembly and signed by Governor Young. Its purpose was to promote the "arts of domestic industry, and to encourage the production of articles from the native elements in this Territory." Annual exhibits of the best agricultural products and manufactured articles were held with the view of stimulating the Saints to industrial pursuits, and premiums were given for the best examples in each

----

[15]*Ibid.*, January 5, 1852.
[16]Brigham H. Roberts, *A Comprehensive History of the Church*, IV, 24, 26.

field. An appropriation of fifteen hundred dollars was made to start the project.

Trouble Between Mormons and Gentiles, and Establishing of Cooperative Stores

But in spite of all the efforts made by President Brigham Young and his associates to establish a self-sufficient economy for his people through home industry, adverse conditions prevented their efforts from being one hundred per cent successful. Numerous difficulties and obstacles were encountered, but only the major ones can be mentioned here.

Hardly had the Saints established themselves in the Great West before the Gentiles began to settle in their midst. The old troubles with non-Mormons which characterized so much of their pre-Utah history were enacted again in their new home in the West. The beginning of this irritation of any marked importance occurred shortly following the arrival of the first federal appointees of the Territory of Utah in 1851. Added to this trouble were the difficulties which arose between the government of the United States and the Saints over the question of the Mormons' doctrine and practice of "plural marriage." By 1856 it had become a political issue in national politics. A year later a federal army of 2,500 soldiers was en route to Utah. The soldiers stayed in the Basin until the outbreak of the Civil War.

Even after the withdrawal of the army, strife continued between the Saints and the federal government. The Mormons' practice of plural marriage was the primary cause of this trouble. In 1862 Congress passed an "anti-bigamy law" in opposition to the practice of polygamy. However, this law was not put into effect immediately, as President Lincoln's policy was to let the Saints alone. But after the passage of this law, a long and bitter struggle continued between "gentiles" and Mormons in the Utah Territory and further legislation was enacted against the latter's religious practices.

Other fundamental points of irritation existed—i.e., continuous bitterness prevailed between church members and Gentile territorial officials, and, as a general rule, Mormons and non-Mormons were antagonistic toward each other. But it is only fair to mention that some of the more honorable of the Gentiles got along splendidly with the Saints.

As days and years passed, a number of non-Mormon merchants established their places of business in Salt Lake City. But as bitterness and rivalry between Gentiles and the Saints increased, one of their main channels of expression was in the field of industry. President Young, in a communication to the Gentile merchants dated December 21, 1866, made it clear that Mormons were willing and happy to trade with non-Mormons if their relationship toward each other could be conducted on a Christian basis. But he definitely objected to having the Saints give their trade to those Gentiles and apostates who were trying to destroy both himself and the church. Quoting from Brother Brigham:

> It matters not what a man's creed is . . . he will receive kindness and friendship from us, and we have not the least objection to doing business with him; if in his dealings he acts in accordance with the principles of right and deports himself as a good, law-abiding citizen should.[17]

The Mormon President instructed the Saints in a discourse two days later as follows:

> We advise you to pass by the shops and stores of your enemies and let them alone, but give your means into the hands of men who are honest men, honorable men, and upright men—men who will deal justly and truly with all. Shall we deal with Jews? Yes. With those who call themselves Gentiles? Certainly. We calculate to continue to deal with them.[18]

It was during this period of strife that the Saints established throughout the various settlements a chain of cooperative stores—Zion's Cooperative Mercantile Institution, incorporated 1869, being the parent institution. They were established to make it possible for church members to trade with each other rather than with their enemies. Brigham Young and his people claimed that it was "cooperation for self-defense." Another purpose of cooperation was to keep home industry thriving in the face of the influx of cheaper states' goods brought into the territory with the coming of the Union Pacific railway. Of course the cooperative system extended to manufacturing as well as to merchandising.

No doubt commendable results were obtained by the Saints in President Young's time in establishing home industries. Two years prior to his death (1875), the United States census showed that Utah industries alone, not counting mining, were producing nearly $5,000,000 worth of merchandise annually. It is true that many of the early industries of Utah met with failure while others attained a marked degree of success.

There is a possibility that if Brigham Young's ideas on home

---

[17]Cited in Joseph Fielding Smith, *Essentials in Church History*. 537.
[18]*Ibid.*, 538.

industry had been rigorously adhered to by all Mormons—both during his time and down to the present day—the Saints of God would be enjoying today considerable more economic independence and prosperity. But a variety of contributing factors have resulted in the ownership of many Utah industries falling into the hands of Gentiles and in many cases into the hands of large industrial corporations not located in the state. Our story does not deal with that phase of Mormon history but must close with the presentation of Brigham Young's views on home industry and his efforts to make his people completely independent in their new home in the Great West. His were the views and efforts of a remarkable leader, a keen organizer, a devout and unselfish prophet of God, exerting every energy for the temporal and spiritual salvation of his people.

Chapter XV

EARLY INDUSTRIES IN UTAH

First Sawmills and Gristmills in Utah

In view of Brigham Young's policy on home industry, presented in the last chapter, it is not surprising to find that in early Utah history attempts were made to establish a great variety of industries, some of which were adaptable to conditions of the Great West while others were not. The establishing of industries began almost immediately upon arriving in the Basin.

Machinery for sawmills and gristmills was brought across the plains by the first pioneer groups in 1847. According to Archibald Gardner's journal, his mill was the first to saw lumber in the Salt Lake Valley. The Gardner family arrived in the Basin on October 1, 1847, and settled that winter north of the city at the Warm Springs. In the words of Mr. Gardner:

> I had only two wagons crossing the plains and broke one of them up to make the crank and other irons for a sawmill which we set up at the Warm Springs in the fall. The flume for it was a log hollowed out. I brought two saws for an up-an-down-saw mill with me across the plains. Due to the water being warm there was not sufficient power to turn the wheel. The men helped it around and three boards were turned out. We set the mill up at the grove on Mill Creek, seven miles south next spring. It was what was termed a "muley" mill (the up-and-down saw type) and was operated by an overshot wheel. The mill was built without nails. Wooden pins and mortices were used instead. All shafts, bearings, cog wheels, etc., were of wood, our mountain maple. Here we turned out the first lumber sawed in Utah.[1]

It was probably winter or rather early in the spring when the Gardner mill was established, as an entry of March 6, 1848, in the *Journal History of the Church* stated:

> Brother Chase has a saw mill in operation on the spring a short distance from the Pioneer Garden. Archibald and Robert Gardner have a saw mill already sawing on Mill Creek. Brother Amasa Russell has leave to put up a frame for the carding machine near Gardner's saw mill.[2]

Gristmills were also put into operation shortly after the arrival of the Saints in the Basin. Quoting from Archibald Gardner's journal: "We next erected the second flour mill in Utah, 1849.

[1]Cited in Delila Gardner Hughes, *The Life of Archibald Gardner*, 42.
[2]*Journal History of the Church*, March 6, 1848, Ms.

Brother John Neff's being the first. The machinery for Neff's mill had been brought with the first company of Pioneers."[3]

As soon as each new community was founded by the Saints, sawmills and gristmills were built according to the needs of the people, as all lumber and flour had to be supplied locally in those pioneer days.

DOMESTIC INDUSTRIES

Brigham Young's policy of encouraging domestic manufactures and the ingenuity of the Saints when necessity forced them to supply their own needs resulted in a variety of industries springing up in all the new Mormon communities. On April 7, 1851, in a general epistle, the Mormon Colonizer numerated some of the noteworthy accomplishments in domestic manufactures and encouraged the Saints to continue their good work. In the words of Brother Brigham:

"The Deseret Pottery" is in successful operation, some good light yellow ware was drawn from the kiln, June 27th, and white ware is soon expected. It is anticipated that the valley materials for making crockery and china ware, will be equal to any other place; and that the pottery will soon be able to supply this market. Good potters are wanted. A carding machine is in operation and doing extensive business in this valley; also one in Utah [Valley], and others in progress.

There are four grain and five saw mills in operation, or nearly completed in Great Salt Lake county; also two grain and two saw mills in San Pete county; one grain and one saw mill in Iron county; and one saw mill in Tooele county; and an increasing desire and exertion to promote domestic manufactures prevails throughout the territory.[4]

According to the governor's message to the legislature in December, 1852, considerable advancement had been made in industry in the five years of Mormon residence in the Basin. He reported:

Domestic Manufactures, I am happy to state, are in flourishing condition; considerable quantities of leather and crockery having found their way into market, and a large amount of clothing has been made, principally by the hands of the "good housewife", who thereby adds dignity to her station and reflects credit and honor upon her household. Specimens of iron have also been forwarded from the works in Iron county, which for the first run, was exceedingly flattering. It separates well, but owing to the sulphur in the coal not being sufficiently extracted, was thereby injured; but a little experience in combining materials, and continued effort, it is believed, will soon produce that article in great abundance, and of good quality. . . . I am also happy to announce the arrival in our territory, of the machinery for the manufacture of sugar from the beet. The machinery, and operators who have come

---

[3]Hughes, op. cit.
[4]Brigham Young, "Sixth general Epistle . . . to the Saints," Millennial Star, XIV, 23-24.

together from the "Old World," and being under the direction of energetic, enterprising, and able men, will doubtless soon furnish an abundant supply of that article, for the wants of the people.[5]

SUGAR INDUSTRY

The supply of sugar brought from the States was soon consumed, and the ingenuity of these frontiersmen was taxed in making a substitute. A common substitute was provided by cooking parsnips, carrots, or beets until a thick syrup was formed. Watermelon sugar was also produced. Then sugar cane seed was brought to Utah from which cane was grown and the juice crushed out for molasses. Often the portion of this substance which hardened in the bottom of the barrel was used for sugar.

None of these substitutes completely satisfied the Mormon leaders. As early as 1851 John Taylor was studying the beet sugar industry in France from the angle of production possibilities in Utah. President Young had admonished the elders sent on missions in 1849-50 to be alert in the observation of industries and enterprises that could possibly be established in the Great Basin. Elder Taylor received a letter from President Young urging him "to get ideas and machinery if necessary to send to 'Deseret' to further and build up her industries."[6] Brother Taylor and his companion, Philip De La Mare, immediately visited the sugar beet district at Arrac, in northern France. After a careful investigation and study of the factories, machinery, and soil conditions, the conclusion was reached that the sugar beet industry could be carried on successfully in Utah.

Thereupon John Taylor and four companions organized the "Deseret Manufacturing Company" in Liverpool (1851), with a capital stock of $60,000.00. To Elder Taylor was assigned $10,000 of the stock for being the chief promoter of the company. He contracted and supervised the manufacturing of the machinery, which work was done by the firm of Faucett, Preston and Company, at a cost of $12,500. "It is claimed for it that it was first class machinery, the best that could be obtained, and certainly it was the product of one of the most reliable and foremost manufacturers of machinery in England. Such was its weight that it required over 200 yoke of cattle to haul it across the plains to Deseret."

"Many were the difficulties encountered in carrying this first sugar plant to 'Deseret'—the first beet sugar plant for Utah, and also, so far as known, imported into or erected within the United

[5]*Deseret News*, December 25, 1852.
[6]Philip De La Mare, *History of the Deseret Manufacturing Co.*, Ms.

States."[7] First, and unexpectedly, there was the payment of a $5,000 government tariff at New Orleans. Then the fifty-two wagons, manufactured at Omaha for the purpose of bringing the machinery across the plains, broke down shortly after leaving Fort Leavenworth. They were replaced by forty heavy-weight Santa Fe wagons, which proved to be strong enough to convey the sugar beet machinery to Utah.

Finally, in the Governor's message to the legislature in December, 1852, Brigham Young announced the arrival in the territory of some of the best machinery obtainable in Europe for the manufacture of beet sugar, accompanied by "energetic, enterprising, and able men" from the "Old World." Also five hundred bushels of beet seed had arrived with the machinery and European workmen.[8]

Prospects looked very encouraging at first,[9] but when the machinery was put into operation the workmen were unable to refine sugar from the beets, because the soil in Utah had changed the beets' chemical makeup. The sugar company was unable to carry on the enterprise, so it was eventually dissolved and taken over by the Mormon Church. Brigham Young and his associates felt that such an important industry should not be allowed to fail if there was a way to make it succeed. "Before them were visions of a mighty commonwealth and their faith in the future was firmly supported by a determination to build it for themselves."[10] The machinery for making sugar was set up in Provo. Later it was moved, being placed in an adobe building erected on Parley's Creek southeast of Salt Lake. That section of the valley thereafter became known as Sugar House.

Several fruitless attempts to refine sugar were made in the fall of 1853. The fact that new experienced workmen were brought from Europe did not assure the success of the enterprise.

For two more years tons of beets were raised and gallons of molasses made from the beets, but the expert sugar makers from Europe, as well as local helpers, did not succeed in making the sugar crystallize. "At least one hundred thousand dollars had been spent in a desperate effort to produce sugar from the sugar beet, but without success."[11]

Finally the attention of the church leaders was diverted into other channels, and the beet sugar industry was not revived again

――――
[7]Brigham H. Roberts, A Comprehensive History of the Church, III, 396-397.
[8]Millennial Star, XV, 105.
[9]Deseret News, October 16, 1852.
[10]John G. Crook, The Development of Early Industry and Trade in Utah, 79, Ms.
[11]Ibid., 81.

SUGAR FACTORY AT SUGAR HOUSE, UTAH, ERECTED 1853

COTTON MILL AT WASHINGTON, UTAH, ERECTED 1866

until shortly after the death of Brother Brigham. With increased understanding of chemistry, there was discovered a method of changing the alkaline content of the beets so that the sugar would crystallize. From that time, sugar made from beets has been one of the major industries of Utah.

Although on the surface it may appear that the attempt made in colonial Utah to manufacture sugar from beets was expensive, and to a certain extent a failure, yet "this is a strong testimony to the financial and moral and physical courage, and the largeness of views, and the spirit of daring enterprise of the Latter-day Saint men of early Utah."[12] The qualities shown in their endeavor at this enterprise are the same qualities which caused them to conquer the desert and leave their names in history as great colonizers, practical people, and men of vision.

Even after the first effort to produce sugar from beets in Utah failed, sugar cane continued to be grown extensively. In 1855 Richard Margetts made a cast iron roller to crush the juice from the cane in order to make sugar and molasses. "Sugar mills were brought by ox teams in the fifties, and Wilford Woodruff had one on his farm, and was producing sugar and molasses for the market in 1857."[13]

Cotton Industry

The first attempt at raising cotton in Utah was in 1851 in the Salt Lake Valley. But it was only in the Dixie country that cotton was successfully grown. In 1854, at Santa Clara, one quart of seed was planted, yielding enough lint to produce thirty yards of cloth. "A sample of this cloth was exhibited in Governor Brigham Young's office in Great Salt Lake City (1855), and Major Hunt, Indian Agent, a Virginian, declared it was as good as any he had ever seen."[14] Cotton production at Santa Clara had increased so much within the next two years that Zodoc K. Judd made a cotton gin.

At the April conference, 1857, Brigham called twenty-eight families, composed mostly of converts from the Southern States, to settle Washington, four miles from Saint George. They were joined by fifty families from San Bernardino that fall and were very successful in raising cotton. In January, 1858, Brigham Young selected a group of colonists to settle on the Virgin River for the specified purpose of establishing a cotton farm. At Saint George a large cotton mill was built by President Young in 1866. Smaller

[12]Roberts, op. cit., 401-402.
[13]Levi Edgar Young, Founding of Utah, 198.
[14]Saint George Stake, 1847-1873, 16, Ms.

factories were put into operation at Toquerville, Parowan, and other towns. "Cotton became so plentiful that it was shipped to California."[15]

FLAX, SILK, AND WOOLEN INDUSTRIES

Attempts were made—successfully and otherwise—to establish numerous other industries. Flax raising in Utah was begun in 1847 and continued for several years. Governor Young secured mulberry trees from France in 1855, upon which silkworms were raised. Some silk was produced, but, as the climate proved unfavorable, silk went into the list of unsuccessful experiments.

One of the most important industries in the Basin was the production of wool and the manufacture of woolen goods. During the first few years in Utah the making of woolen cloth was carried on domestically by the women. A public carding machine was set up just south of Salt Lake City in 1848, a step toward establishing factories. In 1852 the Utah Legislature responded to Governor Young's request for the development of industries by appropriating $2,000 for a woolen factory on the Jordan River. Brother Brigham and two others were to "award premiums to persons who manufactured the largest number of articles for practical use." That same summer Matthew Gaunt's mill produced the first factory-made woolen goods in the Basin. Within the next four or five years, factories were established in other communities, the Provo woolen mills being the largest west of the Mississippi River. The woolen industry has continued to grow until at the present day Utah is known for her numerous and excellent woolen factories.

DOMESTIC MANUFACTURING OF OTHER ARTICLES

Besides manufacturing practically all of their clothing in Utah pioneer days, "the people manufactured soap, brooms, candles, molasses, beverages, wooden bottles, combs, dyes, and many other useful articles."[16] Cabinet shops were established and furniture was made from native lumber. The leather and iron industries were established also. A discussion of them is given in later chapters.

AGRICULTURE, STOCK RAISING AND HORTICULTURE

Of course the industry stressed most by President Brigham Young was that of agriculture. The Mormons have always been

---
[15]*Ibid.*
[16]Young, *op. cit.*, 193.

basically an agricultural people, deriving the major portion of their livelihood from the soil.

Closely connected with agriculture was stock raising. Thousands of acres of arid land in the Great Basin afforded pasturage, especially for winter feed, while the numerous mountain ranges were excellent summer grazing lands. Brother Brigham was not slow in recognizing the possibilities of the livestock industry; neither was he slow in utilizing the natural resources for that purpose, with the result that every Mormon community made use of the pasture lands for miles in each direction from its agricultural lands. Church herds of cattle and sheep, cooperatively owned community herds, as well as hundreds of individually owned herds contributed toward making the Saints self-sustaining and prosperous. The livestock industry, then, became a major one in the Basin.

In colonial Utah, fruit growing soon became an important industry. Orchards producing all kinds of fruits adaptable to temperate climate, not only added beauty to each city lot, but served to supply an abundance of food. Many of the settlers devoted a portion of their farm lands to producing fruit also. In fact, fruit trees, as well as shade trees, were so characteristic of the Mormon communities during Brigham's period that observers never failed to comment on that fact.

Chapter XVI

THE LEATHER INDUSTRY

Brigham Young and the Leather Industry

The outdoor life of the frontier required the use of a great deal of leather in equipment and clothing. Since the Mormons were far from the base of supplies, it was necessary that they learn to replace that which was worn and to provide new articles of clothing. Brigham Young advised the Saints to be resourceful:

> If you cannot tan a fox or wolf skin, shoot or trap the fox or wolf, and come to us we will tell you how to tan it, and one or two will make your babe a warm frock, and three or four will make your woman a warm petticoat, a much better one than you can buy for gold at any store in Deseret. Save all your hides and deliver them to your tanner, and if he cannot pay you for them, give them to him, and then peel or shave some bark to tan them with, and in a few days he will exchange some leather with you for some more hides and bark, which will cost you nothing but the improvement of your few leisure moments in some useful industry; then you will be in town for shoes, and not be obliged to run to St. Louis for the next change of feet protectors.[1]

Beginning of the Leather Industry in Utah

Among the early immigrants to Utah there were men skilled in the manufacture of leather, but they found tanning materials very scarce. The barks to be found in the Basin were different from those that the tanners had previously used, so that they experienced considerable difficulty in their work.[2]

The first man to begin the tanning business in Salt Lake City was Samuel Mulliner. At a general conference in 1850 his first leather, made from a calf-skin, was exhibited. On June 14, 1850, Mulliner made the following announcement of his business in the *Deseret News*:

> Samuel Mulliner hereby notifies the citizens of Deseret that he has entered the tanning business and solicits the cooperation of all who feel interested in home manufacture. He wishes to state that it will be just as necessary for the citizens to bring bark and sumac as it is for tanners to make the necessary preparations for making leather. Owners of sawmills will please save all the bark they can, stripping all green pine trees which come to their mills.—Wanted immediately fifty cords of pine or oak bark for which the

---

[1]Brigham Young, *Latter-day Saint Journal History*, January 24, 1852, Ms.
[2]Edward W. Tullidge, *History of Salt Lake City*, 670.

highest prices will be paid.—Wanted ten hundred weight of sumac threshed and cleaned. . . . As the season for peeling bark is nearly past, the bark must be produced immediately. For further particulars apply to the subscriber at his shop on E. Temple St., opposite Reese's Store.[3]

Shortly after, Samuel Mulliner advertised in the *Deseret News* that all those who wished boots and shoes without having to pay for them could peel bark and exchange it with him for finished leather. He gave instructions on how to peel the bark and suggested that someone enter the business of raising sumac, a product much needed in the tanning business.

At that time Mulliner and his partner, Allen, had in their vats 220 sides of leather that could not be completely tanned without more bark. So they urged very strongly that someone furnish it, feeling that by the proper development of the leather industry $100,000 could be saved from going to a foreign market each year.

DEVELOPMENT OF THE INDUSTRY

President Brigham Young became concerned about the slow development of the leather industry. Early in January, 1852, he advised the Saints in Europe who were tanners to migrate to Utah and to help in this work. His letter stated:

Experiments at tanning hides, and making leather, have, as yet, been very limited in the valley. Much leather is needed in this country. . . . If some of the brethren who are tanners, would come home and attend to their calling here, they could receive the blessing of many souls. Some attempts are now making at this business, but more help is wanted. Brethren, the harvest here is great, but the laborers few.[4]

Others soon joined in the tannery business. As early as 1852 a tannery was built at Paragonah, while Ira Ames and Alexander Brian opened one in Salt Lake City in 1853, subsequently known as the Pugsley's Tannery. Phillip Pugsley, a native of England, "had learned the process of tanning leather, a knowledge and skill which was of great value in the new territory."[5] He and Isaac Young were hired to Ames' tannery for a year. After the death of Isaac Young and until the "move south" in 1858, Pugsley operated this business on shares with Ira Ames and supervised the work in Golding and Raleigh's tannery.

The fifteenth ward tannery, founded by the merchant Hockday and sold to Nathaniel Jones and James W. Cummings in 1856, announced its beginning with the following advertisement:

---

[3]*Deseret News*, June 14, 1851.
[4]Brigham Young, "Sixth general Epistle . . . to the Saints," *Millennial Star*, XIV, 17-25.
[5]John G. Crook, *The Development of Early Industry and Trade in Utah*, 20, Ms.

Fifteenth Ward Tannery—Leather, Leather.

We take this method of informing the citizens of this place and surrounding country that the Fifteenth Ward Tannery is now in operation and
designs keeping on hand a large and well-assorted stock of leather of every
description which shall not only surpass anything heretofore manufactured
in the territory, but shall equal, if not surpass, anything brought to this
market for sale. The mechanical branch of this business will be carried on
under the direction of A. L. Toussig who has been engaged for years in the
manufacture of leather in Austria, Russia, France, England and the U. S. He
has thoroughly satisfied himself by this trial that the very best article of leather
can be furnished from the material with which this country abounds. . . .[6]

During the "Utah War," Captain Pugsley was left with a
detail to guard Salt Lake City. At times he was the only man in
the city, but he kept the tannery going. After the Saints had returned from the "move south," Pugsley purchased Ames' share in
the tannery. He was the only man in the city who had gathered
bark that winter, so when other tanneries resumed business he sold
bark to them.

Among other new tanneries in 1858 was a factory established
by President Young, Feramorz Little, and John R. Winder. The
Mormon President also operated a saddle and harness manufacturing shop, and a shoe shop. The last mentioned was on his own
premises just north of Eagle Gate, in which he employed about a
dozen workmen to make boots and shoes for his family and his
numerous employees.[7]

There were also a number of leather factories operating on
a smaller scale in many of the towns throughout the territory. According to the United States census reports of 1868-1870, Salt Lake,
Millard, Sanpete, Weber, Utah and Beaver counties had leather
industries working at good profits. One very successfully operated
tannery was established in 1866 at Brigham City by Apostle Lorenzo Snow. A letter dated October, 1875, explains the general
methods of financing such enterprises:

We erected a tannery building two stories high, forty-five by eighty feet,
with modern improvements and conveniences, at a cost of $10,000. Most of
the materials and mason and carpenter work were furnished as capital stock
by such persons as were able and who desired an interest in our institution.
The larger portion of the work was done during the winter season when no
other employment could be had. One-fourth was paid in merchandise to such
as needed it. We gained by this method additional capital, as well as twenty
or thirty new stockholders without encroaching much on anyone's property
or business. This tannery has been operated during the past nine years with

⁶*Deseret News,* February 10, 1856.
⁷Tullidge, *op. cit.,* 677.

success, and reasonable profits, producing an excellent quality of leather worth from $8,000 to $10,000 annually. We have in connection with our business a boot and shoe shop, also a saddle and harness shop. We draw our dividends in the articles manufactured at these two departments. . . .[8]

Effect of the Coming of the Union Pacific Railroad

Although the leather produced in these tanneries was not of the very highest quality during the early part of Utah colonial history, it proved very successful in supplying the pioneer communities. But the coming of the Union Pacific Railroad had a deleterious effect on the leather industry just as the high prices of the Civil War, a few years earlier, had stimulated it. The scarcity of proper tanning material, the expense of adequate machinery, and the fact that much tanning material had to be imported in order to produce even a fair quality of goods made it impossible for the Utah products to compete with States' goods. Furthermore, because the demand was great the leather was seldom allowed to remain long enough in the vats to get thoroughly tanned before it was used. These factors resulted in a grade of leather goods inferior to that imported from the States, and thus the term "valley-tan" became a derogatory expression applied to any home-made article.

As the Saints in increasing numbers bought the imported goods, the continuance of the leather industry was threatened. To meet this and other emergencies, Brigham Young organized the Zion's Cooperative Mercantile Institution with branch establishments throughout the territory in the various communities. Under the direction of this organization the leather business was revived and continued to be one of the important home industries.

[8]Edward W. Tullidge, *Quarterly Magazine*, II, 401.

CHAPTER XVII

UTAH FORTY-NINERS

Brigham Young's Ideas Relative to Mining

President Brigham Young had very definite ideas as to the relative value of the various metals to his people and was not hesitant in expressing those ideas. Mormon literature of his day is replete with his opinions on the undesirability of finding gold and the necessity of mining iron and coal. Realizing the importance of certain kinds of minerals to the proper development of a Mormon empire, Brigham Young instructed the Saints only two months after their arrival in the Salt Lake Valley:

> Should the brethren at any time discover any specimens or beds of chalk, lime, coal, iron, lead, copper or any other minerals, we wish they would report the same to the Council, who will keep a record of the same with the specimens, the place where found, and by whom, which record may be of great worth hereafter.[1]

Accordingly, a careful record was kept of all discoveries made by the Saints as they visited various parts of the Great Basin during the formative period. Exploring parties were sent out on various occasions in search of minerals. Coal, iron and lead were particularly sought.

Samuel Brannan, Gold, and California

But an event occurred in 1848 which rather upset the equilibrium of the world—the discovery of gold in California. Naturally some of the Mormons "caught the gold fever."

In fact, nine of the twelve white men who were working on James Sutter's mill when gold was discovered on January 24, 1848, were discharged members of the Mormon Battalion.[2] Other Battalion members joined them later, but when Brother Brigham advised them to return to the Basin, they willingly obeyed.

Not so with Samuel Brannan. He, having arrived at "Yerba Buena" (San Francisco) on July 29, 1846, with 238 Mormon colonists, after completing an eventful voyage from New York via Cape Horn in the ship *Brooklyn*, took an active part in the gold

---

[1]Brigham Young, "First general Epistle . . . to the Saints." *Latter-day Saints Journal History*, September 8, 1847. Ms.
[2]Henry W. Bigler. *Journal* (Bancroft Library), January 24, 1848. Ms.; H. H. Bancroft. *History of California*, VI, 33.

rush and urged President Young to bring the Saints of God to the Pacific Coast. But the Mormon prophet, fearing that such a move might result in the absorption of church members in the mass of humanity that was immigrating to the coast and, probably, in the loss of their religion, flatly refused Brannan. Brigham knew that if he took his people to California the seclusion for which he had been seeking would be lost, and the Saints would again be open to Gentile persecution. History has proved his judgment to have been correct as is evidenced in what happened to Sam Brannan and his Mormon associates who stayed at the gold fields. Of Mr. Brannan it is written:

> Brannan participated in the early scenes of California's pioneer life—the discovery of gold; the wild speculations in San Francisco real estate; became the organizer of mining, milling, and railway companies, purchased a great distillery, and became a large land proprietor both in California and in Sonora, Mexico; and for a time was known as the richest man in California. . . . In the midst of these activities, however, he acquired habits of intemperance: "and he became as well known for his dissolute habits and drunken freaks as he had been for his wealth and ability." Domestic troubles led to divorcement from his wife who had accompanied him to California in the *Brooklyn;* he afterwards remarried to a Mexican woman. Under unlucky speculations his vast fortune melted away, and for a number of years before his death he was "a sorry wreck, physically and financially".[3]

Desire of Some of the Saints to go to California

Some of the early reactions of a few of the Saints in the Basin regarding the desirability of Brigham Young and his people migrating to the gold field in California were reported by James Brown, one of the Mormon pioneers of 1847, in the following words:

> The winter of 1848-49 was quite cold. . . . As the days grew warmer the gold fever attacked many so that they prepared to go to California. Some said they would go only to save a place for the rest of us; for they thought Brigham Young too smart a man to try to establish a civilized colony in such a "God-forsaken country", as they called the valley. They further said that California was the natural country for the Saints; some brought choice fruit pips and seeds, but said they would not waste them by planting in a country like the Great Salt Lake Valley; others stated that they would not build a house in the valley, but would remain in their wagons, for certainly our leaders knew better than to attempt to make a stand in such a dry, worthless locality, and would be going on to California, Oregon or Vancouver's Island.[4]

Brigham Young's Attitude

The cry was raised by many of the Saints: "To California—

---

[3] *Ibid.;* B. H. Roberts. *A Comprehensive History of the Church.* III, 39.
[4] James Brown. *Autobiography,* 119-123.

To the Gold of Ophir our brethren have discovered! To California!" But President Brigham Young had different ideas on the subject. December 7, 1848, he wrote: "Some few have caught the gold fever. I counseled such, and all the Saints to remain in these valleys of the mountains and make improvements, build comfortable houses and raise grain."[5]

You will do better right here than you will by going to the gold mines. Some have thought they would go there and get fitted out and come back, but I told them to stop here and get fitted out. Those who stop here and are faithful to God and his people will make more money and get richer than you that run after the god of this world; and I promise you in the name of the Lord that many of you that go thinking you will get rich and come back, will wish you had never gone away from here, and will long to come back, but will not be able to do so. Some of you will come back, but your friends who remain here will have to help you; and the rest of you who are spared to return will not make as much money as your brethren do who stay here and help build up the Church and Kingdom of God; they will prosper and be able to buy you twice over. Here is the place God has appointed for his people.[6]

I will commence at the north and go to the south settlements, and pick out twenty-five of our inhabitants as they average; and another man may take fifty of the gold diggers, off hand, and they cannot buy out the twenty-five who have tarried at home. Before I had been one year in this place, the wealthiest man who came from the mines, Father Rhodes, with 17,000 dollars, could not buy the possessions I had made in one year![7]

And again, in a public discourse delivered on October 1, 1848, President Young expressed himself very pointedly and gave reasons for not wanting the Saints to go to the gold fields. He said:

If we were to go to San Francisco and dig up chunks of gold, or find it here in the valley, it would ruin us. Many want to unite Babylon and Zion, but it is the love of money that hurts them. If we find gold and silver, we are in bondage directly. To talk of going away from this valley for anything is like vinegar to my eyes. They who love the world have not their affections placed upon the Lord.[8]

Brigham remarked that if the people knew how to make good use of gold he could tell them where plenty of it was. But gold would not help them develop the country. Early in the spring of 1849, he remarked:

I can stand in my door and can see where there is untold millions of rich treasures of the earth—gold and silver. But the time has not come

[5]Cited in Preston Nibley, *Brigham Young—The Man and His Work*, 126.
[6]Brown, *op. cit.*, 122.
[7]*Millennial Star*, XIII, 17, 18.
[8]Brigham Young, *Latter-day Saint Journal History*, October 1, 1848, Ms.

for the Saints to dig gold. It is our duty first to develop the agricultural resources of this country. . . . As for gold and silver and other rich minerals of the earth, there is no other country that equals this; but let them alone; let others seek them, and we will cultivate the soil; for if the mines are opened first, we are a thousand miles away from the base of supplies, and the people would rush in here in such great numbers that they would breed a famine. . . . Then, brethren, let the mines alone until the time comes for you to hunt gold, though I do not think this people will ever become a mining people.[9]

When the Saints shall have preached the gospel, raised grain, and built up cities enough, the Lord will open up the way for a supply of gold to the perfect satisfaction of his people; until then, let them not be over-anxious for the treasures of the earth are in the Lord's storehouse, and he will open the doors thereof when and where he pleases.[10]

From the time gold was discovered in California, the Mormon leaders detested thoroughly the gold-fever and definitely forbade the Saints to join in the California movement or to search for the precious metal in the Great Basin. On February 24, 1849, Robert Grew presented a petition signed by himself and seven others, asking permission to go to the gold fields under the sanction of the First Presidency of the Church. Upon their refusal he readily accepted their counsel and remained in Utah. Five months later Brigham Young made the following remark in a sermon: "I hope the gold mines will be no nearer than eight hundred miles. If you Elders of Israel want to go to the gold mines, go, and be damned."[11] Mormon records show that not many of the "Elders of Israel" went. In the words of Daniel Tyler:

The enlightened virtue of their rulers saved the people and the fortunes of Deseret. A few only went away—and they were asked in kindness never to return. The rest remained to be healthy and happy, to "raise grain and build up cities."[12]

This rather unusual yet almost universal acquiescence of the Saints in the opinion of the Mormon leaders, especially in Brother Brigham's, was described in a letter written by one of the Saints to his friends in England. Quoting:

The counsel of Brigham Young, the present governor of the territory, is followed to the very letter, and men's determination to obey his mandates is stronger than the love of life, or worldly enjoyment, or the fear of death itself. This struck me more than any other thing after I came to the valley.[13]

[9]Brown, op. cit., 122.
[10]Millennial Star, XI, 246.
[11]Young, op. cit., July 8, 1849. Ms.
[12]Daniel Tyler, History of the Mormon Battalion, 105.
[13]Cited in Nibley, op. cit., Deseret News, February 23, 1935.

Two of the apostles wrote the following warning words to the president of the European mission, probably with the hope of preventing any of the foreign Saints from migrating to Utah with a mistaken conception:

> Those who anticipated entering into a harvest field of gold on their arrival here, must meet with disappointment. *Gold is not the God of the Saints.* They seek to build up the Kingdom of God by industry, by building cities, raising grain, gathering the Saints, and in fact, by devoting their time, means, and talents, whether in preaching or labour of their hands, in the service of their God. The exaggerated accounts of gold mines in the Valley, and an over-plus of the metal imported from California are entirely unfounded. A coal mine would be a welcome sight to us here, but a gold-mine we neither have found nor seek to find.[14]

THE UTAH FORTY-NINERS

It was under Brigham Young's direct supervision that a group of "Forty-niners" arose in Utah. Like the California Forty-niners, they were frontiersmen who were willing to face the rigors of a new country. But the Utahns were searching for iron and coal—not gold. They were working to develop a commonwealth and to serve their Church and their God rather than to earn a fortune for themselves.

Brother Brigham very definitely stated just what the Utah Forty-niners desired—"*coal, iron, and hard labor.*" After comparing the wealth and power of England and Spain and the sources of that wealth and power, he remarked:

> What is the wealth of England? Is it gold? No. If the English had found gold instead of stone coal, they would have been sunk in degradation. The sun never sets upon their dominions. Coal, iron and hard labor have been the wealth, the power, and the strength of England.[15]

As the iron supply brought across the plains diminished and industry increased, the demand for that metal became urgent. The prosperity of the people, yes, almost their very existence depended upon an adequate supply. Brigham Young asserted, "Iron we need and iron we must have. We cannot well do without it, and have it we must if we have to send to England to get it."[16]

SETTLEMENT OF PAROWAN AND CEDAR CITY

Late in 1849 a mountain of iron ore was discovered by

---

[14]George A. Smith and Ezra T. Benson to Orson Pratt, in *Latter-day Saint Journal History*, September 29, 1850, Ms.
[15]Young, *ibid.*, July 8, 1849.
[16]Brigham Young, *Journal of Discourses*, II, 282.

Parley P. Pratt's exploring expedition in the Little Salt Lake Valley about 250 miles south of Salt Lake City. The report of Pratt on returning to the Mormon Mecca in 1850 was considered favorable to the settlement of that section of the country as soon as circumstances would permit, the main purpose of the colony being to establish an iron foundry. The First Presidency published in the Deseret News of July 27, 1850, a call for volunteer colonists to Iron County. The article stated:

> Brethren of Great Salt Lake City and vicinity who are full of faith and good works; who have been blessed with means; who want more means and are willing to labor and toil to obtain those means, are informed by the Presidency of the Church, that a colony is wanted at Little Salt Lake this fall; that 50 or more good effective men with teams and wagons, provisions, and clothing, are wanted for one year.
>
> Seed, grain in abundance and tools in all their variety for a new colony are wanted to start from this place immediately after the fall conference, to repair to the valley of the Little Salt Lake without delay. There to sow, build and fence; erect a saw and gristmill, establish an iron foundry as speedly as possible and do all other acts and things necessary for the preservation and safety of an infant settlement.[17]

Apostle George A. Smith was selected by the Moromn Colonizer as the one to establish this important settlement. October 27, 1850, Smith called for one hundred men to accompany him on this mission.[18] Three weeks later another notice was published in the Deseret News, giving names of some chosen to go and calling for a hundred additional volunteers.[19] Ten days before Christmas a meeting was held at Fort Utah (Provo), that being the place of rendezvous, at which Apostle Smith was sustained by a unanimous vote to be the president of the company. Smith said:

> I hope our ears will not be saluted with swearing or the taking of the name of the Lord in vain. We want no gambling. We are going to gather the Saints and build up the kingdom of God. We should act as though we are on a mission to preach the gospel. The Sabbath day should be observed in all cases; six days we should labor and we should rest on the Sabbath.[20]

In accordance with Brigham Young's instructions, when the company reached Payson, an inventory was taken and sent back to the President. This inventory is given here to show the detailed amount of supplies necessary in the establishment of a new colony.

There were 120 males, 31 females, over 14 years of age, and 18 children under 14. Total of 169.

---

[17]Deseret News, July 27, 1850.
[18]Ibid., October 27, 1850.
[19]Ibid., Nov. 16, 1850.
[20]George A. Smith, Parowan Stake, Wards, December 15, 1850, Ms.

Provisions of seed grain, etc., as follows: flour, 56,922 lbs.; wheat, 35,370 lbs.; corn, 3,486 lbs.; oats, 2,163 lbs.; barley, 1,267 lbs.; potatoes, 3,240 lbs.; and groceries, 1,228 lbs.; total, 103,676 lbs.

Following equipment: carpenters tools, 9¼ sets; blacksmith tools, 3½ sets; mill iron for sawmill, 1 set; whip saws, 3; plows, 5⅞; hoes, 98; spades and shovels, 110; axes, 137; scythes and grain cradles, 72; grass scythes 45; lights of glass, 436; nails, 190 lbs.; stoves 55.

Arms, ammunition, etc.; 1 brass cannon, 6 pounder; 129 guns; 52 pistols; 9 swords; 1001 rounds of ammunition and 44 saddles.

General outfit of foregoing pioneers: Wagons, 101; carriages, 2; oxen, 368; horses, 100; mules, 12; cows, 146; beef cattle, 20; dogs, 14; cats, 18; chickens, 121.

Military organization: 25 cavalry, 32 infantry, and 13 men having the cannon in charge.[21]

The company left their camp on the Provo River, December 16, 1850, and arrived at Center Creek, Iron County, January 13, 1851. They built cabins, planted crops and initiated the work necessary to a new commonwealth. They were joined by incoming Saints until on May 12, the population of Parowan—a name suggested by President Young—numbered 360.

Immediately after the first colonists arrived, a council convened to appoint a committee to explore the canyon and another group to more fully explore the valley. Six days later George A. Smith was able to inform President Brigham Young that they had explored "the iron regions the past few days, and Brother Caruthers pronounces it of a fine quality."[22] Within a few days a road was made up Center Creek Canyon and preparations were made for the beginning of the iron industry. Coal was found nearby. The first job of blacksmithing with stone coal was done by Bringhurst, Burr, and Frost, by welding an axletree for one of Brother Brigham's party on May 12. "The coal was of first rate quality and answered all the expectations of the people."[23]

A second settlement was established in Iron County in the fall of 1851. November 3, George A. Smith and others camped on a spot on Coal Creek which had been selected by Parley P. Pratt two years previously for settlement. This site was nineteen miles southwest of Parowan. The following day William H. Dame surveyed a town plat about a mile due north from the present location of Cedar City. Apostle Smith "dedicated the ground . . . to the service of God in the manufacture of iron, machinery, etc.,

[21]George A. Smith, *Saint George Stake, 1847-1873,* 5-6, Ms.
[22]George A. Smith to Brigham Young, in *Latter-day Saint Journal History,* January 19, 1851, Ms.
[23]*Ibid.,* March 12, 1851.

that the necessities of the Saints might be supplied and the territory of Utah built up."[24]

EARLY DEVELOPMENT OF IRON INDUSTRY

November 5, 1851, a company of "English, Scotch, and Welsh miners and iron manufacturers" was organized at Parowan to settle Cedar City for the purpose of manufacturing iron.[25] Within two weeks after their arrival they discovered another good coal deposit within seven or eight miles of the settlement. Iron ore was also found in rich abundance less than a mile from the fort they had recently erected.

In a letter dated June 27, 1852, Henry Lunt wrote from Cedar City to the effect that for the past month the colonists had been conducting successful experiments in preparation for making iron.[26] A good blacksmith shop had been built and, Lunt stated, the iron work for the machinery was progressing rapidly. In order to supply themselves with the required amount of iron, the workmen had used their wagon tires, expecting to replace them from the iron works. The settlers were very hopeful that before many weeks they would have plenty of metal of their own manufacture.

That summer a small furnace was erected and two pairs of blacksmith bellows were used to demonstrate that iron could be successfully manufactured. Burr Frost made enough nails to shoe a horse. A pair of andirons, commonly known as "dog irons," were cast from the native ore in September and exhibited at the October conference (1852) by Apostle George A. Smith. He preached the "first Iron Sermon" to the assembled thousands.

Confidence was established in the ability and skill of the ironworkers, and the future prospects of the industry seemed reasonably bright to the settlers.[27] On October 5, 1852, Henry Lunt wrote from Cedar City to the editor of the *Deseret News* as follows:

The prospects of manufacturing that all-important iron is excellent. I would that we had five hundred good men at this time to develop the rich resources of this beautiful vale and I am satisfied that iron to almost any amount could soon be manufactured. The machinery is of the best kind and works well. It would do for a much larger furnace than the one erected.[28]

President Brigham Young responded to this letter by issuing a call at the October conference, 1852, held in Salt Lake City,

[24]*Parowan Stake, Wards,* November 4, 1851, Ms.
[25]*Ibid.,* November 5, 1851.
[26]*Latter-day Saint Journal History,* June 27, 1852, Ms.
[27]*Deseret News,* December 11, 1852.
[28]*Ibid.,* November 6, 1852.

for one hundred families to go to Iron County. These colonists were composed of recent converts from Scotland, Wales and England, and were skilled iron workers, coal miners, blacksmiths and farmers. They arrived in Cedar City during November and December and proved to be a valuable acquisition to the iron industry. About the time of their arrival George A. Smith wrote to the *Deseret News* as follows:

> A temporary road has been worked to the coal veins, about six miles up the creek. A number of new veins of coal have been discovered by Mr. Gregory, late from the collieries in England. It will require a heavy amount of labor to complete the road and open the coal veins so as to be made available. An iron mountain, about seventeen miles from Cedar City, recently discovered by Mr. Shirts, is a mixture of iron and black lead. There is a good furnace built at Cedar City, where forty hands are wanted immediately to run it and for the lack of which it stands idle.[29]

It was evident that in spite of the natural resources available, the industry was far from successful as yet. Progress was extremely slow notwithstanding the great amount of energy expended by the iron workers to solve the problem relative to the production of iron and in spite of the spurts of apparent success in certain of the processes, there were three major factors lacking—capable management, adequate capital, and sufficient trained workmen.

[29]*Ibid.*

Chapter XVIII

THE DESERET IRON COMPANY

Founding of Deseret Iron Company

In January, 1852, only one year after George A. Smith had arrived at Parowan to establish the iron industry, Brother Brigham and his counselors wrote a letter to Franklin D. Richards, the retiring president of the European Mission, recommending that he organize a company for the manufacture of iron in the Great Basin. President Young had manifested much concern over the possibilities of the Saints producing their own iron; therefore, he was going to exert every effort possible to make that industry successful and productive in the Great West. He had recently declared:

> We shall never give up what we list to perform. The Lord guiding and directing us, we shall continue our operations, until we manufacture everything we wish to eat, drink, and wear, in the midst of these mountains; so that we shall not be under the necessity of going to any other place in the whole world, to get anything we wish to consume.[1]

Probably the most nearly insurmountable problem that had confronted the Utah Forty-niners was that of accumulating the necessary capital for the development of the iron industry. The Mormon leader instructed Richards to solve this difficulty by selling stock to the wealthy members of the Church in Europe, as well as to those who had migrated to the Mormon Mecca.

Also, disappointments and losses had been encountered by Smith and his associates at Parowan because of lack of capable managers and trained workmen in the iron industry. Being in a position to draw from the world at large, Brother Brigham was determined to secure the needed managers and a sufficient number of trained workmen. So he further instructed President Richards that expert workmen should be selected from converts to Mormonism who had learned the details of manufacturing iron in the British Isles and Sweden. They should immigrate to Zion at an early date and contribute their share to the building of the Mormon commonwealth. Quoting from the instructions to Franklin D. Richards:

If a company of brethren could be formed in England, Wales, Sweden, or any other country, to come and make iron from ore (magnetic ore of the

[1]*Millennial Star*, XVII, 7.

best quality), and machinery for rolling, slitting, and cutting nails, and drawing off wire, it would be one of the greatest auxiliaries for advancement in building up the valleys of the mountains; and the presiding elders in those countries are instructed to examine this subject, and forward such a company with the least possible delay.[2]

In accordance with the foregoing recommendations, Apostles Franklin D. Richards and Erastus Snow commenced operations in London at their church conference, April 6, 1852. They spent the remainder of the month in visiting the wealthier converts in the British Isles and in observing various iron works in England, Wales, Scotland, and Ireland, from which they obtained all the information they could on the subject of making iron from magnetic and other ores.[3]

Consequently the "Deseret Iron Company" was organized in Liverpool, April 28, 29, 1852, with a subscription of 4,000 pounds in stock to be paid on or before January 1, 1853. Richards and Snow were appointed "Managers and Agents for the company." A constitution was drawn up in which was written:

1. We the undersigned do hereby unite ourselves in a firm or company to be known as the Deseret Iron Company.

2. The design of said company is to procure a tract or tracts of land in Utah Territory containing iron ore, coal, water privileges, etc., and thereon to erect works for the manufacture of iron, and all such articles made of iron, as the wants of that community and the wisdom of the company may determine.[4]

Iron Works in Cedar City Taken Over by the Company

Nine days after the organization of the company, Snow and Richards left England for Utah, where they reported their work to President Young. He approved what had been done and advised that the agents effect the organization in Iron County as quickly as conditions would permit.

Typical of the Mormon pioneer leaders, Erastus Snow and Franklin D. Richards did not wait in Salt Lake until the stockholders sent them money upon which to carry on the business. They immediately began operation, standing surety for the expense involved until they could be reimbursed. In the words of Erastus Snow:

There being no funds in the Company's Treasury, and as subscriptions of stock could not be made available under about one year, and being anxious to

---

[2]Brigham Young, "Sixth general Epistle . . . to the Saints," *Millennial Star,* XIV, 20.
[3]*Millennial Star,* XVII, 2.
[4]*Minute Book of Deseret Iron Company,* 7, cited in John C. Crook, *The Development of Early Industry and Trade in Utah,* 45, Ms.

set the business of the Company in operation without delay, we proceeded on our own credit to loan money, and with money and credit to purchase the goods with which we commenced the business of the Company in this country.[5]

In November, 1852, the two apostles went to Cedar City. They found it advisable to take over the interests of the iron works previously established there in order to promote the best interests of the Deseret Iron Company. The improvements, interests and rights of the earlier iron workers were purchased by the agents of the new company for $2,865.65. These interests consisted of a small blast furnace, the coal mine of Coal Creek Canyon, the water privileges of Coal Creek, and a tract of land extending from Cedar City to the mountains eastward. Reporting the foregoing transaction, December 2, 1852, Henry Lunt stated that "there has been a thorough organization for the manufacture of iron under the name of the Deseret Iron Company. A large sum has already been subscribed and expensive contracts made."[6]

Before returning to Salt Lake, Snow and Richards appointed John C. S. Smith to superintend "experimentation on the ores." Erastus Snow reported the business carried on by Richards and himself as follows:

A reason for their [Smith and the others who began iron manufacturing before the opening of the Deseret Iron Company] not progressing more rapidly or succeeding better in the manufacture of iron may be found in their lack of experience in its elementary processes and of union in their organization.

As a final closing up of matters, we purchased their works on Coal Creek for the Deseret Iron Company and opened the books of the company for subscriptions of stock and there and then received subscriptions from those who felt the greatest interest in the business, to the amount of several thousands, after which we employed such other desirable workmen as did not take stock and placed the little furnace, already built, under the management of Mr. Adams, who had had many years experience as furnace keeper in Pennsylvania and in Great Britain. We also employed Mr. James from the Victoria Iron Works, Wales, to construct a small air furnace in which to try the experiment of fluxing the richer ores without the blast; and further directed that operations be carried forward with charcoal and dry pitch pine wood (which abounds in that vicinity) until a better quality of coke could be produced from the stone coal. This alteration seemed to be warranted by the experiment already made in the furnace which was heated up with pitch pine wood; the first iron that came into the smelting hearth was far superior to that smelted after the furnace was charged with their miserable coke. John C. L. Smith, president of the stake, whom we regarded as a judicious and persevering man, was made superintendent and from past experience we feel warranted in indulging in the hope of soon furnishing an excellent quality of iron. We surveyed a tract of land for the Deseret Iron Company east of Cedar

[5]*Millennial Star.* XVII, 2.
[6]Henry Lunt, *Deseret News,* December 25, 1852.

City to the mountain, embracing several sites in the creek for furnaces, foundries, a forge with wire-drawing works, and a nail factory, all of which works it is the purpose of the company to erect; already a commencement is made with a capital near forty thousand dollars.[7]

DEVELOPMENT OF IRON INDUSTRY

In December, 1852, a Mr. Bladon discovered a solid four hundred pound lump of pure malleable iron of a very superior quality, which caused much excitement among the iron workers. Henry Lunt expressed a fear that the ore was too rich for them to work properly. In his own words:

Mr. J. James has been testing the ore with chemicals and finds certain ingredients not common; consequently it will require different fluxing and that no limestone will be wanting. The greatest difficulty in my opinion is that the ore is so very rich that we are not acquainted with a system easy and simple enough to convert it into pig metal.[8]

During the winter of 1852-53 the workers constructed an excellent air furnace as well as an expensive frame casting house.[9] They prepared great quantities of pitch pine wood and charcoal with a view to putting the furnace into operation in the early spring. During March, 1853, 2500 pounds of an excellent grade of iron were produced. However, for this amount of iron there were consumed six hundred bushels of charcoal.[10] On a visit to the iron works the following month, Snow and Richards concluded that the experiment proved charcoal would not answer for fuel, as it was too expensive.[11]

Governor Young was greatly interested in the success of the Deseret Iron Company. Besides recognizing the urgent need for iron in the territory, he knew that the law which he signed on January 17, 1853, incorporating the new company, approved an appropriation by the Utah Territorial Legislature of $7,000 to aid in opening coal mines. The Legislature had purchased two shares of stock in the iron company and the Church had also purchased two.[12] Brigham Young, as governor of the Territory of Utah and President of the Church, was the determining factor in the appropriation and in the purchase of these four shares of stock. The territorial appropriations were placed at his disposal. He appointed Erastus Snow to go to Cedar and expend the money as ordered.

[7]Erastus Snow, *Ibid.*, December 25, 1852.
[8]Lunt, *op. cit.*, December 25, 1852.
[9]*Deseret News*, March 19, 1853.
[10]*Ibid.*, April 2, 1852.
[11]*Ibid.*, October 15, 1853.
[12]*Millennial Star*, XVII, 5.

James A. Little and Philip K. Smith were appointed to open up coal mines so that a cheaper fuel could be procured. Within ten days after they commenced work they discovered several veins of coal. One vein of special richness, which was traced for several miles on the precipitous side of a mountain far above the valley, contained several feet of pure coal with about two feet more separated from the main body by a very thin stratum of rock and clay. A wagon road was made to this deposit at an expense of $6,000.[13] Now it seemed that the workers had all necessary factors at their command with which to produce iron cheaply and rapidly.

REVERSES, 1853

But this optimistic outlook was not to continue long. In July, 1853, the outbreaking of the Walker War necessitated the suspension of operations, as all the energies of the colonists were needed in preparing for self-defense against the Indians. The settlements had to be fortified, and hay, grain and other provisions had to be brought into the fort in preparation for winter.

This setback to the iron industry was followed shortly by another severe blow. September 3, 1853, a tremendous flood swept down Coal Creek, carrying bridges and dams before it. The torrent forced down huge boulders, some of them weighing from twenty to thirty tons.[14] The site of the iron works was inundated to the depth of three feet. Large amounts of charcoal, lumber and wood were carried away, and the property that remained was greatly damaged. After this disaster the workers rebuilt the dam and made necessary repairs during the autumn so that the works could again be put into operation.

Snow and his associates were not dispirited, but they realized better what obstacles they would be confronted with. Only two months after the disaster wrought by the "terrible flood," director Snow optimistically reported to the stockholders as follows:

The flood admonishes us of some of the difficulties to be encountered in supplying the furnace from the mines of Coal Creek. . . .

By our last advices we are informed of the accession of new members, the subscription and payment of additional stock, and a general increasing interest in the Company's welfare throughout the British Churches. . . .

It is with a lively sense of gratitude that we acknowledge the blessings of our Heavenly Father upon our labors, in crowning them with such abundant success.[15]

- - - -
[13]Ibid., Deseret News, July 30, 1853.
[14]Journal of Discourses, II, 281-282.
[15]Millennial Star, XVII, 3-4.

OFFICERS OF THE COMPANY

In November, 1853, the first general meeting of the Deseret Iron Company, after its incorporation by the Territorial Assembly, was held in Cedar City. Erastus Snow presented a report of the company's activities up to that date and asked that he and Richards be released from their position as "Managers and Agents" of the company. This was done by unanimous vote of those present; then officers were elected in accordance with the provisions of the charter. Erastus Snow was chosen as president; Franklin D. Richards, secretary; Thomas Tennant, treasurer; Isaac C. Haight, Vincent Shurtleff, Christopher Arthur, and Jonathan Pugmire, trustees.[16] Toward the close of the month the board of directors appointed Isaac C. Haight to be general manager of the company's affairs.

ACTIVITIES OF COMPANY IN 1854

During the latter part of May, 1854, the iron workers began to construct a furnace twenty-one feet square. It was completed by September 24, at a cost of $3782.45. The water wheel was enlarged four feet and a new blowing appartus was installed. By the first of the year of 1855, four large coke ovens were completed and two more were under construction. It was the intention of the company to supply six additional coke ovens.[17]

A quotation from a letter written by Manager I. C. Haight at Cedar City, September 24, 1854, to Franklin D. Richards in Liverpool, shows the undaunted faith and unrelenting efforts put forth by the Mormon frontiersmen to establish home industry.

We all feel sanguine in the expectation of making iron this winter. We want a good engine, and then I think nothing will hinder us. I hope the brethren in England and Wales will come forward to our assistance, and take shares, and send an engine and goods to help us. A little assistance now would do us a deal of good. The brethren of Parowan and this place are uniting their small means to take shares and help us along. Most of the hands are willing to work as long as they can keep spirit and body together. And if we could only get clothing for them, they would do very well.[18]

The editor of the *Millennial Star* added the following comment:

We have now given a short history of the operation of the Deseret Iron Company, but it is still a very imperfect account of the privations, sacrifices, and labours that have been endured in the effort to establish this important

[16]*Ibid.*, 4.
[17]*Deseret News,* January 4, 1855.
[18]I. C. Haight to F. D. Richards, in *Millennial Star,* XVII, 6.

branch of industry. Like everything else commenced or accomplished for the benefit of this kingdom, it has called forth the energies, prayers, and faith of the Saints. As every enterprise must prosper which is necessary for the progress of the Lord's people, so we believe this will, notwithstanding the difficulties which have hitherto surrounded it. . . . We feel assured that iron will soon be produced in sufficient quantity to commence supplying the wants of Utah, and make a profitable return to those who have made investments in the Company. . . .[19]

MAJOR EVENTS IN IRON INDUSTRY FROM 1855-1857

At no time had there been brighter prospects for the iron industry than in the spring of 1855. In April the large furnace started operation, making as much as 1700 pounds of good iron in twenty-four hours.[20] But it again became apparent that there was a shortage of help. This fact caused the following announcement to be sent to Salt Lake City:

One hundred and fifty men are wanted immediately in this country to carry on the iron works successfully. Those most needed are wagoners, miners, colliers, lime burners, lumbermen, quarrymen, brick and stone masons, carpenters, joiners, machinists, charcoal burners, and furnace men. Fifty additional teams are necessary to keep the furnace supplied with fuel and ore. The people are in high spirits on the iron subject; the furnace having been kept successfully in operation two weeks satisfied the most sceptical that nothing was wanting but to continue the charge as the furnace was "blown out" simply for want of fuel.[21]

Near the time this call was made, Brigham Young visited Cedar City. His keen eye and mind aptly analyzed conditions. In a public discourse on May 27, 1855, he stated:

The men have done as well as they possibly could do, considering the circumstances and inconveniences. There has been a great lack of capital to develop rapidly so great an industry, also there has been a shortage of suitable clothing and bedding, but in spite of these handicaps, the work has progressed almost as well as the same kind of industry in the older states where capital and labor are plentiful. . . .

It is very injurious for a large and expensive furnace to "blow out", as they call it; hence policy requires that the blast be continued as long as possible. No furnace can be heated for two or three weeks and then "blown out" or stop, without risk of spoiling the furnace or destroying its lining; and it frequently so injures the furnace that it has to be wholly or at least partially rebuilt. When it costs from $1,000 to $5,000 to prepare a furnace to bear a long blast, it is a great loss to any company to have it "blow out" in a short time. . . .

I will send two teams and teamsters. We need fifteen good teams with men who are willing to take hold and quarry out the ore and coal, get wood

---

[19]*Ibid.*, 6-7.
[20]John C. L. Smith, *Deseret News*, April 19, 1855.
[21]*Ibid.*

and lime or anything else that is wanted. In addition to these teams and teamsters, we need twenty to twenty-five more good men to go in the early part of the season so that the blast can be kept running for several months, or at least until they are obliged to stop in consequence of a deficiency of water.[22]

The Deseret Iron Company met one obstacle after another during the next few years, resulting in its disintegration. Circumstances over which the Saints had no control finally caused the failure of the iron industry.

First, the extremely cold weather of 1855-56 hampered the process of manufacturing, for Coal Creek was frozen and the snow lay in the canyon so deep that coal could not be secured for three months. Although a pair of thirty horse-power engines was brought from Salt Lake City and new machinery was set up to supersede Coal Creek for motive power, the loss of time and the added expense were too great to be borne by a young company which had made no profits.[23] As a natural result, the output of iron soon diminished. In fact, by 1857 the iron works had almost completely shut down, being considered by many people as a failure. Therefore during that year a number of families who were previously engaged in the manufacture of iron moved from Cedar City.

Dissolving of Deseret Iron Company

The following year Johnston's army brought ample supplies of iron into the territory, so that there was little demand for the home manufactured product. Also, the attention of the Mormon leaders was occupied with new problems of gigantic proportions. Later, the Union Pacific Railroad imported iron at a cost much smaller than that at which it could be produced by the Saints under existing conditions. Therefore, the Deseret Iron Company was dissolved, and the manufacture of that metal lay practically dormant until recent years, during which it has been revived. At the present time the mining of coal and the manufacture of iron are two important industries of Utah.

Appraisal of Achievements

The efforts made by the Utah Forty-niners to manufacture iron on a large scale, and under such difficult circumstances, bear testimony to the undaunted faith, acute vision, the determination of purpose and the tenacious will of those hardly empire builders of

[22]*Journal of Discourses*, II, 281-282.
[23]*Deseret News*, March 5, 1856.

the Great West. They were efforts of no mean order. The descendants of those stalwart Mormon pioneers have every reason to look upon the assiduous struggle and achievements of their noble ancestors with pride and gratitude.

While the fact is recognized that the Deseret Iron Company was forced into extinction, yet it cannot be denied that the Utah Forty-niners made a noteworthy effort toward building the West. Cedar City did not share the fate of the industry for which it was founded. The townsite had to be moved twice, but in spite of trouble with the Indians and losses through devastating floods and the loss of the iron industry, it thrived as it was located in an excellent agricultural section. It is at present the prinicpal city of Iron County, and the important tourist center of southern Utah.

COKE OVENS USED IN UTAH DURING EARLY MINING OPERATIONS

CHAPTER XIX

THE SETTLEMENT OF SALT LAKE VALLEY

OBJECTIVE

It is not the purpose of this chapter to give more than a brief summary of the colonization of Salt Lake City and valley as several excellent histories on that subject have already been written. Only a few points which have a direct bearing on Mormon colonization in general and the development of Brigham Young's colonial policies will be discussed. In dealing with specific problems and policies in other chapters of this study, references are made to the parent colony as occasion requires. But for a complete account of the history of this region the reader is referred to such books as Edward W. Tullidge's *History of Salt Lake City*, or any of the other standard histories of Utah.

SALT LAKE CITY—UTAH'S COLONIAL LABORATORY

July 24, 1847, the day that Brigham Young with the main body of the first pioneers arrived on the site of Salt Lake City, is celebrated by the Saints as a memorial day to commemorate the beginning of Mormon colonization of the West. Only three days after arriving in the valley and settling on City Creek, the leader of the Saints informed his people that they could explore as far as they wished but that they would be convinced that the right place for their most important settlement had been selected. Time has vindicated Brigham's judgment.

From its infancy, Salt Lake City was the typical Mormon settlement and from it the others were ruled. Here the director of the colonial movement—surrounded by a group of intelligent counselors and helpers—resided and worked out his policies. Salt Lake City became the laboratory in which President Brigham Young experimented and, to a certain degree, perfected the methods and policies followed in nearly four hundred other communities established under his tuition. The problem of how to protect themselves from the Indians; how to cope with a desert country; how to equitably distribute the natural resources among his followers; how to develop a self-sustaining organization; and a thousand other such problems were solved in this laboratory.

Salt Lake City was the parent colony from which settlements spread in every direction. Later hub colonies were established at various strategic points throughout the Basin, but there was always only one center—the home of the Prophet and leader of the Saints. The Mormon Mecca was connected with these other colonies by a network of wires, as it were, at the center of which sat Brigham, manipulating them with skill and judgment.

FOUNDING OF BOUNTIFUL, FARMINGTON, KAYSVILLE, CENTERVILLE, BIG COTTONWOOD, MILL CREEK, SOUTH COTTONWOOD, SUGAR HOUSE, AND DRAPER

After Salt Lake City was established, the rest of the colonies in the valley did not follow exactly the typical Mormon fashion of directed colonization but came about much as settlements on other American frontiers did. Land settlement spread from the parent colony; therefore Salt Lake City was not only the center of all Mormon colonization but also the hub city of the valley.

Some of the new towns in Salt Lake Valley were begun as the result of a search for pasturage for a portion of the 5,000 head of cattle which were brought to the Basin by the first pioneers. In search of grass and to preserve the nearer food in accordance with President Young's instructions, the cattle were herded at some distance from the city in various directions and as far north as the present site of Farmington. The following are Brother Brigham's instructions to the Saints in the Basin in September, 1847:

We recommend that you herd your cattle on the south of the valley, or in the valleys south, west or north, reserving the feed in your vicinity and toward the Salt Lake.[1]

Perrigrine Sessions arrived in the Great Salt Lake Valley on September 26, 1847. Three days later, in company with Samuel Brown, he camped on the site where Bountiful was subsequently built. They had with them about three hundred head of cattle. Sessions built a shanty for himself and brought part of his family to Bountiful in December of that year. The following spring five other families joined them. Thus Bountiful, a city situated about ten miles north of Salt Lake City and lying between the Wasatch Mountains and the Great Salt Lake, has the distinction of being the second settlement established in the Great Basin by the Saints.

[1]Brigham Young, "First General Epistle." *Latter-day Saint Journal History*, September 8, 1847. **Ms.**

A little later the same fall, Hector C. Haight arrived on the creek seven miles farther north in Davis County with his cattle. Throughout the winter of 1847-1848 he herded them near the present site of Farmington. He dwelt in a tent at first but early in 1848 Haight and his son built a cabin, the only one in Farmington until other settlers moved there in the fall of 1848. From that time forward Farmington was considered a colony.

Samuel Oliver Holmes is credited with being the first settler of Kaysville. He purchased a small cabin from a trapper in 1849 about a mile southwest of the present town site, where he planted and raised a crop that year. The following spring William Kay— the man after whom the town was named—accompanied by others, settled near Holmes' claim, forming a nucleus for a city.

Settlers also located on a creek between Farmington and Bountiful in the spring of 1849. They called their town Centerville. Thus within a little over a year after the arrival of the Saints in the Salt Lake Valley four thriving settlements had been established in the rich table-lands of Davis County north of Salt Lake City. All of them became important Mormon communities.

While settlers were locating north of Salt Lake City, others were also spreading out into the valley in other directions. After spending the winter of 1847-1848 in the fort at Salt Lake, a number of families led by John Holladay started out in the spring to search for suitable places for locating farms. They settled on Big Cottonwood Creek about nine miles southeast of the center of the Mormon Mecca. Their colony was at first called Holladay's Settlement and later Big Cottonwood. It was patterned on regular Mormon style with the cabins close together in a villiage, the fields surrounding them.

Early in the spring of 1848, John Neff located a mill about two miles below the mouth of the canyon subsequently named Mill Creek. During the summer he constructed the first flour mill built in the Great Basin, with the exception of a small grain-chopper built hurriedly by Charles Crisman at the mouth of City Creek Canyon. Neff moved his family to the mill site in the fall of 1848. The Gardner family, including Robert Gardner, Senior, Archibald Gardner and Robert Gardner, Junior, and their families had also located on Mill Creek in the spring of 1848. They built a sawmill that same spring and the following year Archibald Gardner built a gristmill.[2] Other settlers located farther down the stream in 1848, creating the town of Mill Creek.

---

[2]Delila G. Hughes, *Life of Archibald Gardner*, 41-47.

In October, 1848, Apostle Amasa M. Lyman arrived in Salt Lake Valley in charge of a company of Saints. He located them on a tract of land lying between the two Cottonwood creeks, about ten miles southeast of the center of Salt Lake City. Following the Mormon land system, they surveyed a tract of land about one mile square and divided it into ten-acre lots, distributing it among the settlers. This town received the name of South Cottonwood.

During the years 1848 and 1849 several other towns, forming a semi-circle to the south, were established. The Sugar House colony was located near the mouth of Parley's Canyon, east and a little south of Salt Lake City; the Jordan settlements were situated in the valley southwest of the parent colony; and Draper was located in the extreme southeastern end of the valley seventeen miles from the hub city.

A DESCRIPTION OF SALT LAKE VALLEY, ITS SETTLEMENTS AND SETTLERS, BY A GENTILE IN 1849

During the first two years of the Saints' occupancy of the Great Basin, while settlers were locating on all the best sites in the Salt Lake Valley, the parent colony itself had grown into a rather impressive city. A Gentile who passed through the Great Basin in 1849 wrote, under date of July 8, the following account of what he observed:

The company of gold-diggers which I have the honor to command, arrived here on third inst., and judge our feelings when, after some twelve hundred miles of travel through an uncultivated desert, and the last one hundred miles of the distance through and among lofty mountains and narrow and difficult ravines, we found ourselves suddenly, and almost unexpectedly, in a comparative paradise.

We descended the last mountain by a passage excessively steep and abrupt, and continued our gradual descent through a narrow canyon for five or six miles, when suddenly emerging from the pass, an extensive and cultivated valley opened before us, at the same instant that we caught a glimpse of the distant bosom of the Great Salt Lake, which lay expanded before us to the westward, at the distance of some twenty miles.

Descending the table-land which bordered the valley, we saw extensive herds of cattle, horses, and sheep, grazing in every direction, reminding us of that home and civilization from which we had so widely departed—for as yet the fields and houses were in the distance. Passing over some miles of pasture land, we at length found ourselves in a broad and fenced street, extending westward in a straight line for several miles. Houses of sun-dried brick were thickly clustered in the vale before us, some thousands in number, and occupying a spot about as large as the city of New York. They were mostly small, one story high, and perhaps not more than one occupying an acre of land. The whole space for miles, excepting the streets and houses, was in a high state of cultivation. Fields of yellow wheat stood waiting for the harvest, and Indian corn, potatoes, oats, flax, and all kinds of garden vegetables, were growing in profusion, and seemed about in the same state of forwardness as in the same latitude in the States.

At first sight of all those signs of cultivation in the wilderness, we were transported with wonder and pleasure. Some wept, some gave three cheers, some laughed, and some ran and fairly danced for joy—while all felt inexpressibly happy to find themselves once more amid scenes which mark the progress of advancing civilization. We passed on amid scenes like these, expecting every moment to come to some commercial center, some business point in this great metropolis of the mountains; but we were disappointed. No hotel, sign-post, cake and beer-shop, barber pole, market-house, grocery, provision, dry goods, or hardware store distinguished one part of the town from another, not even a bakery or mechanic's sign was anywhere discernible.

Here, then, was something new: an entire people reduced to a level, and all living by their labor—all cultivating the earth, or following some branch of physical industry. At first I thought it was an experiment, an order of things established purposely to carry out the principles of "Socialism" or "Mormonism"; in short, I thought it very much like Owenism personified. However, on inquiry, I found that a combination of seemingly unavoidable circumstances had produced this singular state of affairs. There were no hotels, because there had been no travel; no barbers' shops, because everyone chose to shave himself, and no one had time to shave his neighbor; no stores, because they had no goods to sell or time to traffic; no center of business, because all were too busy to make a center.

There was abundance of mechanic shops, of dressmakers, milliners, and tailors, etc.: but they needed no sign, nor had they time to paint or erect one, for they were crowded with business. Besides their several trades, all must cultivate the land, or die; for the country was new, and no cultivation but their own within a thousand miles. Everyone had his own lot, and built on it; everyone cultivated it, and perhaps a small farm in the distance.

And the strangest of all was, that this great city, extending over several square miles, had been erected, and every house and fence made, within nine or ten months of the time of our arrival; while at the same time, good bridges were erected over the principal streams, and the country settlements extended nearly one hundred miles up and down the country.

This territory, state, or, as some term it, "Mormon Empire", may justly be considered as one of the greatest prodigies of the age, and, in comparison with its age, the most gigantic of all republics in existence, being only its second year since the first seed of cultivation was planted, or the first civilized habitation commenced. If these people were such thieves and robbers as their enemies represented them in the States, I must think they have greatly reformed in point of industry since coming to the mountains.

I this day attended worship with them in the open air. Some thousand of well-dressed, intelligent-looking people assembled; some on foot, some in carriages, and on horseback. Many were neatly, and even fashionably clad. The beauty and neatness of the ladies reminded me of some of our best congregations in New York. They had a choir of both sexes, who performed extremely well, accompanied by a band who played well on almost every instrument of modern invention. Pearls of the most sweet, sacred, and solemn music filled the air; . . . After this, came a lengthy discourse from Mr. Brigham

Young, president of the society, partaking somewhat of politics, much of religion and philosophy, and a little on the subject of gold, showing the wealth, strength, and glory of England, growing out of her coal mines, iron, and industry; and the weakness, corruption, and degradation of Spanish America, Spain, etc., growing out of her gold, silver, etc., and her idle habits.

Every one seemed interested and pleased with his remarks, and all appeared to be contented to stay at home and pursue a persevering industry although mountains of gold were near them. . . . Such, in part, was the discourse to which we listened in the strongholds of the mountains. The Mormons are not dead, nor is their spirit broken. And, if I mistake not, there is a noble, daring, stern, and democratic spirit swelling in their bosoms, which will people these mountains with a race of independent men, and influence the destiny of our country and the world for a hundred generations. In their religion they seem charitable, devoted, and sincere; in their politics, bold, daring, and determined; in their domestic circle, quiet, affectionate, and happy; while in industry, skill, and intelligence, they have few equals, and no superiors on the earth.

I had many strange feelings while contemplating this new civilization growing up so suddenly in the wilderness. I almost wished I could awake from my golden dream, and find it but a dream; while I pursued my domestic duties as quiet, as happy, and contented as this strange people.[8]

---
[8]New York Tribune, October 9, 1849.

Chapter XX

THE COLONIZATION OF WEBER VALLEY

The Miles Goodyear Claim

Although the Great Basin was almost completely uninhabited by white men in 1847, there were several trappers and hunters in the region, collecting beaver and other fur, their camps being on various rivers. One of the trappers, Miles Goodyear, had established himself upon the Weber River about forty miles north of the site that was later Salt Lake City. Goodyear, who was in the employ of the Hudson's Bay Company, obtained from the Mexican Government, in about 1835, a grant of land which embraced a large portion of what is now Weber County, Utah.[1] Here he lived for the twelve years preceding the advent of the Mormons, hunting, trapping, and trading with the Indians.

The Hudson's Bay Company had built a fort upon the Weber River several years before Goodyear came to the region. He took possession of this vacated fort, strengthened and enlarged it, and made it the most pretentious one between Fort Hall and the Mexican forts farther south. Attached to the north end of the original enclosure, Goodyear made a second stockaded enclosure of the same dimensions as the original fort.

The original Goodyear fort covered about one-eighth of an acre of land, and was made very strong; it was built so close to the river's edge that water could be obtained without much risk, even during times of special danger from Indians. Cottonwood logs out on the lowlands along the Weber River were used in its construction and most of the ends were round and a foot or more in diameter; some of them were split in half. The logs, placed upright, sunk firmly in the ground and their tops sharpened, were from twelve to fifteen feet high above the ground and set close together. Loopholes were made in the outside wall and doors and windows on the inside. Within the enclosure were three small log houses.[2]

Purchase of Goodyear's Property

Brigham Young, being very anxious to gain possession of all the best sites in the Basin and realizing the value of this particular one, suggested before returning to Winter Quarters in the fall of 1847 that the Goodyear claim be purchased. Goodyear had already offered to sell for $2,000 cash. Accordingly the High

[1] *Ogden Herald*, December 27, 1919.
[2] *Ibid.*, December 27, 1919.

Council appointed Ira Eldredge, Daniel Spencer and Henry G. Sherwood as a committee for the purpose of collecting money to buy the claim. The committee reported two days later that it was unable to raise sufficient money. November 16, Mr. Goodyear visited Salt Lake where further consultations took place regarding the purchase of his claim by the Mormons.

About the time that Goodyear made this visit, James Brown returned from California where he had been sent to collect money which was due certain members of the Mormon Battalion group. In his journey Brown visited Goodyear's Fort, observing the excellent possibilities for a settlement there.

James Brown, accompanied by Amasa M. Lyman, Jedediah M. Grant and others, visited the Weber River, "to view this important situation for the planting of new settlements, and to advise with him [Goodyear] relative to its purchase." They "undoubtedly reported the prospects for northern settlements to the High Council left in charge of the parent colony, presided over by Father John Smith, General Charles C. Rich and John Young, brother of President Brigham Young."[3] The council decided that the Goodyear claim and property on the Weber should be purchased. Accordingly, on January 6, 1848, Captain Brown entered into negotiations with Miles Goodyear for all the land he claimed. About a week later the purchase was made, Goodyear receiving 3,000 Spanish pesos, worth $1,150 in United States money, for the land and improvements he owned in virtue of the Spanish grant. In addition to the farm-lands, this purchase included a fort, seventy-five head of cattle, a similar number of goats, six horses, and twelve sheep. In the words of Edward W. Tullidge:

> The money thus brought into the country during the absence of the Pioneers, gives an evident reason of the commencement of colonization in the North, on the Weber River, a year before it began in the south with the Provo colony. It was the money obtained by Captain Brown that enabled him to make the purchase in question, and hence to start a colony in the North, which further strengthens the historian's opinion that it was a part of the colonizing plan of President Young, given to Captain Brown when he sent him to California to collect the Battalion pay.[4]

Captain Brown made the purchase of the Goodyear lands with the gold which he had brought from California. However, it was not the portion belonging to the soldiers that he used, but his own money, part of which he had received while in military service and part of which he made as a business gain on his trip to California.

³Edward W. Tullidge, *History of Utah*, II, 7.
⁴*Ibid.*

Founding of Ogden by the Mormons

Almost immediately after making the purchase, James Brown and his family moved into the old Goodyear Fort where later during the year other colonists joined them. Quoting from Andrew Jenson, assistant Church historian, who identified the site of Goodyear's Fort on May 2, 1920: "This fort was situated at or near the intersection of what is now Twenty-eighth Street and the Weber River."[5] It was located on the east side of a knoll fifty feet high which caused the Weber River to swing slightly westward. This site furnished a splendid lookout if an enemy should approach and also made it possible to locate the fort on the water's edge. The following year, on account of the river overflowing its banks, Brown moved the cabins to higher ground about forty rods southeast from Goodyear's Fort. The new site selected was where Mr. Ranks, who had migrated to California the previous year, had formerly built a house. Brown moved part of his family into the deserted building. The majority of the former inhabitants of the Goodyear Fort now moved to this new location. They built their houses in fort style enclosing about a hundred yards square. The Goodyear Fort was entirely deserted, everything being taken to this new location which was called Brown's Fort or Brownsville.

The pioneer cabins constructed in these forts were composed of cottonwood logs, with roofs of poles, rushes and dirt. Only a few of the houses had puncheon floors, made by splitting logs in two and smoothing the split sides. The other cabins had dirt floors.

Food became very scarce in the Great Basin the first winter that the Mormons were there. In February, 1848, Captain James Brown sent Thomas Williams, Alexander Brown and Ephraim K. Hanks to Fort Hall, 160 miles distant, to purchase flour. They obtained six hundred pounds at twenty-five dollars per hundred. Two hundred pounds were to supply the colonists at the Weber while the remainder was taken on to Salt Lake City.

That same spring Captain James Brown, his sons Alexander and Jess J., and hired help, prepared ground and planted a few acres of wheat. The captain also planted turnips, cabbage, potatoes, corn, and a few watermelons, from seeds which he had brought from California on mules. Goodyear and his men expected that the crops would be a total failure and tried to discourage Brown when he was preparing to plant them. Regardless of the discouragement received from the mountaineers, Captain Brown and his

---

[5]Andrew Jenson, "The Building of Utah and Her Neighbors," *Deseret News*, December 19, 1934.

sons tended the crops carefully and were successful in producing that first season on the Weber one hundred bushels of wheat and seventy-five bushels of corn, besides cabbage, turnips, potatoes, and watermelons. In addition to this, the family milked about twenty-five cows which they had purchased from Goodyear, and from the milk manufactured the first cheese produced in Utah by the Mormons. Mary Black Brown, one of the Captain's wives, made the cheese, several thousand pounds being produced the first season.

ASSISTANCE OF JAMES BROWN TO PEOPLE OF SALT LAKE CITY IN 1848

The crop produced on the Weber by Captain James Brown and his sons in 1848 was of vital importance in tiding over the starvation period in Salt Lake City until another crop could be raised the following year. Under those dire conditions when foodstuff was so scarce, potatoes sold from six to twenty dollars per bushel and the market price of wheat was five dollars per bushel. But Captain Brown's generous nature would not permit him to charge the Saints such an excessive price. He sold flour in Salt Lake and Ogden for four dollars per hundred. He also killed a large number of his fat cattle to tide over the destitute brethren. In bringing the people through that second winter in the Great Basin without a large casualty list, "historians will . . . attribute much of the good results to the presiding care of Brigham Young and the semi-communistic example of such pioneers as Captain James Brown, who with an unstinted hand fed to the people his breadstuff, and his beef and butter and cheese from his bountiful dairy."[6]

PLAGUE OF CRICKETS

The main cause of such a shortage of food in the Basin in 1848 was the plague of crickets. The story has often been repeated of how those insects came in hordes to ravage the crops the following summer (1848); and how gulls came from the islands of the Great Salt Lake and saved the crops from utter destruction by feasting upon the crickets until full, disgorging, and feasting again until the enemy was exterminated. At the present time there stands on Temple Square in Salt Lake City a monument erected in honor of the birds that saved the Mormon Pioneers from starvation. Mr. Daniel Tyler reported the cricket plague in the following words:

Wingless, dumpy, black, swollen-headed, with bulging eyes in cases like goggles, mounted upon legs of steel wire and clock springs, and with a general

[6]Tullidge, op. cit., 13.

personal appearance that justified the Mormons in comparing him to a cross of the spider and the buffalo, the Deseret cricket comes down from the mountains at a certain season of the year, in voracious and desolating myriads. It was just at this season that the first crops of the new settlers were in the full glory of their youthful green. The assailants could not be repulsed. The Mormons, after their fashion, prayed and fought, and fought and prayed, but to no purpose. The "Black Philistines" mowed their way, even with the ground, leaving it as if touched with an acid or burnt by fire.

But an unlooked for ally came to the rescue. Vast armies of bright birds, before strangers to the valley, hastened across the lake from some unknown quarter, and gorged themselves upon the well-fatted enemy. They were snow white, with little head and clear dark eyes, and little feet, and long wings, that arched in flight "like an angel's." . . . They disappeared every evening beyond the lake; but returning with sunrise, continued their welcome visiting till the crickets were all exterminated.

This curious incident recurred the following year, with this variation, that in 1849 the gulls came earlier and saved the wheat crops from all harm whatsoever.[7]

This plague of crickets of 1848, added to the drought which killed much of the crops, almost reduced the Pioneers to starvation. The little wheat and other vegetation not destroyed by the two enemies heretofore mentioned was almost entirely killed later by frost. Only the patriarchal and cooperative organization of the Mormons saved the lives of these frontiersmen.

Captain James Brown retained only two or three hundred acres for himself of the immense tract of land that he purchased from Miles Goodyear along the Weber River. The remainder he turned over to other colonists without price and without question of their rights as fellow settlers. This action was completely in accord with the Mormon land policy, as has been previously outlined. Brigham Young informed his followers the second day after their arrival in the Great Basin that they had no land to sell nor to buy, that land should be measured out for city and farming purposes according to their needs, but that they must be industrious and take care of what they received. In the words of Edward Tullidge:

So Captain James Brown, though he had purchased the Goodyear claim, to give the colonists undisputed occupation, was living up to the strict order of the community; he had no land to sell to his brethren; it was theirs for legitimate settling without money and without price.[8]

Within two years after the purchase of the Goodyear lands (1848-49) some twenty to thirty families had cast their lot with Captain Brown in Weber Valley. The majority of them located at Brownsville on the Weber, but a few families settled north of

[7]Daniel Tyler, *The Mormon Battalion*, 103-104.
[8]*Ibid.*

SEAGULL MONUMENT ON TEMPLE SQUARE, SALT LAKE CITY

COALVILLE, UTAH, 1869

the Ogden River (about two or three miles northeast of Goodyear Fort), where Ezra Chase and his sons, settlers of 1848, had previously located.

BRIGHAM YOUNG AND PARTY AT OGDEN, 1849

President Brigham Young and party visited the frontiersmen in Weber Valley in the fall of 1849. They spent two or three hours during the morning fishing in the Ogden River. Thomas Bullock wrote:

> Here we were regaled with plenty of mountain trout . . . Ogden's Fork is about a rod wide and eighteen inches deep, the water being soft and clear and the banks of the river lined with willows, rose bushes and small trees. Ezra Chase said that the land was very productive in grain. A short distance below, he said, it will yield a hundred bushels of crickets to the acre and fifty bushels of mosquitoes.[9]

The party then returned to Brownsville where a meeting was held at which Brigham Young, Heber C. Kimball, and Jedediah M. Grant gave the pioneer settlers timely instructions. The following day the president granted Captain James Brown the right to build a bridge across the Weber River and another across the Ogden with the privilege of collecting toll from all parties who should cross these bridges.

The Mormon Colonizer was always concerned as to the best location for each settlement. It was his practice to visit a settlement soon after its founding to see if the people had chosen the best available location. If they had not he would choose a site for them and would often plan the city himself. While on this trip to Weber Valley (September 3, 1849) he carefully selected the site for Ogden City. Thomas Bullock, the President's secretary, gave the following account:

> President Young, Heber C. Kimball, Jedediah M. Grant, Thomas Bullock and others went on to the top of the sand-hill to view or select a location for a town. After staying about an hour, it was decided that the town should be laid out on the south side of Ogden's Fork at the point of bench land, so that the waters from the Weber River and Ogden's Fork might be taken out for irrigation and other purposes.[10]

The return trip to Salt Lake City was accomplished in typical fashion. Upon arriving at Warm Springs just north of the city, the president's company fell into order of procession that they might return to the capital city in a manner worthy of the Gov-

[9]Thomas Bullock, *Latter-day Saint Journal History*, September 2, 1849. Ms.
[10]*Ibid.*, September 3, 1849.

ernor and President. In the words of Bullock: "The band played as we traveled through the streets, and at the Council House it played the 'Sweets of Weber,' a song composed by Heber C. Kimball. The company then dispersed to their respective homes."[11]

ACTIVITIES OF LORIN FARR IN WEBER VALLEY

Brigham Young was an excellent judge of men, as his success in colonization testifies. His choice of the leader for Weber Valley was a happy one but was not made until some time after the valley was settled—a procedure Brigham often followed. In the words of Andrew Jenson:

> Soon after the return of President Young and his pioneer compeers, with the body of the Church from Winter Quarters, Brigham Young, being desirous for the rapid growth and efficient government of the young colonies, sent Lorin Farr to take charge of affairs in Weber County.[12]

Farr arrived in Weber Valley early in the year of 1850. He had been residing at Salt Lake since September 21, 1847, having crossed the plains in Daniel Spencer's company, which company was the first to arrive in the Basin after the original Pioneer band. "Lorin Farr, though not the pioneer of the Weber colony, may very properly be considered the founder of Ogden City, of which he was the first mayor. Under his fostering care and judicious administration the city grew up."[13] In the capacity of mayor he served continuously for twenty years without pay. For a number of years he was a member of the Utah Legislature. He built the first gristmill and sawmills in Weber County, obtaining his waterpower from the Ogden River. He was foremost in promoting and in effecting all of the early irrigation projects, not only in Ogden, but also in the neighboring settlements.

March 5, 1850, the first branch of the Church of Jesus Christ of Latter-day Saints in Weber County was organized and received the name of the Weber Branch. Lorin Farr was appointed president. The following year, January 26, 1851, he was appointed president of the Weber Stake which was formed at that time. Thus Brother Farr was the ecclesiastical as well as the civil head of Ogden throughout its formative period. For the majority of these public services he worked without economic remuneration.

In accordance with Brigham Young's Indian policy, in February, 1850, soon after the arrival of Lorin Farr in Ogden, the first

---

[11]*Ibid.*, September 4, 1849.
[12]Jenson, *op. cit.*, December 28, 1934.
[13]*Ibid.*

company of militia in Weber County was organized. All of the male members of the infant settlement were enrolled. Cyrus C. Canfield, who had served as a lieutenant in the Mormon Battalion, was elected captain with Francillo Durfee as first lieutenant.

Lorin Farr and his associates early in 1850 constructed Farr's Fort to protect themselves against the Indian attacks, as the red men north of the Ogden River were beginning to molest the settlers. It was located one and a half miles northwest of the mouth of Ogden Canyon, just north of the Ogden River. Five acres of land were enclosed in the fort by the houses, which were joined end to end facing the inward square. The spaces between houses were stockaded with pickets placed deep into the ground and extending upward some twelve feet. However, the north wall of the fort was never completed. A schoolhouse and store stood in a central place in the fort. As was a common practice in Mormon communities, the schoolhouse was one of the first buildings erected and served for both church and school. Mr. Walton and Sanford Bingham conducted educational work there in 1850. During the Indian troubles of 1850-1852 practically all the settlers on the north side of the Ogden River lived in Farr's Fort, but the following year the majority of them moved out.

As had been pointed out, Lorin Farr erected the first sawmill and the first gristmill in Weber Valley. These he established shortly after his arrival in 1850. They were located about one and a half miles northwest from the mouth of Ogden Canyon, or about seven hundred feet northeast of Farr's Fort. A canal named Mill Creek was constructed from his millsites to the Ogden River about a mile distant. The gristmill was completed in time to grind all of the wheat raised in 1850 and continued in operation on that site until 1862, at which date it was moved nearer to the center of the city. After moving the Farr flourmill, Lorin Farr and two associates utilized the site for a woolen factory.

About the time that Lorin Farr came to Ogden in January, 1850, the General Assembly of the State of Deseret passed an ordinance for the construction of a road from Ogden to Provo. This ordinance read as follows:

Section 1. Be it ordained by the General Assembly of the State of Deseret that a state road, eight rods in width, be located from Ogden, the county seat of Weber County, south, passing the Temple block in the Great Salt Lake City, and terminating at the town of Provo, the county seat of Utah County.[14]

In order to carry out the provisions of this ordinance and to

[14]*Latter-day Saint Journal History,* February 20, 1850, Ms.

arrange for the construction of the road, Governor Young sent Apostle Ezra T. Benson to Weber Valley about five weeks after the ordinance was enacted. The following is taken from a letter from the president under date of March 4, 1850:

> We send you Brother Ezra T. Benson to counsel, instruct you and gladden your hearts, organize you and set you in order; listen to his counsel, and you will surely be blessed.
> We purpose having a state road laid out this spring and worked through, and wish the bridge Captain Brown purposes building to be placed where said road will cross the river. Brother Benson will consult Captain Brown and the brethren where they would prefer having it, and we will have the road run accordingly. We are coming down to see you and lay out a city as soon as the weather will permit.[15]

SUMMARY: LAND SETTLEMENT OF WEBER VALLEY TO FALL OF 1854

In compliance with his promise, Brigham Young, Heber C. Kimball, Orson Hyde and others, in August, 1850, formally laid out the city of Ogden and named it after the river on which it was situated. Quoting from the *Deseret News* of September 7, 1850: "President Young and his associates, as mentioned in our last, returned on Saturday evening, same week, having located the corner stake, and given a plan for the City of Ogden, in Weber County."[16] The site of Ogden was between the forks of the Ogden and Weber rivers on the site selected by the President's party the previous year. The president then urged the people to move immediately to their city lots, build substantial dwellings, a meetinghouse, a schoolhouse, and to fence their lots and plant trees. It was Brigham's intention to make Ogden the headquarters of the northern settlements.

So rapid was the growth of that new community that by October, 1853, its Church population, including North Ogden and the East Weber branches, was 1515 souls. The statistical report read at the general conference of the Church on the foregoing date is as follows: "The Ogden First Ward contained 449 souls belonging to the Church; Ogden Second Ward, 633 souls; Ogden Third Ward, 200 souls; (North Ogden) and East Weber, 233 souls."

Before the end of 1851 settlers on the Weber had scattered out as far as the mouth of Weber Canyon. Here a branch of the Church, originally called East Weber, later known as Easton, and still later as Uintah, was organized.

15Brigham Young, *Deseret News*, March 4, 1850.
16*Deseret News*, September 7, 1850.

Erastus Bingham located on a land claim which he had taken up in what is now the Lynne Ward, north of Ogden, in the spring of 1851. This place subsequently became known as Bingham's Fort, after the construction of the fort in the fall of 1853. Several other settlers joined Bingham in the spring and summer of that year.

Apostle Wilford Woodruff wrote in journal form to the *Deseret News* the observations he made while visiting the settlements in Weber Valley in the fall of 1854, picturing the thrift and success of those young settlements.

November 30, 1854. I rode to South Fort. In the afternoon I visited their school, which is taught by a female, and has some thirty-five scholars who are making good improvement; and held a meeting in the evening. About twenty-five families are here gathered around a hollow square of forty rods, but their wall is not made.

December 1. I rode to East Weber Fort, stopped at Bishop Wadsworth's and preached in the evening. This fort is sixty rods by twenty, contains some thirty-five families and has a school. The wall is nearly finished and the buildings are on each side of a street running east and west through the center.

December 2. I rode to Ogden City and preached in the evening to a full house. This is the county seat of Weber County and is a flourishing place containing some 150 families. The city wall will enclose one mile square and is to be built of earth eight feet high, three feet wide at the bottom and eighteen inches at the top; but very little is yet built. They have two schools with about 120 scholars, one adobe school house, thirty by twenty feet. There are many good dwellings in this city; also two stores, on of which has been recently built by Captain James Brown. They have raised during the past season about 10,000 bushels of wheat.

December 3, I rode to Bingham's Fort and preached in the morning. This Fort contains 732 inhabitants, is very flourishing and is surrounded by an abundance of good farming land. . . . Two schools are about to commence. . .

After meeting at Bingham's Fort, I rode to Ogden Hole (North Ogden). . . . This is one of the most flourishing settlements in the Territory, according to the number of inhabitants. The soil is very rich and fertile, and water abundant. They number forty-seven families, and have raised 16,000 bushels of wheat. . . . A thrashing machine was in operation when I was there. Their school has fifty scholars. . . .[17]

[17]Wilford Woodruff, *Deseret News*, December 11, 1854.

CHAPTER XXI

FORT UTAH

DESCRIPTION OF UTAH VALLEY

Immediately south of the Great Salt Lake Valley, separated from it by a low range of mountains cut through by the Jordan River, lies one of the most beautiful valleys in the Great Basin—the Utah Valley. The scenery is magnificent—a contrast of perpetually snow-capped mountains, a sparkling fresh water lake, broad fields of agricultural lands bordered by pastures and canyon streams, the largest of which is the Provo River. The most majestic of the peaks is Mount Timpanogos, which rises twelve thousand feet above sea level.

This region lying between the Wasatch Mountains and Utah Lake contains some of the most productive soil in the Rocky Mountains. The climate is delightful and well adapted to the growing of fruits of every description and the different kinds of grains and hay that are grown in temperate regions. Because of its natural advantages, and because it was settled in typical Mormon style, it furnishes a good example of Brigham Young's colonization policy.

According to earliest records of Utah Valley, it had long been a favorite home of many Indians. These tribes who inhabited it at the advent of the Mormon pioneers "were known as the Pah-Utahs or Pah-Utes, 'Pah' meaning 'water' in the native dialect. They lived mostly on fish found in the lake and in adjacent streams."[1] They were a nomadic group.

Many of the streams, lakes, valleys and mountains in Utah were given the tribal name of groups of Utes or of Indian chiefs. Thus Utah Lake, named after these nomads, was also known by the name of Lake Timpanogos. The mountain standing in the eastern side of Utah Valley still bears the name of Mount Timpanogos. Sanpete Valley was named after the Sanpitch Indians; Uinta Valley and mountains and the town of Kanosh were named after Indian chiefs. The towns of Parowan, Paragonah, Kanab, Panguitch, Tintic and others also have Indian names.

----

[1]Andrew Jenson, "The Building of Utah and Her Neighbors." *Deseret News, January* 18, 1935.

The Establishing of Fort Utah—Mormon Methods of Colonization

Before arriving in the Great Basin, President Young and his associates lost no opportunity to collect information upon the region toward which they were headed. The Mormon frontier settlements being located in Missouri during the active part of the fur trading period furnished the Saints an opportunity to gain much valuable information directly from the trappers. The first company of the Pioneers under the leadership of Brother Brigham met James Bridger just east of his fort on the Black's Fork in Wyoming. The President was so intent on increasing his information about the Great Basin that he immediately gave orders for camp to be made, although it was mid-afternoon. He spent the afternoon and evening in asking a thousand and one questions of Jim Bridger—a trapper who knew the Salt Lake and Utah valleys and adjacent region better, possibly, than any other living man.

After Brigham Young's arrival from Winter Quarters in the fall of 1848, he lost no time in investigating the possibilities of Utah Valley, with a fixed determination to utilize them. January 6, 1849, the Church Presidency decided to send Amasa M. Lyman with eight companions "to Utah Valley to learn its capabilities for a stock range and that when the cattle went, forty or fifty men should go with them; that Isaac M. Higbee, John S. Higbee and William Wadsworth constitute a committee to seek out suitable fishing places in the Utah Lake, establish fisheries and supply the market."[2]

Six days later Apostle Lyman reported to President Young that it was not advisable to take cattle into Utah Valley at that time,[3] mainly because of reports of the thieving inclinations of the Indians in that district.[4]

By the time two months more had passed, President Brigham Young and his counselors had reached the decision to plant a colony in Utah Valley for the purposes of agriculture and fishing. In making the plans for its establishment, the great Mormon Colonizer was formulating a precedent—a definite system—which he used time and time again in developing his extensive colonial empire. A study of this procedure helps one to understand Brigham Young's foresight, his power over his people, and his success as a founder of a commonwealth.

A council meeting of the leading Church officials was held in

---

2*Latter-day Saint Journal History*, January 6, 1849, Ms.
3*Ibid.*, January 12, 1849.
4*Ibid.*, February 27, 1849; March 5-6, 1849.

the house of Heber C. Kimball in Salt Lake City, March 10, 1849. They voted unanimously "that a colony of thirty men settle in Utah Valley this spring for the purpose of farming and fishing and of instructing the Indians in cultivating the earth and of teaching them civilization."[5] Several names were suggested as part of the colony at that meeting. Within the next four or five days the Church officials carefully selected other brethren, many of them with families, and added them to the original list. Thirty-three families, numbering in all about one hundred fifty individuals, were called directly by President Young and enrolled for the establishment of a settlement in Utah Valley. These brethren honored the authority of their leader by willingly consenting. The strength of a great leader depended upon the willingness of the group to follow.

Although Brigham Young was actively engaged in several important projects at this time, he gave each of them his individual attention, neglecting no detail. He requested twenty-nine of the brethren who had been called to settle Utah Valley to meet at his office on March 13, 1849, for the purpose of receiving instructions. John S. Higbee, one of the group who had visited Utah Valley in 1847 with Parley P. Pratt, was selected president of the company. His brother Isaac Higbee was appointed as first counselor and Dimick B. Huntington as second. The following day the Presidency of the Church and other leading officials spent the complete day "counseling with regard to Utah Valley farming, fencing, etc."[6]

President Brigham Young and his counselors followed the practice of informing the Saints in various parts of the world in general epistles as to the movements and achievements of the colonists in the Great Basin. In a general epistle dated April 9, 1849, the following paragraph appeared:

About thirty of the brethren have recently gone to Utah Valley about 60 miles south, to establish a small colony for agricultural purposes and fishing, hoping thereby to lessen the call for beef which at the present time is rather scarce, at an average of seven to eight cents per pound, but will improve with the vegetation.[7]

The company arrived at the Timpanogos, or Provo River, on April 1, 1849. About three miles before reaching the river, they were confronted by a Ute Indian named Angatowata, who placed himself across their trail and commanded the Mormons to proceed

[5]*Ibid.*, March 10. 1849.
[6]*Ibid.*, March 14, 1849; March 17. 1849.
[7]*Ibid.*, April 9, 1849.

no farther. It took interpreter Dimick B. Huntington a full hour to convince the Indian that the settlers and the Indians might try living together, that the whites would be the friends of the red men and would assist them in every way possible.[8]

Upon reaching the Provo River, the colonists crossed to the south bank and selected a site for their fort about a mile and a half east of Utah Lake and about two miles west of the present site of Provo. The spot chosen was on the level floor of the valley where the water could be taken from the Provo River and applied to the farm lands with the least labor and expense. This general procedure was followed as each new colony was founded.

The bottom lands surrounding their selected site were dark and rich and abounded with grass suitable for grazing. Bunch grass grew plentifully between their camp and the lake. There was a heavy growth of large cottonwood and box elder trees along the river with a large supply of cedar extending some four or five miles north in a belt about half a mile wide. Numerous pine groves were to be found on the mountain sides and in the canyons, accessible, however, only after much labor had been exerted in making roads into the rugged canyons.

Farming lands were immediately opened on the rich bottom lands on the west, south and east of the place selected for the fort, most of the farms being on the west side towards the lake. Water from a spring about seventy-five rods northeast of the fort ran southwesterly, passing close to the south end of the fort.

Erecting the Fort

Under the direction of President John S. Higbee, Isaac Higbee, Dimick Huntington, and Captain Jefferson Hunt of Mormon Battalion fame, Fort Utah was constructed. The group began work on the fort April 3, two days after arriving at Provo River, and in about six weeks it was completed. The fort consisted of a stockade enclosing a parallelogram, "about twenty by thirty rods, enclosing an ancient mound near the center."[9] The outer walls of the east, north, and west sides of the fort were composed mostly of cabins built of cottonwood logs in a continuous line. Pickets twelve feet high were set solidly together to form the south wall and to fill any spaces between cabins. Light was admitted into each cabin through two windows—one at the back and one at the front. Coarse cloth was used to cover the windows, as the settlers had no glass. On

[8]George W. Bean, *Journal*, April 1, 1849. Ms.
[9]*Latter-day Saint Journal History*, May 10, 1849. Ms.

the mound in the center of the fort, a bastion, or raised platform, about fifteen feet high, was erected. A twelve pound cannon was placed on this bastion and fired on different occasions in order to impress the natives with a proper respect. A corral was built on the east in which the cattle were kept at night. In addition to this general stock corral, private corrals were built behind the respective cabins with gates or back door openings.

Selecting a Site for the Settlement, and Establishing an Ecclesiastical Government

Like most Mormon colonies, during the first few months of its history the settlement at Fort Utah was under the direction of an ecclesiastical organization and administration, the settlers enacting what laws they needed by their vote at public meetings. John S. Higbee was the ecclesiastical head of the colony at first but was replaced in about two months by his brother Isaac Higbee. The following letter announcing the appointment of Isaac Higbee to the leadership of the Provo settlement was written by President Brigham Young:

> Great Salt Lake City
> May 28, 1849.
>
> To Isaac Higbee, president of the settlement in Utah Valley.
> Dear Brother:
> At a council of the Presidency, Twelve, and others held in the Recorder's office in this city, last evening, upon the suggestion and request of John S. Higbee to be released from the duties of the presidency of your place, it was unanimously voted that Isaac Higbee should be the president in his stead. You will therefore take due notice of your appointment, choose your counselors and receive the necessary ordination at the earliest convenient opportunity.[20]
>
> (Signed)
> Brigham Young.

In the winter of 1849-1850, when, under the State of Deseret, civil machinery was set up to assist the ecclesiastical government already in operation, Governor Young appointed President Isaac Higbee to be chief justice of the newly-organized Utah County. As was often the case in Mormon colonial history, upon the organization of civil government, the presiding ecclesiastical official received the head appointment.

About five months after the establishing of Fort Utah, Brigham Young in company with Willard Richards, Thomas Bullock, Truman O. Angell, John S. Higbee, and three or four ladies, paid a visit to the newly established settlement. They arrived at the Provo

---

[20]*Ibid.,* May 28, 1849.

FORT UTAH, CONSTRUCTED IN 1849

CHIEF KANOSH–PAUVAN VALLEY–KANOSH, UTAH

CHIEF WALKER AND HIS BROTHER ARAPENE

River toward evening of September 15, 1849. Thomas Bullock wrote:

> At length we came in sight of the grove in which lies the fort, when the old pioneer gun belched forth our introduction to the fort. The brethren were collecting their cattle for the night when we arrived. On crossing the island in the river, we saw some very beautiful timber. We then crossed the Provo River, a fine stream, five rods wide and from sixteen to twenty inches deep.[11] . . .

One of the primary purposes Brother Brigham had in making this early visit to Fort Utah was to select the best location for a town, as he had done in Weber. On this occasion the party in three carriages, accompanied by five men on horseback, left the fort on Monday, September 17, to locate the town site. They found what appeared to them to be an excellent place about two miles east of the fort. Brigham Young made this selection "on account of its elevation above the line marked by the overflow of the Provo River which in the early summer overflowed the bottom lands."[12] After selecting the site, the president's party decided on the dimensions of the blocks and city to be established there. That evening:

> At early candle-light the brethren met in Captain Hunt's house to converse about the southern country and the prospects of settling it. Many questions were asked in regard to routes, traveling, locations, incidents, etc., and the prospects before the Saints caused quite a good feeling. . . . September 18 . . . Young and party left the fort and arrived at Great Salt Lake City the same evening.[13]

INDIAN POLICY

Before sending colonists to Utah Valley, the President had been informed that the Indians in that district were rather numerous and hard to get along with. About three weeks after the arrival of the colonists at Fort Utah, April 18, 1849, Dimick B. Huntington, the Indian interpreter, wrote to the President as follows: "There are quite a number of Indians in this vicinity; they appear very friendly at present, but they are very uncertain."[14] The following month he wrote that the Indians were more numerous at the settlement than they were a month earlier, that numbers were coming in from all quarters, but that they were as yet friendly.[15]

In response to Huntington's letter, on May 19, Brigham wrote to the brethren to finish Fort Utah as soon as possible, to keep continually on their guard and not admit the Indians inside their fort,

[11]*Ibid.,* September 15, 1849.
[12]*Utah Stake Manuscript History,* September 17, 1849.
[13]Thomas Bullock, *Latter-day Saint Journal History,* September 17-18, 1849, Ms.
[14]Dimick B. Huntington to Brigham Young, in *ibid.,* April 18, 1849.
[15]*Ibid.,* May 18, 1849.

unless it were a few unarmed ones at a time. He urged that they could not be too cautious or too well prepared for defense, for they might be deceived by the appearance of the Indians. At any moment, if they were not on guard, they might suffer loss.[16]

Upon careful consideration of the Indian conditions in Utah and to prevent any occasion for an Indian uprising, the Mormon pioneer leaders decided to have regularly appointed men to trade with the natives. President Young sent word to Isaac Higbee that Dimick B. Huntington and Alexander Williams were appointed to do the trading with the Indians for the entire group of settlers:

> All other persons are prohibited from attempting to trade with them or they will be fined by the Bishop for a breach of obedience. It was also ordered (at a council meeting of the First Presidency and Apostles) that Brothers Huntington and Williams should be paid double wages for the days that they were actually engaged in trading and to let the brethren have the skins, furs, etc., at the cost, when trading is done in the fort or vicinity, but if they have to travel a great distance in order to trade, then they make their own arrangements; at the same time they are requested to keep their minds directed towards the benefits of the brethren and not be oppressive in the charges. . . .
> It will be better for our settlement not to be so familiar with the Indians; it makes them bold, impudent and saucy and will become a source of trouble and expense to you. Keep them at a respectful distance, all the time, and they will respect you the more for it.
> Your affectionate brother in the Gospel,
> Brigham Young.[17]

SKIRMISH WITH THE INDIANS

In spite of all the precautions taken by the leaders to prevent trouble, Indian hostilities did develop which became very serious for the infant colony. Unfortunately, some of the colonists were really to blame for beginning this trouble. August 1, 1849, when the colony was only four months old, Richard A. Ivie, Y. Ruffus Stoddard and Jerome Zabriskie met an Indian called Old Bishop a short distance from the fort. Ivie immediately asserted that the shirt the Indian was wearing had been stolen. He tried to take the shirt, whereupon a scuffle ensued in which the Indian was killed. The men, fearing the results, weighted the body with rocks and sank it in the river.

The Indians became suspicious, instituted a search, and found the body. Immediately they were greatly excited. First they demanded the murderers, but their request being refused, they asked

---

[16]Brigham Young, *ibid.*, May 19, 1849.
[17]Brigham Young to Isaac Higbee, in *Ibid.*, May 26, 1849.

for compensation in cattle and horses. However, the whites did nothing to satisfy their demands. Shortly after this horses and cattle were found with arrows sticking in them, and on several occasions persons were shot at while a short distance from the fort. The attitude of the red men became so belligerent that the settlers prepared for defense. They organized a militia with Peter W. Connover as captain and conducted military drill daily. It became necessary to post guards at night and to have armed horsemen to care for the stock in the daytime. But cattle were stolen from time to time and the Mormons were ordered off the land under serious threats in case they failed to leave.

Open warfare was probably averted for a few months by the appearance of a large company of gold-seekers en route to the gold fields by way of southern California. This group camped alongside the fort for four or five weeks. Having plenty of arms and ammunition and enough powder to supply the cannon, they were a great aid to the colonists. However, after the California immigrants left, conditions became so critical that toward Christmas open war seemed inevitable. Isaac Higbee reported to Brigham Young the condition at Fort Utah in the fall of 1849. President Young answered as follows:

Salt Lake City,
October 18, 1849.

Dear Brother:

In reply to your letter of the fifteenth instance, requesting counsel concerning the Indians, we reply: Take care of your corn, brethren, and grain of all kinds, and pursue the course proposed in our former letters and counsel to you. Stockade your fort and attend to your own affairs, and let the Indians take care of theirs.

Let your women and children stay in the fort and the Indians stay out; for while you mix with them promiscuously, you must continue to receive such treatment from them as they please to give. This is what we have told you continually, and you will find it true.

Let any man, or company of men be familiar with Indians, and they will be more familiar, and the less influence you will have with them. If you would have dominion over them for their good, which is the duty of the elders, you must not treat them as your equals. You cannot exalt them by this process. If they are your equals, you can not raise them up to you.

You have been too familiar with them; your children have mixed promiscuously with them; they have been free in your houses and some of the brethren have spent too much time in smoking and chatting with them, instead of teaching them to labor. . . . You had better finish your fort; bring all your grain into it, and continue to live in it at present. And when the town is laid out, build thereon, as you have means and the way shall open. May the Lord bless you with wisdom and direct your course in all things.

(Signed)
Brigham Young.[18]

———
[18]*Utah Stake Manuscript History*, October 18, 1849.

Feeling that the Federal Government should take the lead, or at least cooperate in protecting the citizens engaged in making new settlements, Governor Young reported the conditions in Utah Valley to Captain Howard Stansbury. He in turn reported to the army officials at Fort Hall, but snow was too deep for men to be sent to Utah Valley at that time.

January 31, 1850, Isaac Higbee reported to Brigham Young that troubles were becoming very critical at Fort Utah, and "that the brethren were agreed in asking the privilege of defending themselves and chastising the Indians."[19] The Church authorities decided to grant the settlers their request. On February 1, Brigham Young, accompanied by Daniel H. Wells, general of the Nauvoo Legion (the local militia), George D. Grant, and Thomas Bullock called again upon Captain Stansbury in Salt Lake City. Stansbury advised that the local militia be called into service and offered Lieutenant Howland and Dr. Blake of his staff as representatives of the government to accompany the expedition.

The following day General Daniel H. Wells called out the militia. Volunteers were asked to join the force at Cottonwood, where Major Andrew Lytle took command. February 6, the company marched to Fort Utah and there joined Captain Peter W. Connover of the Utah Valley militia. Early the next morning the combined company started toward the fortified camp of the Indians who, hearing of the proposed attack, had taken possession of James Bean's log cabin near the river and had also entrenched themselves in the river-bottom brush and trees about one and one-half miles east of the fort.

Dimick B. Huntington had a long talk with Chief Stick-in-the Head before the whites made an attack. A treaty of peace probably could have been made even at this juncture if it had not been for Chief Big Elk and his band of young warriors. They opened fire on the militia and commenced the battle. Brigham Young gave an account of this fight and its outcome in a letter to Orson Hyde at Kanesville, Iowa, and also to Orson Pratt, Liverpool, England, under date of February 28, 1850:

A portion of the Indians, entrenched in the brush near Fort Utah fought two days, with loss of some of their warriors, and one of our brethren, and a few wounded, now convalescent. On the night following the two day's fight, the surviving Indians retreated to the mountains, whither they were pursued. Peace was offered them and other clans of the same tribe in various canyons around the Lake, but they all said they would fight till they died—they would

19Isaac Higbee, to Brigham Young, in *Latter-day Saint Journal History*, January 21, 1850. Ms.

have no peace when our men proceeded to slay their warriors and take their squaws and papooses prisoners. Many of the Indians fled and could not be found. Peace was apparently restored after killing some twenty or thirty Indians, and the women and children prisoners were distributed among the citizens, clothed, fed, and taught to work. There are many tribes called Utahs from many of whom we have heard, and they appear satisfied with our course, and say 'the Lake Utes are bad Indians' . . .[20]

Brigham Young, accompanied by several others, visited Fort Utah again in the spring of 1850. He arrived there May 21 and remained four days. George D. Grant, Lewis Robinson, Ephraim K. Hanks and Hiram B. Clawson were appointed to trade with the Indians, while the latter were represented by two chiefs, Arrapeen and Talbow. President Young expressed his displeasure with the spirit of levity and gambling shown by the colonists at Fort Utah in their dealings with the red men. After visiting several chiefs in order to strengthen good feeling between the Indians and the colonists, President Young and party left Fort Utah on May 24 for the Mormon Mecca.

[20]Brigham Young to Orson Hyde, in *Ibid.,* February 28, 1850.

CHAPTER XXII

DIRECTED COLONIZATION INTO UTAH VALLEY

SETTLEMENT OF PROVO

"On Saturday, March 23, 1850, President Brigham Young and Elders Thomas Bullock and William M. Lemon, counseling together, agreed to lay out a city in Utah Valley to be called Provo."[1] Fort Utah, supplying the nucleus for the settlement, had been in existence one year. Accordingly another group of colonists was sent by Brother Brigham from Salt Lake City to Fort Utah to reinforce the original settlers and assist in founding Provo.

The site decided upon for the new city was two miles up the river on higher ground. In fact, President Young had selected this spot on his visit to Utah Valley the previous year. The colonists' first efforts were exerted in constructing a new fort on the land now known as North Park or Sowiette Park. This fort was built on the same pattern as Fort Utah which was described in the preceding chapter, except that the enclosure covered about eleven acres of land or more than a full city block. In the middle of the fort was erected a large building fifty feet in length, which was used for both school and meeting purposes and served as a recreation hall as well. Upon completion of this building the President came from the Mormon Mecca to dedicate it. One of the first public projects of each Mormon settlement was to erect such a building.

CHIEF SOWIETTE—A THREATENED INDIAN ATTACK

Shortly after fifty families had established themselves in their new fort, Chief Walker with about four hundred warriors made plans to massacre the settlers. His terrible design would probably have been executed had it not been that old Chief Sowiette, who was friendly to the Mormons, interfered. "When Walker made known his plans, Sowiette answered him by saying, 'And when you and your men get there [to the fort], you will find me and my men helping the Mormons.'" In gratitude to Sowiette, the name of the site of this fort has recently been changed from North Park to Sowiette Park.[2]

---

[1]*Latter-day Saint Journal History*, March 23, 1850. Ms.
[2]Andrew Jenson, "The Building of Utah and Her Neighbors," *Deseret News*, January 25, 1850.

Surveying, Incorporating, and Early Growth of Provo

Provo City was incorporated by an act of the General Assembly of the State of Deseret on February 6, 1851. Two months later the City of Provo was created. Andrew J. Stewart made the survey of Plat A, in which was included the site selected by Brigham Young in 1849 and surveyed by William M. Lemon in 1850. The city plot was one mile square, containing eleven blocks each way, each block being twenty-four rods square, with eight lots to a block. The streets were six rods wide, with the exception of Main Street, running north and south, and Center Street, running east and west, which were eight rods wide.

The colonists commenced building on the city lots soon after the survey was completed in 1851. Before that year had ended Provo had become quite a thriving town, containing several presentable adobe houses. A letter dated January 4, 1852, stated that twenty adobe houses had been erected during the past three months.

It was not long before all of the lots of the first survey of Provo (Plat A) were taken. As the population increased new surveys were made. Plats B and C were added to Plat A on the east, and later Plats D and E were added on the north. The present city of Provo is composed of these four surveys.

Industries

During 1851 industries began to develop rapidly in this infant settlement. Isaac Higbee and James A. Smith built the first gristmill, and Thomas Williams opened the first store. Alanson Norton and Shadrach Holdaway established a carding mill on the north side of the Provo River. This was the beginning of the textile industry for which Provo became famous. January 4, 1852 a tannery was opened by Samuel Clark.[3] A month later a pottery factory, the second in the Territory of Utah, was in full operation.[4] Also in February, David Cluff, Senior, of Provo, announced that he had opened a cabinet shop in which he manufactured furniture out of the finest cottonwood, boxwood and box elder. April 18, 1852, a general epistle of the Church stated, "The country is supplied with wooden bowls from a factory at Provo."[5] Apostle George A. Smith, who was at the time presiding over the Saints in Utah Valley, reported the following to the *Deseret News*, September 27, 1853:

Provo contains over two hundred families, three sawmills, one gristmill,

---

[3]*Deseret News*, January 4, 1852.
[4]*Ibid.*, February 7, 1852.
[5]*Latter-day Saint Journal History*, April 18, 1852, Ms.

one shingle machine propelled by water, one carding machine and fulling mill, and one manufactory of brown earthenware.   There is also a turning lathe for turning wooden bowls, one thrashing machine, propelled by water power, and two cabinet shops.   A meeting house, eighty feet by forty-seven, to be finished with a gallery and steeple tower, has been commenced.   Last week I let the brethren who are newcomers have fifty town lots, which cost them only the expense of recording and surveying—one dollar and a half each. Bishop Blackburn is about finishing the tithing house, thirty-six feet long by twenty-four wide, two stories high with good cellar underneath.

Provo River affords a great amount of water power for machinery.   We occasionally get a taste of trout from Utah Lake, which are very fine.[6]

George A. Smith had come to Utah Valley in July, 1852. On May 19 a letter, signed by many of the Saints in Provo, was written to the First Presidency of the Church asking that he be sent to preside over affairs in Utah Valley. The Saints felt that they should have at least one of the general authorities of the Church living in their section of the country. In response to this request, Brother Brigham came to Provo two months later, and on July 17, called a meeting in the bowery "during which Elder George A. Smith was appointed by unanimous vote to preside over the Saints in Utah County."[7]

WALKER WAR

July 19, 1853, the Walker Indian War broke out, having its beginning in Utah Valley at Springville and Payson. For several months all of the Mormon settlements were in the greatest of danger, many of them suffering losses from the Indians. On October 26, Captain John W. Gunnison, of the United States topographical Engineer Corps, and seven companions were killed by Indians on the warpath. A number of Mormons in various communities throughout the Great Basin lost their lives during these troubles with the natives. Next to the Black Hawk War, it proved to be the most severe Indian uprising experienced by the Mormon colonizers. In the spring of 1854, Governor Young succeeded in making peace with Walker.

These Indian troubles forced the people of Provo who had scattered out on farms to settle more compactly together. Following the advice of President Young and Apostle George A. Smith, the settlers began the construction of a mud wall around the city for protection against the hostile natives. The wall was to be from four to six feet wide at the bottom, two feet at the top, and from

⁰George A. Smith Deseret News, September 27, 1853.
⁷Latter-day Saint Journal History, July 17, 1852, Ms.

twelve to fourteen feet high. According to Mormon practice, the work of building the wall was apportioned among the colonists in proportion to the number of city lots owned. For the next two years work was continued upon the wall, until the west, south, and part of the north sides were completed, but as the Walker War abated and danger from the Indians became less, the work was discontinued. At that time the population of Provo was 1,359.

FOUNDING OF AMERICAN FORK

Within one year and a half after the establishment of Fort Utah, several other thriving settlements had been established in Utah Valley destined to furnish homes for hundreds of Mormon families. The years 1850 and 1851 saw the establishment of American Fork, Lehi, Pleasant Grove, Springville, Spanish Fork, Payson, and Alpine, others being formed later.

American Fork was the first established in this valley after the founding of Provo. The American Fork Creek had long been a favorite camping place for the Indians, and later for pioneers traveling from their base of supplies in Salt Lake City on their early journeyings to the south. However, no attempt was made to found a colony there until the summer of 1850. Stephen Chipman, Arza Adams, and others came out from Great Salt Lake Valley to Utah Valley to fish and hunt. They camped upon the American Fork stream and located a ranch there. They returned to Salt Lake with glowing descriptions of the beauty of the valley and its facilities favorable for colonization.

In the fall of the same year they returned with a surveyor and laid out farms on the American Fork Creek for the prospective settlers in what they termed the Big Survey. They cultivated the big field cooperatively, but later divided it into small tracts among the settlers. The so-called Big Survey was about two miles square, extending south of the present American Fork townsite.

Stephen Chipman, Arza Adams, Noah R. Guyman, and about half a dozen other men built houses near a cottonwood grove shortly after arriving that fall. The population of the infant community was augmented by the arrival of several other families early in the spring of 1851. On May 25 an ecclesiastical government was put into operation, with Leonard E. Harrington as bishop, Arza Adams and James Guymon as counselors. The following month, June 28, American Fork was organized as a precinct under the provisional government of the State of Deseret. It soon became a flourishing agricultural center.

Founding of Lehi

Canute Peterson, David Savage, Charles Hopkins, and four or five others from Salt Lake, who had heard favorable reports about the land around American Fork Creek, set out in July, 1850, on an exploring expedition for the purpose of locating themselves homes. "They proceeded immediately to this little stream, but were surprised to find, on their arrival, that it was already pre-empted by Washburn Chipman, Arza Adams and others who laid claim to all the land and water in that vicinity."[8]

Peterson and his followers, not being able to agree with Chipman and his associates, left American Fork Creek and stopped on a small creek three miles west which they named Dry Creek. They spent the remainder of the day in exploring the surrounding country. At Dry Creek about one mile east of the Jordan River and three-fourths of a mile north of Utah Lake, they discovered a spring, "which they christened Sulphur Springs on account of the peculiar taste of the water. This spring later became the center around which the first settlers located."[9]

The members of the party were favorably impressed with the land in that vicinity, so they surveyed an extensive tract with the intention of returning and making a permanent settlement. Early in September, 1850, in company with a few additional friends, they were back again at Sulphur Springs. Israel Evans, Charles Hopkins, and several other families joined the little colony at the spring before November had passed. There they spent the winter of 1850-1851. Crude log cabins were hastily constructed, but the settlers were so few that only part of a fort was erected. They made temporary shelters for their animals and cut some grass for hay. Although the amount was insufficient, the cattle wintered well, as the season was mild.

In the spring of 1851 several families arrived, settling on other small springs which were discovered near. One group of these colonists became known as the Lott Settlement.

When this colony on Dry Creek was only a few months old, President Brigham Young selected a strong pioneer leader, ordained him a bishop, and sent him to preside over these Saints. This man was David Evans. February 15, 1851, he and his family arrived on Dry Creek about three miles up stream from Sulphur Springs, locating near other families who had recently moved from the latter

---

[8]Hamilton Gardner, *History of Lehi*, 11-12.
[9]*Ibid.*, 12-13.

site. The remainder of the families at Sulphur Springs soon joined the small colony on the creek, which they named Evansville in honor of their new bishop. Evans' home was located in the central part of the present city of Lehi. Hamilton Gardner described David Evans in the following words:

He was destined to play the leading part in the growth of the community for many years. . . . He had previously been ordained a bishop in Nauvoo by Joseph Smith, and had now been sent by Brigham Young to preside over the Saints at Dry Creek. Bishop Evans was a typical pioneer. Possessing the same rugged qualities which distinguished his chief, President Young, he was eminently fitted to direct the work of founding a community. Devoted to his Church, honest, upright, but determined and aggressive, and withal characterized by the rare gift of leadership which, above everything else, was imperative for a pioneer commander, he knew how to direct the colonists to obtain the best results. In his dealings with his fellows he was plain and outspoken, but always just and fair. Altogether, Bishop Evans was precisely the kind of a man needed to meet the situation.[10]

Under Evans' direction, wheat, corn, squash and potatoes were planted in the spring of 1851. It soon became imperative to find irrigation water elsewhere, Dry Creek not being able to supply enough to mature the crops. "As the only supply available was the stream in American Fork Canyon, the prodigious undertaking of digging a ditch seven miles long from the mouth of the canyon to Lehi was begun under the initiative and direction of Bishop Evans."[11] Because of poor tools, sun-baked soil filled with cobble stones, scarcity of food, and other disagreeable frontier conditions, the men would undoubtedly have abandoned the project had it not been for the influence of the Bishop. His humor, tact, and diplomacy inspired the people to continue the ditch to its completion.

Late in the fall of 1851 Lorenzo H. Hatch, Abram Hatch, and Nathan Packer built a flour mill at the mouth of American Fork Canyon, the first mill in the north end of Utah County. Within a year after its completion it was burned down, but on advice of Willard Richards, it was immediately rebuilt, and served the people for many years.

Over thirty families had arrived in this vicinity during 1851. Most of them stopped at Evansville, but some went on to the Lott Settlement. The inhabitants of Evansville were greatly augmented in the spring of 1852 by the arrival of more colonists. Finally, a petition was approved by legislative act February 5, 1852, which

[10]*Ibid.*, 30-31.
[11]*Ibid.*, 35.

incorporated Evansville under the name of Lehi. This name was taken from the important Book of Mormon character. In October, 1853, the population of Lehi was 458.

FOUNDING OF PLEASANT GROVE

Contemporaneously with the establishment of Lehi and American Fork in the summer of 1850, another colony was established in Utah Valley between Provo and American Fork. Pleasant Grove, situated on Battle Creek, lies at the foot of Timpanogos Mountain on a plain sloping westward from the foothills toward Utah Lake. The soil is very rich, producing fine orchards, berries, and grains. The beautiful site of Pleasant Grove was early known to the Saints. It became especially well known in March, 1849, owing to a skirmish with the Indians who were camped near the mountain stream on which Pleasant Grove was later situated. A group of renegade Indians had been molesting the settlers in the southern part of Salt Lake Valley, so Brigham Young sent Captain John Scott with thirty or forty men in pursuit of them. The Indians were overtaken at their camp. A battle ensued with the loss of four Indians and no whites. This was the first battle which the Mormon pioneers fought with the Indians after arriving in the Great Basin. After this skirmish the creek on which it was fought became known as Battle Creek.

Philo T. Farnsworth, William Henry Adams, and John Mercer were the first white men to lay claim to land on Battle Creek (subsequently Pleasant Grove) for agricultural and pastoral purposes. They visited that place in July, 1850, and selected land. On their return trip to the Mormon Mecca they met Calvin W. Moore, Orlando F. Herron, and Joseph Moore coming with a herd of stock. These herders built a cabin on the bank of Battle Creek near a beautiful grove of cottonwood trees, giving rise to the name Pleasant Grove.

September 13, 1850, George S. Clark, John Greenleaf Holman, Lewis Harvey, Charles Price, and several other colonists arrived at Battle Creek with their wagons and supplies ready to make a permanent settlement. They immediately built a small fort consisting of log houses near the grove where the herders had previously built their house. Several other families joined the settlers at this place early in 1851, so that by the time President Young came to their settlement in February to organize an ecclesiastical government, a nucleus for a rather substantial colony had been formed.

After this visit, only a month passed before Brigham and a

group of leading Church officials again came to Pleasant Grove. The occasion for this trip was to effect a number of organizations in the different infant settlements in Utah Valley. On March 18, 1851, Thomas Bullock, Brigham Young's secretary, wrote:

> On entering Utah Valley we beheld the increasing industry and improvements in rescuing the waste lands from their desolate condition. Twelve months ago not a house or fence was to be seen on the north side of the Provo; but now we behold villages springing up, fences to inclose thousands of acres of excellent land and detached farmhouses, with the busy sounds of hum of happiness. We passed through Evansville [Lehi] and McArthursville [American Fork] and were arrived in Pleasant Grove as the sun was setting and were received into the houses of George S. Clark and John G. Holman for the night.[12]

Seven months later, after another tour of Utah Valley, the following appeared in the *Deseret News*:

> In the forepart of August, 1850, there was no sign of improvements from Jordan Canyon to Provo River; now there are many buildings at Dry Creek [Lehi], American Fork, Battle Creek, and nearly all the extensive area included between the road on the east, the lake and Jordan on the west, and Dry Creek and Battle Creek is surveyed into farming lots, and upon a large portion of it good crops were raised this season.[13]

Most of the people who had built close together in the "old fort" at Battle Creek during the first several months of the colony's infancy moved out upon their farms in 1851. Meetings were first held in the private house of William Stevens until a schoolhouse, a small adobe building, was erected in 1852.

In accordance with instructions given by Brigham Young, the Saints at Pleasant Grove were building a new fort when the Walker War broke out in 1853. July 23, the Indians stole twenty-three horses from a corral standing in the middle of the fort. The following day the people evacuated their farms and flocked into the fort for protection, moving many of their houses and the schoolhouse into the fort later.

The population of Pleasant Grove increased steadily. On September 4, 1851, only a year after the colonists arrived, it contained 96 people. Two years later, in October, 1852, there was a total of 290 Church members there.

An event occurred at Pleasant Grove in December, 1853, which illustrates one of Brigham Young's methods of colonization. George S. Clark, who had been acting as bishop from February,

---

[12]Thomas Bullock, *Latter-day Saint Journal History*, March 18, 1851. Ms.
[13]*Deseret News*, II. 11.

1851, to December, 1853, and who had been particularly successful as a leader, was called by the Mormon Colonizer to take fifty families from Pleasant Grove, American Fork and Lehi to Cedar City to help strengthen the southern settlements, and to give his experience and personality as assets to further Brigham's colonial project.

FOUNDING OF ALPINE

Another colony, located in the extreme northeast corner of Utah Valley, six miles northeast of American Fork, was also settled in 1850. William Hooper and Quincy Knowleton had located a cattle ranch on the present site of Alpine in 1849 but the first colonizers, ten or twelve families, arrived in the fall of 1850. Joseph Dudley and Roswell Stevens were among them. January 19, 1855, Alpine, at first called Mountainville, was granted a city charter by the Utah Legislature, being one of the smallest incorporated cities in the United States.

FOUNDING OF SPRINGVILLE

Also in 1850, colonies were established under the direction of President Brigham Young on all of the important canyon streams in Utah Valley south of Provo. Springville, Spanish Fork, and Payson were all founded in the fall of that year. The first of these is located 53 miles southeast of Salt Lake City and about six miles south of Provo. It is very picturesquely situated. The soil is extremely fertile, the climate pleasant, and the scenery varied.

As early as February 1, 1849, a company of Mormon explorers under the direction of Oliver B. Huntington camped upon a creek where Springville was established the following year. They put iron hobbles on one of their mares and turned their animals out to graze for the night. The hobbles were lost near the creek, and the following day the animals were found grazing toward the mouth of Spanish Fork canyon. From then on the creek was called Hobble Creek.

William Miller and his wife came down into Utah Valley from Salt Lake City in the summer of 1850 in search of a good place to build their home. They went as far as the Peteetneet Creek (Payson) and then returned to the Mormon Mecca, having found no other place that impressed them as being so desirable a place as did Hobble Creek. Therefore, shortly after Miller returned to Salt Lake he visited President Young and informed him of his desire to locate in that part of the Basin. It was there decided that as soon as Aaron Johnson and a company of Saints who were then crossing the plains should arrive in Salt Lake, Brigham would send them with Miller to Hobble Creek to establish a settlement.

Upon the arrival of Aaron Johnson, September 2, 1850, with his train of 135 wagons, he was informed by William Miller "that his home in the mountains was already selected for him, and that arrangements had been consummated for him and his company to go to Utah Valley to form a settlement." In order to satisfy Johnson as to the advantage of Hobble Creek he and Miller mounted their horses and visited that spot. They agreed while there that the future city should stand exactly where it now stands.

Shortly after they returned, President Young went down to the Emigration Square in Salt Lake City where Johnson's company was camped. He designated the first eight wagons and told their occupants that they should go to the selected locality and build a fort, which would be made into a town in the near future. The eight families, in obedience to his orders, arrived on the present site of Springville, September 18-19, and began to construct the fort enclosing one and one-half acres. In less than a week after they arrived they had also built a schoolhouse of logs. Seventeen other families soon joined the original group, making a total of twenty-five that spent the winter of 1850-51 in the Springville fort.

President Brigham Young never let an infant colony remain long without paying it a visit to inspect its location, or to establish an ecclesiastical government, or to see if the officers he had appointed were functioning properly and efficiently. Therefore, on March 20, 1851, he and his party arrived at Springville. Thomas Bullock, the clerk of the company, gave the following account of the visit:

> When we were near the beautiful Spring Creek we were met by two companies of horsemen, bearing a flag. These companies opened columns and received us, and then returned to escort us into the fort of Springville, where the whole male population paraded in a line to receive us. After visiting several beautiful springs and examining some of the richest soil that man can wish to see in any part of the world, we returned to supper at William Miller's.
>
> At seven in the evening, the schoolhouse was filled by the people who were addressed by the presidency until nine p. m.; and they afterwards ordained Asahel Perry as president of the branch at Springville and Noah Packard and Stephen C. Perry as his counselors—Aaron Johnson to be the Bishop of the branch, with William Miller and Myron N. Crandall as his counselors.[14]

In the spring of 1851 a townsite was surveyed and the people, who had lived in the fort during the winter, began to build upon

---

[14]Thomas Bullock. *Latter-day Saint Journal History*, March 20. 1851. Ms.

their city lots. All newcomers for the next two years also constructed homes on city lots. Finally, in July, 1853, the Walker War, which practically had its origin in Springville, forced the people to move close together for protection. Eight blocks of Springville were selected for another fort. Houses, connected by an adobe wall and a stockade, were built around the enclosure, and a corral was constructed in the center. For the next two years the colonists lived in the fort, passing through many dark and gloomy days, as the Indian uprisings were numerous.

Meanwhile, from the fall of 1850 on, the colony continued to grow. The immigration of 1852 nearly doubled the population. By October, 1853, the numerical strength of the Springville Ward was 799 people.

FOUNDING OF PAYSON AND SANTAQUIN

The next site selected for colonization was the Peteetneet Creek eighteen miles south of Provo and seven miles south of Utah Lake. This creek was named after an Indian chief. In the fall of 1850, directed by the President, a little immigrant train of three families led by James Pace pitched their camp in the northwest extremity of the present city of Payson on October 20. Early in December they were joined by six more families. These nine families formed the nucleus of what later became a very thriving city.

Only two months after the Saints arrived at Peteetneet, Apostle George A. Smith and party, en route to the Little Salt Lake Valley in Iron County, stopped with them for three or four days—December 18-21, 1850. Among other business attended to was the appointment of a president of the branch. Apostle Smith advised the settlers "that each man should take a small piece of land, fence it, and till it well, in order better to apply the water"[15]— a bit of advice given to each colony. In a letter to President Brigham Young, under date of December 20, 1850, Apostle George A. Smith described the activities at Peteetneet:

> While we were here waiting for the rear wagons, the people of this place came together and were organized into a branch. Brother James Pace was appointed to preside; Brother Andrew J. Stewart was appointed clerk. The branch will be known by the name of the Peteetneet Branch, and numbers thirty-five members, old and young. . . .
> Great credit is due Captain James Pace for the energy he has manifested in making this settlement, twenty miles from any other. From this location

[15]George A. Smith, *Latter-day Saint Journal History*, December 20, 1850, Ms.

under his direction a fine and intensive settlement may soon be looked for by the pioneers of the mountains.[16]

Later the name of the settlement was changed from Peteetneet to Payson in honor of James Pace. When the change first took place, it was spelled "Pacen," but later was changed to "Payson." The Mormon leader visited there early in the spring of 1851 and again on October 24, of that same year. On the latter visit, the scribe of the party stated that the town had been laid out on both sides of Peteetneet Creek about one and a half miles below the canyon. During the next two years the settlement was increased by the arrival of colonists to the extent that the settlers were able to secure a charter from the Utah Territorial Legislature, January 21, 1853, legally forming a city. By October, 1853, Payson and Summit, a small settlement nearby—now named Santaquin—had a total population of four hundred twenty-seven according to the official report read at the general conference of the Church.

FOUNDING OF PALMYRA AND SPANISH FORK

Spanish Fork, another city of importance in Utah Valley twelve miles south of Provo, also had its inception in 1850. Situated on the Spanish Fork River, it was principally an agricultural and fruit growing community, as are all the surrounding towns. Spanish Fork was plotted in a style typical of all settlements planned by President Brigham Young, with its square blocks, wide streets, and shade trees on each side of the street growing along the banks of small streams of water.

Father Escalante, the first white explorer to visit the Great Basin, camped on the Spanish Fork stream in 1776.

Later, when trappers and mountaineers carried on a trade between Santa Fe and California, many of them came over what was known as the Old Spanish Trail, which passed directly through the canyon to the east. Thus the city of Spanish Fork received its name from the canyon and river, which in turn derived their names from events of early Mexican history in that section of the country.

The first Mormon to take up land on the Spanish Fork River was Enoch Reese, one of the earliest of Utah's merchants. In 1850 he laid claim to four hundred acres of land on the river bottoms and sent Charles Ferguson and George Sevey there in the fall of that year with two hundred head of cattle.

Early in the spring of 1851 groups of colonists arrived on the

---

[16]*Ibid.*

Spanish Fork River, broke land and planted crops. These first settlers located in scattered formation on the river bottoms, but more or less in two groups. William Pace and others built their cabins in what was called the upper settlement, but the majority of the colonists found claims on the river about three miles below, and about a mile and a quarter southwest of the present city of Spanish Fork. This lower settlement later received the name of Palmyra. In the spring of 1851 small ditches were hastily dug to convey water from the Spanish Fork River to their farm lands. But in the fall of that year the settlers constructed a large canal, locally known as the South Canal, which taps the Spanish Fork River one mile above where it crosses the present state road. The initial groups of colonists were continually being augmented by incoming settlers.

Apostle George A. Smith was sent as director to Palmyra August, 1852. Within three months after his arrival the population numbered seventy-five families. Apostle Smith directed the laying out of the city and construction of a fort. He wrote as follows to Samuel W. Richards, the editor of the *Millennial Star*, 1852:

> I have sought out the location for the city of Palmyra, on the Spanish Fork River, Utah County, and procured the survey of 360 lots, containing one hundred rods of ground each, and temple square of thirteen acres, and four school squares of two and a half acres each. Streets, six rods wide. The public scquare commands a view of all the settlements in Utah Valley, except Mountainville, and is one of the most delightful spots in the mountains."[17]

Only a few buildings were erected on the Palmyra City plat before the Walker War in July, 1853, which event forced the people to build their houses in fort formation. They were joined by the colonists from the upper settlement on the Spanish Fork River. The statistical report of October, 1853, lists four hundred twelve people at Palmyra.

In the spring of 1854, a number of them left Palmyra to return to their farms farther up the river. That fall a fort was constructed and the following spring a city plot was surveyed which they named Spanish Fork.

These cities and other less important ones in Utah Valley were not haphazardly built. Unlike many frontier towns, they were the result of an organized, controlled and supervised project.

---

[17]George A. Smith. *Millennial Star*, December 26, 1852.

Chapter XXIII

SETTLEMENT OF TOOELE AND RUSH VALLEYS

Founding of Tooele

Tooele Valley was originally named "Tule," the Spanish word for a water-flag which grew in abundance near the shores of the Great Salt Lake. When first writing the name, a clerk spelled it "Tooele," which form has been used ever since. This valley is bounded on the north by the shores of Great Salt Lake and on the east by the Oquirrh Mountains. For many years Tooele Valley was a favorite rendezvous for the Indians, especially the Goshute tribe, who assembled there. Most of the early trappers and explorers visited this valley and knew it well. The Donner company also passed through it in 1846 on the way to California.

President Young, with several of the apostles, visited Tooele Valley just a few days after his entrance into the Great Basin and soon utilized its pasture, as well as that of Rush Valley just beyond, for cattle. On July 17, 1849, Brigham, accompanied by about a dozen other men, made a second trip into Tooele Valley. After a reconnoitering tour around the hills, the President's party estimated the valley to be about twenty-five miles long and fifteen miles wide. Standing in its center was a pile of rocks like a fort which they named Adobe Rock.

In the same year, Captain Howard Stansbury, United States government surveyor, soon after his arrival in the Great Basin, commenced his exploration and surveys of the Great Salt Lake. He built a small adobe house by a spring in Tooele Valley about thirty rods west of Adobe Rock. Here his herders lived while they cared for the government mules and other stock. Sometime during the summer of 1849, John Barnard brought a herd of cattle into the valley and used the house built by Stansbury for his dwelling.

In October, 1849, Ezra T. Benson employed two brothers, Cyrus and Judson Tolman, and Phineas Wright, a millwright, to go into Tooele Valley for the purpose of building a mill. Shortly thereafter Francis X. Lougy, Samuel Meecham and others followed. These pioneer-settlers of Tooele located near the mouth of Settlement Creek Canyon about a mile southwest of the present site of Tooele City. They built several cabins joined together on the east side of the creek.

Some of these workers, while on a trip to Salt Lake, visited President Young, who encouraged them in their labors and promised them help in building up the new settlement. In fact, the Mormon leader was very anxious for the success of the Tooele colony. He was also personally desirous of securing timber that was suitable for shingles; therefore, he sent scouts from Salt Lake to explore the canyons and mountains for shingle and saw timber. Upon their return the explorers reported to the President that there was no shingle timber and very little timber of any kind to be found in the Tooele mountains. Shortly after this incident, Cyrus Tolman visited Brother Brigham at the Mormon Mecca and in the course of the conversation was informed of the lack of success of the exploring party. Tolman asserted that he knew that there was plenty of both saw and shingle timber in the canyons. The President immediately made a contract requiring Tolman to bring a load of shingle timber to the city—"a contract that Cyrus fulfilled in a few days to the satisfaction of Brigham."

Just about this time Young gave orders for Ezra T. Benson to build both a sawmill and gristmill in Tooele Valley. The original intention was to erect the equipment upon Settlement Creek, but finding insufficient water there for the operation of the mills, Benson chose a site on Twin Springs about nine miles north, near the place where the county gristmill now stands at Milton.

Brother Benson was accompanied to the valley by John Rowberry, his wife and five children, and Robert Skelton. They brought with them Ezra T. Benson's livestock. With the arrival of this group, about a dozen families were now in Tooele Valley and spent the winter of 1849-1850 there. The first winter was a very hard and cold one for the new colonists. The snowfall was extremely heavy. In the words of one of the settlers:

> One of the snow storms swept over the valley for forty-eight hours, and drifted the snow as high as the tall willows that grow along the creek. Two feet of snow had to be shoveled out of some of the cabins before the settlers could start a fire. The poor cattle died and the stronger teams suffered. They sought shelter from the storms along the willow drifts and there they were found frozen stiff. But the settlers made the best of it. The most of them were even content and happy, and they met together and sang praises to God; and encouraged each other with the bright future before them when the spring time would come and the summer work would begin again.[1]

While the Mormons in Tooele were cheerfully struggling through the cold winter of 1849-1850, Governor Brigham Young

---

[1]*Manuscript History of Tooele Stake,* January 23, 1850.

and his associates were planning for the permanence and future betterment of the young settlement. In connection with his multitude of other activities, the President had a great portion of his attention turned toward the needs of his fellow colonizers. On January 28, 1850, the General Assembly of the Provisional State of Deseret ordered that a state road be constructed from the Temple Block in Salt Lake to the Tooele settlement. Three days later Governor Young signed an act which divided the territory in the State of Deseret into six counties; namely, Great Salt Lake, Utah, Weber, Little Salt Lake (Iron), Sanpete, and Tooele.[2]

The following fall, September 27, 1850, in a general epistle of the First Presidency, the Saints were informed that a company had been chartered by the General Assembly of Deseret for the purpose of running a regular line of coaches between Ogden and Sanpete, and also from the capital to Tooele County by way of the lake.[3]

A few days after the establishment of Tooele County, Apostle Benson was sent there for the purpose of effecting an ecclesiastical organization. John Rowberry was appointed presiding elder with Phineas R. Wright and Judson Tolman as his counselors. Two months later, April 24, 1850, Rowberry was ordained president.[4]

As early as the season would permit, the settlers began their spring work by grubbing brush and preparing their land for planting. The people at Tooele, like the Mormons in the other communities, fenced cooperatively.

"The settlers took up the small field which they divided amongst themselves into small lots which they commenced to plow and improve. They fenced their small field in 1850 but enlarged it the following year."[5] Fifty acres including the seven acres plowed by Cyrus Tolman in the fall of 1849 were plowed and planted to wheat which produced an abundant harvest.

Later during the summer and fall the settlers were joined by other home seekers, Jacob Hamblin, the most famous scout and Indian missionary in the Church, arriving in the fall of 1850. There was plenty of land for all, but, as was the condition in many of the new Mormon communities, many of the colonists were afraid that they would be crowded out by scarcity of water. At that time the best judges in the settlement put the extreme limit of land that could be watered by Settlement Creek at three hundred acres.

[2]*Latter-day Saint Journal History,* January 28, 1850, Ms.
[3]*Ibid.,* September 27, 1850.
[4]*Ibid.,* April 24, 1850.
[5]*Manuscript History of Tooele Stake,* February 15, 1850.

They estimated that from eight to fifteen families would be all who could be supported by the water supply. However, either the estimate was extremely erroneous, or the amount of water in the creek increased considerably, as the people in Tooele and in the other towns under similar conditions declared it did. At any rate, before the end of 1850 there were over twenty families in the new settlement, and it continued to grow.

DIFFICULTIES WITH THE INDIANS

From the first arrival of Mormons in Tooele Valley and for several years afterward, the settlers had almost continuous trouble with the Indians. The natives became very aggressive, beginning their depredations early in the spring of 1850 by stealing cattle from the settlers. "The Indians were in a position and a frame of mind to run the first few settlers out any day; and it was only the addition of numbers in the spring (1851) that prevented that very plot being carried out."[6] The situation developed to such a critical degree that a posse was sent from Salt Lake in April under the direction of Orrin Porter Rockwell to help settle the Indian troubles. On April 22, 1851, a report of the activities of the posse stated:

> Indians having been very troublesome in driving off stock in Tooele Valley for some past, a company of men under Orrin Porter Rockwell who were sent out after them captured some thirty Utah Indians. At night the prisoners attempted to escape, but were fired upon by L. D. Curtis, an emigrant. The Indians returned the fire, killing him instantly, the ball lodging near the heart. All but four of the prisoners escaped. A reinforcement of twenty-five men were immediately sent to assist Rockwell's command in pursuing the Indians.[7]

The posse returned to Salt Lake City on May 1. It had followed the Indian trail for a considerable distance but had not seen the camp nor the Indians with the stolen stock.

After the killing of Curtis a guard was sent out from Salt Lake to protect the colonists while they built a fort at Tooele during the summer of 1851. The fort was located about half a mile southwest of the present meetinghouse, enclosing about three acres of land with houses on three sides and a corral on the north. At this time there were twenty-five families in the settlement. Troubles with the natives continued. September 22, 1851, five months after the killing of Curtis, Governor Young wrote to the Saints:

---
[6]James Dunn, *Tooele Transcript*, January 30, 1903.
[7]*Latter-day Saint Journal History*, April 22, 1850, Ms.

Several depredations have been committed by the Indians during the summer, mostly in Tooele Valley where it is computed that more than $5,000 worth of cattle and horses have been stolen and destroyed. So great was the destruction of property that annihilation of the settlement seemed inevitable unless the savages were met and resisted, which resulted in the death of one white man and a few Indians, which produced a cessation of theft for a season.[8]

GROWTH OF TOOELE

A few months later relationship with the Indians had improved, and the Mormon colonizer had more assurance that the Tooele settlement was going to be successful. In his message to the Utah Legislature on January 5, 1852, Governor Young stated: "There is a successful settlement now established on the west side of Tooele where the Indians had become so troublesome that it was feared that none could be maintained."[9] Conditions on March 25, 1852, were summarized by President John Rowberry:

We have built a meetinghouse twenty-four feet square. Our meetings are well attended. We have had no lawsuits nor bishops' courts to contend with. Peace and good will prevail in our midst which causes the gratitude of our hearts to flow to the Giver of all good. We have a school of about thirty scholars. We have a good sawmill in operation and a gristmill (in process of) building. There are a few spinning mills and looms in this place, but having no sheep, these things consequently remain almost still. The Saints here have been subject to many inconveniences, having to pull up stakes and fort; together with the repeated aggressions of the Indians at a time when most of them were making a beginning in the valleys of the mountains; yet they show forth by paying up their tithing as fast as they can and hearkening unto the teachings of those that are sent to counsel that they are determined to endure as good soldiers. They are very busily engaged at present putting in all the grain they can in order that they may reap a bountiful harvest. There is a very prosperous settlement at Grantsville, twelve miles west of this city, surrounded by a vast quantity of good land and would accommodate a great many more settlers which would be a benefit to those already there, on account of schools, etc.[10]

The following spring, 1853, a gristmill known locally as Edward Mill was built at the mouth of Settlement Canyon. This was the first flour mill in Tooele Valley, the nearest one up to that time being John Neff's in Mill Creek, Salt Lake County. After running some years, this first mill was permitted to go into decay, but later two other mills were built in successive order on the same site.

In the fall of 1853, a townsite was surveyed in the Tooele

[8]Brigham Young, "General Epistles . . . to the Saints," ibid., Sept. 22, 1851.
[9]Brigham Young, Manuscript History of Tooele Stake, January 5, 1852.
[10]John Rowberry, Latter-day Saint Journal History, March 25, 1852. Ms.

settlement by Jesse W. Fox, and the people began to locate on their city lots. However, when settlers in other localities became seriously threatened with danger during the Walker War, Governor Young sent messengers with the word for all colonies to enclose themselves in forts. Brigham's advice was followed. The new Tooele fort was located on the town plat, enclosing four central blocks of the city survey. The houses were moved from the old fort and from the places where the people had already commenced to settle on their land, into this new fort. Early in 1854 the people began the construction of a mud wall around their fort. Alexander Gee wrote on December 11, 1854, from Tooele to the *Deseret News* as follows:

> The wall is now half finished around the city and unlike most places where the people have commenced to wall in their cities, we have not a patch here and there, but as far as it is built it is finished, and I am proud to say that it is as substantial and handsome as any I have seen in all the settlements I have ever visited.[11]

The population continued to increase. The Mormon Colonizer strengthened the city of Tooele as he did others, by calling colonists from the better established places. At the general conference of the Church held in Salt Lake City on October 7, 1853, President Young instructed Apostles Wilford Woodruff and Ezra T. Benson to gather fifty families to add to the number in Tooele Valley. According to an official report dated March 29, 1853, the Church population of Tooele City numbered 602 persons.[12]

After the Mormons had permanently established the city of Tooele, they began to spread out in the valley and in Rush Valley by founding several other communities. Between the year 1849 and the coming of Johnston's army in 1857, Tooele, Grantsville, Lake View, Batesville, E. T. City, Clover and Lake Point were established.

FOUNDING OF GRANTSVILLE

Contemporaneously with the settlement of Tooele, other pioneers were bending every effort toward land settlement on Willow Creek, creating the town of Grantsville. Thomas Ricks and Ira Willis, who were herding stock for Brigham Young, Edwin D. Wooley, and other Salt Lake stock owners, built a herdhouse on what is now the street in front of the Grantsville Coop store in the fall of 1849. They used the ground on which the town now stands and the surrounding country for grazing purposes.

[11]Alexander Gee, *Deseret News*, December 11, 1854.
[12]*Latter-day Saint Journal History*, October 7, 1853. Ms.

But the first men who brought their families there with the intention of making a permanent settlement were Harrison Severe and James McBride, brothers-in-law. They had crossed the plains in the summer of 1850, had camped a short time at Warm Springs north of Salt Lake, and then upon hearing that Apostle Ezra T. Benson was building a mill in Tooele Valley had determined to try their fortunes in that direction. In October, 1850, they arrived at Tooele City but remained there only one night. Upon learning that there was a stream of water called Willow Creek on the west side of the valley where there was plenty of feed for cattle, they removed to that location. The two men constructed cabins of timber and willows which afforded shelter for their families during the winter.

In February, 1851, as the winter had broken up and left the soil in condition for plowing, Severe and McBride went on the range to hunt their oxen for that purpose. To their dismay they found that the Indians had stolen them. These frontiersmen concluded that as their cattle had been stolen, and as there were only two families in the new colony, it would be best for them to return to Salt Lake and wait for a more fitting opportunity to settle the place. Fear of the Indians did not keep them away long. In the autumn of that same year the two men moved their families and belongings back to Willow Creek. They were joined by six other families from the Mormon Mecca. This small group of pioneers hauled logs from the east side of the valley to build their houses in fort form.

Early in the spring of 1852 a townsite was surveyed at Willow Creek by Jesse W. Fox of Salt Lake under the direction of George D. Grant, a brother of Jedediah M. Grant. The little settlement was subsequently named Grantsville in honor of George D. Grant. The site selected was about six miles south of the south shore of the Great Salt Lake, eleven miles northwest of Tooele, and forty-four miles by nearest road southwest of Salt Lake City. The settlers in 1852 did not locate in the stockade that had been built the previous year but chose the surveyed townsite lots. But at the time of the Walker War they moved their houses into fort style as they had been directed to do.

The little group at Willow Creek felt that the Mormon Colonizer had not given them exact justice in his distribution to the various settlements of immigrants as they arrived in the city of the Saints. They recognized the Mormon leader's hand of authority and pleaded with him for assistance in making their struggling frontier settlement become a reality. Thereupon on August 30, 1852, Benjamin Baker, President of Willow Creek settlement (Grantsville), wrote the following to Brother Brigham:

> We, the citizens of the above named place, feel to write you a few lines, stating the situation of our settlement. At the present time we number about eight men strong and about forty-five Indians, out of which there are about sixteen able men, and according to the best information that we can get from the Indians, there are about seven of the same tribe remaining in the mountains, including men, women and children, all of whom seem to be perfectly friendly and not disposed to steal; but we know not how soon they may change, as Indians are very treacherous, and we would like to have your counsel on what further to do with them, as we have a great many of them now, and they have become a burden on our hands to feed and take care of. As there are but few of us here to protect ourselves, we are obliged to use them more than kindly for fear of offending them, and they become embittered against us and become our enemies.
>
> We would further request that you would send a dozen or more families to settle and strengthen our place, as there will, we think, be water enough to support that many. We would furthermore request that all those owning land in this place to either settle on their land, or cause it to be settled with families that will become permanent settlers, in order to strengthen our place and support schools, as we do not feel safe with the few in number that are here; not only that: we have children here growing up, but not enough to support a school, and unless those who are owning land in this place settle, or cause their land to be settled, we never can have a school, as most of the land in this place is owned by those living in the City, and they do not intend settling it, either themselves, or cause a family to settle on it, according to the present prospects; and we would request your honor to use your influence to have those that own land to settle it, or give way to those that would settle, as they hold the best land in this place, and we do not feel safe with so few in number.[13]

Judging from results President Young responded to the request. New colonists were supplied to meet the demands of the circumstances. A little over a year later (October, 1853), the Grantsville settlement contained 159 Church members.[14] Two years later the official statistical report gave the number of settlers as 251, from which time it grew into one of the two most prosperous cities in the valley.

FOUNDING OF E. T. CITY AND MILTON

Tooele City served as a hub settlement for the colonization of the surrounding territory. Lake View and Batesville were organized with very small groups in 1850 and 1851. Peter Maughan left Tooele and settled what became known as E. T. City in 1854. He

[13]Benjamin Baker, to Brigham Young, in *ibid.*, August 30, 1852.
[14]*Deseret News*, October 15, 1853.

became the ecclesiastical head of the settlement, to which a number of pioneers came the following year. A hotel was started, a store was opened, and many other improvements were made. It looked for a while as if E. T. City would become a flourishing village, until much alkali was brought up from the ground by irrigation and during high water most of the crops were destroyed. Then many of the settlers became discouraged and moved away. Today under the name of Lake Point it is a small farming community located eleven miles east of Tooele.

Milton was begun by Ezra T. Benson who built a sawmill on what was then called Twin Springs.

SETTLEMENT OF RUSH VALLEY

John Bennion wintered his cattle in the north end of Rush Valley just south of Tooele in 1854-1855 and built a cabin directly west of Rush Valley Lake, about eighteen miles southwest of Tooele City. In the fall of 1855 William A. Hickman, Enos Stookey and Luke S. Johnson, once a member of the quorum of Twelve Apostles under Joseph Smith, settled where Bennion had spent the previous winter, the last named occupying Bennion's cabin. Early in the spring of 1856, because of fear of Indians, they moved back to Tooele, but in April they returned and located on the main stream entering Rush Valley from the west. Other settlers followed and small farms of about ten acres each were planted. In honor of Luke S. Johnson, they named the little hamlet Johnson's Settlement. This town was subsequently named Clover.

Acting under the advice of George A. Smith, most of the people left Johnson in 1867 and settled two miles farther down the creek. The new site was named Saint Johns in honor of Bishop John Rowberry who directed the moving of the colonists from the Johnson site to Saint Johns in the autumn of 1867. This community became the principal one in Rush Valley.

Under the tuition of the Mormon paternal system, land settlement had been extended into two more valleys with a number of thriving communities springing into existence. Cities of the Saints were spreading throughout Zion, helping to bring about the realization of Brigham's dream of a Mormon empire.

CHAPTER XXIV

SANPETE VALLEY

CHIEF WALKER'S REQUEST

Walker, the Utah Indian Chief from Sanpitch Valley, with twelve of his tribe, met in council at Salt Lake City with President Brigham Young and some of the other leading Church officials on June 14, 1849. These Indians had come to request the Mormon leader to send colonists down to their land to make settlements and teach them to live as the white men lived. Walker remarked, "I was always friendly with the Mormons, as I hear what they say and remember it. It is good to live like the Mormons and their children. I do not care about the land, but I want the Mormons to go and settle it."[1] Explorers were sent to the valley two months later, and after visiting various localities they recommended the present site of Manti for the proposed colony.

CALLING OF MISSIONARIES TO SETTLE SANPETE VALLEY

Having acted favorably upon their report, early in the fall of 1849 Brigham Young proceeded to make necessary arrangements for selecting the colonists. Patriarch Isaac Morley, commonly called Father Morley by his people, Charles Shumway and Seth Taft were notified at the October general conference that they were to form the presidency of the proposed settlement. The following day, in conformity with the regular Mormon custom of common consent, the whole conference voted in favor of making a settlement in Sanpitch Valley. Brigham Young recommended that the settlers be selected mostly from young men with their families. Preparations had advanced far enough that a week later (October 13) the First Presidency were able to announce in a circular letter that fifty to one hundred families were expected to start for Sanpete Valley within a few days.

FOUNDING OF MANTI

October 28, 1849, Father Morley left Great Salt Lake City with a company for the proposed site. As his company traveled along, it was augmented until it finally consisted of 225 people—125 men and 100 women.

---

[1]*Latter-day Saint Journal History,* June 14, 1849. Ms.

The company traveled from the Mormon Mecca southward into Utah Valley, passing by a small Mormon colony at Fort Utah; then it continued southward to the present site of Nephi. Turning to the east, it passed through a range of mountains via Salt Creek Canyon and pitched camp in the Sanpitch Valley (later called Sanpete) on November 22, 1849. There a council was held relative to the advisability of remaining where they were then encamped. Father Morley, a man in whom the qualities of good sense and leadership were coupled with great fortitude, "felt constrained to proceed about three miles southward and pointing with prophetic finger to an eminence rising in the distance said, 'There is the termination of our journey in close proximity to that hill. God be willing, we will build our city.'"[2] Several of the company felt that this was not the best spot. One member of the group gave vent to his feelings in the following expression: "This is only a long, narrow canyon, and not even a jack-rabbit could exist on its desert soil!"[3] But Father Morley opposed the continuation of the journey, saying in his usual "terse and predictive manner," "This is our God appointed abiding place; and stay I will, though but ten men remain with me."[4] Considering the Mormons' willingness to follow leadership, one need hardly say that they remained on the place Morley had chosen.

The settlers commenced making themselves shelters to live in. A few of them began to build log houses, others made dugouts, while still others were content to live in their wagons for awhile. Fearing that winter would be upon them before they would be able to provide sufficient protection elsewhere, Father Morley advised them to move to the south side of the hill. Those who had shelters completed when the first snow began to fall considered themselves lucky indeed, while those who were still camped on the creek with their wagon boxes set up on end with covers stretched across them soon discovered that their temporary refuges were entirely inadequate to protect them from the winter storms. They were now willing to follow the advice of their leader and prepare themselves dugouts in "Temple Hill."

SUFFERING OF CHIEF WALKER AND THE SANPITCH INDIANS DURING WINTER OF 1849-1850

Not long thereafter, on December 13, Father Morley and his group were visited by Chief Walker, with some five to seven hun-

[2]Adelia Belinda Cox, *Manti Sentinel*, August 1, 1889.
[3]*Ibid.*
[4]*Ibid.*

dred warriors. The Indians pitched their tents about one mile away. They stayed near the Sanpete settlement throughout the winter, showing a very friendly attitude toward the Mormons. Both the Indians and the whites suffered intensely from excessively cold weather and scarcity of food. The Indians fed upon the dead carcasses of the colonists' cattle. One of the early settlers of Manti states that "The major portion [of the cattle] that were brought to the valley had died of starvation and cold but, stiff and stark in death, they were undoubtedly more serviceable to the settlers than they would have been living; probably saving the lives of the colonists by keeping the Indians in good humor, as they utilized all the carcasses for food, and considered the white people princes of generosity, in giving them all of the beef."[5]

February 20, 1850, in a letter to President Young, Patriarch Isaac Morley described the poor circumstances of these Indians. Many of them had died of measles. Walker had sent for Brother Morley to come and help heal their sick. He and his people had supplied those afflicted with medicine and had given them what other assistance he could. "The settlers, notwithstanding their limited supply of provisions, could not refrain from administering to the Indians who would sometimes cry for hunger."[6] Although many of the Utes at that time, especially around Provo, were on the warpath, Walker wanted the Saints to stay in Sanpete Valley, attesting his friendship by sending messengers throughout the country to his Indian subjects to advise them to be friendly to the Mormons. He also advised the whites not to travel in companies of less than eight or ten, well armed, and to keep a good watch at night. Father Morley, who baptized Walker on March 13, made the following comment:

He has been very friendly; his sick are made well for which he feels glad; they want "tiegup" or food, and are hardly willing to take a denial. Our bread stuffs are wearing away and most of our cattle are too feeble to do any hauling. If we had corn or bread stuffs of any kind, we could sell it for skins and relieve the wants of the natives, which would continue a good friendly feeling between us. Walker does not want us to go away, but to stay here and be friends and work, and his Sanpitch folks, he says, will learn to work and raise their food.[7]

DIFFICULTIES ENCOUNTERED IN BRINGING FOOD SUPPLIES FROM SALT LAKE CITY TO MANTI

The winter of 1849-50, one of the coldest in Utah's early history,

[5]Ibid., August 1, 1889.
[6]Isaac Morley to Brigham Young, in Latter-day Saint Journal History, March 15, 1850, Ms.
[7]Ibid., February 20, 1850.

was felt severely by these frontiersmen. Snow began falling shortly after they arrived in the valley and continued to fall until by midwinter it had reached a depth of three feet on the level. The weather remained bitterly cold. Just before the settlers arrived the Indians had wantonly burned most of the grass in the Sanpitch Swamps, so that by Christmas there was none left in the close vicinity for the cattle. The snow continued to increase at such a rate that the colonists were forced to transfer their cattle in a body to some warm springs about two miles south. The men and the boys would shovel snow from the grass all day for the sustenance of their starving beasts. The horns of their animals were sharpened by filing to enable them to protect themselves more effectively against the ravenous attacks of coyotes and wolves. Of 250 head of cattle, only one hundred survived.

The settlers themselves, like the cattle and the Indians, were in need of food. Shortly before Christmas Morley sent twelve men back to the Mormon headquarters for supplies. On their return trip they were detained a few days at Fort Provo on account of Indian hostilities in that part of the territory. Two Indians, Tabian and Ammon, brothers of the great war chief Walker, volunteered to join the party and assist in conducting them safely to the Sanpete settlement. The company arrived in Salt Creek Canyon in January, 1850, but, unfortunately, heavy snows prevented them from continuing farther.

To the great surprise of the colonists, Tabian arrived in their settlement with the startling news that "a white man was lying beyond Sanpitch at the foot of the west hills, in a nude, exhausted and almost dying condition." Immediately a relief party on snowshoes was sent across the valley to his rescue. Upon reaching him, the rescue party learned that he and the Indian had been sent for help by the returning supply party which was imprisoned by the snow at the forks of Salt Creek Canyon. The white man reported the snow on the divide to be from eight to ten feet deep on the level and twenty feet in the hollows and drifts. The constant breaking through the crust of the snow had worn his clothing to shreds. With his clothes in tatters, barefooted, and totally snowblind, he was borne by the relief party to the settlement.

The Indian, serving as the guide, directed some men to the supply train in Salt Creek Canyon. The supplies were brought on hand sleds to the settlement as they were needed. Part of the company helped in this work, and part acted as guards over the remaining goods. Most of the supplies were moved during the winter, but March arrived before the wagons could be removed.

Suffering at Manti During First Year

Food being scarce in the settlement, young Theophilus Shoemaker, a youth of generous disposition, decided to return to Salt Lake City where he might obtain employment and thus earn his subsistence. As he expressed to his associates, he was young, strong and robust and what would be required for his sustenance could be reserved for the use of women and children. Thereupon, he put on some snowshoes and started alone on a very dangerous journey. At Obanion springs in Juab Valley he met a hostile party of redskins and was murdered—the first white man from Sanpete to be killed by the Indians.

The Pioneers had almost all they could do throughout the first winter to tend fires and take care of the cattle; yet they were able to accomplish a little toward making themselves more comfortable. On February 20, 1850, Morley wrote to Brigham Young:

> We have put up about twenty houses, but some of our people live in tents and in caves of the earth. The lines are measured off for a fort, but only a little work has been done on it. . . . We draw our wood on hand sleds, half mile—good wood and enough of it too. Pine trees are plentiful within four or five miles of us. We are erecting a schoolhouse, twenty by twenty-five feet, of beautiful pine logs, which I think will be finished in a few days.[8]

President Brigham Young, in a general epistle to the Church under date of April 12, 1850, made the following comment:

> As we anticipated in our last letter, about sixty families, under the presidency of Patriarch Isaac Morley, left this place in October, and commenced a settlement in Sanpete Valley, 134 miles south. They have suffered many inconveniences through the deep snows and severe frosts for want of houses and other necessaries common in old settlements, and have lost many of their cattle; but they have laid the foundation of a great and glorious work, and those who persevere to the end in following the council of heaven, will find themselves a thousandfold richer than those who have made gold their counselor and worshiped it as their God. Their cattle, now living have been sustained by their shoveling snow from the grass, and feeding them with their provisions and seed grain, and we have sent them loaded teams to supply their necessities until after seed time. They have been surrounded by a tribe of Indians who appear friendly, and who have suffered much from the measles, since they have been among them, and many have died, as have also most or all of the tribes in the mountains; and those who live urged the brethren to remain among them and teach them how to raise grain and make bread; for having tasted a little during their afflictions, they want a full supply. There is plenty

[8]*Ibid.*

of firewood easy of access; some of the best of pine, bituminous coal, salt and plaster of paris at this settlement, or its immediate vicinity.[9]

As spring opened up, the people busied themselves in planting crops. By the early part of May they had planted 250 acres of wheat, as well as some oats, barley, and potatoes. While waiting for their crops to mature, they were sustained by ten loads of grain collected at Salt Lake under the direction of the bishops of that city, as was mentioned in Brigham's letter. Also Nelson Higgins and three companions took four loads of shingles to the Mormon Mecca (June 19) to trade for food supplies and grain. Later during the summer a number of loads of shingles and lumber were sent from Sanpete.

BRIGHAM YOUNG'S PARTY AT MANTI

President Young with several of the leading Church officials made his first visit to the Sanpete Valley during the summer of 1850. Arriving on August 4, they "were saluted by the firing of cannon and welcomed heartily by the brethren of the fort, who extended a most liberal hospitality to their distinguished visitors."[10] An early settler of Manti stated that "the magnetism of his presence always produced like enthusiasm where he visited, and meetings and banquets were the order of the day."[11]

The following day President Young and Heber C. Kimball chose a site for a city, which William M. Lemon immediately commenced surveying. Old settlers of Sanpete maintain that Brother Brigham on this occasion pointed out a site for a Temple on the spot where the Manti Temple now stands. The visiting brethren asserted that the crops in Sanpete were the best they had seen in the Great Basin.

When, on August 8, President Young and his company left and were traveling through Salt Creek Canyon, they found ten men under the direction of Titus Billings at work repairing the road. President Young had offered the settlers of Sanpete two hundred dollars to make a good road through that canyon. It was quite evident that they were losing no time nor sparing energy in accomplishing the task.

The following month, at a general conference in Salt Lake, President Young spoke of the desirability of strengthening the Sanpete colony and making it a hub settlement for that section

---

[9]Brigham Young. "General Epistle to the Saints." *Latter-day Saint Journal History*. April 12, 1850. Ms.
[10]*Manuscript History of Sanpete Stake*. August 4. 1850.
[11]Cox, *op. cit.*

of the country. He called for volunteers to return with Father Isaac Morley. After listening to this call, Morley arose and frankly stated that he wanted only good men and good women to go to Sanpete Valley, "And that he desired that no man should dwell in that valley who was in the habit of taking the name of God in vain." Whereupon President Young remarked, "I have it in my heart to ask the congregation if Father Morley shall have the right and privilege to select such men as he wishes to go to Sanpete."[12] A vote was called and Morley was given the privilege of selecting one hundred men, with or without families as he saw fit. Thus was established the precedent of allowing the head of the colony to choose his own group—a plan used in many succeeding colonies.

DEVELOPMENT OF INDUSTRIES

Brigham Young had no intention of establishing groups throughout the Great Basin and then letting them remain isolated from the parent colony. On the contrary, he planned to have them connected by roads and later by railroads. As early as September 27, 1850, the leader's plan was disclosed in a general epistle to the Saints. "A company is already chartered by the General Assembly of Deseret for the purpose of running a regular line of coaches between Ogden and Sanpete, to commence as early next spring as the traveling will permit, and to be extended as fast as the settlements extend."[13]

Efforts were made also to secure aid from the Federal Government to establish postal service between the various Mormon colonies. President Young received a letter from Delegate John M. Bernhisel at Washington, D. C., under date of October 2, 1850, containing the information that he had succeeded in obtaining the establishment of a post route from Great Salt Lake City, via Fort Utah, to the settlement in Sanpete Valley.

While efforts were being made to establish a postal route to the parent colony, industries were developing in Sanpete Valley. On December 12, 1850, Dan Jones wrote as follows: "Stones for gristmill have been brought from an unopened canyon twelve miles north as by magic since I came here, and will be grinding next week. Also a skeleton of a sawmill is under way."[14]

Charles Shumway in a letter to the Mormon Colonizer stated that he had the timber all out for framing the gristmill and

---

[12]Brigham Young, *Latter-day Saint Journal History*, September 6, 1850, Ms.
[13]Brigham Young, "Fourth general Epistle . . . to the Saints," *ibid.*, Sept. 27, 1850.
[14]Dan Jones, *Deseret News*, December 12, 1850.

suggested that the President become part owner of the mill by furnishing the irons. Brigham Young responded to Shumway's suggestion by shipping mill irons and leather for elevators and belts to Sanpete, December 28. The sawmill and the gristmill were built at the mouth of City Creek Canyon about forty rods apart and both were completed the following month.

Brigham Young and his counselors announced April 7, 1851, in a general epistle that charters had been granted by the General Assembly of Deseret to Provo City in Utah County, Ogden City in Weber County, Cedar City in Iron County, and Manti City in Sanpete County. "This is the first time that the name Manti was applied to the Sanpete settlement in Church literature."[15] President Morley, who was given the honor of naming this settlement, selected Manti, a Book of Mormon name.

PRESIDENT'S PARTY AGAIN AT MANTI

The Mormon leader made his second visit to Manti in April, 1851, to organize the Sanpete Stake of Zion and in November of that same year made a third visit. On this occasion Manti was described as follows by the President's scribe:

This city is beautifully located on the east side of Sanpete Valley on both sides of City Creek and near a spur range containing an inexhaustible supply of limestone, easy of access and admirably adapted for laying into walls of buildings and burning into good lime. This settlement has a large two-story council house built of limestone, several handsome two-story adobe houses, many one-story dwellings, a good gristmill, a sawmill, and stock, grain and produce of various kinds. Good salt is obtained from springs ten miles south on the left bank of Sanpete Creek, and also from beds and springs about thirty miles south. Coal has been brought in by the Indians from the eastern rim of the Basin against the headwaters of City Creek, but other fuel is so plentiful, and so easily procured, that no search has been made for coal. The pine of this region makes such superior lumber that much of it is hauled to Great Salt Lake City.[16]

Only six months passed before President Brigham Young again visited the Saints in Sanpete Valley. One can better appreciate the effect upon his followers of the visits of this great Mormon leader by referring to some of the expressions of the Saints when their esteemed President honored them with a visit. May 13, 1852, Andrew L. Siler at Manti wrote the following: "Brother Brigham Young and company came like a brilliant planet and illuminated our little world nearly two days and passed on, leaving a happy influence behind him. Our esteemed President,

[15]Andrew Jenson, *Manuscript History of Sanpete Stake*, 22.
[16]*Latter-day Saint Journal History*, November 2, 1851, Ms.

Father Morley, and many of the brethren from this place went with him south."[17]

THE FORT AND GROWTH OF MANTI

For two years following its establishment there had not been at Manti a regular walled fort. The houses, wagons, dugouts, and other shelters had been placed as close together as possible for protection. But as rapidly as they could in connection with their duties, the people of Manti erected a very substantial stockade. The walls were built of limestone. June 18, 1852, Andrew L. Siler wrote from Manti, "We have a fort enclosing one hundred square rods about half done. The wall is to be eight feet high and two feet thick with bastions and portholes every rod."[18] The actual thickness of the wall was three feet at the bottom, tapering off to twenty-two inches at the top.

As the population of Manti increased within the next two years, the size of the fort was increased. When Governor Young returned October 15, 1854, the fort enclosure was 408 rods with a wall three feet thick and eight feet high built of rock. Brother Brigham instructed the people to make their wall fifteen feet high in order to make themselves more secure from the Indians who were at that time on the warpath. The Walker War had been in progress for over a year, the center of the trouble being in Sanpete, Sevier, Millard and Juab counties. In his typical manner, the Mormon leader said, "I want you to turn out as one family and finish the wall."[19]

It might be said that by 1853 the initial period of Mormon colonization in Sanpete Valley had been passed through. A hub colony had been thoroughly and successfully established under the typical Mormon pattern. Its population was 647 people.[20] Wide streets had been laid out, with streams of water on either side along the edge of the sidewalk and rows of shade trees along their banks. Beautiful private gardens, orchards, and farms were flourishing. Another group of Saints had made the "desert blossom like a rose."

FOUNDING OF SPRING CITY AND MOUNT PLEASANT—INDIAN TROUBLES

President Brigham Young did not cease his activities of estab-

[17]Andrew L. Siler, *Deseret News,* May 29, 1852.
[18]Andrew L. Siler, *Manuscript History of Sanpete Stake,* 28.
[19]Brigham Young, *ibid,* 58.
[20]*Deseret News,* October 8, 1853.

lishing communities in Sanpete Valley with the successful founding of Manti but continued as long as there were available mountain streams and attractive town sites. In the fall of 1851 he advised James Allred, known as Father Allred, "to select a place for a settlement where he could locate with his numerous posterity and kindred and preside over them."[21] Accordingly early in the spring of 1852, Father Allred examined the tract of land lying along Canal Creek eighteen miles northeast of Manti and finally chose the present site of Spring City for his colonization project.

Four days later, on March 22, 1852, Father Allred together with his sons, Andrew J., James T. S. and some younger boys, and Charles Whitlock came from Manti to the chosen site and commenced to make improvements. James T. S. Allred brought with him a log house sixteen feet square, which the settlers placed on Canal Creek. The following day the first house of Spring City was completed and ready for occupation.

Almost immediately, ninety acres of land were fenced, and thirty-nine acres cleared, planted and sowed, from which a good crop of wheat, oats, corn, potatoes, melons and other vegetables was reaped in the fall. During that first summer, J. T. S. Allred surveyed a tract of land containing about one hundred acres into five-acre lots, on which plat throughout the summer several more families, mostly Allreds, built their cabins.

President Brigham Young visited the little colony on Canal Creek in April. Reuben W. Allred was ordained Bishop and appointed to preside over the place, with Wily P. and James T. S. Allred as his counselors. He advised the settlers to build a fort for protection against attacks from the Indians. Conditions soon showed that the President's advice was wise and timely. That very summer about three hundred Sanpitch Indians came and interfered with their farming operations and threatened to kill the settlers. It was only by the greatest tact that James T. S. Allred, who could speak the Indian language, was able to pacify the warriors. This was partly accomplished by giving the Indians a small wage to help the settlers in their farming and fencing.

But this friendship with the Indians was suddenly broken by the outbreak of the Walker War in July, 1853. The settlements in Sanpete were soon found to be in the greatest danger. July 19, the Indians made a raid upon the Pleasant Creek settlement (now Mount Pleasant), where about a dozen families resided. They immediately moved, with all they could save, into

---
[21]Young, op. cit., Spring City, 1.

the Allred Settlement. Both groups of colonists moved their cabins in fort style, closing the openings between the houses with a rock wall. This fort was completed July 28, 1853.

The day after the fort was completed about four hundred Indian warriors of the Walker band made a raid on the settlement and drove off about two hundred head of cattle and thirty head of horses. Only two or three horses and a few calves were left. The Manti Saints sent teams and a squad of well-armed horsemen to remove the 118 settlers from the Allred Settlement to Manti.

That fall James Allred and Reuben W. Allred, while attending the October general conference of the Church in Salt Lake City, learned that a large number of Danish Saints had arrived in the city on September 30. Due to the Allreds' influence, President Young sent these Danish Saints to strengthen the Allred Settlement. Consequently the name of the settlement was changed to "Little Denmark." The original settlers moved back from Manti, and the entire group made preparation for wintering on Canal Creek by enlarging the fort, cutting hay, and attending to other necessary work. But their plans were not to be realized. Because of increasing trouble with the Indians, the settlement was abandoned a second time, December 18, 1853, not to be resettled until 1859.

In the winter of 1851-52, Madison D. Hambleton and Gardner Potter built a sawmill at the mouth of Pleasant Creek Canyon, five miles north of Spring City. About a half dozen families settled on that creek in the spring of 1852. They erected a cluster of houses immediately below the present townsite of Mount Pleasant and commenced clearing the land. The crops which they raised were excellent, and their success attracted other pioneers. At first the little colony was known as Hambleton's Settlement, but it grew rapidly into the rather important city of Mount Pleasant.

FOUNDING OF EPHRAIM

One of the finest and most attractive towns inhabited by Latter-day Saints in Sanpete Valley is Ephraim. It is beautifully situated on Pine Creek close to the base of the Wasatch Mountains, in the center of the valley. Ephraim is seven miles north-east of Manti. The city is planned out in regular Mormon fashion of ten-acre blocks with streets six rods wide.

The first settler of Ephraim was Isaac Behunin who located on Pine Creek in the fall of 1852. That following winter Behunin, his wife and nine children lived in a dugout. He raised a good crop on forty acres of land in 1853, but that fall, because of the Walker War, he was forced to move his family to Manti.

In February, 1854, Isaac Behunin sold his claim to Calif C. Edwards. Immediately a number of families who had had to abandon Allred's Settlement on Canal Creek (Spring City) made preparations to establish a community on Pine Creek. Before taking their families to this new site, twenty-five men under the direction of Captain Sanford Allred, who acted under order of Major Nelson Higgins, commander of all the Sanpete militia, arrived on Pine Creek on February 4, 1854, to build a fort.[22] These frontiersmen had learned the necessity of being well-protected against the natives. By the end of March they had finished the fort and had built enough accommodations that they were able to move their families from Manti.

At the time of the establishment of the colony, Reuben Warren Allred, who had acted as bishop of the Allred Settlement, was placed in charge of the ecclesiastical affairs of the community. Fort Ephraim grew rapidly. Within two years after its establishment, January, 1853, it boasted a population of 311 persons. July 9, of that year, one of its colonists wrote, "There are about eighty families here, and fifty of that number speak the Danish language; the remainder are Americans, English and Welsh."[23]

SETTLEMENT OF SANPETE, AN EXAMPLE OF DIRECTED COLONIZATION

The settlement of Sanpete County is a good example of the methods involved in colonization under the direction of President Brigham Young. First the valley was carefully explored by scouts sent out from Salt Lake, and the site was selected for the initial colony. Then a group of missionaries, painstakingly chosen by Brigham Young, established that initial colony, which served as a hub from which other towns were established, thus preserving a base of supplies much nearer to the territory to be settled than was the parent colony, Salt Lake City. Throughout the whole process of colonization, immigrant Saints, as they arrived at Salt Lake City, were distributed throughout the territory to strengthen recently established communities. On certain occasions, those who had already shown themselves to be successful colonizers led groups to found new settlements. For that reason some of the same names, such as the Allred brothers, appear in the initial period of several colonies.

---

[22] *Millennial Star*, XVII, 476.
[23] *Manuscript History of Sanpete Stake*, Ephraim, 3.

CHAPTER XXV

THE MORMON STATION

PASSING OF BATTALION MEMBERS THROUGH CARSON VALLEY—
MURDER OF CAPTAIN BROVITT BY INDIANS

In the year 1847 the Mormons first came in contact with that part of the country known as Carson Valley, located in the western part of the present state of Nevada. July, the same month that Brigham Young and his first company arrived in the Salt Lake Valley, the Mormon Battalion was honorably discharged at Los Angeles. The majority of the soldiers immediately started the journey to the Great Basin to join the Saints established there.

Having traveled up the coast and across California to Sacramento and then eastward as far as Pleasant Valley, they decided that Captain Brovitt, Daniel Allen, and Henderson Cox should go ahead in order to search out the most passable route for the soldiers to follow across the Sierra and then through the desert of Nevada. The fact that they had been warned of the danger from Indians did not prevent the three from endeavoring to carry out their scouting project.

After leaving their thirty-seven companions in Pleasant Valley, Brovitt and his two associates successfully crossed the summit of the mountains and then traveled as far as the head of Carson Valley. They now decided to return to report their explorations to their companions. But upon arriving at a place subsequently called Tragedy Spring near the top of the mountains, they were killed by Indians who badly mutilated their bodies.

After waiting some time for the return of the three scouts, the battalion members determined to continue their journey toward Great Salt Lake Valley with the hope of meeting Brovitt and his companions as they traveled through the mountains. To their dismay and sorrow they found the mutilated bodies of their comrades. They buried the remains and then continued on their way.

They entered Carson Valley and traveled down the Carson River some distance. But upon finding that this stream bore too far to the south, they left it and directed their course northward, thereby reaching the emigrant road on the Truckee River. They followed this route eastward to the headquarters of the Saints.

The favorable report regarding Carson Valley which these

men gave contributed a share in arousing interest in that section of the country as desirable for future land settlement. Other events which quickly followed created a greater interest in western Nevada.

FOUNDING OF MORMON STATION (GENOA)

The first Mormon settlement in Carson Valley was the outgrowth of a business enterprise launched in the spring of 1849. It was first known as Mormon Station, and later was sometimes referred to as Reese's Station. Ultimately, however, it grew into a city named Genoa.

Many of the people in the large stream of immigration attracted toward California as a result of the discovery of gold in 1848 were in dire need of provisions by the time they reached the Great Basin. Brigham Young and his followers at Salt Lake gladly exchanged grain and vegetables with these "forty-niners" for clothing, farm implements, and other supplies, the groups mutually benefiting by the trade. Naturally this lucrative business did not confine itself to one city. "But Mormon and other traders soon posted themselves along the line of travel to the mines, and particularly in the valley of Carson River, where, in 1849, they founded the first settlement in what is now the state of Nevada."[1]

In April, 1849, a company of eighty men was organized at Salt Lake City under Captain DeMonte with the intention of going to the mines in California for a short time and then returning to Utah. The majority of the company were non-Mormons; however, there were approximately fifteen Mormons in the group, most of whom were ex-Battalion members who had been in California the previous year and had passed through Carson Valley on their way to Salt Lake City. Hampton Sidney Beatie was appointed clerk of the company. According to Beatie, this group of Mormons did not ask the advice of the Church authorities before going.[2]

The members of the company took their own teams and supplies. Upon arriving at the Carson River, Hampton Sidney Beatie and six of his companions sensed the economic possibilities of establishing a supply station for the passing immigrants and were left there by the other members of the company. They took possession of the site of the present town of Genoa, and Beatie and his companions erected a house. "The cabin was a double-logged, one-story house, about twenty by sixty feet, con-

---

[1]Hubert Howe Bancroft, *History of Nevada*, 65-67.
[2]Hampton Sidney Beatie, *The First in Nevada*, 4, Ms.

taining two rooms."[3] Luckily for their supplies it did not rain
that summer, as their house had neither floor nor roof. They
built a corral for their stock, but unlike groups sent out by Brigham
Young, they planted no crops and made no fences.

LUCRATIVE TRADE

When their building was completed, Beatie and one of the
Blackburns were appointed by their companion to go over the
Sierras by Carson Pass to the American River to purchase supplies.
There they received more information on the large immigration
to California expected that summer, so they sold three of their
six yokes of oxen for a high price and with the proceeds purchased
"flour, dried fruit, bacon, sugar and coffee." They returned to
the Mormon Station by the old route through Carson Canyon
and quickly disposed of their cargo.

Beatie and Blackburn again journeyed over the mountains to
the California mines for a larger supply of provisions. This time
the adventurers took fifteen pack animals and crossed the mountains by way of another pass three miles south of Beatie's place.
Besides trading for provisions, they bartered for horses and mules
and anything else that might be needed.

By the end of the summer of 1849 Beatie and his companions
who had stayed in the Carson Valley found that they had made
more money by trade than their companions who had gone on
to the mines. Indeed, they would have become rich that summer
if they could have procured sufficient provisions to supply the
needs of the passing emigrants. In the words of Beatie:

> Flour at that time was worth $2.00 a pound, fresh beef $1.00, bacon
> $2.00. A friend of mine went over the mountains and left a yoke of cattle with
> me, and one day I got a thousand dollars for one of those oxen in the shape of
> beef. We had not sufficient flour to sell out in large quantities, and therefore
> we used to deal it out in small quantities, thereby benefiting more people.
> One time a captain of a train of emigrants came along and wanted to buy five
> hundred pounds of flour at $2.00 a pound, but I refused him, not having
> sufficient to deal out in such large amounts.
>
> There was a good deal of emigration that year and a great amount of
> suffering. For a few loaves of bread I could get a good horse.[4]

In the fall of 1849 Beatie and four companions at the Mormon
Station were joined by ten of their former company from the
mines in California. These fifteen men returned to Salt Lake

— — — —
[3]Ibid., 5.
[4]Ibid., 6.

City, arriving there October 19. They brought to the Great
Basin from California and Carson Valley about one hundred head
of horses.

The third group of Mormons to visit Carson Valley and to
bring favorable reports to the Saints at home was Apostle Amasa
M. Lyman and about thirty other brethren. In the latter part
of August, 1850, they passed through Carson Valley on their way
back to Salt Lake from the gold mines in California. "They
gave a flattering report of the natural resources in said valley
to their co-religionists. This report undoubtedly had much to do
with the selection of Carson Valley by the Latter-day Saints the
following year."[5]

JOHN REESE: PURCHASE OF MORMON STATION; TRADING ACTIVITIES

After Beatie returned to the headquarters of the Saints, he
was given employment by the Reese brothers as clerk in their
store. Colonel John Reese and his brother Enoch were enterprising
merchants in Salt Lake who had come there prepared to establish
a store. No doubt it was Beatie who interested them in the
business advantages of Carson Valley, and there is a possibility
that he was associated with them to some extent in the enterprise.[6]

Beatie sold his claim in Nevada to a man named Moore, who
"probably sold it in 1851 to John Reese. It is certain that one
of the Mormon party kept possession until Reese came."[7] Reese
stated that he bought Beatie's claim "from a man who pretended
to own it. I suppose he was one of the party and had come
through there on his way back from California. I gave him about
fifteen or twenty dollars for it."[8]

In the spring of 1851 John Reese left Salt Lake for the
purpose of establishing a trading station in Carson Valley on the
overland road. He took ten wagons loaded with "eggs, bacon,
flour, seed grain and seeds of all kinds."[9] There were sixteen in
Reese's company, some of them teamsters, a few others being passengers bound for the Coast.

The party arrived at the Mormon Station June 1, 1851. Reese
took up a ranch located in the place now called Genoa,
although this part of Nevada was then part of the territory of Utah.
About fifty yards from where Beatie's house had been, Reese and
his hired men commenced building a log cabin, "that when com-

[5]*Manuscript History of Nevada*, 3.
[6]John Reese, *Mormon Station*, 3. Ms.
[7]Bancroft, *op. cit.*, 65-67.
[8]Reese, *op. cit.*, 4.
[9]*Latter-day Saint Journal History*, April 10, 1851, Ms.

pleted was the only house in what is now Nevada." At the time of his arrival, "there was no one living there [at the Mormon Station], no house, no ruins of a house, or the vestige of one to be found. Those who had occupied the place in 1849-1850 had folded their tents like the Arab, in the fall of the last year, and silently stolen away, leaving the torch of the Indian to efface any indication of their ever having been there."[10]

The house built by John Reese was a hotel, store, and dwelling combined. It was made of logs, two stories high, and about fifty by thirty feet in size. The upper story was divided into two large rooms, while the lower story contained such rooms as the kitchen, dining-room, and the storeroom. A stockade corral, enclosing something over an acre of ground, was also put up at the cost of two thousand dollars. It was made strong as a protection against Indians.

It was still early enough in the season for the colonel and his party to fence, plow, and sow a patch of turnips. The generous crop demonstrated the productiveness of the soil and encouraged the colonists to put in a variety of products the next year. They fenced and plowed a field of some thirty acres and planted it in "wheat, barley, corn, and watermelons in one side and mixed things all around." Luckily for Reese there proved to be a great deal of immigration in 1852. His crops produced abundantly, yet he could not raise enough to supply the demand, which was so great that he could get one dollar for a bunch of turnips which could be bought for ten cents in Salt Lake. Other products sold in proportion.

More colonists arrived in Carson Valley during the summer and fall of 1851. The majority of them were non-Mormons from California, but a few followers of Brigham arrived at different times during the year. Israel Mott and his wife left Salt Lake for Mormon Station in May, 1852. They settled four-and-one-half miles up from Mormon Station on the overland road. "Mrs. Mott was the first permanent lady settler in Carson Valley."[11]

As time passed and population increased, industries developed. A blacksmith shop was established by Henry Van Sickle and his brother. December, 1852, John Reese and Israel Mott were granted a five-year franchise privilege of putting a toll bridge on the Carson River and of repairing the mountain road on condition that they expend one thousand dollars on this project before July

[10]*Manuscript History of Nevada,* 11.
[11]*Ibid.,* 12.

1, 1853. In the spring of that year a post-office had been established at Mormon Station.[12] The following year John Reese and Thomas Knott both built gristmills and sawmills.

Before that time flour had been freighted from Salt Lake and was worth twenty-five dollars per hundred pounds. After the mill was put into operation, flour sold for as low as six dollars per hundred.

CREATION OF CARSON COUNTY

January 17, 1855, the Utah Legislature approved an act creating Carson County. By this act the new county was given representation in the State Legislature. Brigham Young, the governor of Utah Territory, was given authority to appoint a probate judge for Carson County. He selected Orson Hyde and instructed him to organize the county, divide it into precincts and conduct an election. January 18, the Utah Legislature divided Utah into three judicial districts and appointed Honorable George P. Styles, United States Judge for Utah Territory, to preside over district number three (Carson County).

In consequence of their recent appointments, Apostle Hyde, Judge Styles, and Joseph L. Heywood, United States Marshal for Utah Territory, with Enoch Reese and an escort of thirty-five men, left Salt Lake City early in May, 1855.[13] They arrived at Mormon Station on June 15. Of their work Brigham Young in his message to the Utah Legislature on December 11, 1855, said:

> In accordance with a law passed by the Assembly in 1854-1855, the Honorable Orson Hyde repaired to Carson County, accompanied by the Honorable Judge Styles and the Honorable Marshall Heywood and in connection with authorized persons from California, approximately established the boundary lines between this Territory (Utah) and the State (California), in the region of Carson Valley, and fully organized that county.[14]

SUPERVISING OF CHURCH ACTIVITIES BY ORSON HYDE

Up to this point in the history of the Mormon Station the settlement of Mormons in Carson Valley had not been directed as a special colonization movement by Brigham Young and the other Church officials. But now, in the spring of 1856, Brother Brigham evidently designed to settle systematically the agricultural parts of western Utah (Carson Valley) by his followers. Thereupon a company of colonizers left Salt Lake May 7, 1856, and it

[12]Latter-day Saint Journal History, May, 14, 1853, Ms.
[13]Deseret News, May 20, 1855.
[14]Manuscript History of Nevada, 25.

was followed by others, with the result that the Saints were in a majority before the election occurred on August 5 of that year. William Jennings, one of the missionaries called by President Young to settle Carson Valley, stated that there were from 150 to 250 Saints called at the time he received his call. The purpose of the mission was to "build up the country" and establish a midway station between the Mormon Mecca and the Pacific Coast. The new settlers provided a type of colonists unlike those already there. The Mormons brought their families with the intention of building homes. Before the arrival of these missionaries, the population of Carson Valley was almost entirely male.

Preparatory to the planned Mormon colonization of 1856, Orson Hyde surveyed a town site at Mormon Station in the spring of that year and named the place Genoa in honor of the birthplace of Columbus. The incoming Saints settled at Genoa and at other points, making two or three new settlements, one of which was Franktown. They built a number of houses along the Carson River and in the Washoe Valley.

Before the arrival of Apostle Hyde there were no Mormon meeting-houses in Nevada. But during the year of 1856 he directed the constructions of such buildings in all the towns that had been established by the Saints. Both a meeting-house and a schoolhouse were erected at Franktown. In order to supply the people with lumber, Elder Hyde built a large lumber-mill at Franktown in the fall of 1856. The irons for the mill were brought from California.

In Carson Valley, as in all other Mormon colonies, a Latter-day Saint ecclesiastical government was organized and put into active operation. Saturday, October 4, 1856, the brethren who had been chosen as high councilors at the conference a week earlier met at the home of Thomas H. Parks to effect the organization of a "high council for the stake of Zion in Carson Valley."[15]

CARSON VALLEY, AN OUTPOST GATHERING PLACE FOR MORMON PROSELYTES

That valley was accounted by the Saints at that time as being of much future importance and value. It was their purpose to build up the western country as an outpost of the Mormon empire and as "a gathering place for the Saints from California and Oregon." Brigham Young and his associates realized that it lacked the natural resources and economic advantages of Oregon

---

[15]*Ibid.*, 30.

and California, yet these states were near enough for the Saints in western Utah (Nevada) to receive benefits from them in trade. Carson Valley was to serve as a half-way station between Salt Lake and the Pacific Coast. This desert country, like other parts of the Great Basin, suited Young's purpose far better as a place to establish Latter-day Saints and particularly to retain them as true Church members than did California or Oregon.

Mormon missionaries were continuously proselyting among the people along the Pacific Coast, instructing their converts to gather with the Saints in Carson Valley. It was near at hand, yet far enough from the main non-Mormon centers that the Saints were able to establish, control and develop their own institutions. January 3, 1857, in a letter to Chester Loveland, president of the high council at Carson Valley, Brother Brigham expressed in definite terms his purpose in sending colonizers there: "We shall not recruit that place from here. Carson Valley is a subsidiary gathering place to collect the Saints to from California and Oregon, and if there are not enough there now for those purposes, then all had better come home. It is not our wish for you to abandon the place."[16] All of the members of the high council voted to remain in Carson Valley and let the "mission carry out the designed will of the Presidency to make this a gathering place for the Saints from California and Oregon."[17]

The Mormon's Abandonment of Carson Valley

Several months passed by, and the Mormon Station continued to grow. Then in the fall of 1857 President Young suddenly called the missionaries home. The United States army under command of Colonel Albert Sidney Johnston was on its way to Utah with the purpose, the Saints understood, of wiping them out. Remembering their former troubles, Brigham decided that they should all be together to protect themselves from the army, or as a group move south. Along with several other outpost missions, therefore, the Mormon Station was abandoned. The Saints disposed of their property as best they could. Those who were lucky enough to find buyers sold at a great loss. The majority of them returned to Salt Lake City in the fall of 1857, but a few did not leave Carson Valley until the following spring. Colonel John Reese remained at the Mormon Station only one year after the last of the missionaries had gone. After some difficulties in clearing

---

16*Ibid.*, 36.
17*Ibid.*, 37.

the title to his ranch, he sold out, abandoned the Station and returned to the City of the Saints in 1859.

Although the Mormons had now all been called home from Carson Valley, Brigham Young had demonstrated his ability to establish colonies at an extensive distance from the base of supplies. The Mormon midway station to the Pacific and subsidiary gathering place was lost before Brigham really had time to adequately develop the possibilities of Carson Valley for his avowed purpose. If the Colonizer's plans had not been hampered at various times by outside influence such as the coming of Johnston's army and Indian wars, the dream of even a more expansive empire than the one he established would have been realized.

CHAPTER XXVI

FILLMORE THE CAPITAL OF UTAH

LOCATION AND DESCRIPTION OF PAUVAN VALLEY

Extending northward from near the south rim of the Great Basin in Iron County through Beaver, Millard, and Juab counties to Utah and Cedar valleys—nearly 150 miles in length and nearly half that distance in width—lies the great Pauvan Valley. It received its name from the "Pah-van-te" tribe of Indians who resided in that locality. This extensive valley consists of several smaller ones, more or less vaguely defined, some of which are little Salt Lake Valley on the south, Preuss Valley, Lower Sevier River Valley, Parowan, Beaver, Fillmore, Juab and Tintic valleys. The eastern edge of the Pauvan is bordered by the principal range of the Wasatch Mountains, which are known by the sectional names of Parowan, Beaver, Pauvan, and Sanpitch mountains. On the west this valley extends into the desert.

MORMONS' EARLY CONTACT WITH AND OPINIONS OF PAUVAN VALLEY

Numerous mountain streams served as watering places for the earlier travelers and later furnished Brigham Young sites on which to build a line of settlements throughout the length of the Great Basin. The Mormons were not the first people to use those mountain streams. There is no doubt that the Indians had definite trails from one stream to another as they traveled along the valleys west of the Wasatch Mountains. Later the Spaniards frequented the Great Basin and followed the Indian trails. Leading southward from Spanish Fork Canyon in Utah Valley to the Pauvan Valley, and on southward, was a route known as the Old Spanish Trail when the Mormons first arrived in the Great West. In the words of Levi Edgar Young:

The State Road [Route No. 91] was at first an Indian trail, for the Shoshones were accustomed to trade with the Navajos in the days before the white men came, and it is possible that a trail led through Utah from Santa Fe, New Mexico, to Fort Boise, in Idaho, and was used by the Spaniards who traded with the fur-traders of the north, and exchanged leather, saddles, and bridles for beaver furs and buffalo-skins.[1]

After thorough exploration, Pauvan Valley was early chosen

---

[1]Levi Edgar Young, *Founding of Utah*, 236-237.

as one of the best possibilities for land settlement. One of Brigham Young's chief concerns was to get an outlet to the sea—a Mormon Corridor—and the settlement of the Pauvan Valley would further that project. Because of the extent of the valley and of the lack of knowledge of the amount of water available, the Mormon explorers far over-estimated its possibilities and resources, i. e., under existing geographical and climatic conditions. Such a vast level country would, these frontiersmen believed, support an enormous population.

Pauvan Valley had the advantage of being centrally located in the Great Basin. Furthermore, the early spread of colonies had been much more rapid and extensive southward from the Mormon Mecca than northward. Even before 1851 had passed San Bernardino, some 700 miles southwest of Salt Lake, had been established. Therefore, Pauvan Valley was geographically a logical center for Brigham Young's empire at that time.

Every group of Mormons who visited the valley before it was colonized recommended Pauvan as an ideal place in which to build towns. Jefferson Hunt passed through it in 1847 and again in 1848, in going to and returning from California. He recommended it to Brigham Young. In 1849 Addison Pratt mentioned Chalk Creek in Pauvan Valley as a possible site for a Mormon settlement. Some of the men of Parley P. Pratt's exploring company spent the winter of 1850 on that creek. They felt that it was an excellent site for a Mormon town. Several months later, George A. Smith, while en route to settle Parowan, wrote to the Mormon leader to the effect that "many farmers of our camp would have been perfectly satisfied to have remained" at Chalk Creek. Brigham Young himself made numerous trips to the new frontier communities, spending a great deal of time traveling from Salt Lake City southward. He fully endorsed the opinion of those who had previously visited Pauvan Valley relative to its desirability for land settlement.

Selecting a Site for the Capital City of Utah

So enthusiastic were the reports Brigham received that he determined in 1851 to establish the capital city of his empire in Pauvan Valley. Preparatory to founding the settlement, the Utah Territorial Legislature passed an act designating Chalk Creek as the site for the capital of the territory. The text of this legislative act, signed by Governor Brigham Young on October 4, 1851, follows:

Section 1. Be it enacted by the Governor and Legislative Assembly of the Territory of Utah: That that portion of Iron County, known as Pauvan Valley, is hereby formed into a county, to be called Millard County. Said county to contain the limits of Pauvan Valley.

Section 2. Be it further enacted, that Anson Call is hereby appointed to organize said county; and it is hereby made his duty to organize the same, according to the provisions of an ordinance to provide for the organization of Iron County, passed by the Legislature of Deseret.

Section 3. The sea of government of the Territory, in said county, shall be called Fillmore City.[2]

Anson Call and Company, Establishing Fillmore

Anson call then was designated to lead a group of home seekers to Chalk Creek, to organize Millard County, to be probate judge, and to establish what was to be the capital city of Utah. He was a personality of significance in Utah colonial history. Like President Young, Call was a man of great shrewdness and executive ability, endowed by nature to be a leader of men. Even as early as six months previous to the passing of the foregoing legislative act, Bishop Call had been selected by Brigham Young to collect colonists for the purpose of founding a Mormon settlement in Pauvan Valley. But now his responsibility was much greater. In his journal he stated:

The First Presidency of the Church gave me a mission to return from Parowan to Salt Lake City and raise fifty families to settle the Pauvan Valley. I accordingly returned in June, (1851), and found all well at home. I went to work to raise the company. I also carried on my farm in Davis County. . . . The camp was generally poor, consisting of brethren who had just emigrated from the States and England.[3]

A little over two weeks after Chalk Creek was designated as the location for the seat of government, Governor Brigham Young left Great Salt Lake City for Pauvan Valley to select the site for the territorial capital. A detailed account of the journey was published in the Deseret News of December 13, 1851. In the words of that report:

Tuesday, October 21, 1851, Presidents Young and Kimball, with several of the company, left Great Salt Lake City for the purpose of locating the site for our seat of government.

Wednesday, October 22, the company all met at the house of Abraham O. Smoot ten miles south of the city, consisting of Presidents Young and Kimball, the committee for locating the site, viz; Orson Pratt, Albert Carrington, Jesse W. Fox, and William C. Staines, Elder George A. Smith, Bishop

2Acts, Resolutions and Memorials, etc., of the Legislature of the Territory of Utah, 224.
3Anson Call, Journal, 41-43.

Robinson, Z. Snow, U. S. Associate Judge, Major Rose, Indian Sub-Agent, General Daniel H. Wells, H. S. Eldredge, Marshall, and others. In all, fifteen men and three boys, with carriages, baggage wagons, horses and mules; a party well armed and considered sufficiently strong in case any band of Indians should be hostile. . . .

Tuesday, October 28, moved our camp one and one-half miles up Ntiguin (Chalk Creek), and on its left bank. From present and previous observations, the site for the seat of government was located in the immediate vicinity of our camp about one mile above the ford, and four or five miles below the mouth of the canyon, on both sides of the creek and at the western terminus of the table lands. Observations for latitude and declination were taken, and several readings of the barometer and thermometers were noted. An inexhaustible supply of sandstone and limestone, well adapted to building purposes was found at the base of the mountains, about five miles from the site, to which it can be easily conveyed down a long, gentle slope. At the suggestion of President Young the site . . . is called Fillmore city, and commands an extensive view of the rich valley, and varied mountain scenery; and in a northwesterly direction there is no obstruction to the view but the dim distance.[4]

The Mormons doubly honored President Millard Fillmore by naming their new capital city after his last name and designating the new county Millard. They believed that President Fillmore deserved that distinction because he had shown a friendly attitude toward them and had inaugurated for them a territorial government. A toast given by Daniel H. Wells on July 4, 1853, in honor of Fillmore, aptly expressed the Mormon feeling toward him. In the words of Mr. Wells:

Ex-President Fillmore: May his retirement be as happy and prosperous as his administration was successful and glorious; and the American people learn to know and appreciate their good men before they lose them.[5]

Chief Kanosh and His Pah-van-te Tribe

Within a day or so after Call and his associates arrived on Chalk Creek, they were visited by a few Pah-van-te Indians. Their chief remarked "that he was not fond of roaming, and wished to be instructed in tilling the soil. The chief and part of those Indians reside upon Corn Creek (15 miles south of this site) and have there raised corn, beans, pumpkins, squashes, potatoes, etc., year after year, for a period that dates further back than their acquaintance with the whites."[6] The camp historian also remarked that "The few Indians who appeared at the city professed great friendship, and promised good behavior to Bishop Call and company

---

[4]*Deseret News,* December 13, 1851.
[5]Cited in Brigham H. Roberts, *A Comprehensive History of the Church,* IV, 11.
[6]*Deseret News,* December 13, 1851.

who were on the ground, ready to build a fort forthwith—a work preparatory to fencing fields, and building up a city."

The Pauvan Indians were among the most friendly of the Utah tribes. Their chief was named Kanosh. He was good to the Mormons. "He did all he could to prevent trouble with the whites, and gave his word that he would always protect the colonizers, which he always did."[7] Chief Kanosh was an unusually intelligent and influential native. In June, 1865, at the close of the Black Hawk war, the leaders of the whites and fifteen important Indian chiefs signed a treaty of peace. "Kanosh was the only Indian who was able to attach his signature to the document, a fact of which he was very proud. The rest of the chiefs attached their marks."[8]

Founding and Growth of Fillmore

After choosing the site for Fillmore, the next matter of importance for the Mormons in Pauvan Valley was to survey the city lots and the farming lands. The decision having been reached to make the capital city an exact duplicate of Great Salt Lake City— that is, to make square blocks of ten acres each and subdivide them into eight lots of one and one-fourth acres, with streets eight rods wide—Jesse W. Fox began the survey of Fillmore on October 28, the very day that the site was selected. The distance from Salt Lake was computed to be 151 miles. Two days after selecting the site, President Young and company left Fillmore to return to the parent colony. Before leaving Brigham had instructed Call and his associates to construct a fort near the spot which he had designated as State-house Square.

With Bishop Anson Call as leader, a thriving, typical Mormon community came into existence within a very short time, as is evident from several letters and reports from Fillmore within a few months. Call stated: "We then built a school-house, established a school within fifteen days of our arrival. . . . I was counseled by Brigham to erect mills. I immediately commenced building a sawmill."[9] November 24, only one month after their arrival, Call informed Brigham Young that the settlers had erected, according to the President's instructions, a corral two and one-half acres in extent. Not being able to make a stockade the fall of their arrival on account of the dryness and rockiness of the ground, the settlers erected their houses in close formation, making a fort in the shape

---

[7]Young, op. cit., 287-288.
[8]Ibid.
[9]Call, op. cit., 41-43.

of a triangle.[10] They also constructed a wagon road into the canyon east of the settlement, at a cost of 150 days' work, to make accessible the timber which was plentiful in the mountains within five or six miles of their camp.

Early in 1852 Dimick Huntington was sent into Pauvan Valley by Governor Young, who was also superintendent of Indian affairs, to settle some difficulties that had arisen between the red men and the settlers. Upon returning to Salt Lake he reported to the governor that the colonists at Fillmore had been plowing and sowing for the past ten days, that the ground was broken easily, and that the people were highly pleased with the farming land, it being better than they had at first anticipated. Huntington also took the report to Brigham that the colonists were "in great want of a good blacksmith . . . one that has a good set of tools to work with, one or two would meet a good liberal patronage in this place; also a tanner and a currier."[11] The Mormon Colonizer always hastened to satisfy the needs of the colonists.

During the following winter, 1852-1853, two day schools were taught and one evening school. A gristmill was completed and put into operation, which was of great advantage to the members of that frontier community. Previously they had to haul their grain to Nephi or Manti to have it ground into flour.[12]

The Mormon capital city grew rapidly during the early years of its settlement. Some of the leading church and state officials took up lots in Fillmore, convinced that it was going to be an important center of Mormon population, as it had been selected for the seat of the government. Brigham Young's message to the Territorial Legislature, January 5, 1852, gave reasons for moving the capital from Salt Lake City to Fillmore. He stated:

"The location is far more central to the territory than Salt Lake City; the Pauvan Valley will sustain a large and dense population; locating the seat of government there would encourage settlers to go there and very much facilitate the settlement of all other suitable places in that region. Under all these circumstances the location of the capital at the place selected appears judicious upon its own merits, and will unquestionably advance the already prosperous and vastly increasing resources of the territory."[13]

No doubt the governor's message had its effect in causing a number of leading citizens to move to Fillmore. By October, 1853, only two years after its establishment, there were 304 church mem-

[10]*Deseret News*, November 24, 1851.
[11]Dimick B. Huntington, *Deseret News,* February 8, 1852.
[12]*Deseret News*, March 27, 1853.
[13]*Ibid.,* January 10, 1852.

bers in that community.[14] Colonists continued to arrive in large numbers, "many being called from other settlements to cast their lot with the people of Fillmore in order to make that place as strong as possible." In 1853 Anson Call was succeeded as president of ecclesiastical affairs in Fillmore by John A. Ray.

THE STATE HOUSE

While the citizens of Fillmore were taking care of the problems of home and community building, they were also exerting every effort within their power, working cooperatively, upon a State House which they had been counseled by Governor Young to build. They hauled sandstone and limestone from the base of the neighboring mountains for the building. Samuel P. Hoyt reported on January 15, 1852, that a new stone-quarry had been discovered on the left fork of Chalk Creek, and a road had already been built to it.[15]

During the following summer, work was continued on the State House in whatever time was not absolutely required in eking out a livelihood. By November of 1852 the foundation was completed. According to various witnesses, these pioneers were building so well that the result of their efforts would stand almost indefinitely. When George A. Smith passed through Fillmore, he reported to the *Deseret News* that "the foundation of the State House is the best foundation in the Territory, and does credit to the builders."[16]

The citizens, during the fall, were all occupied in harvesting their crops, so they gave up the idea of finishing the walls of the State House until the following spring. However, Brigham Young sent a group of masons and other workmen from Salt Lake to speed the construction. When the colonists had completed their farm work, they cooperated with the builders by hauling rock, sand, lumber, scaffold poles, and by burning lime. The work progressed so rapidly that on December 9 they had completed the walls; then the workmen returned to Salt Lake. The foreman reported in regard to the State House: "The whole building is built of rock, laid in lime mortar, making it the most substantial building in the Territory."[17]

Work was continued on the edifice, and the south wing of it was completed by December, 1855, at a cost of about $32,000. It

[14]*Ibid.*, October 6, 1853.
[15]*Ibid.*, January 15, 1852.
[16]*Ibid.*, November 10, 1852.
[17]*Deseret News*, December 15, 1852.

still stands in practically as good condition as when the pioneers erected it.   The dimensions of that wing were forty-one feet four inches wide, by sixty-one feet eight inches long.   There were a basement and two stories. The basement was ten feet high, the first story twelve, and the second story fourteen feet six inches, making a total of nearly forty feet up to the spring of the arch. According to Colonel Albert G. Brown:

> The design of the architect is for a very magnificent edifice in the shape of a Greek Cross, with a rotunda sixty feet in diameter. Only one wing has been completed, but this is spacious enough to furnish all needful accommodations. The material is rough hammered sandstone of an intense red.[18]

However, the design of the architect was never completely fulfilled. Later conditions and developments made it unnecessary to construct more than the one wing.

HOLDING OF UTAH LEGISLATURE AT FILLMORE IN 1855

On December 7, 1855, Governor Brigham Young and most of the members of the Legislative Assembly arrived in Fillmore. Three days later the fifth annual session of the Legislature of Utah convened in the new State House.   Heber C. Kimball was elected president and Jedediah M. Grant speaker.   The following day Governor Young delivered his message to the council and the house. Besides those already mentioned and the members of the legislature, there were present that winter in the half-built frontier town: Secretary Almon W. Babbitt, Judges J. F. Inney, G. P. Stiles, and W. W. Drummond of the supreme court; marshal of the territory, J. L. Heywood, T. R. King, probate judge of Millard County, and Apostles Amasa M. Lyman and Erastus Snow.   For forty-two days the session of the legislature continued.   On January 18, 1856, it was adjourned and most of the officials returned to the Mormon Mecca.[19]

SEAT OF GOVERNMENT MOVED TO SALT LAKE CITY

This was the only session of the legislature which ever met in Fillmore, for it was by now evident that Salt Lake City was industrially and socially the real center. Therefore, Fillmore was abandoned as the capital of the Territory of Utah, and the legislature met at Salt Lake City from then on. The following resolution, signed by Governor Brigham Young, December 15, 1856, gave other reasons for the change from Fillmore to Salt Lake:

---
[18]*Atlantic Monthly* (May, 1859), 573.
[19]*Deseret News*, December 19, 1855

Whereas the General Government has failed to make an appropriation for the completion of the public buildings at the seat of the government of this Territory; And whereas the Territory has already expended thereon upwards of ten thousand dollars over and above the amount appropriated by Congress; And whereas we deem it advisable to change the seat of government from Fillmore to Great Salt Lake City, until the public buildings are further completed; And whereas suitable accommodations can be furnished in Great Salt Lake City; And whereas it is our duty to pursue that regard to legislation best calculated to promote the public interest: Therefore, be it resolved by the Governor and Legislative Assembly of the Territory of Utah, that the seat of Government is removed from Fillmore City to Great Salt Lake City; until otherwise provided by law. And be it further resolved that the Supreme Court hold its annual sessions in Great Salt Lake, so long as the seat of Government remains at that place.[20]

Fillmore's importance as the capital city was thus taken away, but home seekers still found it a desirable town. It grew to considerable size as the hub colony of Millard County. It is at the present time a typical Mormon agricultural community.

[20]*Ibid.*, December 15, 1856.

STATE HOUSE AT FILLMORE, UTAH

Chapter XXVII

THE NORTHWARD ADVANCE OF MORMON SETTLEMENTS

Founding of Willard and Brigham City

The advance of Mormon colonies northward during the Utah colonial period was somewhat slower than that southward. Climate probably had much to do with the rapid southward movement of the Saints, as farming was their chief concern. But the greatest factor was Brigham Young's desire to establish a line of settlements through the Basin to the ocean, over a route which he believed would be the most feasible for transporting the Saints into his empire, the "Mormon Corridor." At any rate there was, before the spring of 1851, a Mormon settlement some 250 miles south of Salt Lake City, with many others at intervening points, and a group of colonists was being dispatched at that time to settle San Bernardino. But northward there were very few, and the most distant one was only about fifty-nine miles from Salt Lake City.

Gradually, however, the people began to learn that the land north was just as productive as that south, and that farming conditions were as promising. The first settlement north of Weber County was begun on March 31, 1851, when five families went to the present site of Willard, originally known as North Willow Creek, fifteen miles north of Ogden. The men immediately commenced plowing and putting in grain. They erected five log cabins north of the creek, about a quarter of a mile northwest of the present meeting-house of Willard.

Sometime during 1851 Henry G. Sherwood and Cyril Call surveyed the land for the settlers on North Willow Creek. In the fall and during 1852 the number of settlers was augmented by the arrival of several more families. The foundation of another Mormon colony had been laid and another frontier district opened to land settlement.

By the spring of 1851, home seekers were also located twenty-two miles north of Ogden and seven miles north of Willard on Box Elder Creek, near the mouth of the Box Elder Canyon. This settlement, originally known as Box Elder but subsequently named Brigham City, is today one of the principal cities of northern Utah. It is beautifully situated at the base of the Wasatch Mountains near the northeast corner of the Great Salt Lake. Today it is noted for its fine fruits; in fact, no part of Utah excels it in quantity and quality of its peaches, plums, apricots, apples, and all kinds of berries. Most of its people are engaged in horticulture, farming, and stock raising. It is laid out with wide, straight streets, intersecting each other at right angles. The main street, extending in a straight line from the southern to the northern extreme of the city, is one of the finest in Utah.

Among the settlers who arrived there in 1851, William Davis built the first house on Box Elder Creek near the center of the present Brigham City. Jefferson Weight, Benjamin Tolman, and George F. Hanson erected their houses immediately thereafter. These colonists were joined by several other families during the summer and fall of 1851, making a little village composed of eight or nine families.

Molested by Shoshone Indians

In the vicinity surrounding the infant colony lived about 500 Shoshone Indians. Although they appeared to be friendly, their proximity caused a great deal of uneasiness to the little band of home seekers. Right at that time Indian troubles threatened the general extermination of small groups of settlers on all the frontier districts of the Great Basin. These Shoshones around Brigham City were continually asking the whites for all kinds of foodstuff, and wanted everything to which they took a fancy. In order to protect themselves and avoid trouble, the settlers built a fort in the fall of 1851. It was called Davis Fort, subsequently known as the Old Fort after a larger one was built in 1853.

Growth of Brigham City—Apostle Lorenzo Snow

In April, 1852, an ecclesiastical organization was effected. William Davis was ordained a bishop to preside over Box Elder. At this time the infant settlement was directly under the ecclesiastical control of Ogden where a stake organization was in existence.

In the spring of 1852 the settlers moved out of the fort upon their farms which had been surveyed by Henry G. Sherwood in May of the previous year. In contrast to the extremely small farms of only several acres each cultivated by the settlers under the Mormon land system, the first farms at Brigham City ranged from forty to eighty acres in size. The policy of owning rather large tracts of land was not to endure long, however, even in this colony. Two years later President Young sent Jesse W. Fox to survey a townsite and also the farming land. The latter survey became known as the Big Field. It "was surveyed principally into five-acre lots," again applying Brigham Young's policy of small farms.

At rather frequent intervals during 1852 and 1853, colonists, among whom were many Scandinavian immigrants who had crossed the plains that summer, were sent by Brother Brigham from Salt Lake to augment the infant colony on Box Elder Creek. In July, 1853, the settlers at Brigham City received an order from Governor Brigham Young to move again into a fort owing to the outbreak of Indian hostilities. Consequently a second fort was built near the center of the infant city; the walls were composed of log houses built close enough together to enclose the fort on three sides, the south end only being open. Nearly all of the white men on Box Elder Creek spent the winters of 1853 to 1855 in the fort. Some remained longer.

Until the fall of 1853 Box Elder had "lacked a master spirit to guide its affairs." Reports reached President Young that conditions needed improving in this frontier settlement and that an increase of numbers was desirable. Accordingly, at the October conference at Salt Lake, Apostle Lorenzo Snow was called upon to gather fifty families and send them to Box Elder early the next season (1854). In choosing a strong leader to revive the little colony and develop a frontier district, no better choice could have been made than that of Lorenzo Snow. He was a man of marked ability, strong personality, and great friendliness. Later he became President of the Church of Jesus Christ of Latter-day Saints.

Following his appointment, Apostle Snow became very active in sending colonists to strengthen the settlement on Box Elder Creek. Most of them arrived in the spring of 1854 and were assigned city lots and five acres of farming land. In May of the following year (1855), Apostle Snow moved his family to Brigham City, where he had been sent by the President to preside over the Box Elder Stake of Zion. Jonathan C. Wright and Samuel Smith acted as his counselors from 1855 to 1857.

President Lorenzo Snow gave a very interesting account of affairs in Brigham City at and shortly after his arrival. His description is quoted here at length as it pictures in a vivid way the reception given President Brigham Young by the Mormons when their beloved leader honored them with a visit. Snow stated:

When I arrived in Box Elder County, I found the location where Brigham City now flourishes in a very unprosperous condition. . . . At first, in locating there, I only took a portion of my family, as a small and incommodious adobe hut was the only tenement attainable. During the summer and fall I succeeded in erecting a house, one story and a half in height, thirty feet by forty. It being impossible to obtain shingles, I covered the building with slabs and for two winters the rattling of those slabs, put in motion by the canyons breezes, supplied us with music in the absence of organs and pianos. I had thus covered the roof of my house, but before my front door was in, and all my floors laid, and before any plastering was done, our house was the stopping place and the home of President Brigham Young and his company of tourists, whenever they visited these northern settlements.

To manifest due respect, and a proper appreciation of those visits, which were productive of a vast amount of good to the Saints scattered throughout the Territory, I introduced a precedent which was widely adopted and carried into effect, until railroads superseded those lengthy carriage drives. To perpetuate a remembrance of this unique order of reception, I will give a description of the original one, as follows:

On learning the precise time when the party would arrive, I arranged a programme for the occasion. In the first place, a set of hands was detailed to put the roads in good condition for carriages, by clearing away stones, filling crevices, repairing bridges and causeways, etc. Much care and labor were devoted to organizing the escort to meet the President's long train of carriages some miles from the city. We had not the means in those early days of our history to be very elaborate in furnishing equipment as would have gratified our vanity, but what we lacked we supplied in ingenuity and enterprise, in fixing up what our means and circumstances would admit.

We selected forty or fifty intelligent, interesting looking young gentlemen, dressed in gray uniform, each carrying a lance, the top of which was pointed with shining material, from which gay ribbons floated gracefully in the breeze. These young gentlemen were mounted on our finest horses and properly instructed and disciplined for the occasion. Next, we selected sixteen or twenty fine intelligent young ladies, had them dressed in white, with corresponding decorations. These were seated in wagons, each drawn by two span of horses, properly caparisoned. All the members of the escort were carefully instructed respecting a proper manner of giving a salute on meeting the visiting party, the various branches of the escort bearing flags and beautiful banners with appropriate mottoes. All were preceded by one or two carriages occupied by the authorities and leading men of the city, the whole led by a martial band under the direction of the city marshal.

In connection with the foregoing arrangement, the children, in their Sunday attire, gathered from all parts of the city, and many from adjacent settlements, were formed into lines on each side of the street, and as the company entered, it was conducted through these long lines of children to my house, amid loud cheers, the ringing of bells and waving of banners.

The effect of this display on President Young and party was truly thrilling. They were taken by a surprise of the most impressive character. Thus an example was set which has been extensively followed, until carriage riding has, to a great extent, yielded to that of railroads.[1]

In June, 1855, a number of families moved out of the fort and erected houses on their city lots. Thomas Mathias built the first

[1]Lorenzo Snow, *Latter-day Saint Journal History,* June 10, 1855, Ms.

log cabin and John D. Reese built the first adobe house on the city plat. At that time Frederick Kesler was operating a mill situated on the northeast corner of the city plat. That summer Joel Edmunds and Henry Ettlemon erected a sawmill in Box Elder Canyon, which was in active operation by October 13.

Lorenzo Snow perceived that his pioneer associates needed more to enrich their lives than merely the development of industry. The journalist stated: "Up to this time the only music that saluted the ears of the settlers on Box Elder Creek was the mountain breezes, and Elder Snow seeing the necessity of something better to entertain the people turned his house into an amusement hall. A dramatic association was formed which entertained the people during the winter of 1855-1856."[2]

The "Move South"

Affairs progressed very satisfactorily at Brigham City under the direction of Apostle Snow until the coming of Johnston's army in 1858. At this time the city was nearly evacuated by the people moving south, most of them going as far as Utah County where they settled temporarily. The exiles took along enough flour to last them for a year or more, as the crops raised in Box Elder in both of the preceding years had been very bounteous.

Samuel Smith remained in the town with a company of minutemen to guard the place against Indians. About 600 of the red men were encamped in the neighborhood of the settlement at that time. The danger of an attack seemed grave enough to warrant President Snow's leaving about forty men sufficiently equipped with firearms and well prepared to fight the natives if they were forced to do so. However, after a short time the Indians left Box Elder Creek and went northward. With this immediate danger removed, most of the men who had been left to guard Brigham City journeyed to the south to join their families.

The guards were instructed by Governor Young to burn Brigham City in case the soldiers on entering the valley proved hostile. Similar instructions were received by colonists in the other settlements that were to be evacuated. The country was to be left as desolate for the incoming army as it had been ten years earlier when the Saints of God first entered the Great Basin.

But by the time the army entered the Salt Lake Valley in the spring of 1858, an amicable agreement had been reached between the federal government and the Mormons; therefore, the latter were

----

[2]*Box Elder Stake History,* 18. Ms.

not forced to burn their newly constructed houses. As soon as peace was restored, the former inhabitants of Brigham City returned home. They found their property safe, the guards not having had occasion to burn it.

LORENZO SNOW AND COOPERATION

Under the direction of Lorenzo Snow, Brigham City became one of the most progressive and thriving cities in the Great Basin. Probably the most successful project conducted by Apostle Snow while residing in that frontier community was the cooperative system that he inauguarated and supervised. In the shoe factories and similar establishments, enough merchandise was manufactured during the winter months, while the people had spare time, to provide for all their private needs, and the surplus was disposed of on the market.

FOUNDING OF PERRY AND HARPER

While Brigham City was still in its infancy, two or three small settlements were established a short distance from the larger one. Several home seekers from Salt Lake City came into Box Elder County in 1852 and decided to make a settlement on Three Mile Creek. In April, 1853, William Plummer Tippets with his family located there. Later, other families joined him, and the little settlement subsequently known as Perry was established.

John Gibbs and George Foster came to Brigham City in the spring of 1852 and selected a spot five or six miles northwest of it for settlement. About a dozen families had collected there by the fall of 1853. The following fall (1854) President Brigham Young, who was also president of the Perpetual Emigrating Fund Company, sent Anson Call to establish a farm to furnish profitable employment for the poorer Saints who had been brought from Europe that season by the Emigrating Fund. Call opened a large farm about eight miles from Brigham City and two or three miles from where John Gibbs and his associates had previously located. The converts sowed fifty acres of grain that fall, and a number of them wintered on the place in 1854-1855.

"In 1855 President Brigham Young counseled Anson Call to build a fort on his farm for the security of the people against Indian depredations." Consequently a stone wall, three feet thick and eight feet high, was constructed around a piece of land 120 feet square. Early in 1856, Call engaged Thomas Harper, for whom the settlement was subsequently named, to manage the farm. In the spring of 1858, prior to the "move south," the Saints planted extensive acreage, but later were forced to abandon everything for about three months when they were called to evacuate the settlements. In the fall most of the settlers returned and found that the grain had matured and that they were assured of a good harvest.

Founding of Wellsville and Mendon

Land settlement spread north and east of Box Elder County into Cache Valley. The first colonists to arrive there did so only a year before the coming of Johnston's army. Two infant villages —Wellsville and Mendon—were founded just in time for the colonists to join in the "move south." Yet there were enough settlers to show that Brother Brigham intended to have Cache Valley populated as rapidly as conditions would permit.

Wellsville was first settled by Peter Maughan, his wife and six other families, the colonists being sent there from Tooele, September 15, 1856, by President Young. Mary Ann Maughan, wife of Peter, said, "We left Tooele County early in September, 1856. Brother Brigham Young said that all the brethren who wanted to go with Brother Peter (Maughan) could do so; some were glad of the chance; six of the brethren with their families started with us."[3]

In the spring of 1858 the "move" took place and Maughan's Fort (Wellsville) was temporarily evacuated on about March 19, 1858. The people returned that autumn and other colonists were sent with them to build a city.

In 1857, about one year after the first settlers arrived at Wellsville, Alexander B. Hill and Robert Hill took up farms at the present site of Mendon. After the "move south" several families arrived during the latter part of April and the beginning of May, to form a nucleus for another farming community.

The following year (1859) President Brigham Young began to direct his attention to the agricultural possibilities of Cache Valley which had scarcely begun to be utilized before the "Utah War." Many people on their return from the "move south" were looking for a spot to locate where good land and water were plentiful. Cache Valley supplied that spot. Also, in 1859, the emigration from Liverpool, which had been temporarily closed during the period of the trouble with the federal government, was re-opened.

---

[3]*Hyrum Stake History, September 15, 1856. Ms.*

"On their arrival in the Basin, the English-speaking immigrants were as naturally attracted to Cache Valley as the Scandinavians were toward Sanpete."

FOUNDING OF LOGAN

In April, 1859, settlers located on the present site of Logan and established what proved to be the most important city in northern Utah. In June they were joined by other families who had been advised by Peter Maughan to settle at Logan. Mr. Maughan had been appointed by Brigham Young to preside over the Saints in Cache Valley; therefore he took an active part in directing land settlement in that region. During the first summer and fall, log houses, a fort, and a school house were erected in the infant settlement. Church services were held for the first time in the latter building on December 18.

In August, 1859, William B. Preston, a young man who was destined to rank as chief among the founders of Logan and as its first bishop, arrived, in company with the Thatcher family, on the present site of Logan. He said to his brother-in-law, John Thatcher, "John, this is good enough for me!" Thereupon they unloaded their goods and began work.

Three months later Apostles Orson Hyde and Ezra T. Benson traveled to Logan to effect the organization of a ward. They asked Peter Maughan to suggest a man who he considered would be a good bishop. He pointed to Preston's house and said that the young man who resided there had worked night and day ever since his arrival. Apostle Hyde remarked that William Preston would do for bishop, and soon thereafter he was notified of his appointment.

The Thatcher family are considered also among the most important of Logan's founders. In 1859 Hezekiah Thatcher was believed to be the wealthiest man in Utah with the exception of Brigham Young. He had obtained his wealth at the gold fields in California. During the winter of 1858-59 he sent his wagons, with his sons J. W. and A. D. Thatcher, and his son-in-law, William B. Preston, to California for merchandise. Upon their return they took their goods into Logan to help build Cache Valley.

Following the general Mormon practice, lots were surveyed and then divided among the settlers. Sawmills, gristmills, and other similar industries were established during that year. James Ellis and Benjamin Williams sawed the first lumber in the fall of 1859.

The city of Logan was favorably and beautifully located. It grew rapidly. Even by the close of the first year of its existence it contained 256 people, and that number was greatly multiplied each succeeding year.

After the establishment of Logan, the northward advance of Mormon settlements continued at a rapid pace. Within the next five or six years some twenty to twenty-five settlements were established in Cache Valley and in southern Idaho. President Young directed his main colonizing efforts in that section of the Basin during the early sixties. The northern settlements—sometimes called the granary of Utah—proved to be excellent farming communities, equaling if not surpassing President Young's expectations.

Chapter XXVIII

FORT BRIDGER AND FORT SUPPLY

Green River Valley

The Green River Valley lies eastward from the Great Salt Lake Valley. They are separated by the towering range of the Wasatch Mountains. Between those two valleys extends a long narrow canyon through which trappers and scouts found their way into the Great Basin. Later the Donner Party heading for California, the Mormon Pioneers, the Forty-niners, and other adventurers and home seekers in the Great West traversed that route on their westward trek.

Why Mormons Desired Control over James Bridger's Property

In 1843 James Bridger, who for some years had been a renowned mountaineer and trapper, built a fort on Black's Fork, a tributary of Green River. Here he was living at the advent of the Mormon colonizers. Bridger claimed a Mexican grant of land thirty miles square, but "under the Mexican laws he was allowed only nine miles square." Brother Brigham considered Bridger's location to be a site of considerable importance on the Mormon Trail; therefore, it must be secured by the Saints and maintained as an outpost and supply station on the main highway of travel before entering the Great Basin.

Governor Young's reasons for desiring to own Fort Bridger are apparent. Thousands of immigrants were traveling to Salt Lake City each year, and an outpost in which they could rest and replenish their supplies just before making the last 126 miles of difficult journey through the mountains would be of untold benefit. Also, by 1853 the Mormons in the Basin were having a considerable amount of trouble with the mountaineers, especially those who lived in the Green River Valley. By 1853 the Walker Indian War was on, affecting most of the Mormon settlements in the Great Basin. "It was believed by Brigham Young that James Bridger and other mountaineers were at the bottom of much of the ill-feeling manifested by the red men, and that they were incited to attack the Mormon settlements."[1] In the words of J. Cecil Alter:

----

[1] Orson F. Whitney, *History of Utah.*

James Bridger was an arrowhead in the flesh of the Mormon leaders, fixed as he was in a position of authority and influence at Fort Bridger; and every time the arrowhead was agitated the Church authorities flinched.   Brigham Young bore the Bridger barb for some time before endeavoring strenuously to rid himself and the country of the old scout, and to people the scar with those whom he preferred to trust.[2]

MORMONS AND THE MOUNTAINEERS

The Mormons had established ferries on the various streams along the Overland route and had provided stores of goods and livestock at various places where the emigrants could replenish their diminishing supplies while traveling toward the Basin. But on the various streams in the Green River Valley, the mountaineers were pretty much in control of supplying the needs of the passing emigrants.

Some of the Mormons were not content to see all the lucrative business go to the enrichment of the Gentiles. Early in the spring of 1853, W. A. Hickman, a Utah attorney, left Salt Lake City with a good supply of merchandise with a view to establishing a trading post on some good spot east of the entrance to the Basin. About the first of May he located on the Green River, a favored position which gave him opportunity to intercept all emigration before it reached Fort Bridger. During that summer he claimed to have cleared about $9,000 in three months' time.

In the winter of 1852-1853, the Utah territorial legislature granted a charter to Messrs. McDonald, Thompson, and Hawley, of Salt Lake City, to operate the emigrant ferries on Green River. Naturally the mountaineers, including James Bridger, "resented the act of certain Utah interests in horning into the lucrative business," as they had for many years operated the ferries. They had no intentions of turning their prosperous business over to the Mormons, so they enforced what they thought were their rights with their guns. "In this manner they stood the Mormons off, reaping approximately $300,000 in tools during that summer."[3]

ATTEMPT TO ARREST JAMES BRIDGER

When the Mormon traders returned to Utah that fall (1853), they reported that James Bridger was selling powder and lead to the Indians and inciting them to kill the Saints. Governor Brigham Young, being also Indian agent, feared that the Indian wars in

[2]J. Cecil Alter, *James Bridger*, 244.
[3]*Ibid.*, 246.

Utah might result in the sending of a federal army to the Basin against the natives. As this would hamper the freedom of the Mormons, he caused affidavits to be made out for the arrest of the mountaineer. "The sheriff was ordered to confiscate Bridger's dangerous goods, and deliver the old scout to Utah a prisoner."[4]

When a posse of 150 men arrived at Fort Bridger, Jim was not to be found and his Indian wife claimed not to know where he had gone. After carrying out the orders regarding the property, the posse went on to the Green River, where they engaged in a battle with the mountaineers at the ferries. Two or three of the latter were killed and much of their property, which included whiskey and several hundred head of livestock, was disposed of by the posse. When the sheriff and his assistants returned to Salt Lake City with the livestock, the word "was given out authoritatively from that time that the Mormons were in Green River valley to stay, and that Bridger was out to stay, or his influence was at most greatly minimized."[5]

Surveying Bridger's Property

But James Bridger himself seemed not to be entirely of that opinion. Hardly had the posse left the Green River Valley before the old scout and John M. Hockaday, a government surveyor, began a land survey of the country claimed by Bridger. On November 6, 1853, the survey was completed. The plat contained 3,898 acres. The following spring, March 9, "a true copy of the original" was filed with the General Land Office in Washington, D. C.

After completing the survey of the Fort Bridger lands, the mountaineer took his family and settled on a farm at Little Santa Fe, Jackson County, Missouri, near Kansas City. James Bridger never returned to reside in the fort again, although he did make other trips into the Great West.

Founding of Fort Supply

Just before the posse left Utah on their man hunt around Fort Bridger, at the general conference of the Church of Jesus Christ of Latter-day Saints, Orson Hyde was appointed by the Church officials to select colonists and supervise the founding of permanent Mormon settlement in the neighborhood of Fort Bridger. On October 7, the last day of the conference, Apostle

―――
[4]*Ibid.,* 246-247.
[5]*Ibid.,* 249.

Hyde read from the stand the names of thirty-nine persons selected to accompany him on that mission. Conforming to Mormon practice, those called were sustained by the vote of the Saints assembled at that meeting.

The company was organized at the State House in Great Salt Lake City, with John Nebeker as captain or president, on November 2, 1853. It arrived at Fort Bridger eleven days later. Every person who had been called responded. The following articles and supplies were considered necessary to the establishment of this settlement:

> Two men to a wagon; three hundred pounds of flour, seventy-five pounds of seed wheat, half a bushel of oats and forty pounds of seed ends of potatoes, and a peck of barley to the man. There was one milch cow and a beef creature to the wagon. Besides this the company brought along all necessary teams, arms and ammunition for defense and game, with seed corn and every variety of garden seed, fruit seeds, etc.; also various kinds of tools and implements for farming and mechanical operations.[6]

No sooner had Orson Hyde got the first company on its way toward the contemplated settlement than he busied himself in raising another company to follow the first. In less than two weeks a group consisting of fifty-three men well fitted out with supplies had been raised by voluntary subscription. Thus Apostle Hyde had used the two methods—appointment and volunteering—commonly practiced by the Church in selecting colonists.

This second company, made up of mechanics and workmen of many trades, was well equipped with tools and implements in abundance, and with blankets, leather, nails, and other things essential to founding a colony. Besides this equipment, they had twenty-six wagons, from two to five yoke of oxen to each wagon, fifty head of beef cattle, and nearly as many milch cows. On November 16, 1853, three days after the arrival of the first company at Fort Bridger, the second group left Salt Lake.[7]

When the Mormon colonists arrived at Fort Bridger, they found about a dozen mountaineers there who were very "surly and suspicious." Having had two or three of their number killed by the posse from Salt Lake City at the Green River ferries only a few days previously, these rough mountain men had the spirit of murder lurking in their minds. The Mormons were informed that about twenty additional mountaineers, together with

[6]Andrew Jenson. "Fort Bridger." *Utah Genealogical and Historical Magazine*, January, 1913.
[7]Alter. *op. cit.*. 251.

FORT SUPPLY, ESTABLISHED IN NOVEMBER 1853, NEAR FORT BRIDGER

MAIN STREET SCENE, SALT LAKE CITY, 1865

a tribe of Ute Indians, were settled a short distance away on Henry's Fork.

Therefore, these new-comers felt that their welcome at Fort Bridger had not been very cordial and that it would be better for them to select another site upon which to establish their settlement. They traveled about twelve miles southwest of Bridger and located on Willow Creek, a tributary of Smith's Fork. The site was about two miles above the confluence of the two streams. Here they were joined by the second group sent out from Salt Lake, and together they established a town known as Fort Supply. "The name, Supply, was prophetic in a sense, indicating the aims of the settlement, which were to supply the oncoming emigrants with such home-grown foodstuffs and supplies as the country could afford." In speaking of the arrival of the second group, one of the original members remarked that, "On November 26, 1853, Captain Isaac Bullock came in with fifty-three men and twenty-five wagons. When they joined us our company was ninety-two strong, all well armed, and when our blockhouse was completed we felt safer than ever."[8]

Building a Blockhouse

The plans for the blockhouse were made by James S. Brown; and within two weeks the project was completed. This house had four wings or rooms of equal size, uniting at the corners, thus forming a center room. This room was built two stories high, the lower one being used for storage and the upper for a guard-house from which position the surrounding country could be overlooked. All of the rooms in the stockhouse were provided with portholes.

During the first winter at Fort Supply the weather was extremely cold, the thermometer registering thirty degrees below zero in January. A few of the cattle froze to death. But the snow fall was light—no deeper than one foot on the level, and the west winds cleared many of the hillsides of snow, making it possible for the animals to get the grass.

Success Under New Frontier Conditions

The Saints were again confronted with a new type of frontier, 7,200 feet above sea level. Doubts were entertained by many as to the possibility of maturing crops at such a high altitude. The following account appeared in the Deseret News on June 22, 1854:

---

[8]James S. Brown. *Life of a Pioneer*, 307.

By our latest advices from Green River Ferries, and Fort Supply, dated the seventeenth and twentieth inst., we learn that matters are moving on quite harmoniously; but the question whether farming can be carried on there to advantage is still undetermined.[9]

A small crop was raised in 1854, but in the fall of that year it was still a question whether or not farming could be made successful. However, the Saints proved that point beyond doubt the following year. July 2, 1855, George Boyd reported in Salt Lake City that he had just come from Fort Supply and "that the settlers there had seventy acres of wheat looking successfully fine."[10] A good account of what had been accomplished at Fort Supply in 1855 and the agricultural possibilities of that high altitude are plainly stated by George A. Smith. No man in the Mormon group had seen more colonies in the making or had actually participated in the establishment of more settlements than had Apostle Smith. For this reason his observations are of exceptional importance and accuracy. In Smith's own words:

After a cold and unpleasant journey we arrived at this place on the evening of the 26th (April, 1856). We went up the Black Fork road, through a very fine and rich bottom, capable of producing the choicest grain, vegetables and fruit, and were surprised to find that Fort Supply was seven thousand and two hundred feet above the level of the sea. . . . A two-story house used for a court house and other public purposes, twenty-five neatly constructed dwellings, and substantially made corrals and stockyards were evidence of the energy and taste of the people and also the fruitfulness of the soil, for we saw nine stacks of wheat in one yard, and several stacks of hay and oats keeping the wheat stacks company. . . . Cattle, horses and sheep wintered over seven thousand feet above the level of the sea and north of latitude forty-one degrees. Some of them which last fall were too poor to travel and left by the immigration, are in fine condition, although the snow has been drifted so deep as to entirely cover the stockade. An adjoining field of two hundred acres is enclosed with a fence worthy of being patterned after by any settlement that I have visited in the Territory; it is built of substantial poles laid up in Virginia fence style with stakes and riders. This enclosure has a great variety of soil and a large additional field will be made this spring. . . . A gristmill will be in operation in a few weeks. . . . The success of this settlement, at so great an altitude, shows conclusively what may be done with some of our mountain valleys, those which have been considered a couple of thousand feet above the level of cultivation.[11]

PURPOSES FOR SETTLING FORT SUPPLY

From letters written and from events that transpired within six months after Fort Supply was established, it is quite evident that

[9]*Deseret News*, June 22, 1854.
[10]*Fort Bridger and Fort Supply*, 6, Ms.
[11]George A. Smith, *Deseret News*, April 28, 1856.

the founder of the Mormon empire had called those missionaries to settle Fort Supply with definite purposes in mind.

Brother Brigham had instructed the colonists to serve as missionaries to the Indians for the purpose of teaching them Mormonism and civilization, and with an aim of eliminating Indian troubles. The young men among the colonists were instructed to marry the native girls, if the Indians would permit them "to take the young daughters of the chief and leading men."[12] However, conditions were not conducive for those instructions to be followed very extensively by the Mormon missionaries in any of their missions. Cases of Mormons marrying Indian women were rather few in Utah colonial history.

Shortly after establishing the settlers at Fort Supply, Apostle Hyde—acting in harmony with President Young's orders—selected certain members of his group and sent them to do missionary work among the Blackfoot Indians.

A purpose previously mentioned for settling the Green River Valley was to establish an outpost station where Saints could replenish their depleted food supplies prior to the last 126 miles of difficult mountain travel before entering the Basin. The name—Fort Supply—implies that purpose. A letter written in Salt Lake City, June 29, 1854, indicated that the Mormon leader was searching for a good route from Fort Supply to the Basin where the immigrants' livestock could find pasturage en route. It stated that Brigham Young, Heber C. Kimball, and Jedediah M. Grant were going to the mouth of Provo Canyon to make a new road to Fort Supply for the use of the immigrants. Such a road would lead up Provo Canyon and through a country where there was good pasturage for cattle. It would direct the immigrants immediately into Utah Valley from which place they could spread to the north and south.

Additional Colonists

So greatly interested was the Mormon leader in the success of the pioneer settlement at Fort Supply, that, on February 24, 1856, he called directly from the stand in the tabernacle at Salt Lake a large number of families from the older settlements in Utah to strengthen that Mormon outpost. In making the call, Brigham selected a few families from several towns in proportion to the size of the town. This call gives one an insight into one of the

---

[12]James S. Brown, *Life of a Pioneer*, 304.

methods employed by the president in strengthening the infant colonies. The report on this missionary assignment shows that two families were selected from Springville, twelve from Provo, two from Tooele, twenty-four from Great Salt Lake City, one from Payson, one from Nephi, and one from American Fork.[13]

SENDING ASSISTANCE TO THE HANDCART COMPANIES, 1856

An excellent opportunity for service was given the Saints at Fort Supply in the fall of 1856. One thousand immigrants in two handcart companies followed by two wagon trains had been overtaken out in the middle of Wyoming by an early and bitter winter. In October Governor Young, fearing for the safety of these companies as the weather became cold, called for volunteers to go with wagons and supplies to the rescue. Along with a number of wagons from Salt Lake City,[14] ten wagons were sent from Fort Supply with clothing and provisions for the belated immigrants. The author's grandfather was the teamster of one of the wagons. Brigham Young remarked in a sermon at Salt Lake on November 30, 1856, that:

Night before last we received a messenger from those two independent trains by whom we learn that they are living on their cattle on Green River. The brethren at Fort Supply are striving to get them as far as Fort Bridger. The two wagon companies, still out, we are sending for and will supply flour to such as may have to tarry at Fort Bridger and Fort Supply.[15]

FOUNDING OF SUPPLY CITY—PURCHASING OF FORT BRIDGER

In the spring of 1857, T. D. Brown surveyed a new city plat about three miles north of Fort Supply and seven miles southwest of Fort Bridger on the bench between Black's and Smith's forks. This town site was named City Supply. About a dozen houses were built there during that spring and summer.

In the meantime, the Mormons had purchased Fort Bridger and were carrying on activities there similar to those at Fort Supply. The claim has been made by certain writers and ofttimes repeated that Brigham Young purchased Bridger's property in 1853. Lewis Robinson has been credited with being the purchaser for the Church, at the stipulated price of $8,000.

The fact that James Bridger left his premises in the fall of 1853 and did not return makes it rather difficult to ascertain the

[13]*Latter-day Saint Journal History,* February 24, 1856, Ms.
[14]*Ibid.,* November 9, 1856.
[15]Brigham Young, *Deseret News,* November 30, 1856.

details of the transaction. If the purchase was made that year (1853), Bridger was not acquainted with the fact. As soon as he completed the survey of his homestead in November, he moved his family to Jackson County, Missouri. Then he went to Saint Louis to work through official channels at having his survey papers filed with the Federal Land Office. This filing was done on May 9, 1854. He also spent some time investigating the methods for acquiring titles to his homestead. He had never received a clear title from the Mexican government. These facts are evidence that Fort Bridger was not purchased by the Mormons, at least not from James Bridger, in 1853. The purchase took place at a later date.

In the winter of 1853-1854 Green River County was organized. It included Fort Supply, Fort Bridger, and the ferries on the river. W. I. Appleby was appointed probate judge and William A. Hickman county sheriff. The latter was also made prosecuting attorney, assessor, and tax collector. Brigham assigned Hickman to use his influence in quieting down the mountaineers in that section of the country.

In the spring of 1855 more Mormon colonists were sent to the Green River Valley. They settled at Bridger and took over the old fort. A little over two years later (autumn of 1857), Hickman wrote in his journal, in reference to the events at Fort Bridger and the coming of Johnston's army, that:

> The post was then, and had been for two years, owned by the Church, and in possession of Mr. Robinson, who had charge of the same from the time of its purchase, I having been one of the carriers of the heavy load of gold it took to purchase said place with the (live) stock and goods thereon.[16]

This is good circumstantial evidence that the Mormons purchased Fort Bridger, yet even at that time (1855-1857) James Bridger was in another part of the country. The old scout, in all probability, did not participate in the transfer of Fort Bridger, but the sale was probably made by Louis Vasquez who was a part owner of the fort with Bridger. Under date of October 18, 1858, in the *Journal History of the Church* is recorded:

> Louis Vasquez, of the firm of Bridger and Vasquez, executed a bill of sale of Fort Bridger, and acknowledged of $4,000 on August 3, 1855, and $4,000 this day (October 18, 1858)—also acknowledged before Samuel A. Gilbert, clerk of Third District Court, that Hiram F. Morrell was his lawfully appointed agent and that he fully approved of the acts and doings of said Morrell in the sale of said property.[17]

---

[16]Cited in Alter, *op. cit.*, 256-257.
[17]*Latter-day Saint Journal History*, October 18, 1858. Ms.

Besides being one of James Bridger's partners, Vasquez owned agricultural land nearby, but it is probable that this land was within the original Fort Bridger area. No doubt other mountaineer squatters had claims in that neighborhood also. It is not definitely known what party or parties profited by the $8,000 paid by the Mormons for the Fort Bridger property. It seems that Vasquez received the payment. Judge William A. Carter, who came to Bridger in 1857 with Johnston's army and who "virtually succeeded James Bridger (and Lewis Robinson) in charge of the trading post and the ranch lands under Bridger's survey," believed that Jim Bridger received the money.[18] To complicate the maze of evidence, Bridger wrote a letter to General B. F. Butler, then United States Senator, asking him to secure government compensation for his losses at Fort Bridger. Among other things he stated:

I was robbed and threatened with death by the Mormons, by the direction of Brigham Young, of all my merchandise, livestock, in fact everthing I possessed, amounting to more than $100,000 worth, the building in the fort partially destroyed by fire, and I barely escaped with my life.[19]

But Brigham Young understood that he and his people had not robbed the mountaineer but had purchased his holdings and had paid what they considered full value for the property. In fact, after the United States army had taken over Fort Bridger, President Young took steps to have his claims of having purchased the fort recognized by the federal government and to receive compensation for Mormon losses there. "The War Department told Coutant that 'The Mormons set up a claim to the land on which the post was located on the ground of a conveyance from James Bridger, who was said to hold a Spanish grant for the same.' "[20] Coutant also wrote, "President Young had made repeated applications to have his claim allowed."

During the summer of 1855 the Mormons constructed a few buildings at Fort Bridger, and a heavy wall of cobblestone masonry was erected. This replaced the original picket wall of logs which stood on end, serving as a corral for the protection of the animals. They also "made other improvements on the ranch at an expense of about twelve thousand dollars. . . . Fort Bridger was quite an important Mormon outpost."[21] But its importance was not to endure long.

[18]Alter, op. cit., 258-259.
[19]Senate Report No. 625, Fifty-Second Congress, First Session.
[20]C. G. Coutant, History of Wyoming (Laramie, 1899), cited in Alter, op. cit., 258-260.
[21]Jenson, op. cit.

THE "UTAH WAR"—MORMON LOSSES

In September of 1857, Fort Bridger, Fort Supply, and Supply City were deserted by the Mormons because of the approach of Johnston's army. George A. Smith reported that on September 29, 1857, he met east of Bear River some "fifty families fleeing from Fort Supply and Fort Bridger, with ox and horse teams, and their herds of cattle," returning to Salt Lake City.[22] Upon deserting their property in Green River County, as they had been directed to do by Governor Young, the Mormons burned it. This they considered necessary as a partial safeguard against the oncoming federal troops so that they should not be feeding the army which threatened to exterminate them.

At six o'clock in the evening of October 3, Fort Bridger was set on fire, Lewis Robinson applying the torch. On October 6, it was reported that Fort Supply and Fort Bridger were in ashes and that the members of the Mormon military expedition sent from Salt Lake by Governor Young were subtly engaged in burning grass, timber and everything consumable by fire, in that part of the country. Jesse W. Crosby, one of the Mormons who participated in the campaign against Johnston's army, reported:

The company to which I belonged left Salt Lake City September 25, 1857. We took out our wagons, horses, etc., and at twelve o'clock set fire to the building (Fort Supply) at once, consisting of one hundred or more good hewed log houses, one sawmill, one gristmill and one thrashing machine, and after going out of the fort we set fire to the stockade work, straw and grain stacks, etc. After looking a few minutes at the bonfire we had made, thence on by the light thereof.

I will mention that owners of property in several cases begged the privilege of setting fire to their own, which they freely did, thus destroying at once what they had labored for years to build, and that without a word.

We then went our way a few miles and stopped to set fire to the City Supply, a new place just commenced; there were ten or fifteen buildings perhaps, and warmed ourselves by the flames. Thus was laid waste in a few hours all the labor of a settlement for three or four years, with some five or six hundred acres of land fenced and improved.

Our work of destruction was now finished and we moved silently onward and reached Bridger a little after daylight and found it in ashes, it having been fired the night before.[23]

"The total loss and damage sustained by these Mormon Pioneers in this case were about $300,000."

----

[22]George A. Smith, *Latter-day Saint Journal History*, September 29, 1857, Ms.
[23]Jesse W. Crosby, *Fort Bridger and Fort Supply*, 30, Ms.

Federal Army at Fort Bridger

Immediately upon the arrival of the army, Colonel Albert Sidney Johnston took possession of Fort Bridger in the name of the United States and declared it and the surrounding country, including the farming lands of Fort Supply, to be a military reservation.

Thus passed out of existence the full fruits of a noble and successful effort of a pioneer group to gain a livelihood under the most austere frontier conditions. This experiment, directed by the great Mormon Colonizer, had become successful to the point that had it been permitted to continue, Fort Supply would very probably have become a flourishing farming settlement, whereas, at the present time, there is nothing left of Fort Supply except stumps in the ground as remnants of what the Saints built there in 1853 to 1857. At Fort Bridger the only evidence of Brigham's people having been there is that a portion of the Old Mormon Wall remains today.

Chapter XXIX

BRIGHAM YOUNG'S INDIAN POLICY

Origin of the American Indians

The Mormon Church, from the time of its institution in 1830 until the present, has had an unusually friendly attitude toward the American Indians. Church members have regarded the aborigines of the western hemisphere as their brothers, on the ground that the Book of Mormon teaches that their ancestry runs back to the blood of Israel—God's chosen people.

The Book of Mormon claims to be an account of the origin of American Indians and a record of their history wherein they had intimate contact with the Nephites, a race of white people who lived in ancient America for 1000 years contemporaneously with their dark-skinned brothers. The one race of people were called Nephites after their leader Nephi, and the other race took upon themselves the name of Lamanites after Nephi's older brother Laman.

The Book of Mormon is a story of a perpetual struggle between those two races.

A terrific war broke out between the two peoples and continued to the utter destruction of the white race. Moroni, the last Nephite prophet, lived to see the extermination of his race. He was the last of a long line of keepers of records which he completed 421 A. D. and deposited in a place of safety. Fourteen hundred years later, September 22, 1827, he gave those records to the Prophet Joseph Smith from which the Book of Mormon was translated.

Basis of the Mormon Indian Policy

The Lord had promised the Lamanites that one day they would receive the Gospel of Jesus Christ and the record of the Nephites; and at that day the God of heaven and earth would remember the promises that He had made to His people, the Israelites; and the Lamanites, being Israelites, would receive their share of the blessings.[1] Some of them would assist in building the "New Jerusalem."[2] In regard to the Book of Mormon, the Lord told the Prophet Joseph:

> And this testimony shall come to the knowledge of the Lamanites . . . that [they] might come to the knowledge of their fathers, and that they might know the promises of the Lord, and that they may believe and rely upon the merits of Jesus Christ.[3]

Naturally, after publishing the Nephite record and receiving the foregoing revelation, Joseph and his associates felt a keen interest in the Lamanites and an impelling desire to teach them the Gospel of Jesus Christ. They also wanted to place in their hands the Book of Mormon. Therefore, only six months after the Church of Jesus Christ was organized, the Mormon Prophet sent five missionaries from Fayette, New York, to the Indian territory west of Missouri.

Brigham Young's Attitude and Indian Policy

Thus the start was made and the Indian policy set in the days of the Prophet, but not a great deal more was done relative to giving the Lamanites the Gospel until after the trek to the Great West. In the valleys of the mountains, President Brigham Young carried on an extensive missionary work among the red men. Brother Brigham's Indian policy had its origin in the philosophy of the Book of Mormon and of the teachings of the Church, and the western frontier gave him opportunity to express that policy.

When Young and his exiled followers were preparing to migrate westward, he sought earnestly to imbue the Mormons with a feeling of friendship toward the Indians. He knew that his people would be thrown into contact with thousands of them, and that by observing the correct policy toward them he felt that peace and security would be shared alike by each group.

---

[1]*Book of Mormon,* 2 Nephi 30:3-6; 5:21.
[2]*Ibid.,* 3 Nephi 21:22-29.
[3]*Doctrine and Covenants,* Section 3:18-20; 10:48; 48:24.

In a way the Mormons and the Indians were kindred people, having had similar experiences. The Saints had been driven from state to state by their neighbors. The majority of them had been persecuted and some of them had been murdered. The Lamanites also had been driven from their homes by the white men, their lands had been stolen, "game had been wasted, and feelings of hatred had been fostered until the dictum had been reached that no Indian is a good Indian until he is dead." Brother Brigham felt deeply the numerous injustices which had been heaped upon the natives by the settlers of the United States. In his own words:

We shoot them down as we would a dog. Now, this is all wrong, and not in harmony with the spirit of Christianity. In only one instance, that of William Penn, has Christian treatment been accorded them. But even aside from the aspect of Christian duty, I am satisfied it will be cheaper to feed them, than to fight them.[4]

Such was Brigham Young's Indian policy thereafter. The just and friendly way in which his people treated the natives of the Great Plains had its effect in the kindly treatment accorded the Mormons by the red men. Thousands of the Saints from year to year passed through the lands of the Sioux, Shoshones, Omahas, Utes and other Indian tribes, and history affirms that hardly a Mormon was killed by the Indians. On the other hand, many an emigrant headed westward over the same route followed by the Saints was massacred by the Lamanites.

There were a few Indian uprisings in early Utah history, but their numbers were insignificant and the loss in property and life very little when one considers the fact that the Mormons settled in the heart of the red man's country, 1,000 miles from any other white settlements. This unusual absence of Indian hostilities in Utah colonial history can be attributed to Brigham's Indian policy. When it was followed to the letter, difficulties were always averted. But many of the troubles that did occur were instigated by disobedient Mormons or unscrupulous Gentile emigrants.

We shall now discuss some of the important features of the Saints' treatment of the Lamanites.

---

[4]Cited in *Memoirs of John R. Young, Utah Pioneer of 1847,* 55

To Feed, Teach, Educate, Civilize, and Christianize the Red Men

It has already been mentioned that Brigham felt that it would be cheaper to feed the Indians than to fight them. But the Mormon leader had no intention of making parasites and beggars out of the natives. He continuously instructed his people to teach them to work and the value of earning their own goods. They were to be taught the Gospel of Jesus Christ—and an important part of the Gospel is to support one's self and family in harmony with the laws of thrift and truth. The following statement from the journalist at Parowan expressed clearly the Mormon policy: "President George A. Smith advised the brethren not to give anything to the Indians, but to let them understand that those things they might want have a value."[5]

The Mormons in all the new frontier communities of the Great West were instructed by Brother Brigham to assist in educating and civilizing the natives in their respective districts. Thus we read in the early Utah manuscripts such statements as the following report of Dimick B. Huntington's trip to Fillmore in February, 1852. He said: "A portion of the citizens have been over on Corn Creek ploughing and sowing wheat for the Indians. They returned yesterday."[6] At Santa Clara the whites and Indians farmed cooperatively and divided the returns equally.

In many of the new communities, Indians were hired to help the white men work. Brigham felt that such a policy was the best way to keep the natives contented. In 1852, shortly after Spring City had been settled, about 300 Sanpitch Indians came to the little community and threatened to kill the colonists. James T. S. Allred had had considerable experience in dealing with the natives. He could speak their language and knew how to pacify them. After talking to them for some time he succeeded in breaking down their hostile attitude by hiring them to assist the settlers in farming and fencing their farms.[7]

There are cases in Utah history where Brother Brigham had the different families in a community take the responsibility of feeding and clothing certain Indians and teaching them to work. Apostle Wilford Woodruff visited Weber Valley in 1851 and gave the following report:

5Parowan Stake and Wards, January 19, 1850, Ms.
6Dimick B. Huntington, Latter-day Saint Journal History, February 8, 1852, Ms.
7Sanpete Stake, July, 1852, Ms.

Here (Brigham's Fort) and at Ogden I saw the Indians who were lately distributed among the people for the purpose of bettering their condition by feeding and clothing them and teaching them to work. Most of them were at these two forts and were very sad and uneasy, fearing that some evil was designed against them, and while we were holding meeting many left their wickiups standing and went down to Weber river. But since receiving a letter from Governor Young they have become more reconciled and have returned.[8]

In the fall of 1853 Apostles Erastus Snow and Franklin D. Richards visited Iron County. Upon arriving at Cedar City, they appointed Joel H. Johnson and sons to do special instructive work among the Lamanites in that section of the country. Quoting from the manuscript:

Joel H. Johnson and sons were appointed to carry on farming and to teach the Biede Indians how to cultivate the ground for their support. Brother Johnson's son, Nephi, having as good a knowledge of the Indian language as any in the country, was sustained as Indian interpreter and was engaged in the winter of 1853-54 teaching the people of Cedar the dialect of the natives.[9]

On Christmas day, 1853, about 300 Piute Indians—men, women, and children—were entertained by the Mormons at Cedar City. "The brethren preached to them in their own language and made them a donation of an ox together with some vegetables and flour, after which they returned to their camp rejoicing."[10]

By the time the Saints had been in the Basin less than six years, President Brigham Young and his counselors felt that some progress had been made in teaching the natives to be self-supporting. In a general epistle to the Church they urged all the settlers to do what they could to cultivate good will between the natives and the whites. Christian ethics, they taught, should regulate all their dealings with the red men just as with each other. In the words of the epistle:

There have been less disturbances and outbreaks among the Indians than during previous seasons; some are beginning to know the value of bread, and are willing to labor a part of their time, and learn how to work to raise corn for themselves; and we recommend to all the settlements to cultivate this spirit, and learn the Indians to raise grain, and live by their labor, rather than steal, starve, or live by begging, as the game is scarce on their hunting grounds.[11]

INDIAN ADOPTION VS. INDIAN SLAVERY

When the Mormons first came to Utah they found very few children among many of the weaker tribes of the Great Basin.

[8]Wilford Woodruff, *Deseret News*, December 3, 1851.
[9]*Deseret News*, February 2, 1854.
[10]*Ibid.*
[11]Brigham Young, "Eighth general Epistle...," *Millennial Star*, XV (February 19, 1853), 113-117.

They soon learned that Mexicans and bands of Utes had repeatedly
made raids upon various groups of Indians for the purpose of
taking their children to California or Mexico to be sold into
slavery. Sometimes the Indians even sold their women and children
into slavery for firearms and horses. Chief Walker and his warriors
reaped their share of profits from this slave trade.

Governor Young, who was also Indian agent for the Utah
Territory, decided to put a stop to such traffic in human beings.
He and his people did what they could to prevent raids upon the
weaker tribes of Indians. Brigham felt that if any of the natives
desired to sell their children, it would be best for good Mormon
families to purchase them and educate and Christianize them.
Therefore, in 1852:

> He caused an act to be passed by the Utah Legislature legislating the
> enforced apprenticeship of Indian children. This act permitted families to
> take over Indian Children from Indian parents who were determined to sell
> them to the Mexicans. A year later, in 1833, because of the abuse of this act,
> a proclamation was issued, ordering the arrest of all strolling parties of
> Mexicans.[12]

The following is quoted from an address given by the Mormon
leader to the people of Parowan, June 28, 1851, only six months
after the founding of that frontier community:

> He advised them to buy up the Lamanite children, as fast as they could,
> and educate them and teach them the Gospel, so that not many generations
> would pass ere they would become a white and delightsome people. He re-
> marked that the Lord could not have devised a better plan, than to have put
> the Saints where they were, in order to accomplish the redemption of the
> Lamanites.[13]

There are a number of cases on record where Mormons followed Brigham's advice. Jacob Hamblin reared an Indian boy.
President Young himself took care of native children, one of whom
was named Sally. She was rescued from Chief Wanship's warriors,
who were torturing her by cutting the fleshy parts of her legs,
arms, and body and thrusting firebrands into the wounds. The
girl recovered and lived for years in Brigham Young's home. Later
she married Chief Kanosh.[14] A good description of the actual
working of Brigham's Indian policy was depicted by Anson Call,
one of the prominent Mormon colonizers. Shortly after he settled
Fillmore, early in 1852, he wrote in his journal:

---

[12]Gates and Widtsoe, *The Life Story of Brigham Young,* 137.
[13]*Deseret News,* June 28, 1851.
[14]Gates and Widtsoe, *op. cit.,* 136-137.

We were surrounded in every direction by different tribes who annoyed us much by a constant begging. Occasionally small bodies of Spaniards were passing who were buying up Indian children for the purpose of making slaves of them. Indians obtained them by gambling and stealing them from the different tribes they were at war with.

This I taught them to be wrong at every opportunity that presented itself, and not to sell the children to the Spaniards but to sell them to the "Mormons" and we would clothe them and educate them. . . . Kanosh, the chief, gave me his son about eight years of age who I agreed to clothe and send to school for three years and then give him back to him again. I washed and clothed him and he commenced the school. His mother came and the boy wept and wanted to go with her and she prevailed with the chief and accordingly took him.

I bought an Indian boy, who was a prisoner of one of the Indian Chief Walker's men. They told me he was a Piute. I named him Dan. I judge he was betwixt three and four years of age. I also bought a Piute girl from one of the Parowan Indians, who I judge to be two years old. I named her Ruth. I started to the Legislature 18th November. I fetched with me my two Indian children and gave them to my wife, Mary, who was much pleased with the present.[15]

To Build Forts

Although Brigham Young advised his people to treat the Lamanites as Christian brethren and always to avoid bloodshed, he realized that his people were in constant danger of Indian attacks, especially in the new frontier communities. Therefore, one of the definite principles in Brigham's Indian policy was for every group of colonists who selected a site for a community to erect as their first building a fort. They were instructed to live in the fort until the community became large enough to furnish security against the red men. The following quotation from George A. Smith is typical of many similar statements which could be cited from Brother Brigham and the other leaders of Mormon land settlement:

After a tedious but prosperous journey we have at last reached our destination. We are an outpost 250 miles from Salt Lake City, and if any difficulty occurs with the natives we are expected to fight our own battles, guard against intruders and make a permanent settlement.

The buildings we erect here shall be built in compact form or in military fashion and style, in order to provide safety for those outside as well as those inside. This is my advice and council. It is unpleasant I know but it is also unpleasant to have one's back stuck full of arrows. You are all as near to me as my own brothers, and when the country is settled and safe you can spread out.[16]

Governor Young's advice was followed very carefully in regard to building forts in all the new communities. Occasionally some

---

[15]Anson Call, *Journal*, 41-43, Ms.
[16]George A. Smith, *Parowan Stake and Wards*, January 19, 1850, Ms.

family or families moved out of the fort against the general Church policy, and sometimes the settlers seemed to their President to be rather slow in completing their forts. These minority cases drew from Governor Young a stern rebuke shortly after the outbreak of the Walker War. In the words of the Mormon prophet-leader:

> I went to every settlement and attempted to encourage them to fort but failed to accomplish anything toward getting them to obey the word of the Lord on this matter. . . . Walker found that the people cared nothing for God, nor the instructions of Brother Brigham and Brother George A. Smith, so he said, "I wonder if you will mind me," and in less than one solitary week he had more than three hundred families on the move; houses were thrown down in every direction, and I presume one hundred thousand dollars worth of property wasted.[17]

President Young felt that it was best to keep the Indians out of the forts and not to become too familiar with them. The colonists were warned that they "could not be too cautious nor too much prepared for defense, for they might be deceived by the apparent overkindness of the Indians and at an unguarded moment suffer loss."[18] In the words of the Mormon leader:

> It will be better for our settlements not to be so familiar with the Indians; it makes them bold, inpudent and saucy and will become a source of trouble and expense to you. Keep them at a respectful distance, all the time, and they will respect you the more for it.[19]

TRADING AGENTS

Another definite point in Young's Indian policy was to have all the trading done between the Mormons and the Lamanites by authorized Mormon agents. In accordance with the Governor's orders, Dimick B. Huntington and Alexander Williams were given exclusive trading rights with the Indians at Provo. Any other person caught attempting to trade with them was "fined by the Bishop for a breach of obedience." The men appointed to be the trading agents received double wages the days they spent in trading with the Indians. On the other hand, they were to let the brethren have the skins, furs, or any other articles obtained from the Lamanites at cost.

Brother Brigham's purpose in establishing this policy was "to keep a uniformity of prices and prevent exorbitant demands from the Indians." He refused to permit any of his people to take unfair

[17]Brigham Young, *Deseret News*, October 15, 1853.
[18]Brigham Young, *Journal History of the Church*, May 19, 1849, Ms.
[19]*Ibid.*, May 28, 1849.

advantage of the less civilized natives. Even in dealing with the Indians, business must be done on an equitable and Christian basis.

INDIAN MISSIONS

A very important factor in the Church's Indian policy was the creation of Indian missions. In a manner similar to what had been done by the Catholic missionaries during the early colonial days of North and South America, Mormon missionaries established themselves among the Indians in various parts of the Great Basin for the avowed purpose of educating the Lamanites and teaching them the Gospel of Jesus Christ. Incidents of the faithfulness and fearlessness of those missionaries, in their dauntless efforts to better the living conditions of the natives, are comparable to the experiences of Father Kino in northern Mexico, or Father Serra in California, or Father De Smet, who spent thirty years among the Sioux, Shoshone and other tribes of the Great Plains and Rocky Mountains.

Between 1852 and 1858 President Young sent groups of missionaries to the Indians in southern Utah, northern Arizona, southern Nevada, Wyoming, and northern Idaho. These missions will be discussed in later chapters. There were several other important Indian missions in addition to the ones referred to. A brief account of some of them is presented here.

Henry W. Miller and four companions were called by the First Presidency at the April conference in 1855 to go as missionaries to the Indians in the middle west—Missouri and Arkansas. Upon reaching the Missouri River, two of the elders were assigned to labor among the Delawares while Miller and the other two did their work with the Cherokee nation. The elders assigned to the Delaware tribe met with very little success, so they joined the other missionaries. For five years they labored among those Indians with excellent results. Many baptisms were made, forty-three within the first two years. But the labors of the missionaries were suddenly drawn to a close by the authorities of the reservation who ordered them to leave.

During those five years, the elders had also done considerable work among the Creek Indians. Two branches of the Church had been organized: the Princess Creek Branch and the Nephi Branch.

By 1860 forty-eight Creek Indians had become members of the Church. The missionaries were also forbidden to do further work among the Creek Indians, so they returned to Utah.

The year of Brigham's death, 1877, a second effort was made
to do missionary work among the Creeks and Cherokees. The time
employed on this mission was rather short—only six months. The
two elders met much opposition, Hubbard died, and his companion, Elder Dalton, returned to Utah.

SKULL VALLEY INDIAN MISSION

Another mission of importance was the one established in the
western part of Tooele County. In 1869 William Lee, who had
been an Indian Agent for ten years, was sent by President Young
to locate a farm for the Lamanites in Skull Valley. Colonel H.
Head, superintendent of Indian Affairs in Utah, was so interested
in the movement that he furnished machinery, wagons, and oxen
for the natives. The following year a branch of the Church was
established, its membership consisting mainly of farm hands and
of a few settlers who had moved into Skull Valley.

But three years later, August, 1873, President Young decided
to devote special attention to the converting of the Indians of
Tooele County to the Gospel. Therupon he called William Lee
to be a missionary. The following month Lee began his labors
by baptizing three Indians at Grantsville. By the next spring he
had baptized fifty.

The success that Elder Lee achieved among the Lamanites
was phenomenal. In May, 1874, he went to Deep Creek. In less
than a month he had baptized 400 Indians. Within the next year
the number that had joined the Church had been increased to over
1,000. President Young instructed Lee to seek out such places in
Skull Valley and at Deep Creek as could be used for ranches to
be operated by the Indians. An article in the *Deseret News* of
September 15, 1875, indicated that Lee had followed the President's
instructions and that the natives in the Tooele Indian Mission
were learning rapidly lessons of civilization from the white men.
Quoting from the article:

> The Indians, we learn from Bishop John Rowberry of Tooele County
> Valley, have raised and harvested, this season about four hundred bushels
> of wheat and a quantity of potatoes, and those who have been similarly engaged
> in the vicinity of Deep Creek have been about as successful in the same
> direction.
> Those Indians who have been baptized are greatly inproving, having a
> great aversion to even the thought of anything in the shape of fighting, which
> feeling they manifested during the late Indian scare sensation. When the
> trouble occured in Spring Valley, Nevada, a number of Indians who did not

want to get mixed up with any trouble moved towards Deep Creek, and those who were located at the latter place and had been farming for fear that there might be hostilities and that in case there was trouble other Indians might force them to join, they at once left their farms and took to the mountains to avoid such a contingency.

The desire to beg is also leaving those Indians who are adopting civilized habits, and they want to do their own farming and be independent.[20]

For the next seven years Elder William Lee continued to make favorable reports of the progress, thrift, and integrity of the converts in his mission. In his own words: "The Indians were enlarging their fields and had raised a fair average of grain; they were very firm in the faith of the Gospel, and had depreciated the use of liquor."[21]

But by 1882 Lee complained that the white men, including the government agents, had been giving the Indians so much help that it was undermining their morale. He was putting forth strenuous efforts to induce the Lamanites to purchase their land with their own money. Some of them followed his advice, while others felt that the land belonged to them without paying for it. The purchase of the land by the red men at this time became necessary because the federal government had opened the Uintah Indian Reservation and was moving the natives there. Thus the majority of the Lamanites were taken from the Tooele Mission to Uintah County, but some of them remained on their farms, purchased them, and lived as the white men lived.

We shall now turn our attention to some of the most important Mormon Indian missions and become acquainted with the personalities who were outstanding in building them.

Chapter XXX

THE SANTA CLARA INDIAN MISSION

Calling of the Missionaries

Probably the most important and successful of the Mormon missions, established to help civilize the Lamanites and teach them the Gospel, was the one founded in 1854 on the Santa Clara River south of the rim of the Great Basin. Among the various groups called at the October Conference in 1853 by the First Presidency of the Church to build new settlements or to strengthen older ones was a party of twenty-three missionaries chosen to labor among the Indians in southern Utah. Apostles Parley P. Pratt and Orson Hyde organized these elders into a company at Salt Lake City and appointed Rufus C. Allen to be president, with David Lewis first and Samuel F. Atwood second counselor. Having just returned in 1853 from a mission to Valparaiso, Chile, Allen was well prepared to direct such a proselyting enterprise among the natives. Jacob Hamblin, noted Mormon scout and Indian interpreter, was one of the important members of the company.

Locating at Harmony, Utah

The party left Great Salt Lake City, April 8, 1854, and arrived at John D. Lee's settlement, called Harmony, in the southwestern part of Utah, May 16. At that time there were some twelve to fifteen families located there. Lee and his group had been sent to southern Utah two years earlier by President Brigham Young. They had already done some work among the natives, as "the Sunday preceding the arrival of the newcomers, the Indian School at Harmony showed an attendance of ten Indian children."[1]

In accordance with instructions received before leaving Salt Lake the missionaries stayed at Harmony until President Young and company arrived toward the latter part of May. In instructing the missionaries relative to their dealings with the Indians, President Young said "that if the Elders called as missionaries to the natives desired to have influence they must associate with them in their hunting expeditions and other pursuits."[2] He wished them to use a different policy from that of colonists, whom he had advised to have no dealings with the Indians except through agents.

---

[1] *Manuscript History of Saint George Stake, 1847-1873,* 12.
[2] *Ibid.*

President Young also told the newly arrived Indian missionaries to stay with Lee and his colonists for the time being, and for the whole group to move north about four miles from where Lee's camp was then located and there construct a substantial fort. They were also to dig a canal to convey water for irrigation purposes. Naturally the group thought at that time that the new fort location at Harmony would be the headquarters of the southern Indian mission.

PRESIDENT ALLEN'S FIRST INDIAN MISSIONARY TOUR

On June 5, 1854, President Rufus C. Allen, Jacob Hamblin, William Hennefer, and several others of the missionaries, with Ira Hatch as interpreter, started south to visit the various groups of natives. Arriving near the present site of Toquerville the first day, they found a small, friendly band of Indians and had an interview with Chief Toquer. The next evening as they reached the Rio Virgin opposite the present site of Washington, they came upon another camp of red men. The woman and children immediately hid themselves in the brush, while the men approached the Mormons in a very cautious manner. Mexicans and bands of Utes had repeatedly made raids upon these weaker groups of Indians for the purpose of taking their children into California or Mexico to be sold as slaves, and so they were suspicious and afraid of all white men. However, before long the natives were convinced of the sincerity of the missionaries and became friendly and at ease with them.

The white men camped the following night on the Santa Clara River near the site of the present town of that name. They found a rather large group of Indians living there. The male members of the village numbered about 250, but there were very few children, as most of them had been taken captive. Having been informed by messengers of the attitude of the missionaries, the Santa Clara Lamanites greeted them very cordially.

The natives in the Santa Clara village were eking out a livelihood by farming which was being carried on in a very crude way. Small "patches of wheat, corn, squash and melons" were growing near the village. The farming implements were made of sticks of ash, three feet long, three or four inches wide, with the edges sharpened and running to a point. Taking these crude implements in their hands, the natives would get upon their knees and make furrows for planting by throwing the soil right and left. President Allen and his missionary companions informed the natives that they had been sent there by the "Big Captain," Brigham Young, to teach them how to farm in a better way; and that probably some of the visitors would come among them later to make their homes and help their red brethren. This greatly pleased the Indians. The Mormons explained their Gospel message and "eleven of the Indians were, at their own request, baptized and confirmed as members of the Church."[3]

Within a few days all of the missionaries returned to Harmony with the exception of Jacob Hamblin and William Hennefer, who were left to visit the Lamanites on the upper Santa Clara. In the latter part of June, 1854, Hamblin and Hennefer rejoined their companions.

ESTABLISHING A MISSION IN THE SANTA CLARA VALLEY

Only a short time passed before the missionaries made a second trip to Santa Clara and succeeded in baptizing fifty more Indians. They spent the remainder of the summer of 1854 in visiting and instructing the various groups of natives in that section.

By special appointment, Jacob Hamblin was sent alone among the Indians on the Santa Clara in November, 1854, to use his influence to keep the natives from disturbing the travelers on the southern route to California, a task which he accomplished successfully. After completing his assignment, Hamblin returned to Harmony.

In December, 1854, Rufus C. Allen and counselors designated Jacob Hamblin, Thales H. Haskell, Ira Hatch, Samuel Knight, Augustus P. Hardy and others to establish a permanent settlement on the Santa Clara. They were to take their families along. Two factors made a new colony necessary: the first was that there seemed to be insufficient water at Harmony to accommodate all of the settlers; second, and probably the more important reason, was that they had learned that Santa Clara was a favorite rendezvous of the Indians.

After receiving instructions to settle on Santa Clara River early in December, 1854, Jacob Hamblin and his companions immediately left Harmony for their new field of labor. Upon arriving at the Rio Virgin that night they met a large group of Piute Indians from the Santa Clara village out on a hunting expedition under Chief Tut-se-gab-its.[4] The next day they chose their site at a point on the Santa Clara about five miles northeast of its confluence

---

[3]*Ibid.*, 14.
[4]*Deseret News*, December 1, 1854.

with the Rio Virgin. The Santa Clara Valley was very narrow, being only about three-quarters of a mile wide where the settlement was located. This necessitated dividing the farm lands into extremely small tracts, but the settlers were fortunate in that the soil was exceptionally productive. It was soon found that semitropical fruits such as grapes, figs and almonds, as well as apples, peaches, plums, cherries, and pears, could be grown very well there. The missionaries immediately began the work necessary in founding a community. They erected a log cabin on the upper end of the present site of Santa Clara, constructed a dam across the creek, built canals, and made preparations to begin irrigation when spring should arrive. Chief Tut-se-gab-its and his tribe, numbering about 800, aided the white men in these labors.

By spring the dam, about one hundred feet long and fourteen feet high, was completed, and one hundred acres of land were also prepared for planting. On this land the missionaries fulfilled the promise they had made to the Indians a year earlier, i.e., they taught the natives how to farm in a more scientific way. The Mormons and the Indians cultivated the land conjointly and shared the produce equally. Jacob Hamblin reported: "We raised melons and had the privilege of disposing of them ourselves. I do not think that the Indians ever took any without leave."[5]

Hamblin and his companions were also interested in teaching the natives to raise their standard of living through stock raising. Therefore, on June 2, 1856, they presented a petition to the Washington County court at Harmony asking the privilege of herd grounds at Mountain Meadows on the California road. This petition was granted for the term of one year "under the sanction and protection of the law regulating herd grounds."[6]

The missionaries exerted an increasing influence for good over these natives, but it was impossible to transform them completely. One of the elders wrote:

But the longer the natives watched the praying and praise and cleanliness of the missionaries the more they realized their own low estate, saying to Jacob Hamblin and his companions when urged to improve their mode of life: "We cannot be good, we must be Piutes. We want you to be kind to us. It may be that some of our children will be good, but we want to follow our old customs." Some then again began to paint themselves and abuse their women as they had done before the missionaries went among them.[7]

In the summer of 1856, by request of the Mormon Colonizer,

---

[5]*Saint George Stake* . . . . *op. cit.*, 16.
[6]*Latter-day Saint Journal History*, June 2, 1856, Ms.
[7]*Saint George Stake* . . . , *op. cit.*, 23.

Jacob Hamblin selected several families from Harmony as missionaries to join the Santa Clara group.

George A. Smith visited the missionaries in July. He brought a letter from Governor Brigham Young, advising them to build a fort as protection in case the Lamanites ceased to be friendly. A few months later the fort was completed. Its walls were composed of rock, two feet thick, twelve feet high, and one hundred feet long. The missionaries were assisted in their labors by Elias Morris and other masons from Cedar City. Later, when President Young visited Santa Clara, he declared the fort to be the best in Utah at that time. Apostle Amasa Lyman visited the Indian mission on May 18, 1857, and wrote in his journal:

> Arrived at the Fort just as its inmates were rising from sleep. . . . The brethren at this place have built a stone fort one hundred feet square, inside of which are the crude cabins in which its occupants reside at present. They have some land in cultivation with and for the natives, with whom there seems to exist a good feeling at present.[8]

JACOB HAMBLIN

Up to August, 1857, Rufus C. Allen had been president of the southern Indian mission. Most of that time he had resided at Harmony, having entrusted the direction of the Lamanites at Santa Clara to Jacob Hamblin. On August 4, President Young released Allen and appointed Hamblin to succeed him. The following letter is typical of Brother Brigham's advice on the proper way of dealing with the Indians:

President's Office
G. S. L. C.
August 4, 1857.

Elder Jacob Hamblin:

You are hereby appointed to succeed Elder R. C. Allen as president of the Santa Clara Indian Mission. I wish you to enter upon the duties of your office immediately.

Continue the conciliatory policy towards the Indians which I have ever commended, and seek by works of righteousness to obtain their love and confidence. Omit promises where you are not sure you can fill them; and seek to unite the hearts of the brethren on that mission, and let all under your direction be united together in the holy bonds of love and unity.

All is peace here, and the Lord is eminently blessing our labors; grain is abundant, and our cities are alive with the busy hum of industry.

Do not permit the brethren to part with their guns and ammunitions, but save them against the hour of need.[9]

---

[8]*Ibid.,* 29.
[9]*Ibid.,* 18.

No better choice than Jacob Hamblin could have been made for the director of the Lamanite mission. He was without doubt the most influential and successful Mormon missionary to the Indians while Brigham Young was at the helm. So great was his power with the natives and so highly was he esteemed that he has aptly been called the "Apostle to the Lamanites."

Hamblin was a tall, thin, angular man, with a voice so low that to hear him one had to get very close to him and listen with great attention. This distinctly personal characteristic helped to make him unusually impressive to the Indians. In one of his first contacts with them, the chief came out and made gestures of peace. Hamblin promised him safety, but his superior officer was determined to shoot the natives. Hamblin threw himself in front of the Indian and said, "If any one is to be shot, I will be the first." Throughout his career in dealing with the Lamanites, he always believed that if he dealt justly with them they would never harm him. He was placed in many precarious positions, but each time he escaped unharmed or wounded only slightly. In the words of John Henry Evans:

Although Jacob Hamblin generally carried a gun of some sort, his dependable weapon was prayer and the most absolute trust in God. . . .

He ate with the Indians, he slept with them, he talked their language, he prayed with them for the rains to save their crops, he took one of their boys to rear in his own way, he thought their thoughts, and reasoned in their simple ways—till he knew more perhaps than any other American ever knew of the native, and exerted more influence with them. And it is safe to say that no one has ever fought them with a more effective weapon.[10]

HAMBLIN'S NARROW ESCAPE FROM NAVAJOS

No doubt Jacob Hamblin's greatest influence came through his absolute fearlessness, which was demonstrated in an event that occurred in 1874. Brigham Young sent Hamblin to Arizona, to try to prevent a threatened Navajo uprising against the Mormon settlements in southern Utah.

In January 1874, Hamblin left Kanab alone, on a mission that was intended to pacify thousands of savage Indians. Possibly since Saint Patrick invaded Erin, no bolder episode had been known in history.[11]

He was joined by J. E. Smith and his brother at Moen Copie. About a day's journey farther eastward, the three men arrived at the Navajo village. The Indians, who erroneously believed the

[10]John Henry Evans, *The Heart of Mormonism*, 452-453.
[11]James H. McClintock, *Mormon Settlement in Arizona*, 84.

Mormons had killed three members of their tribe, immediately took the white men prisoners. They then met in a lengthy council to decide the fate of the three men. The natives decided to release the Smiths, who were not Mormons, but they decreed that Jacob Hamblin was to be burned at the stake there in the council room. One of the Smiths described the scene as follows:

> Had we shown a sympton of fear, we were lost; but we sat perfectly quiet, and kept a wary eye on the foe. It was a thrilling scene. The erect, proud, athletic form of the young chief as he stood pointing his finger at the kneeling figure before him; the circle of crouching forms; their dusky and painted faces animated by every passion that hatred and ferocity could inspire, and their pulse upon us; the whole partially illuminated by the fitful gleam of the firelight (for by this time it was dark), formed a picture not easy to be forgotten.
>
> Hamblin behaved with admirable coolness. Not a muscle in his face quivered, not a feature changed as he communicated to us, in his usual tone of voice, what we then fully believed to be the death warrant of us all.
>
> When the interpreter ceased, he in the same easy tone and collected manner, commenced his reply. He reminded the Indians of his long acquaintance with their tribe, of the many negotiations he had conducted between his people and theirs, and his many dealings with them in years gone by, and challenged them to prove that he had ever deceived them, ever had spoken with a forked tongue.[12]

The final results were the release of Hamblin and his companions and the prevention of the threatened Indian uprising. Twenty-one days later Hamblin again met the Navajos and completed the peace between them and the Saints.

August 19, 1857, Apostle George A. Smith and a company arrived at the Indian mission to inform the Mormons in the southern settlements of the approach of a United States army. Smith advised the Saints to save their grain, as the outcome of the trouble was uncertain.

HAMBLIN AND A COMPANY OF GENTILES EN ROUTE TO CALIFORNIA —ESCAPE OF HATCH AND LEAVITT FROM THE MOJAVE INDIANS

Late in the autumn of 1857 a group of Gentile merchants who had been doing business in Salt Lake City, anticipating difficulty between the Mormons and the United States army, were returning to the Eastern States by way of California and the Isthmus of Panama. Before leaving the Mormon Mecca, they obtained a letter from Governor Brigham Young to Jacob Hamblin instructing him to direct the company and their goods safely through to the Pacific Coast.

---

[12]Cited in *ibid.*, 85-86.

Upon arriving at Cedar City, the company of merchants sent messengers with Brigham's instructions to Hamblin. The Mormon scout sent word back for the travelers to continue their course toward California and he would join them where the road passed Santa Clara. But the junction was not effected as had been anticipated. A day or so after the travelers passed Santa Clara, Hamblin hurried to overtake them. While journeying along the Mormon road, he found a man who had been traveling alone in pursuit of the company of merchants with a view of going through with it to California. The unfortunate traveler had been captured by the Indians. They had stripped him of his clothing and were taking him to their camp for the purpose of "having a good time with him as they expressed it," that is, torturing him. In the words of Jacob Hamblin:

> The stranger, seeing my influence with the Indians, begged me to save his life, and said if I would do so, he would serve me as long as he lived.
>
> I replied that I did not wish any reward for saving him. . . . I assured him that it made no difference to me whether he was a "Mormon" or not. I told the Indians to bring back his clothing, which they did, except his shoes, and I took him along with me to the company.[13]

When Hamblin overtook the merchants he found a few Indians around them and the whites were very excited. One of them asked him if he could "save the ship." The Mormon scout replied that he could if they would permit him to run things as he saw fit. This they gladly consented to do.

As it was nearly evening, they asked Hamblin what to do with their animals. To the surprise of the merchants, the "Apostle to the Lamanites" suggested where there was good grass and for them to send two Indians to take care of the animals during the night. As compensation for their services, they were to give the Indians their supper first, and when they brought the animals back the following morning, they were to give each of them a shirt. Such a suggestion sounded ridiculous to the Gentile merchants. But when Hamblin told them that if he were to direct matters he should do so in his own way, they sent the animals out to feed with two Indians as the herdsmen, Hamblin remarked:

> I presume that some of the company did not sleep much during the night. The animals, however, were all brought safely into camp in the morning. After that, the company appeared to feel quite safe, and took much pains to have things move as I directed.[14]

---

[13]Jacob Hamblin, *Deseret News*, May 20, 1858.
[14]*Ibid.*

When they had traveled about sixty miles farther westward, they met a Moapa Indian who told the scout that the red men had gathered at the crossing of the Muddy River with the intentions of making an attack on the passing emigrants. Thereupon, Hamblin started at dawn the following morning and arrived at the crossing of the Muddy nearly two hours earlier than the company. He found the Indians, as had been reported, collected in the vicinity of the crossing with the view of attacking the company when it camped. They intended to kill all the men and collect the spoil. We shall let Hamblin tell in his own words how he saved those merchants from disaster.

I called them together [the Indians], and sat down and smoked a little tobacco with them, which I had brought along for that purpose. I then said: "You have listened to my talk in times past; you believe that it is good to hear and do what I say." They answered, "Yes."

I then told them I was going through to California with some friends, Americans and merchants; and that we had brought along many blankets, shirts and other useful articles. I hoped they would see that none of the animals were stolen, and if any strayed, they would bring them into camp. Some of the Indians did not readily consent to let the company pass in peace.

For further security, I sent for their women and children to come out of their hiding place, where they had been sent for safety, as is the custom of the Indians when preparing for battle.

I had matters in much better shape on the arrival of the company than I found them. I was careful to listen to all the talk of the Indians, and spent the evening and also the night with the largest collection of them, so they could not make any general move without my knowledge.[15]

The emigrants passed the night in safety, and the next morning they continued their journey across the fifty-six mile desert to Las Vegas Springs. There they met Ira Hatch and Dudley Leavitt. They were returning from a mission to the Mojave Indians where they had not fared so well with the natives. The latter had taken the missionaries' horses and belongings and had decided at a council meeting of the warriors that the Mormon elders should die. A Piute Indian had accompanied Hatch and Leavitt from Las Vegas.

Brother Hatch told their Piute friend, who acted as interpreter, to tell the Mojave chief, Chanawanse, to let him pray before he was killed.

The chief consented and Brother Hatch knelt down among the bloodthirsty savages, and asked the Lord to soften their hearts, that they might not shed their blood. He also said more that was appropriate to the occasion. The prayer was repeated in measured sentences by the interpreter.

It had the desired effect. The heart of the chief was softened. He took the brethren to his lodge, and put them at the farther end of it, in a secure place.

---

[15]*Ibid.*

There he guarded them until nearly morning, then told them to go as fast as they could to Las Vegas, eighty miles distant. They traveled this distance on foot, and with but little food. When I met them they were living on mesquite bread.[16]

After leaving Las Vegas, Hamblin and company had no more trouble with the Indians en route to California, but arrived there in safety.

Arrival of Saints from San Bernardino and Las Vegas

While traveling westward, however, they met several companies of Mormons on their way from San Bernardino to Utah. The arrival of Johnston's army in the Great West had caused Governor Young to call the Saints in California and the other outposts back to the Basin. But since Santa Clara was directly in the line of the proposed "move south" and was near other Mormon settlements, it was not abandoned. It served as one of the places for the California refugees to collect.

Following his trip to the coast in company with the Gentile merchants, Jacob Hamblin spent the remainder of the autumn and the winter of 1857-1858 on the road between the Mormon mission at Santa Clara and Las Vegas Springs in assisting the Saints who were moving to Utah.

A number of the people from the vacated cities of San Bernardino and Las Vegas settled in Santa Clara early in 1858, thereby strengthening the Indian mission. They assisted the original settlers in building a schoolhouse outside the fort and built their own dwelling there too, as the fort could not accommodate more people than the initial group.

The Muddy River Mission

In January of 1858, President Jacob Hamblin sent Elder Ira Hatch to the Muddy River with the hope that the marauding Indians of that neighborhood could be induced not to make attacks on the travelers going to and from California. Hatch located 100 miles from any white man, except occasional passersby, and from the nearest settlement—Fort Santa Clara. He camped in a broken down wagon left by the side of the road by Mr. Crismon when freighting from California.

During the two weeks that he was there Hatch was in constant danger from the half-starved copper-colored marauders of the

---

[16] *Ibid.*

desert. They were constantly trying to steal his food. He was obliged to do his cooking in the evenings after the natives had retired to their own camp and keep the food concealed during the day time. Finally the Indians discovered his provisions, cut the sack containing them, and stole his bread and meat, leaving the Mormon only a little cheese.

While the lonely hours were passing during the day time, Elder Hatch would climb to the top of a hill in sight of his wagon to watch for teams crossing the desert. Almost constantly some of the Indians loitered around near him and amused themselves ofttimes by pointing their arrows at him, sticking them in his clothes, and telling him that they would shoot him full of arrows.

Hatch was not only a man of dauntless courage, but he understood well how to deal with the Lamanites. He would sometimes reply that he "could shoot six of them through with his revolver, while their arrows would only stick in a little ways."[17]

While Elder Hatch was alone on the Muddy, Apostles Orson Pratt, Ezra T. Benson, and other Mormons from California passed by. They considered it unwise for one missionary to be alone, feeling that his position was not only lonely but dangerous. Thereupon, when they arrived at Santa Clara they recommended to President Hamblin to send company to Elder Hatch. Thales Hankell was selected to join the lone missionary on the Muddy. These two elders remained among those Lamanites of the desert until about March 1, 1858; then they returned to the Santa Clara settlement.

VISITING THE MOQUI INDIANS

In the autumn of 1858, Brigham Young instructed Jacob Hamblin to take a company of missionaries and visit the Moqui villages on the east side of the Rio Colorado. Hamblin selected ten of his associates and an Indian named Nahraguts to be the guide, as none of the Mormons had as yet visited that section of the country. Leaving Santa Clara on October 28, 1858, the missionaries followed their Indian guide to the Moqui villages. Here they were hospitably received by the Lamanites, who readily listened to their message but refused to accompany the Mormons back across the Colorado River and join the mission:

They had a tradition that their forefathers had said they must not cross that river until "the three prophets who took them to the region they then lived in should return and lead them out again.". . .

---

[17]*Mission to the Muddy in 1858,* 41-44. Ms.

One of their very aged men related that when he was young, his father told him he would live to see white men coming from the west, who would bring good tidings, and he looked upon the new-comers as fulfillers of this promise.[18]

The largest of these seven Moqui villages was located on a plateau about seven hundred feet above the surrounding country. It was called the Oraibi village. The houses were built of rock and were from one to four stories high. The only entrance into the ground floor rooms was through an opening in the ceiling. Ladders stood against the houses, reaching from the street level to the roof of the ground floor. In times of trouble with marauding bands of Indians or whites, these ladders were drawn up and placed in the houses.

After spending several days with the Moqui Indians, Jacob Hamblin appointed four of his men to remain until early spring with them while he and the other missionaries returned to Santa Clara. Those who remained were to study the language of the Moquis and teach them the Gospel.

This missionary visit to the Moquis in 1858 was the first of a series of such visits. It was the beginning of the intercourse between the Mormons and the Lamanites on the east side of the Rio Colorado and of the exploration of the country which culminated in the establishment of many Mormon colonies in that region.

MURDER OF GEORGE ALBERT SMITH, JR.

In 1859, Hamblin made a second trip to the Moquis, and a third in the fall of 1860. President Young wished the missionaries to stay among those Indians for one year on this trip, and so they provisioned themselves accordingly. Hamblin's company, consisting of ten missionaries and an Indian, left Santa Clara in October. The "Apostle to the Lamanites" seemed to have felt a premonition of impending danger. Quoting his own words: "In speaking at a public meeting the day before leaving, I felt different from what I had ever previously done on leaving home; that something unusual would happen. What it would be I did not know."[19] A depressing feeling that some evil would befall the company bore heavily upon the leader during the entire trip.

Two days after crossing the Rio Colorado, the missionaries met four friendly Navajos, who warned them that they would be killed by hostile Indians at the next watering place if they con-

---

[18]*Saint George Stake* . . . *op. cit.,* 47-48.
[19]*Ibid.,* 59.

tinued on. But as they had exhausted their supply of water and were two days' journey from the river, the missionaries concluded that the only course they could follow was to continue on to the next watering place.

Upon arriving at that point, exactly as they had been warned, they came upon a hostile band of Navajos from Fort Defiance Indian Reservation. George Albert Smith, Jr., the son of the apostle and a member of Hamblin's party, had his horse stolen by the Indians. While trying to recover it, young Smith was mortally wounded by the hostile red men. Three bullets from a revolver pierced the lower portion of his body and four arrows were lodged between his shoulders.

Jehiel McConnell rescued the wounded man from the Indians and carried him on his horse. Smith's pain was so excruciating that the movements of the horse caused cries of agony to come from his lips. This, no doubt, hampered the progress of the fleeing missionaries who, accompanied by the four friendly Navajos, were endeavoring to make their escape. Shortly after sundown, November 2, 1860, the wounded man died. Being hotly pursued by the Indians, the missionaries were forced to wrap hastily in a blanket the body of the deceased lad and hide it in a hollow place in a rock by the side of the trail.

The remainder of the company escaped without further fatality, but not without enduring acute suffering from lack of food, for their supplies had been captured by the hostile Navajos. Even more distressing than the suffering caused by the stealing of their provisions was that occasioned by the loss of one of their faithful companions. They arrived in Santa Clara about a week later.

That winter Jacob Hamblin led another company across the Colorado River to the place where Smith's body had been left and took the remains to Salt Lake City for burial. The author's grandfather, John D. Hunter, was a member of this rescue party.

Hamblin's Trip Around Grand Canyon of Colorado

In 1862 President Young instructed Hamblin to make another trip to the Hopis with the purpose of finding a more accessible route across the Colorado. The Mormon scout's earlier trips had been from Santa Clara via the Paria River to the Rio Colorado, up the course of that stream to the Crossing of the Fathers, and across the river. He was probably the first white man to pass over the

Colorado at that point since Spanish days.[20] At this time Brigham
advised Hamblin to cross the river south of Saint George. Hamblin
and twenty companions transported with an ox team a small boat
to the Colorado and launched it probably at the mouth of the
Grand Wash. After crossing the river, the company traveled for
four days southeast to the San Francisco Mountains, for two days
more to the Little Colorado, and then to the Hopi villages. "This
journey probably was the first that ever circled the Grand Canyon,
for return was by the Ute Crossing."[21]

Growth and Success of Santa Clara Indian Mission

The Santa Clara missionaries did not spend all of their time
in imparting instructions to the natives. As has already been stated,
they very successfully carried on farming cooperatively with the
Indians and laid the foundation for a permanent settlement.

In June, 1859, Apostles George A. Smith and Amasa M. Lyman
organized the Saints at Santa Clara into a ward, ordaining Zadoc
K. Judd to be the bishop. At that time there were some twenty-five
Indian missionaries there.

In the spring of 1861, President Young visited the settlement
south of the rim of the Great Basin, arriving at Santa Clara, May
26. "This visit was specially fraught with encouragement, comfort
and blessing to those already settled in this region."[22] The fore-
sighted Mormon Colonizer advised the people at the mission to
move to higher ground.

The advice was timely but not put into effect quickly enough.
The following January (17th to the 19th) a tremendous flood destroyed the dam and ditches at Santa Clara, washing away the school
and meeting houses, the old fort, and most of the surrounding
houses. It also ruined valuable farming land. So destructive was
the flood that it changed the whole aspect of the country, reducing
the first settlers almost to the position of beginners in a new frontier country. They were forced to work very diligently for some
time to make up the loss.

Having thoroughly investigated the possibilities for colonization in the southern part of his empire and having found the
population very small at the various settlements, the Mormon
Colonizer, at the October conference, 1862, called 339 families
to settle southern Utah. Thirty of these families were assigned to

‐‐‐‐
[20]McClintock, op. cit., 64.
[21]Ibid., 68.
[22]Saint George Stake, ... op. cit.,

the Indian mission to convert it into a permanent Mormon community.

The Santa Clara Indian mission had proven to be a big success. The missionaries had not only taught the Lamanites certain things in regards to living as the white man lived, and had strengthened the ties between the white and red races, but Jacob Hamblin and his associates had explored the country and opened up trails over which Mormon colonists passed to open up land settlement in northern Arizona. As Spain had done earlier, so did Brigham Young send out missionary-explorers, followed by colonists.

Chapter XXXI

THE ELK MOUNTAIN MISSION

Missionaries Called

In keeping with the Mormon policy of teaching the Indians Christianity and the arts of the white man, President Young called forty-one of the Saints to serve as missionaries to the Indians who resided in the vicinity of Elk Mountain, now La Salle Mountains, in Grand County, southeastern Utah. This call was made at the general conference of the Church, April, 1855. The purpose of the Elk Mountain Mission was to educate and convert a tribe of Ute Indians who occupied the vicinity of the little valley on the Colorado River in which Moab is now situated.

On May 21, under the leadership of Alfred N. Billings, who had been appointed president of the mission, the company left Manti, the place of rendezvous. They traveled in military fashion, as was the common practice in the movement of Mormon groups. An inventory showed that the company consisted of:

Forty-one men, 15 wagons, 65 oxen, 16 cows, 13 horses, 2 bulls, 1 calf, 2 pigs, 4 dogs and 12 chickens. The company also carried 14,565 pounds of flour, 28 bushels of peas, 4 bushels of oats, 1 whipsaw, 32 bushels of wheat, 2½ bushels of corn, 33 bushels of potatoes, 22 axes, 6 scythes, 2 iron bars, 6 trowels, 8 hoes, 11 shovels and 5 plows.[1]

Difficulties Encountered En Route

By May 27 the company had crossed a ridge of mountains and come into Castle Valley where the waters began to run toward the Green and Colorado rivers. After traveling over a very rough and wild country, the missionaries arrived at the Green River on June 4 and ferried their wagons across on a boat which had been used by President Billings as a wagon-box. These frontiersmen showed great ingenuity and speed in accomplishing the crossing. At the close of the second day all of their goods, with the exception of two wagons, were across the river. "At one trial trip, the river was crossed, the boat unloaded, rowed back and towed back to the landing in nine minutes. To cross over, one wagon and its loading required three trips."[2]

---

[1]Oliver B. Huntington, *Journal*, June 23, 1855, Ms.
[2]*Ibid*.

But they experienced more difficulty when they tried to swim the cattle through the river. The animals would run into a huddle and then swim round and round, run right over the men and then push to the shore from whence they came. After a day and a half of untiring effort, with the result of swimming only twenty-five head of cattle across the river, the pioneers were forced to take the remainder over with a boat, towing two at a time. By ten o'clock of June 8, all other equipment was over the river and the company was again on its way toward the Rio Colorado. They encountered many difficulties en route, some of which were recorded in the journal of the secretary of the mission, Oliver B. Huntington. Of one day's journey he wrote:

Sunday, June 10: Road extremely sandy, traveled eight miles; the day most exceedingly hot. Most of the teams were near giving out, when they came to the canyon descent leading to Grand River. One of John McEwen's oxen gave out and was left near the head of this canyon, which, being of fast descent and extremely difficult, gave rest to the cattle. They reached the "Jumping-off place" just at sunset, which is nearly three miles from the head of the canyon. The cattle had not had a drop of water or food since morning, and labored hard in a heat that was nearly equal to a torrid zone. This canyon is narrow, crooked, and rough with rocks, the road following the bed of the canyon where it is either sand or rock. The jumping off place is a perpendicular ledge, twenty-five feet high, down which William Huntington and Jackson Stewart, the year previous, let five wagons with their loads by ropes, taking their wagons to pieces. The knowledge of this induced President Billings to take a company of twelve horsemen in the morning and move rapidly to the canyon; all the way down these men worked a road, and at the jump-off they worked a road over a point of the mountain covered with very large rocks; in half a day they completed a very passable road where in the morning it had seemed impossible even to pass with wagons. By doubling teams up and all the men that could be spared to steady the wagons down we got all our wagons down safely about nine o'clock at night; three miles more took us to Grand River the first water our stock got since morning.[3]

SITE SELECTED—TEACHING THE INDIANS THE GOSPEL

President Alfred Billings, accompanied by five other missionaries, crossed the Grand River (Colorado River) on June 10 for the purpose of selecting a site for the mission. About the center of the valley below Elk Mountain, they came upon the lands cultivated by the Indians, where they found ten acres planted to corn, melons, squashes and pumpkins. The Indians had cleared the brush and grass off the land and made small holes with sticks to put the corn into the soil. They did not work the land more than this, but they occasionally irrigated by flooding it. There were

---

[3]*Ibid.*, June 10, 1855.

but a few Indians to be seen in the valley that day, most of them having gone to the mountains to hunt.

After careful exploration of the country surrounding Elk Mountain, the company returned to Grand River and decided upon locating east of the stream near the south side of the valley. Within the next ten days they cleared the land of brush and plowed; they constructed a dam in the creek and dug a ditch three miles long to their farms. By June 23, they had practically completed planting their crops, when, toward evening some Utah Indians came into camp. The missionaries took advantage of the opportunity and preached to them. Thus they began their proselyting work among the natives with propitious results.

Sunday, June 24, meeting was called and the Indians invited, they came and the spirit of God was poured out upon all alike. They were anxious to become as we were, live with us and do as we did. The spirit of our work seemed to be already in them.[4]

These favorable conditions did not last long. Soon other Indians returned from hunting in the mountains. A portion of them were hostile to white men. July 10, a few of the prominent Indians forbade the missionaries to build any more on a rock fort which had been begun the previous week. A crisis at this time was prevented by the arrival of one of the chiefs named Saint John, a friendly Indian who "told his men that the Mormons had come to do them good and that there were not enough to harm them if we [Mormons] wanted to. He wanted his people to let the Mormons alone and not steal from them; it was good to live all together."[5] The foregoing event convinced the missionaries that they should concentrate their efforts and complete the fort before trouble occurred. This they did, finishing the fort on July 19. It was sixty-four feet square with walls four feet thick at the bottom and two at the top.

During the following two months the Indians were peaceable, and the Mormons were able to teach them, as they had been sent to do. A number of Indians joined the Church. July 28 fifteen of them were baptized and some of them ordained to offices in the priesthood. About six weeks later, eighteen more were enlisted in the Church.

INDIAN POLICY

Soon after the Indians first began to arrive at the Mormon

---

[4]*Ibid.,* June 24, 1855.
[5]*Ibid.,* July 11, 1855.

camp from hunting, the missionaries abandoned the Indian policy in regard to trading as prescribed by President Young. The journalist states: "Sunday, July 1: laid aside former rules to suit circumstances and traded with the chief and his men."[6] This practice soon proved to be folly, so just one month later a meeting was called to determine what their policy should be. President Billings instructed them that they must again adopt Brigham's policy of sending the Indians who wished to trade to an officially authorized Mormon agent among the missionaries, in order that they might "keep a uniformity of prices and prevent exorbitant demands from the Indians. Every man was agreed with the president in his remarks and agreed to listen to him. Allen Huntington was appointed by vote assistant trader."[7]

Later, during the same month, the missionaries received a letter from Brigham Young requiring all of them to travel and live with the Indians, except enough to defend the fort. At the time the red men seemed pleased with this idea, but circumstances did not allow the company to obey Brigham's request.

BATTLE WITH THE INDIANS

Shortly after the middle of September serious Indian troubles began. The natives commenced their mischief by digging up nearly all the beets and turnips and about one-fourth of the potatoes that the Mormons had cultivated. On the morning of the 23rd the missionaries felt so apprehensive of some greater harm intended that they sent their cattle to a new herding ground. A few moments later a large group of Indians crossed the river and came up to the fort. They were very impudent, asking the missionaries why they had taken their cattle in a different direction that day. After retiring a short distance from the fort, the natives consulted together, and then three of them started for the field in the direction of the cattle. In a few moments James W. Hunt, with a lariat in his hand, started to the pasture for his horses. Charles, a son of Suit-sub-soc-its, or Saint John, followed Hunt. Riding horseback directly behind him, Charles continued telling him to go on ahead and asking him what he was afraid of. The men in the fort could see that the white man, apprehensive of danger, turned his head occasionally toward the Indian.

When they were about a mile from the fort, Charles shot Hunt in the back, using a gun for which he had traded a horse with

---

[6]*Ibid.*, August 1, 1855.
[7]*Ibid.*

Clark A. Huntington that very morning. Charles immediately took Hunt's horses as well as the one he had traded for the gun, joined the rest of the red men, and crossed the river.

Ephraim Wight and Sheldon B. Cutler were herding the stock nearby when Hunt was shot. Cutler raced to the fort and reported the tragedy. Some of the men hurried to assist in bringing the stock to the fort while four of them went after Hunt. They wrapped the mortally wounded man in a blanket and began carrying him toward the fort as carefully as they could.

By the time the rescuers had arrived within a fourth of a mile of the fort, the Indians, shouting their war whoop, recrossed the river and came charging toward the whites and the livestock. A shower of bullets whistled briskly all around the men. Four of them served as a rear guard to their companions, holding the Indians back while the wounded man was carried to the fort where he died shortly afterward. President Billings was wounded by a ball passing through one of his fingers on his right hand. But even under these perilous conditions the Mormons succeeded in corralling most of their livestock.

The gravity of the situation was increased by some of the Indians turning the water so that none could reach the fort, while others set fire to the hay stacks at the north end of the corral. The stacks and corn were consumed by fire, but through constant effort of four or five men in carrying water, the corral, which contained the cattle, was saved. The Indians kept up the shooting, however, from noon until after dark. In the interchange of bullets three Indians were killed, and three missionaries seriously wounded.

The day before this Indian attack, Edward Edwards and William Behunin had gone into the mountains hunting. In the midst of the attack, the Indians declared that they saw the two Mormons returning. Immediately, with Charles at their head, several of them left the fort. Shortly thereafter the report of seven guns was heard, and Charles and his group of warriors returned.

Toward evening the interpreter, Clark A. Huntington, was able to get into a conversation with the Indians. He told them that it was not good to fight and that the Mormons had not come to kill. The Indians answered that three of them had been killed and as many more wounded and that they would not be satisfied until they had killed two more Mormons. They denied killing Edwards and Behunin. Finally, the Indians consented to go away, talk the matter over and return the following morning to settle the difficulty, on condition that the Mormons give them some bread. The missionaries gladly gave the Indians every piece of bread they had, and the natives ceased their firing.

Early the next morning the red men came to the fort and acknowledged that they had killed the two men who were coming from the mountain. They were glad that three Mormons had been killed as three of their men had been also, and the score was even. Their attitude was anything but conciliatory.

ABANDONMENT OF THE MISSION

Conditions were very critical for the small group of missionaries. They were without water. The Indians had sent runners into the mountains for aid in exterminating the Mormons. There was no doubt that the attack would soon be renewed. President Alfred N. Billings called a council and prayer meeting to decide what was best to be done under existing circumstances. The journalist of the mission stated: "We were all willing to stay and fight it out and die together or leave, whichever the President counseled us to do."[8] They respected the authority placed over them to the extent that they were unwilling to desert their missionary activities, even in the face of death, unless they were officially released from that mission by their superior officers. Herein lies one of the reasons for the success of Mormon missionary work and Mormon land settlement of the Great West.

The president's decision was "that under the present existing circumstances he deemed it wisdom to leave for the present." Without stopping to prepare breakfast, the missionaries quickly packed what little they could and left the fort by eleven o'clock on September 24. They had to leave behind them five horses and twenty-four head of cattle.

When they had crossed the Grand River, the missionaries met an Indian, the brother of Saint John and an uncle of Charles. Mr. Huntington told him all that had taken place, why they were leaving, and the amount of property that they were forced to leave behind. This friendly Indian expressed his regrets and said that he would see that they got their cattle and that the two men who had been killed while coming from the mountain should be buried. He and his sons went to the fort, conversed with the other Indians, and then commenced driving the cattle out of the corral. Some of the more belligerent natives began to shoot at the cattle. One Indian cocked his gun at the friendly Indian, who instantly shot

[8]*Ibid.*, September 24, 1855.

him with an arrow. After pulling another Indian from his horse by the hair of his head and severely beating him for saying that he would follow the Mormons and kill one, this Indian, with help from others who sympathized with the missionaries, succeeded in driving fifteen head of cattle away from the corral and sending them to the missionaries.

After leaving the Elk Mountain Mission, the white men traveled as rapidly as they could toward Manti, as they were in constant danger of being overtaken by the warriors. They saw no more of the hostile Indians, however, and arrived safely in the Mormon settlement on September 30, 1855. That was just four months and a third from the time they left Manti to establish an Indian mission on the Rio Colorado.

Among the many thrilling experiences which the Latter-day Saint Indian missionaries encountered, that of the Elk Mountain Mission of 1855 can be classed as the most disastrous and futile of its kind. Yet through all of these difficulties the missionaries showed an attitude of obedience, humility and service. They helped to blaze the trails for future colonization.

CHAPTER XXXII

LAS VEGAS MISSION

DESCRIPTION OF LAS VEGAS AND ENVIRONS

In the fall of 1847 Captain Jefferson Hunt and companions were sent to California by the authorities of the Church for the purpose of purchasing seeds for planting. They went by the route known as the Old Spanish Trail or the Southern Route. From that time forward the Mormon pioneers knew of Las Vegas Springs, and many of them frequently camped there on their journeys to and from California.

Flowing from two springs, a stream of water about three feet wide and fifteen inches deep ran four miles and then spread out and disappeared in the thirsty earth. Bordering the stream for about half a mile wide and three miles long was a grassy patch to which the Spaniards gave the name of Las Vegas or the Meadows. The country for miles distant was dry, barren, and desolate. An article in the *Deseret News* stated:

> The country surrounding Las Vegas is rather peculiar. The mountains which are not very high, are perfectly bare, and not a living shrub is to be seen. The Las Vegas is a stream about four miles in length, deep and narrow; the water in the creek is good but not cold.[1]

The fact that there was no water to be found between this spring and the Muddy River, some fifty-five miles to the northeast, and in other directions from Las Vegas water was just as scarce, made this oasis a very important point on the Mormon Corridor route. Brigham recognized the importance of being in possession of these springs, so he established a colony there.

MISSIONARIES CALLED

A number of missionaries were called by President Young at the April conference of the Church held in Salt Lake City in 1855. Some were assigned to preach the Gospel while others were instructed to make settlements in various parts of the Great Basin. Thirty brethren were sent to found a settlement at Las Vegas, which at that time belonged to New Mexico. William Bringhurst was appointed president of the mission to Las Vegas, William

[1]*Deseret News,* II, 198.

S. Covert his counselor, and George W. Bean Indian interpreter. Brother Brigham Young instructed the missionaries that the main purpose in sending them to Las Vegas was to form friendly relationship with the Indians and to teach them the Gospel. Among other things, President Young said: "We feel exceedingly anxious to lay a good foundation among the Lamanites, and believe the set time has come when they shall be favored. We do know of a surety that the Lord is working upon them and preparing their minds to receive the Gospel."[2]

DIFFICULTIES ENCOUNTERED EN ROUTE

On May 10, 1855, the missionaries left Salt Lake. Traveling southward they met Brigham Young and other Church officials on the 23rd. After receiving words of encouragement and advice from the President, the company continued toward Las Vegas. On June 11 the Muddy River—the last watering place before crossing the intensely hot desert of fifty-five miles to Las Vegas—was reached. Two or three days were spent visiting with the Mormon missionaries on the Muddy, resting teams, fillling kegs and water barrels, and in making other necessary preparations for crossing the desert.

Then, William Bringhurst, with the strongest of the teams and about half of the company, started across the desert. James T. S. Allred was left in charge of the remaining wagons, with instructions to start twenty-four hours later. On account of the intense heat—the temperature ranging around 115F— traveling had to be done at night. Bringhurst and his group arrived at Las Vegas on June 14. To enable Allred and his group to make it across the desert, teams, wagons and water had to be sent back from Las Vegas to meet them.

FOUNDING OF LAS VEGAS MISSION

Immediately upon their arrival the missionaries commenced their labors. In conformity with the regular Mormon practice, they did their work cooperatively. After completing a bowery in which to hold their meetings, some of the brethren laid out the fort and farming lands while others made irrigation ditches. The fort was to be one hundred fifty feet square, located on a slope of the bench a few rods from the stream of water and about three miles east of the springs.

---

[2]Brigham Young, to Las Vegas Mission, *Record of Las Vegas Mission*, July 31, 1855, Ms.

The garden spots were just below the fort on the bottom lands, and next to the garden spots were the farming lands. In accordance with the Mormon land system, the garden lots were a quarter of an acre each in size and the farming land was divided into fifteen five-acre lots and also smaller plots of two and one-half acres each. Almost immediately the gardens were cleared, plowed and planted. By August 4, 1855, a corral, 150 feet long bordering one edge of the fort, was completed. Throughout the summer the men continued on the fort, completing the walls of President Bringhurst's house September 15, it being the first dwelling built in Fort Vegas.

Treaty of Peace with the Natives

In accordance with the purpose of the mission, one of the first things that the settlers of Las Vegas did was to assemble all of the chiefs and make an agreement with them. After receiving permission to make a settlement on the Indians' land, the Mormons promised to treat the natives well in return for good treatment by the Lamanites. Special attention was given to impress the red men with the idea that they should preserve peace and good conduct toward all emigrants traveling through the country, as well as with the settlers. The Indians recounted many instances of unprovoked murders committed by white men who had traveled through that part of the country, but they also assured the Mormons that they were now willing to bury all animosities and once more to try the conduct of the white men. President Bringhurst felt that much had been accomplished by this treaty with the Indians to assure the safety of travel and safety for the United States mail over the Old Spanish Trail, if white men would but treat the natives in accordance with the foregoing agreement.[3]

Description of the Piutes at Las Vegas

The Indians of that section of the country were very friendly as long as the Mormons had food to supply them. Under those conditions the missionaries did not have to leave their fort to preach to the red men but merely wait for them to come into camp. George W. Bean, the interpreter, reported that if the whites only had enough food to feed the natives they could govern and control the Indians to the very letter.[4] But in trying

---

[3]William Bringhurst, *Deseret News,* July 10, 1855.
[4]George W. Bean to George A. Smith, in *Record of Las Vegas Mission,* December 11, 1855, Ms.

to control them the missionaries found that their major problem was to keep the Indians from stealing. One might agree with John Steele, who remarked that he "did not blame them for stealing anything to eat, for there is not anything in all this country for them to eat except mesquite and lizards. The wolves here are as thin as a greyhound that has had nothing to eat for two months."[5]

Throughout the summer of 1855 the Indians helped the Mormons build their fort walls. Even the chiefs willingly worked at anything that they were set at. One thing that bothered the Indians was the fact that the Mormons had no women with them at Las Vegas at that time, so they offered to steal white emigrant women for them. It was only after much persuasion that the missionaries were able to convince the red men that it would be entirely against their wishes and also wrong for the natives to do so.

The missionaries reported that they found one group of Piutes, about fifty in number, near the Colorado River, in a perfect state of nudity except for breech clouts. The men and women were dressed exactly alike. This group had raised a little wheat on a sandbank, and had completed their harvest by the time the white men arrived.

The Piutes around Las Vegas informed the Mormons that the Indians on the south side of the Colorado did not use the bow and arrow in battle but used large clubs with which they fought very savagely. But the Indians north of the river used bows and flint-point poisoned arrows. They made the poison by having a rattlesnake bite a piece of deer's liver which they buried in the ground until it became putrid. They then took it out and dried it. When they used the poisoned deer's liver, they either steeped it in water or rubbed it directly on the arrow points. Whenever those poisoned arrows cut the skin death was a likely result.

Interpreter George W. Bean reported that the language of the Piutes was somewhat different from that of the Utes, though probably at one time they belonged to the same nation. At least according to their traditions, that was true. In the words of Bean:

These say that the Utahs and Pahvantes are branches of this nation, and, if their traditions are true, it must be the case, for they say that the two

[5]John Steele, to George A. Smith, in *ibid.*, October 1, 1855.

great brothers (Shenoub and Tewots) used to live on the mountain close by here. It was here they quarreled and Shenoub, or the devil, took advantage of his older brother, killed him and stole his wife, but after twenty-four hours, some say three days, Tewots came to life again and then commenced the great war which continued until they both left the country but not until they had peopled this and the surrounding country. There is hardly a mountain or canyon that is not reverenced by them upon some account or other.[6]

TEACHING THE NATIVES

The Las Vegas missionaries put forth their efforts to teach the Indians the arts of civilization. Sunday, August 31, 1856, President Bringhurst informed his companions that he "intended starting four companies in the fall, east, north, west, and south, to explore the country and settle every fertile spot capable of sustaining enough men to teach the Indians the art of civilized life, according to the command of President Young."[7]

The first step in teaching the natives the culture of the white man was to change their methods of sustaining themselves. By the first of January, 1857, the brethren had put in about fifteen acres of wheat for the Indians. The latter seemed well pleased with the idea of raising their own provisions instead of having to depend upon hunting in such a barren country. The following year Jacob Hamblin reported that the missionaries had raised on Las Vegas forty acres of corn and wheat, but just as the crop was matured the mountain Indians had come down and stolen the whole of it.[8]

NUMEROUS ACTIVITIES ENGAGED IN

A multitude of activities engaged the attention of the missionaries in that arid region. Lumber was needed badly. Therefore, soon after arriving at Las Vegas in 1855, President Bringhurst directed the exploration of the country for the purpose of finding timber, as there were no trees in those parts with the exception of scrubby, thorny mesquite. Timber was found in the Charleston Mountains about twenty-five miles away. Soon a saw mill was put into operation by James T. S. Allred and James Dickenson.

September 15, 1855, President Brighurst with four or five companions started for California in company with the mail carriers. They took fifteen yoke of oxen there and disposed of them. With the proceeds they purchased horses and mules. On December 2, Bringhurst and his companions arrived back at Las Vegas.

[6]George W. Bean, to George A. Smith, in *ibid.*, December 11, 1855.
[7]*Ibid.*, 83.
[8]Jacob Hamblin, *Latter-day Saint Journal History*, September 10, 1858, Ms.

Almost immediately after arriving from California, the President continued his explorations. During January, 1856, he directed an exploring party to the Colorado, Muddy, and Virgin rivers, contacting all of the Indians they could while on the trip. This expedition was followed the next year by more extensive explorations.

Meanwhile the government established a post office at Las Vegas and gave it the name of Bringhurst, there already being a city named Las Vegas in New Mexico. At that time southern Nevada was in New Mexico. The settlers engaged in other activities such as planting fruit trees, making preparations to teach school, and building a church house—which they never completed.

EXPLORATION OF NATHANIEL V. JONES FOR LEAD DEPOSITS

About the middle of February, 1856, President Brigham Young called Bishop Nathaniel V. Jones to go to the vicinity of Las Vegas for the purpose of exploring that region in search of lead. Specimens of ore had been brought to the Church officials from that district. Jones made preparations for the trip, leaving Salt Lake City on April 14, with the following letter of introduction from Brigham Young:

April 14, 1856
Great Salt Lake City

To the Bishops and Presidents of the Church of Jesus Christ of Latter-day Saints who are beyond Cedar City:

Beloved Brethren:

You are hereby authorized and required to use all reasonable exertions to furnish the bearer, Bishop Nathaniel V. Jones, with such men, animals, tools, etc., as he may call upon you for, to enable him to safely, diligently and successfully accomplish the purposes of the mission upon which he is now sent, viz: to search for and examine into the location, quality and quantity of different ores and metals, as specimens of rich lead ore have already been brought to me from that region, and it is highly desirable that we be able to make our lead, copper, etc., at the earliest practicable date.[9]

Your brother in the Gospel,
Brigham Young.

Jones received very good support from the settlers in the southern towns. He stated that "they responded promptly and cheerfully" to his calls. Provisions and means of transportation were furnished him at Cedar City, and the bishop, Philip K. Smith,

---

[9]Brigham Young, to Bishops and Presidents . . . beyond Cedar City, in *Record of Las Vegas Mission,* April 14, 1856. Ms.

and Ira Hatch, Indian interpreter of the Santa Clara Mission, accompanied Jones to Las Vegas. They arrived at the latter place May 6, 1856, rested a day or two, then visited the place where the specimens had been obtained that President Young had received. After careful examination of the mineral, Jones and his companions concluded that the strata would not pay for the working.

While making further explorations through the country, they were informed by the Indians that large quantities of the same kind of ore were to be found about fifty miles south from that place. This mineral was located. in the tops of the mountains twenty-seven miles southwest of Las Vegas and "about four miles east from the military road leading to California."   Upon careful examination of the mineral deposit, the conclusion was reached that "the mineral to all appearance was inexhaustible; in quantity it was several rods wide and varying from one to four feet in thickness; in places it was much brangled through the rock . . . though in the aggregate it was an exceedingly flattering prospect."[10] Timber for fuel was plentiful, yet two or three difficulties were quite apparent. The nearest running water was twelve miles away, though there was a small spring about one and a half miles from the mineral deposit which could be used for camp purposes. The country was completely devoid of grass which would make the problem of feeding their animals a serious one.

After examining the mineral deposit, the company returned to Las Vegas and thereafter made a six days' exploration trip to the northwest. They found nothing but "one continuous stretch of dry, burnt up mountains and arid sand plains entirely destitute of vegetation or timber."[11] Not feeling it advisable to risk jeopardizing the lives of men and animals in such a country, they retraced their steps to Las Vegas.

On May 22 Jones and his companions began their return trip to Salt Lake City. Upon reaching Cedar City, they stopped off a few days, and there in the mountains south of the Beaver settlement, in company with Bishop Tarlton Lewis and his son, Jones explored for mineral. Deposits of iron ore were found but no other kinds of mineral. From here the company turned their course toward Salt Lake City, where they arrived on June 13, 1856. Their explorations had taken them nearly two months.

Bishop Jones immediately visited Brigham Young and made a full report of the prospects of lead and other matters related to

---

[10]*Record of Las Vegas Mission*, 109-110, **Ms.**
[11]*Ibid.*, 110.

his trip. The Church officials considered the report favorable, so notified Jones a few days later that he was to take a company and proceed immediately to the working of the mines. Jones, with three companions, two four-mule teams, with necessary tools and supplies, left Salt Lake City, July 9, 1856, for Las Vegas, arriving there August 8. On Sunday two days after their arrival, Nathaniel V. Jones presented the following letter of instructions from President Brigham Young to the missionaries:

April 7, 1856

To all whom it may concern:

This is to certify that the bearer, Bishop Nathaniel V. Jones, is counseled to forthwith proceed with a company to the neighborhood of the Las Vegas and to engage in manufacturing lead, and the said Bishop Jones is hereby empowered to call to his aid in the said manufacture and transportation of lead, building of furnaces, mining the ore, etc, such persons as his judgment and necessities may dictate, not only Southern missionaries, but others of the brethren in the Southern settlements, if need be.[12]

Brigham Young.

Jones' Quarrel with Bringhurst

After reading the foregoing letter to the group at Las Vegas, Jones asked for the brethren who had been called to this mission at the last April conference to assist him in working out the lead. President Bringhurst refused to comply with Jones' request for men to work in the mine, so the latter decided to force his project by asking certain of the brethren directly to join him in mining. Those asked by Jones responded, he said, "cheerfully to the call." Necessary preparations were made for mining, and the group set off for their project, where operation was commenced August 14, 1856.

Before leaving for the mine, President William Bringhurst and Bishop Nathaniel V. Jones entered into much discussion and some quarreling. Finally they decided to submit their trouble to President Brigham Young by letter. On August 4, in a letter to Bringhurst, the Mormon Colonizer made the following reply:

We have appointed Brother Nathaniel V. Jones of this City to take charge of this business [mining lead] and superintend the whole matter, so that whatever is done we wish to have it done under his direction. At the same time we wish to have you render him all the assistance in team work and manual labor that you can and he can employ to advantage.[13]

---
[12]*Ibid.,* July 7, 1856.
[13]*Ibid.,* August 4, 1856.

EFFORTS TO MINE LEAD

In the meantime, Jones with his group were endeavoring to carry out their project of opening the lead mines, while Bringhurst was trying to retain his followers as missionaries to the Indians. Considerable difficulties were being encountered in the mining project. Only after a great deal of effort was expended in constructing a trail were they able to take their pack animals up to the top of the high mountain where the lead was located. With great difficulty they hauled the materials for the furnace, except the adobes, about seven miles. September 10, 1856, they put the furnace in blast but soon found that the material would not stand the fire. So Jones decided that time and effort could be saved by going to Salt Lake City and there constructing a bellows and blast furnace instead of experimenting at the mines, even if it would necessitate a trip of nearly 1100 miles. On September 15 the company left for Salt Lake where they arrived October 1.

THOMPSON REPLACING BRINGHURST AS PRESIDENT OF THE MISSION

While Bishop Jones was in the Mormon capital he presented his version of the trouble at Las Vegas between himself and Bringhurst. Brigham Young decided to suspend Bringhurst from office and disfellowship him from the Church until the difficulties were settled.

While Jones was at Salt Lake, Bringhurst made an effort to reestablish his influence over the missionaries. But the spirit of disunity continued among the group at Vegas. On September 19, 1856, William Bringhurst called a meeting for the purpose of "determining who considered themselves missionaries to Las Vegas, for the time had come when the line must be drawn." He said that it was his opinion that Nathaniel V. Jones had misrepresented conditions at Las Vegas to President Young and that the course Jones was following would sooner or later break up the mission. The sympathies of some of the brethren were in favor of Jones while others were for Bringhurst. Before the meeting was concluded, all but three who had opposed President Bringhurst asked forgiveness and accepted his leadership. But Samuel Thompson, Jacob L. Workman, and Eason Barney handed in their names as opponents of Bringhurst.

On November 12, Elijah K. Fuller arrived at Las Vegas from Salt Lake with some information as to how the officials of the Church were regarding the trouble at the mission. He informed

President Bringhurst that Brigham Young would not hear what he had to say regarding the mission but was completely in favor of Jones. Fuller also stated that "President Young had released all the brethren from the mission who were back in the settlements in consequence of that place not being able to sustain more than three or four men."[14] Several of the brethren expressed surprise that the Mormon leader should have believed Jones' report to the effect that Las Vegas could support only three or four men.

A few days before the return of Elijah K. Fuller from Salt Lake, the decision was reached to construct a church house. Each member of the mission was to be taxed thirty-eight dollars for the construction of the building, most of the tax to be paid in the form of cooperative work. William W. Riley was made chairman of the building committee.

Samuel Thompson and his party were entirely opposed to the idea of building such a house at that time. The majority of the missionaries, expecting that Nathaniel V. Jones would arrive in a few days with documents from Brigham Young authorizing the removal of William Bringhurst and the appointment of Samuel Thompson to the presidency of the mission, pushed the building as fast as possible. They felt that the completion of a church house would assist greatly in assuring the success of the mission, "as the upper part of the house was designed to be used as a prayer circle room, for spiritual instruction, and to give the natives their endowments."[15] Finally, after completing the foundation and about three feet of adobes all around, the brethren showed reluctance in performing a job which they felt would never be used, so the work was given up.

On December 4, 1856, Nathaniel V. Jones arrived to continue his work in the lead mines. He brought a letter to Samuel Thompson from President Young authorizing Thompson to take over the presidency of the mission. Jones also delivered William Bringhurst a letter stating why he had been dropped from the mission and disfellowshipped from the Church. In conformity with the regular Mormon practice, the majority of the missionaries readily submitted to the authority of President Young in now accepting Thompson as head of the mission.

Lead Mining Project Discontinued

Jones and his company proceeded to the mines with the

14*Ibid.,* November 12, 1856.
15*Ibid.,* 98.

equipment for smelting the ore. Little work had been done while he was on his trip to Salt Lake. December 25 everything was ready to begin smelting. By great diligence and hard labor about nine thousand pounds of lead had been produced by January 10. The yield had proved to be very disappointing, the mineral only yielding twenty to thirty per cent. All who had seen the mineral deposit before this date had overestimated its value. An excessive amount of dry bone, black jack and sulphur, which caused much of the lead to burn up during the smelting, added to the fact that provisions and food for animals had to be hauled 230 miles, and also that the Indians were causing trouble caused Jones and his associates to finally abandon the lead mine as unprofitable.

For six weeks their mules had to live upon three pints of oats each per day. No hay nor grass was available. Their mules became so hungry that they would eat rawhide, ropes, or anything that they were tied with, excepting chains. Jones reported that most of the Indians of that country had collected at a spring, about three hours distance from them, with the determination of driving off the stock and killing the miners. He stated:

The difficulties attending the working of the mines, together with the hostile feelings of the Indians, I did not consider it wisdom to remain longer. Accordingly, on the 26th of January 1857, we left the mines for the Vegas.[16]

After the miners had returned to Las Vegas, the Indian chiefs were called together, talked to, and given presents. The Indians appeared to feel satisfied but only a few days later one of the chiefs came into the fort again and threatened to kill all of the whites.

Nathaniel V. Jones and his associates explored the surrounding country for other lead deposits but found none which they believed would pay for the working. Finally they reached the decision to abandon the whole business of lead mining in that region. They left Las Vegas, February 17, 1857, and arrived in Salt Lake City, March 22. About a month later Jones submitted his report to President Young.[17]

Thus the Mormons abandoned their project of lead mining around Las Vegas early in 1857. After that date they did not again attempt to reestablish their lead mining project in that district. Yet there is mention in the Mormon manuscripts of occasional small parties stopping at the lead deposits for a few days and smelt-

16Nathaniel V. Jones to Brigham Young, *Latter-day Saint Journal History*, April 16, 1857. Ms.
17*Ibid.*
18*Latter-day Saint Journal History*, February 17, 1858. Ms.

ing small quantities of ore. In February, 1858, William H. Dame and ten other Mormons from Parowan accompanied Apostle Amasa M. Lyman and company as far as Las Vegas. Five of the party built a small adobe furnace and from 300 pounds of ore produced 140 pounds of lead. Then Dame and his group returned to Parowan with the lead, while Lyman and his company continued to San Bernardino, California.[18]

ABANDONMENT OF LAS VEGAS MISSION

Only five days after Jones and his associates abandoned the lead mines and left for Salt Lake City, President Thompson received a letter from Brigham Young which gave the brethren who desired to do so liberty to leave the mission. About a month later the majority of the missionaries left Las Vegas and returned to their homes in the Basin. With their departure, the Latter-day Saint mission at Las Vegas was practically broken up. Yet, a few of the brethren decided not to leave until they were released in a more formal way. They believed that it was still their duty to remain and do all the good they could for the Indians.

However, the entire abandonment of the mission was not brought about until 1858, the main cause being the coming of Johnston's army to Utah. At that time most of the distant settlers were called to the Basin by Governor Brigham Young. Some of the Vegas missionaries were called to labor among the Indians on the Santa Clara, at which place there were about fifty missionaries at that time. At a conference held by the Santa Clara group September 26, 1858, the decision was reached to drop the Muddy and Las Vegas missions for the time being. During the summer of 1858 the Mormons continued to do what they could to help the Indians at Las Vegas take care of their crops.

It seems that the Mormons retained their claims upon Las Vegas at least until 1868. At that date there appeared an advertisement in a newspaper published at Saint George offering Las Vegas ranch for sale. The advertisement stated:

The ranch is fifty-two miles from the Colorado River. The distance to Callsville is fifty-three miles, the upper settlements on the Muddy fifty-three miles, El Dorado Canyon fifty-five miles, Mojave City 120 miles, and Hardyville 114 miles. There is excellent sawing timber in the Charleston Mountains about twenty-five miles distant, the soil is a black, rich loam and will produce any kind of vegetables; there is water to irrigate 400 acres of small grain and range 3000 head of cattle.[19]

[19]O. D. Gass, *Our Dixie Times*, April 15, 1868.

LAS VEGAS, NEVADA
BY F. S. DELLENBAUGH, 1876

CHAPTER XXXIII

THE SALMON RIVER MISSION

CALLING OF MISSIONARIES

Another Mormon outpost was established in 1855, located 379 miles north of the Salt Lake City in the country that was at that time a portion of Oregon, but today is part of Idaho. It was called "The Salmon River Mission."

At the general conference of the Church, April 6, 1855, President Brigham Young called twenty-seven men to establish a mission "among the buffalo hunting Indians of Oregon Country." He instructed them to select a suitable location in the Indian country for the establishment of a Mormon settlement, and to teach the red men the Gospel of Jesus Christ and the arts of peace and civilization.

Thomas S. Smith of Farmington was appointed to be president of the mission. Under his direction the company assembled on the west side of the Bear River in Utah. Shortly after the middle of May the missionaries departed from their rendezvous.

EN ROUTE TO THE MISSION

The missionaries journeyed northward to and through the Malad Valley and then across the divide that separates the waters of the Pacific from those of the Great Basin. Soon they reached Bannock Creek, traveled some twenty miles to Portneuf River, crossed it at McArthur's toll bridge (paying one dollar per wagon), and continued on to the Snake River. Five miles above Fort Hall they repaired an old boat, owned by McArthur and a Mr. Hugo, and used it to ferry their belongings across the river on June 1.

While repairing the boat, the missionaries baptized in the Snake River three Bannock Indian men who had been traveling with them for several days. These were the first converts made by members of this mission.[1]

The company followed the west bank of the Snake River to a point within three miles of the present city of Idaho Falls and then veered northwesterly over a thirty-mile stretch of desert. After suffering from the heat and lack of water, the missionaries reached a stream which they called Spring Creek (Birch Creek), filled

---
[1] *Salmon River Mission,* May 30, 1855, Ms.

some barrels with water, and retraced their steps some distance to take the water to some of their famished animals which they had been forced to leave by the wayside.

At Spring Creek the missionaries met a Bannock Indian named Mattinger and four other natives who were headed for the Salmon River region. Mattinger encouraged the Mormons to locate on the Salmon River, guided their course in that direction for three days, showed them the Salmon River Pass in the distance, and then left the camp and hurried on ahead to inform the members of his tribe of the approach of the missionaries. Learning from the natives that the Salmon River was the fishing grounds of several tribes of Indians, Smith and his companions decided to locate there.

On June 12, they were met by Sow-woo-koo, the Bannock chief, with his wife and child, who had ridden on horseback seventy-five miles to welcome the Mormons and encourage them to settle near his tribe and teach them how to work.

He also stated that the camp was welcome to any land that they might select for farming purposes. He was also very anxious that they not go any farther north than Salmon River.[2]

The following day Colonel Smith and three companions went down the river ahead of the company for the purpose of exploring the surrounding country and selecting a site for the mission. A favorable spot, containing some good meadow and farming land, was located on the Lemhi River which unites with the South Fork of the Salmon River.

Mission Founded

On June 18, the company reached the selected site. The missionaries began to dig an irrigation ditch, plow the ground, and build a stockade which they called Fort Lemhi (now Lemhi) in honor of a Book of Mormon character. The stockade was made of logs twelve feet long, three feet of which were in the ground. As soon as possible they constructed a sawmill, a blacksmith shop, and thirteen cabins in the fort. Two massive gates, nine feet high and ten feet wide, were hung. One was situated on the east and the other on the west side of the stockade.

Four days after their arrival, the missionaries had planted several acres of peas, potatoes, corn, and turnips. Hordes of grasshoppers appeared late in July and ate the crops, which made it

---

[2] *Ibid.*, June 12, 1855.

apparent to the colonists that there would be a scarcity of food before spring. Thereupon President Smith appointed eleven of the group to return to the Mormon Mecca for supplies. They arrived back at Fort Lemhi on November 19, 1855, bringing not only fresh supplies but mail from their relatives in Utah. In December a second party was dispatched to the Mormon settlements for more supplies. This group returned to Fort Lemhi the following spring, bringing with them twenty-two new colonists.

In harmony with the Mormon land policy, on December 7, 1855, President Smith and some of the other missionaries "surveyed off twenty-two five-acre lots south of the Fort, between the first and second creek, which were drawn for according to their numbers by the brethren present. Some of those present drew for those who were absent."[3]

On October 9, 1855, William Burgess wrote to George A. Smith in the Basin a glowing report of the excellent country in which they had located and the possibilities it afforded for extensive missionary work among the Lamanites. Quoting:

We can have access to four tribes, Bannocks, Shoshones, Nepertians, and Flatheads. . . . The Indians are very honest here. . . . They abhor a thief, comparing him to a wolf, and they think a wolf is the meanest animal that is.[4]

Throughout the winter of 1855-56 the missionaries diligently devoted their attention to learning the Shoshonean language and to teaching the natives the Gospel. Favorable results were attained, sixty-five baptisms being performed before Christmas. By April the elders were able to speak quite fluently the Shoshonean tongue. Trade with the Indians was controlled by President Smith in harmony with Brigham Young's Indian policy.

Early in April, 1856, ninety bushels of wheat, barley, oats and peas were planted. When summer came the grasshoppers again destroyed the crops. This forced the colonists to send another expedition to Utah for supplies.

The people at the Salmon River Mission would have experienced intense suffering for lack of food if it had not been for the abundance of fish in the river. Throughout the summer fish was the main food and they dried a supply for winter. They caught tons of them on willow traps, and wagon loads were sent to Utah.

---

[3]*Ibid.*, December 7, 1855.
[4]William Burgess to George A. Smith, in *ibid.*, October 9, 1855.

Brigham Young and Company Visiting the Salmon River Mission

In May, 1857, the missionaries were honored with a visit of Brigham Young, from the Mormon headquarters, accompanied by his counselors, most of the Twelve Apostles, and the Presiding Patriarch of the Church. The President's company was composed of one hundred fifteen men, twenty-two women, five boys, with one hundred twenty-six horses and mules, twenty-eight carriages and twenty-six wagons. No doubt such a caravan of ecclesiastical dignitaries left an everlasting impression on the Mormon frontiersmen when it visited their distant hamlets.

The avowed purpose of this particular trip was "to visit the settlement on the Salmon River, to rest their minds, to invigorate their bodies, and to examine the intervening country."[5] As usual on such trips, Brigham's party made careful "observations relative to distances, fertility of the soil, amount of water, and conditions in general."

Sunday, May 10, a meeting was held at Fort Lemhi, at which the Church officials gave many fine instructions to the missionaries. In the words of Samuel M. Beal:

> Perhaps the most stirring bit of advice was given by Heber C. Kimball and Daniel H. Wells, when they urged the young men to "marry native women, that the marriage tie was the strongest tie of friendship that existed." However, President Young modified this advice to the extent that they should not be in a hurry, and should marry young girls if any.[6]

The advice for the Mormons to marry the Indians was a deviation from the common practice. One other company of missionaries to the Indians—the group at Fort Bridger and Fort Supply, Wyoming—were given instructions to marry "the young daughters of the chief and leading men," but in neither mission was such a practice carried on very extensively. At Fort Lemhi, "several of the young men made overtures to the dusky maidens, but the parents refused to let their daughters go, or at least seemed unwilling."[7]

Before leaving the Salmon River Mission, President Brigham Young complimented the elders on their work, advised them to build a fort enclosure for the livestock and machinery adjacent to the stockade, and promised the colonists that upon arriving back

---

[5]*Deseret News,* June 10, 1857.
[6]Samuel M. Beal, "The Founding of the Salmon River Mission,"*Deseret News* "Church Section," January 1, 1938.
[7]*Ibid.*

at the Mormon headquarters he would send them reinforcements. Thereupon, after the President's party left for Utah, the missionaries enclosed a space sixteen rods square with a wall, built of clay, rocks, and grass, three feet wide at the bottom, two at the top, and nine feet high. In October, 1857, the new contingent of settlers arrived, making approximately 100 colonists at Fort Lemhi.

After making careful observations of the country while on their trips to and from Fort Lemhi, President Young and his associates were well pleased with the possibilities for establishing Mormon settlements northward. Up to this time the major emphasis in Mormon land settlement had been southward from the Mormon Mecca. Immediately following the "Utah War" (1857-1858), northern Utah and Idaho received the major portion of colonists.

ATTACK OF FORT LEMHI BY THE SHOSHONES

At the beginning of 1858 conditions at the Salmon River Mission were very favorable for a permanent Mormon community. The crops had been good that year, and the missionaries and the Indians were on very congenial terms. But within less than three months the mission was abandoned, never to be reoccupied by the Saints. The two factors which brought about the doom of Fort Lemhi as a Mormon colony were the coming of Johnston's Army to Utah and an Indian attack on the Salmon River Mission.

On February 8, 1858, a band of Shoshone Indians were entertained at the fort and given the usual freedom around the premises. They seemed to be on very friendly terms with the colonists. A few days later, John W. Powell, a mountaineer who lived with the Indians, "dressed and painted himself as they did, and was one of them in all their deviltry," warned one of the Mormons that the Indians were planning to attack the colonists.

However, no attention was paid to the warning and no special precautions were taken by the missionaries to protect themselves against an Indian uprising.

On the morning of February 25 at 10 a. m. the Mormons at Fort Lemhi were attending the regular routine of activities when suddenly about 200 Indians made an attack. When the warriors began to encircle the livestock, the herdsmen attempted to drive the cattle into the stockade. George McBride, in a courageous attempt to head off the frightened cattle, got on his horse, " uttered a yell, and dashed over the hill and down among the Indians." He was met by a volley of bullets, one of which lodged in his body, and he fell from his horse dead. The warriors stripped him of his clothes, scalped him and mutilated his body, and took his horse and revolver.

Another herdsman, Orson Rose, dropped into a heavy sage brush when the Indians began the attack. The red men literally riddled the brush with shot, but Rose escaped unharmed. Later he moved from that dangerous spot to the thickets in the creek bottom, where he nestled in seclusion under their hospitable protection until the shades of night time provided opportunity for him to return to the fort.

Some of the other herdsmen were forced to seek protection in the stockade from the bullets of the Indians. But President Smith and Ezra Barnard made one more desperate effort to rescue the livestock. They mounted two horses and hastened in pursuit of the herd. Six warriors turned and opened fire upon them. A bullet passed through Smith's suspenders and lodged in his horse's jaw. The horse lurched and threw its rider off. While he was remounting, a bullet passed through his right arm. Smith and Barnard failed to rescue the cattle but they did succeed in reaching the fort again without further difficulties.

Several other Mormons hid in the brush when the Indians made the attack. Later they left their hiding place and carried Fountain Welch into the fort. Welch had been shot in the small of the back, stripped of his clothes, robbed of his weapons, and struck over the head with a gun, but he was still alive.

Several months previous to the Indian attack, the missionaries had built a second fort two miles south of Fort Lemhi and eighteen men were living in it, presided over by M. D. Hammond.

During the Indian attack, the inhabitants of the lower fort were on their way to Fort Lemhi when they met the Indian warriors. They were immediately fired upon, which resulted in the wounding of L. W. Shurtliff and Oliver Robinson and in the death of James Miller. All but Miller escaped in the brush while the Indians took the oxen and burned the outfit.

When night arrived there were still six missionaries who had not arrived at the fort. Thereupon President Smith sent out a searching party of ten men while the others stood guard and gave first aid to their wounded brethren. McBride and Miller—both dead—and Andrew Quigley, who had been wounded in the shoulder and beaten over the head, were discovered and brought into the fort.

ABANDONMENT OF THE MISSION

Three days later B. H. Watts and E. J. Barnard were sent on horseback to Salt Lake City to report the condition at Fort Lemhi to Brigham Young and find out what should be done. Upon receiving the information regarding the attack and in view of the existent troubles between the Mormons and the federal government with the solution not yet in sight, the Mormon leaders decided to call the settlers at Fort Lemhi and those at the other outpost settlements back to the Basin. It was apparent that the frontier outposts could not be defended at that time, so they must of necessity be abandoned. Brigham Young realized that to attempt to defend the Salmon River outpost would be most difficult, as it was located over 350 miles from the nearest Mormon settlement. The nearest towns to the east were located on the Iowa and Minnesota frontiers and to the west was the settlement in Willamette Valley, and on the north "there was no limit to the endless stretch of barbarism."

B. H. Watts returned to Fort Lemhi on March 21, accompanied by eleven men. Two days later, Colonel Cunningham, with 100 soldiers, wagons, and other necessary supplies arrived, and on March 25, Captain Horton D. Haight, with fifty more men reached Fort Lemhi. The latter two groups were part of the territorial militia. They had been sent by Governor Young for the purpose of moving the missionaries on the Salmon River to a spot of safety in Utah.

The members of the Relief Expedition helped the settlers gather what cattle they could find and make preparations for the abandonment of Fort Lemhi. However, one hundred thirty-six cattle and twenty-nine horses were never recovered from the Indians.

Old Chief Snagg and a number of his tribe who were still friendly to the Mormons were at the fort when preparations were being made to leave. President Smith gave them 1,000 bushels of wheat. "This old fellow and his immediate followers wept upon the departure of the missionaries."[8]

ATTACK BY INDIANS WHILE EN ROUTE TO SALT LAKE

On March 26 eleven men were sent in advance of the main body to inform the Church officials of conditions at Fort Lemhi since the Indian attack. Four days later, while crossing the Port-

---
[8] Ibid.

neuf River, they were attacked by a group of Indians. W. Bailey Lake was shot in the head and instantly killed while trying to cross the stream. Lake's companions protected themselves as best they could in the willows and from that position returned the fire upon the red men. No damage was done to the Indians, as they rode good horses and kept them in motion. However, two of the Mormons' horses were killed, another and a mule wounded, and seventeen other horses escaped, leaving the ten white men only six horses. Leaving nearly everything behind, they hastened on to Salt Lake City, arriving there early in April.

The main body of missionaries left Fort Lemhi on March 27, accompanied by the militia. Snow was deep and the weather was cold and stormy, resulting in much difficulty and suffering en route to the Basin.

Upon arriving in Brigham City on April 11, the settlers from Lemhi were surprised to find that town and the other northern Utah settlements deserted. The people had joined "the move" southward, occasioned by the approach of Johnston's Army. At that point the Lemhi settlers were disbanded; each followed his own course to settle wherever he wished.

The Salmon River Mission was never re-established, but shortly after an amicable adjustment of the Johnston Army episode many of the former inhabitants of Fort Lemhi were numbered among the early settlers of southern Idaho.

CHAPTER XXIV

BIRD'S-EYE VIEW OF MORMON COLONIZATION

SUMMARY OF EASTERN PERIOD OF MORMON FRONTIER HISTORY

Sturdy Mormon frontiersmen contributed their share in the opening of the Great West to civilization. Between 1830 and 1846 the advance of Mormon land settlement was always on the western portion of the American frontier. The first year it was centered around Palmyra in western New York. In 1831 the Saints left their first home and migrated to two new frontier districts—Kirtland, Ohio, and Independence, Missouri. The latter area bordered on the Lamanite territory which had been set aside by the federal government in 1825 as the "permanent Indian country." Here they hoped to build Zion—a "New Jerusalem."

However, the Mormons were not permitted to remain long in either Ohio nor Missouri. Within eight years after locating on those frontiers, they were forced by Gentile persecution to seek a new haven in which to build Zion. Nauvoo, Illinois, was the site selected. But seven years only were the "children of God" permitted to remain in Illinois. Again they were forced to seek a place of security on a new frontier. This time they determined to migrate to a country far distant from white men. They selected a spot in the heart of the desert where they could establish a commonwealth of their own, they hoped, without further strife with Gentile settlers.

The Great Basin, with its many Rocky Mountain valleys, was the place selected by their prophet-leader, Brigham Young. "The country to which they went was one inhabited by roving tribes of Indians; it was so desolate and forbidding that Daniel Webster had declared it unfit for any use except for wild animals."[1]

DR. THOMAS NIXON CARVER QUOTED

Yet, this desert country served as an ideal laboratory for the Mormons to put into effect their theories of empire building. The unusual success at colonization of those pioneer builders will stand in history as one of the noble accomplishments of a group of God-fearing people. In the words of Dr. Thomas Nixon Carver:

[1]Hubert H. Bancroft, *History of Utah.*

I have been interested in the Mormon policy. It is one of the most interesting and instructive experiments in the world. It throws a great deal of light on the art of nation building. It therefore furnishes a laboratory for the study of the science of statesmanship. . . . The great statesman of the Golden Age of Greece "boasted that he could make a small city into a great and glorious one;" but the Mormon leaders did even better than that. They did not have a small city to start with. They started with nothing and built a great and glorious commonwealth. It was necessary for the Mormon Church to train its own people. They not only began with desert land and had to put everything on it, even water; they also had to start with relatively uneducated people. This double task of developing both land and people could never have been performed except by economizing to the nth degree. The results were a marvel of statesmanship. It may have been a bond of a common religion, it may have been superior intelligence and insight. Whatever the source, the result was good.[2]

Effect of Desert and Religion on Mormons

The rugged mountains and the hot, barren desert, coupled with the strenuous conditions of frontier life in the Great West, produced marvelous qualities of leadership in many of the Church members. The desert, the majestic mountains, and the frontier life, however, contributed only their share to the development of leadership. Most important was the religion which these people had espoused which they sincerely believed was the true Church of Jesus Christ and the only church which could assure men exaltation in the kingdom of God.

Land Settlement in Salt Lake, Weber, Utah, Tooele, Sanpete, Carson, Little Salt Lake, Juab, Pauvan, Box Elder and Cache Valleys

The opening of the American frontier by the Mormons in the Great Basin began with the settlement of Salt Lake City in 1847, over 2,000 colonists arriving that summer. During the fall several groups left Salt Lake with their livestock in search of pasturage. They located on canyon streams, some as far as fifteen miles north and others a comparable distance south of the parent colony. Each group of frontiersmen built themselves houses which served as the nucleus for some half dozen towns which later became the major settlements in the valley.

The second valley in the Basin to be colonized by the Mormons was named Weber. Acting in harmony with Brigham Young's suggestion, on January 6, 1848, Captain James Brown purchased from a trapper named Miles Goodyear a large tract of land located

---

[2]Thomas Nixon Carver, *The Westerner*, April 9, 1930.

on the Weber and Ogden rivers, which tract the letter claimed to have obtained from the Mexican government. Shortly thereafter the settlement named Ogden was begun. It was located some forty miles north of the Mormon Mecca. Around this hub colony other towns soon came into existence in Weber Valley. In accordance with the Mormon land policy, Captain Brown retained only a small portion of the land himself and gave the rest to other Mormon home seekers.

The year after Ogden was settled (1849) witnessed the opening of four other valleys to Mormon colonization. The first of these was Utah Valley, which lies directly south of Salt Lake Valley. In April, 1849, thirty-three families, numbering in all about 150 individuals, arrived on the Provo River, about forty-five miles south of the parent colony, and established Fort Utah (Provo). Tooele, the valley directly south of the Great Salt Lake, and Sanpete, which lay nearly 150 miles southeast of the principal city, were settled that fall. Carson Valley, Nevada, was the other frontier opened for colonization that year. By the time 1849 came to a close the Saints had established twenty-six towns in the Great Basin, with five valleys opened to land settlement.

During 1850 seventeen more communities came into existence. They were all located in the same valleys that had previously been opened to colonization. However, plans were underway that year to project land settlement into several new valleys, some of them far distant from the parent colony. At the October conference Apostle George A. Smith was appointed by President Young to establish a settlement in the Little Salt Lake Valley, 205 miles south of the Mormon Mecca, for the purpose of manufacturing iron. Smith, accompanied by 168 colonists, arrived at the selected spot in January, 1851, and founded Parowan. From that hub city, other towns spread throughout the valley.

In 1851 Nephi in Juab Valley, 100 miles south of Salt Lake, was settled; and Fillmore, Pauvan Valley, fifty miles farther south, received its first colonists. Brigham had selected the latter site as the place to establish the capital city for his contemplated empire. At Fillmore a State House was built in which was held the first Utah Territorial Legislature.

Mormon land settlement advanced not only southward in 1851, but communities were established north of the parent colony as well. Sixty miles to the north, Brigham City was located. There Lorenzo Snow managed affairs and put into operation the cooperative system tried earlier by Joseph Smith. From that hub city other settlements in Box Elder county were soon established. In 1856 Cache Valley, which lies northeast of Box Elder, received its first settlers.

MORMON OUTPOST SETTLEMENTS

In addition to advancing land settlement to the valleys located more closely to Salt Lake, the Mormon colonizer surrounded his contemplated empire with outpost settlements far distant from the parent colony. The first of those outposts was the Mormon Station (Genoa), Carson Valley, Nevada, located over 550 miles west of the principal city. It was situated at the foot of the passes over the Sierra and served as a midway station between Salt Lake City and San Francisco on the northern route to the sea. The first settlers were seven Mormon traders, who established a supply station for passsing emigrants. Later, Brigham Young placed the colony directly under Mormon ecclesiastical control and reinforced it with additional settlers. Carson Valley was to be "a subsidiary gathering place to collect the Saints from California and Oregon."

The most distant outpost was San Bernardino, located 750 miles away. In the spring of 1851, Apostles Amasa M. Lyman and Charles C. Rich were sent "to southern California . . . to establish a stronghold for the gathering of the Saints." Accompanied by 500 colonists, they purchased the Rancho de San Bernardino. That site was selected because that portion of California was sparsely settled, and the farming land was excellent. Also, it was far enough from the seaports to escape the immediate influx of Gentiles. It furnished the possibilities of isolation and security with the advantage of easy access to the Sea—two important requirements. At that time Young intended to make San Bernardino a second Salt Lake City—that is, a gathering place for thousands of his followers who could best live under southern California conditions. It was to be the important outfitting post on the Pacific end of the "Mormon Corridor," that is, a line of towns connected by a good wagon road running from Salt Lake City to a sea port. By 1857 thirty communities had been established on this route.

Four years after San Bernardino was settled, Brigham Young strengthened the Corridor route by founding an outpost at Las Vegas Springs in southern Nevada. Since the stream of water from those springs made the only oasis for miles in that extremely arid region, Las Vegas was a frontier settlement of great importance.

Another project in connection with the Corridor route was Young's idea of navigating the Rio Colorado. He began investigating the river in 1855 with the idea of utilizing that stream for cheaper transportation of immigrants and merchandise into Utah Territory. Ten years later (1865) a church warehouse was built on the north bank of the river fifteen miles upstream from the present Boulder Dam, the site being named Call's Landing. Whether or not the Mormons would have made the Rio Colorado a practicable shipping route was never determined, for hardly had the warehouse been completed when their attention was turned to the transcontinental railway then under construction as a transportation agent.

The same year that Brigham Young sent settlers to Las Vegas (1855), he also dispatched missionary-colonists to Moab, located at an opening in the southeastern edge of the Basin. They built a fort near the Rio Colorado, thereby establishing another control settlement for the Mormon empire.

Outposts of marked importance were Fort Bridger and Fort Supply, Wyoming. In 1853, Governor Young sent Apostle Orson Hyde and other colonists to Wyoming for the purpose of purchasing and taking possession of James Bridger's property. Upon their arrival they were not able to find the old trapper but other mountaineers were residing in the vicinity of the fort. It seemed apparent that trouble would soon develop between those two antipathetic groups if the Mormons located at Fort Bridger. Therefore, Hyde took his followers twelve miles to the west and erected a station known as Fort Supply. Two years later the Mormons purchased and took possession of Bridger's property. Those two outposts were located at the eastern entrance of the Basin on the Mormon Trail where immigrating Saints could replenish their exhausted supplies preparatory to the last 125 miles of difficult mountain and canyon traveling.

The last outpost established in 1855 was Fort Lemhi, located on the Salmon River over 300 miles north of the Mormon Mecca, in what was then Oregon and is now northern Idaho. Thus Brigham Young had succeeded within eight years after arriving in the Great Basin in surrounding his commonwealth with control settlements.

Mormon Colonization from 1847-1857

While the Mormon outposts were being established, numerous towns were springing up on favorable sites on the canyon streams adjacent to Salt Lake Valley. Gradually one valley after another received its portion of colonists, the growth being mainly southward during the first period, as the climate in that direction was thought to be more favorable for agriculture than that north-ward. Consequently, in 1857 the community farthest north, excepting Lemhi, was only seventy-five miles from the parent colony. During the first ten years in the Basin, 100 towns were established. The settlements clustered mainly east and south of the Great Salt Lake, of the Jordan River, and of Utah Lake, with a line of communities running in a southwest direction from Juab County to the southwest corner of Utah. Besides these main groups of colonies, a number of Mormons were living in Sanpete County and in the outposts already discussed.

Thus within ten years after the Saints had arrived in the Great West, they had opened colonization activities in a frontier country extending 1,000 miles from north to south and 800 miles from east to west. Brigham Young's plan of preempting the West was being realized.

Mormon land settlement of the Great West under the direction of Brigham Young naturally divided itself into three periods of almost equal length—1847 to 1857, 1858 to 1867, and 1868 to 1877. The first period of colonization was suddenly halted temporarily by the coming of a federal army to Utah in 1857-58. Trouble between the United States government and the Mormons had been brewing since the appointment of the first federal officers for the newly organized Territory of Utah in 1851. It reached its climax in President Buchanan's order sending Albert Sidney Johnston and 2,500 soldiers to the West. When Governor Young learned that federal troops were en route to the Basin, not knowing what the outcome would be, he called the settlers at the outposts back to Utah. Fort Bridger, Fort Supply, Lemhi, Carson Valley, Las Vegas and San Bernardino were all abandoned, resulting in a contraction of the frontier and a reducing of the size of the Mormon commonwealth at the close of the first period of colonizing activities.

Mormon Colonization, 1858 to 1867

With the adjustment of the immediate difficulties between the United States and the Saints, Brigham Young resumed his colonial program with renewed energy and determination. The very first year after the lull in colonization proved to be, with one exception, the banner period in land settlement. Approximately thirty towns were established, two and one-half times the average number founded per year between 1847 and 1877. Slight advancement of the frontier was made in 1859, but new towns were begun near well-established colonies in order to strengthen the valleys centrally located.

In 1860 President Young again began to expand the frontier of his commonwealth. This time the extension of land settlement was much nearer the base of supplies than had been the policy ten years earlier. The expansion was more gradual and principally northward. The agricultural possibilities of northern Utah and southern Idaho had been demonstrated, and one typical Mormon community after another came into existence, until before the year ended the frontier was pushed as far north as Bennington in Idaho.

Also, other frontier districts of importance were opened to land settlements during the early sixties. Mormon towns dotted the Sevier River Valley from the Sanpete settlements to the source of the river. In southern Nevada along the Muddy River, four communities were founded, and three small villages came into existence north of the Rio Colorado in Arizona. Cotton was being raised in a few small towns in southern Utah. Desiring to strengthen that industry, Brigham sent Apostles Snow and Smith with 746 home builders to establish a city on the slope north of the junction of the Santa Clara and the Virgin rivers in Utah "Dixie." The city which they established was named Saint George.

A greater number of villages were founded in 1864 than in any other year while Brigham was at the helm, more than thirty being established. During the period of 1861 to 1868, over 20,000 European proselytes arrived in the Basin in search of new homes. These converts furnished Young with most of his material from which to build new communities. But as the contemplated transcontinental railroad came nearer to Utah, colonization activities slackened, with the result that there were only four new towns in 1866 and five in 1867, as compared to thirty-one in 1864. Thus the building of the railway marked the end of the second period of Mormon land settlement.

The colonizing activities during that period (1858-1867) resulted in the establishment of 135 towns, thirty-five of them in Cache, Box Elder, Bear Lake and Bear River valleys in northern Utah and southern Idaho. Twenty more were located on the Provo, Weber and Ogden rivers and adjacent canyon streams. The Sevier and Virgin rivers and other small streams from central to southern Utah supported forty-five new colonies. Several were located in southern Nevada, with three in Arizona north of the Colorado. The remaining twenty-six were in valleys previously settled.

From the time of the coming of the railway until Brigham's death, the founding of towns was carried on at the relatively even pace of about thirteen per year. However, in 1877, the year of his death, he planted twenty settlements—the greatest number during the third period.

COLONIZATION FROM 1868-1877

This last period (1868-1877) like the first (1847-1857) was one in which Young projected settlements far distant from Salt Lake City. New frontiers were opened. His activities at that time were centered mainly upon developing Arizona. In 1876 there were several groups located on the Little Colorado, and the following year he dispatched Mormons to the Gila River country. But before many Saints arrived in southern Arizona, the great Mormon Colonizer had died, after having successfully directed the establishment of over 360 settlements in the Great West. At least 127 of the number were founded during this last ten-year period. Besides building approximately twenty-five permanent settlements in Arizona, located from the extreme southern to the northern part of the state, the Mormons extended the line of land settlement outward in every direction in Utah and north and west in Idaho. Naturally, a few new communities sprang up in the sections of the country which had been previously colonized.

SUMMARY—A COMPARISON

During the thirty years of his residence in the Basin, the Mormon leader, Brigham Young, successfully founded and witnessed the development of communities in almost every valley of the present state of Utah, as well as many in southern Idaho, Arizona, and Nevada. Most of the towns built by the Mormons were within a rectangular district 500 miles long by 400 miles wide, omitting the Arizona settlements. However, some were as distant as 1,000 miles east of Salt Lake City in Iowa and Nebraska; San Bernardino was about 750 miles southwest of the parent colony, while Fort Lemhi was located in northern Idaho. The total Mormon population at the time of Brigham's death (1877) was approximately 140,000.

The magnitude of this achievement can best be understood by making a comparison between the accomplishments of Brigham Young and his people and those of Spain—one of the most successful of European colonizing countries during the early American

BRIGHAM YOUNG ABOUT 1875

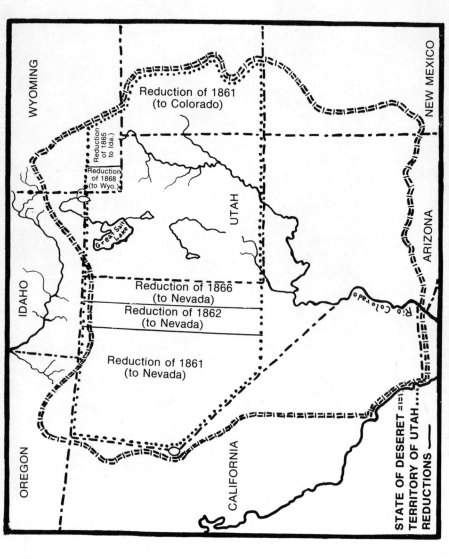

WYOMING

Reduction of 1861
(to Colorado)

Reduction
of 1865
(to Ida.)

Reduction
of 1868
(to Wyo.)

NEW MEXICO

Great Salt Lake

UTAH

IDAHO

Reduction of 1866
(to Nevada)

Reduction of 1862
(to Nevada)

ARIZONA

Rio Colorado

Reduction of 1861
(to Nevada)

OREGON

CALIFORNIA

Rio Colorado

STATE OF DESERET ▭▭▭
TERRITORY OF UTAH......
REDUCTIONS ▬▬▬

REDUCTIONS IN UTAH'S TERRITORY FROM 1849 TO 1868

colonial period. Of course due consideration should be made for the advantage that the Mormon land settlers had over the Spaniards in the improved facilities for transportation and communication and in not being separated from the last frontier by an ocean. Yet the fact that the king of Spain had at his command many thousands of subjects while Brigham Young had to glean proselytes from the world (even across the ocean) through the Mormon missionary system helps to balance the Mormon advantage.

Similar comparisons could be made between the Mormon land settlement and the colonizing activities of France or England during early American history. But none of these comparisons should be considered as absolutely scientific. The following one is presented merely to help make clear the part played by the Mormons in the opening of the Western Frontier.

Lopez de Velasco, official geographer of New Spain, described the Spanish colonization achievement in his report of 1574. "At that time there were in North and South America about 200 Spanish towns and cities, besides numerous mining camps, haciendas, and stock ranches. The Spanish population was 32,000 families, or perhaps from 160,000 to 200,000 persons."[3] Besides the Spanish population there were 40,000 negro slaves and approximately 5,000,000 Indians.

At the time of Brigham's death in 1877, exactly thirty years had passed since he entered the Basin at the head of his first company of Mormon pioneers. At the time of Velasco's report in 1574, eighty years of the most active period of Spanish colonization had gone by. There were over 360 Mormon towns thoroughly established with a total population of approximately 140,000 Saints,[4] while in Hispanic America there were about 200 Spanish towns with a total Spanish population of about 160,000 to 200,000 persons. When one considers that in approximately one-third of the time the number of Mormon towns was much greater and their population almost equal to that of the Spanish colonists, one is led to believe that Brigham Young as a colonizer has no peer in American history.

MORMON COLONIZATION IN MEXICO AND CANADA

But Mormon land settlement did not end with the death of Brother Brigham. Two more frontiers were opened by the Saints,

[3]Herbert E. Bolton and Thomas M. Marshall, *The Colonization of North America, 1492-1783* (New York, 1920), 75.
[4]Joseph Fielding Smith, *Essentials in Church History* (ed. 2. Salt Lake City, 1922), 567.

one in northern Mexico and the other in the Rocky Mountain section of Canada. The expanding of Mormon colonization to foreign nations was a direct result of the persecution inflicted upon the Saints by the United States government in accordance with the "anti-bigamy" laws of 1882 and 1887.

Many of the polygamists took their families and migrated southward to Mexico or northward to Canada where they were free from persecution. The refugees who fled southward settled in Sonora and Chihuahua. In the former state they founded Colonia Morelos and Colonia Oaxaca, while in the latter they established Colonia Diaz, Colonia Dublan, Colonia Juarez, Pacheco, Garcia and Chuichupa. The principal town established by those who fled to Canada was Cardston.

SUMMARY OF THE OUTSTANDING ACHIEVEMENTS OF BRIGHAM YOUNG THE COLONIZER

To summarize some of the outstanding achievements of the founder of Utah: Brigham Young led a persecuted, disheartened group of devout religionists into the center of an uninviting desert country which no other group of people would at that time consider occupying. There, with the helpful cooperation of his sturdy pioneer associates, he colonized an extensive territory. He sent out exploring parties to select favorable sites for the new colonies and often chose the sites himself. He sent balanced groups of industrial and agricultural workers to found these new communities. Brigham personally supervised the laying out of many of the towns into surveyed square blocks with wide streets and the alloting of farming lands and city lots to the Saints.

While he was founding colonies he also provided his followers with civil government, with social institutions for their education and enjoyment, and with the necessary equipment for their economic independence and prosperity. On March 12, 1849, he was elected the Provisional Governor of the "State of Deseret." The following year, September 28, 1850, Utah was made a territory with Brigham as the governor. This position he held until 1858, when he was replaced by Alfred Cumming. While acting as governor, as well as throughout his entire career in Utah as President of the Mormon Church, Brigham Young deserves much credit for the success of federal Indian agents, federal surveys across the Basin, the building of the transcontinental railway, and the construction of the telegraph.

All of the Mormon colonization accomplishments were made

SALT LAKE TEMPLE

SALT LAKE THEATRE, ERECTED 1862

possible partially by adding thousands of colonists to his ranks which he did by sending missionaries to various parts of the United States as well as to Europe, Canada, Hispanic America, India, Australia, and the Islands of the Pacific. He was able to fuse this heterogenous mass of humanity, representing several different races, into a harmonious social unit.

While building homes, developing farms and establishing themselves a government, the Mormon colonists did not neglect the finer side of life. Education, religion, art, drama, and music were fostered for the social development of the people. The Saints built their own theatres and trained their children in the various sciences and in music. Simultaneously with the erection of private dwellings, each group of colonists through cooperative effort constructed a public hall which was used as a church house, a school house, and a place in which dances and dramas were conducted. In October, 1847, the first pioneer group opened a school in an old military tent. Even while these frontiersmen were struggling to construct their first shelters in the Salt Lake Valley, this school was conducted daily. Only two years elapsed before Governor Young signed an act, passed by the first legislative Assembly of the State of Deseret, incorporating a university, later known as the University of Utah.

As early as 1850 the Salt Lake Musical and Dramatic Association was formed, conducting its earlier performances in the Temple Square Bowery. Later, 1852, the Social Hall was built. It was one of the first theatres erected west of the Missouri River. Ten years later the Salt Lake Theatre replaced the Social Hall. It was a remarkable building to be erected on the frontier so soon after the Mormons' arrival in the Basin. Mr. Leavitt concluded, in his *Fifty Years of the American Stage*, that "At the time of its erection, it was not surpassed in magnitude, completeness, and equipment by any other existing house."

Between 1863 and 1867 an unusual structure known as the Mormon Tabernacle was erected. It is elliptical in shape and the roof is a self-supporting wooden structure. Originally the building was fastened together without nails, wooden pins and rawhide being used in lieu thereof. The famous pipe organ was "the largest in the world when built."

But the most important edifice of all erected by the Mormon pioneers is the Salt Lake Temple. Only four days after the arrival of Brigham, he selected the site upon which to construct a house to the Lord. Those persevering frontiersmen hewed massive granite stones out of the mountains fifteen miles southeast of the city and dragged them to the temple site by slow-moving ox teams. Forty years and four million dollars were consumed in the construction of that edifice. A building which would be a credit to a far wealthier and older community of people majestically arose, with its six large towers pointing heavenward, as a monument to the church for which it was erected and to the faith of the people.

Throughout the thirty years, 1847-1877, of Brigham Young's residence in the Basin, he was always, if not the titular head, the actual head of his people. So broad and impressive was his work that practically every phase of Utah life at the present time bears the marks placed upon it by Brigham Young the Colonizer.

Following is a list of the towns established under Brigham Young's direction. The number indicates the location of the town on the corresponding map.

MORMON COLONIES, 1847-1857

1. Salt Lake City, July 24, 1847.
2. Bountiful, September 29, 1847.
3. Farmington, fall of 1847.
4. Parley's Park, fall of 1847.
5. Pleasant Green, fall of 1847.
6. Ogden, January, 1848.
7. Big Cottonwood, spring of 1848.
8. East Mill Creek, spring of 1848.
9. Sugar House, spring of 1848.
10. Centerville, spring of 1848.
11. Bingham, August, 1848.
12. Mound Fort, fall of 1848.
13. South Cottonwood, fall of 1848.
14. North Jordan, December, 1848.
15. West Jordan, December, 1848.
16. Kaysville, spring of 1849.
17. Provo, spring of 1849.
18. Genoa (Mormon Station), June, 1849.
19. Union (Little Cottonwood), 1849.
20. Lynne (Bingham's Fort), 1849.
21. Brighton, fall of 1849.
22. Granger, fall of 1849.
23. Draper, November, 1849.
24. Manti, November 22, 1849.
25. Tooele, fall of 1849.
26. Grantsville, fall of 1849.
27. Harrisville, spring of 1850.
28. Uinta (Easton), 1850.
29. Lehi, August, 1850.
30. Pleasant Grove, July, 1850.
31. Lake View, 1850.
32. Springville, September, 1850.
33. Payson, October 20, 1850.
34. Alpine, fall of 1850.
35. Spanish Fork, fall of 1850.
36. American Fork, fall of 1850.
37. Layton, fall of 1850.
38. Marriott, fall of 1850.
39. Slaterville, fall of 1850.
40. West Weber, fall of 1850.
41. Wilson, 1850.
42. North Ogden, fall of 1850.
43. Lindon, 1850.
44. Parowan, January 13, 1851.

45. Salem, spring of 1851.
46. Herriman, spring of 1851.
47. Brigham City, March 4, 1851.
48. Willard, spring of 1851.
49. Farr West, 1851.
50. Santaquin, summer of 1851.
51. San Bernardino, 1851.
52. Nephi, September, 1851.
53. Fillmore, October 28, 1851.
53a. Cedar City, November 11, 1851.
54. South Weber, November, 1851.
55. Midvale, fall of 1851.
56. Mona, December, 1851.
57. Pleasant View, fall of 1851.
58. Harper, spring of 1852.
59. Paragonah, spring of 1852.
60. Harmony, spring of 1852.
61. Cedar Valley, October, 1852.
62. South Hooper, 1852.
63. Batesville, 1852.
64. Mt. Pleasant, spring of 1852.
65. Spring City, 1852.
66. Butterfield, before 1853.
67. Ephraim, winter of 1852-53.
68. Perry, April, 1853.
69. Fort Supply, November 15, 1853 to October 3, 1857.
70. E. T. City, spring of 1854.
71. Crescent, 1854.
72. Wanship, 1854.
73. Santa Clara, December, 1854.
74. Clover, fall of 1854.
75. Peterson, 1855.
76. Fairfield, spring of 1855.
77. Las Vegas, 1855 to 1858.
78. Fort Bridger, 1855 to 1857.
79. Lake View, summer of 1855.
80. Pine Valley, 1855.
81. Holden, 1855.
82. Morgan, 1855.
83. Moab (Elk Mountain Mission), May 21, 1855.
84. Lemhi (Salmon River Mission), 1855 to 1858.
85. Beaver, February 6, 1856.
86. Franktown, 1856.

87. Wellsville, September, 1856.
88. Mapleton, 1856.
89. Pinto, fall of 1856.
90. Milton, 1856.
91. Washington, May 15, 1856.

92. Mendon, 1857.
93. Meadow, spring of 1857.
94. Peoa, 1857.
95. Goshen, 1857.
96. Gunlock, 1857.

MORMON COLONIES, 1858-1867

97. Heberville (Price), Jan. 13, 1858.
98. Toquerville, spring of 1858.
99. Virgin City, December 7, 1858.
100. Mountain Dell, 1858.
101. Harrisville, spring of 1859.
102. Charleston, spring of 1859.
103. Coalville, May 17, 1859.
104. Plain City, March, 1859.
105. Deseret, spring of 1859.
106. Logan, April, 1859.
107. Providence, April 20, 1859.
108. Minersville, May 17, 1859.
109. Harrisburg, spring of 1859.
110. Fountain Green, July, 1859.
111. Hoytsville, 1859.
112. Eden, 1859.
113. Henefer, 1859.
114. Richmond, July, 1859.
115. Kanosh, 1859.
116. Gunnison, 1859.
117. Millville, fall of 1859.
118. Moroni, 1859.
119. Cheney's Ranch, 1859.
120. Franklin, fall of 1859.
121. Mountain Green, 1859.
122. Smithfield, October, 1859.
123. Deep Creek, spring of 1859.
124. Heber City, spring of 1859.
125. Midway, spring of 1859.
126. South Jordan, March 1, 1859.
127. Fairview, 1859.
128. Grafton, December, 1859.
129. Scipio, fall of 1859.
130. Kamas, spring of 1860.
131. Spring Lake, spring of 1860.
132. Hyde Park, April, 1860.
133. Paradise, spring of 1860.
134. Hyrum, April, 1860.
135. Juab, 1860.
136. Richville, summer of 1860.
137. Avon, 1860.
138. Benjamin, 1860.
139. Rockport, August, 1860.

140. Center, 1860.
141. Adventure, 1860.
142. Harrisville (Weber), 1860.
143. East Porterville, fall of 1860.
144. Morgan, fall of 1860.
145. Huntsville, fall of 1860.
146. Greenville, February, 1861.
147. Little Cottonwood, 1861.
148. Porterville, spring of 1861.
149. Fayette, spring of 1861.
150. Enterprise, summer of 1861.
151. Mountain Dell (Utah), 1861.
152. Rockville, November, 1861.
153. Saint George, December 4, 1861.
154. Duncan's Retreat, 1861.
155. Echo, fall of 1861.
156. Shonesburg, January 20, 1862.
157. Coveville, 1862.
158. Croyden, 1862.
159. Vernon, April, 1862.
160. Hebron, April 27, 1862.
161. Wallsburg, 1862.
162. Northop, spring of 1862.
163. Adamsville, spring of 1862.
164. Springdale, fall of 1862.
165. Zion Park, 1862.
166. Tonaquint, evacuated 1862.
167. Mantua, spring of 1863.
168. Pipe Springs, 1863.
169. Belleview, spring of 1863.
170. Middletown, spring of 1863.
171. Spring Lake, 1863.
172. Petersburg, 1863.
173. Monroe, fall of 1863.
174. Salina, fall of 1863.
175. Paris, fall of 1863.
176. Glenwood, January, 1864.
177. Portage, spring of 1864.
178. Circleville, spring of 1864.
179. Joseph, spring of 1864.
180. Richfield, March 13, 1864.
181. Indianola, 1864.
182. Clinton, 1864.
183. Panguitch, March 16, 1864.

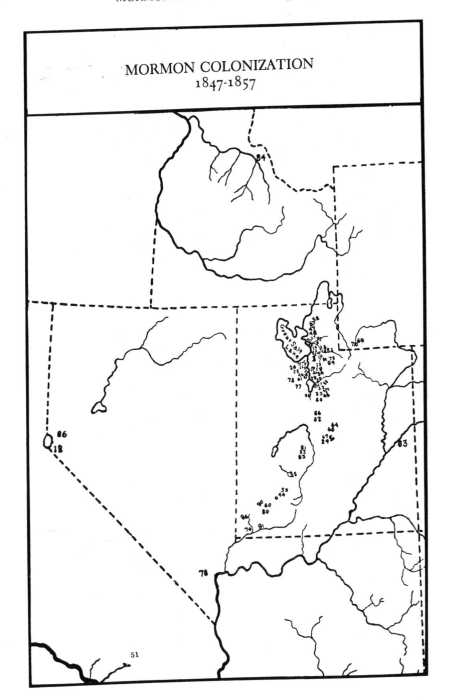

MORMON COLONIZATION
1847-1857

184. Woodland, April 15, 1864.
185. Malad, April, 1864.
186. Marsh, 1864.
187. Bloomington, April 22, 1864.
188. Montpelier, spring of 1864.
189. Fish Haven, spring of 1864.
190. Garden City, 1864.
191. Laketown, 1864.
192. Liberty, spring of 1864.
193. Ovid, 1864.
194. Saint Charles, spring of 1864.
195. Moccasin Springs, 1864.
196. Clarkston, 1864.
197. Glendale (Berryville), spring of 1864.
198. Bennington, spring of 1864.
199. Eagle Valley, July 7, 1864.
200. Mount Carmel, fall of 1864.
201. Easton, 1864-65.
202. Call's Landing, 1864.
203. Eden, 1864.
204. Littlefield (Beaver Dam), 1864.
205. Marysvale, October, 1864.
206. Oxford, fall of 1864.
207. Saint Thomas, January 8, 1865 to 1871. Resettled, 1881.

208. Overton, 1865 to 1871. Resettled, 1881.
209. Saint Joseph, 1865 to 1871. Resettled, 1881.
210. Logandale (West Point), 1865 to 1871. Resettled, 1881.
211. Simonville, 1865 to 1871.
212. Millpoint, 1865 to 1871.
213. Oak City, spring of 1865.
214. Alton, spring of 1865.
215. Pahreah, 1865.
216. Cherry Creek, spring of 1865.
217. Upton, 1865.
218. Woodruff, October, 1865.
219. Spring Valley, 1865.
220. Wardbaro, fall of 1865.
221. Bluffdale, December, 1865.
222. Port Sanford, spring of 1866.
223. Bear River City, January, 1866.
224. Panacca, 1866.
225. Mountain Meadows, n. d.
226. Honeyville, 1866.
227. West Point, March, 1867.
228. Leeds, fall of 1867.
229. Petersboro, 1867.
230. Saint Johns, fall of 1867.
231. Berryville, 1867.

MORMON COLONIES, 1868-1877

232. Alta, 1868.
233. Samaria, February 10, 1868.
234. Oakley, 1868.
235. Levan, spring of 1868.
236. Dayton, summer of 1868.
237. Treasureton, 1868.
238. Kanarraville, by 1869.
239. Newton, spring of 1869.
240. Saint John, spring of 1869.
241. Manila, 1869.
242. Skull Valley Indian Mission, 1869.
243. Eureka, 1869.
244. Quincy, 1869.
245. Meadowville, August 6, 1869.
246. Clifton, fall of 1869.
247. Fairview, fall of 1869.
248. Randolph, March 14, 1870.
249. Trenton, March 17, 1870.
250. Kanab, March, 1870.
251. Chester, June, 1870.
252. Cambridge, 1870.

253. Cannon, 1870.
254. Freedom, 1870.
255. Milford, 1870.
256. Hillsdale, 1871.
258. Georgetown, April 29, 1871.
259. Sandy, 1871.
260. Soda Springs, May 1871.
261. Johnson, spring of 1871.
262. Mound Valley, 1871.
263. Annabella, spring of 1871.
264. Moen Copie, 1871.
265. Pioche, 1871.
266. Mayfield, fall of 1871.
267. Vermillion, fall of 1871.
268. Leamington, fall of 1871.
269. Murray, 1872.
270. Lake Shore, 1872.
271. Preston, spring of 1872.
272. Central (Inverury), January, 1872.
273. Warrena, February, 1852.
274. Hatch, 1872.

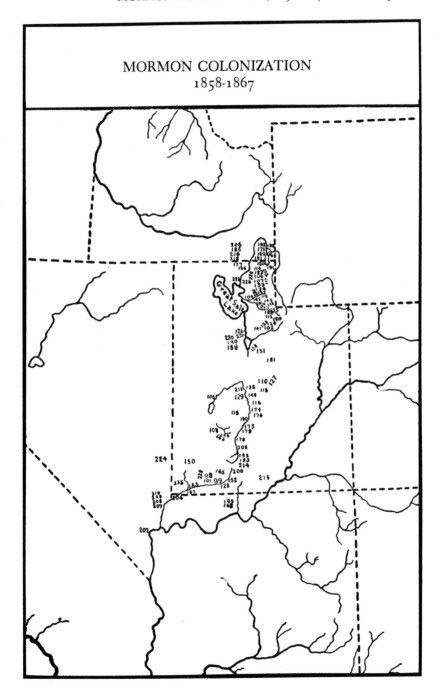

MORMON COLONIZATION
1858-1867

275. Lee's Ferry, 1872.
276. Mink Creek, 1872.
277. Riverdale, 1872.
278. Sterling, 1872.
279. Venice, 1873.
280. Pettyville, 1873.
281. Prattville, April, 1873.
282. Tuba, May 17, 1873.
283. Burrville, June 23, 1873.
284. Whitney, summer of 1873.
285. Bern, August, 1873.
286. Fort Cameron, September, 1873.
287. Elba, 1873.
288. Dingle, 1873.
289. Daniel, March, 1874.
290. Mount Trumbull, February 8, 1874.
291. Elsinore, spring of 1874.
292. Grass Valley, 1874.
293. Koosharon, August, 1874.
294. Cannonville, December 24, 1874.
295. Cleveland, December 8, 1874.
296. Woodland, fall of 1874.
297. Greenwich (Grass Valley), 1874.
298. Wales, n. d.
299. Deweyville, n. d.
300. Curley, n. d.
301. Aurora, March 25, 1875.
302. Redmond, spring of 1875.
303. Albin, May, 1875.
304. Snowville, n. d.
305. Escalante, June, 1875.
306. Orderville, spring of 1875.
307. Washakie (Indian farm), spring of 1875.
308. Nashville, 1875.
309. Mapleton, 1875.
310. Marion, 1875.
311. Mount Sterling, 1875.
312. Chesterfield, 1875.
313. Nounan, 1875.
314. Vineyard, 1875.
315. Argyle, 1875.
316. Fremont, spring of 1876.
317. Grouse Creek, spring of 1876.
318. Saint Joseph (Allen City), March, 1876.
319. Brigham City (Ballenger), March, 1876.

320. Thomas' Fort, 1876.
321. Hunter, 1876.
322. Sunset, March, 1876.
323. Obed, June, 1876.
324. Tonto Basin, July 17, 1876.
325. Timpanogos, 1876.
326. Mill Creek, 1876.
327. Kingston, fall of 1876.
328. Woodruff, December, 1876.
329. Ramah, winter of 1876-1877.
330. Bunkerville, January 6, 1877.
331. Garden Creek, March 21, 1877.
332. Saint David, March, 1877.
333. Benson, 1877.
334. Almo, 1877.
335. Syracuse, 1877.
336. Lanark, October, 1877.
337. Price, fall of 1877.
338. Huntington, fall of 1877.
339. Castle Dale, 1877.
340. Ferron, fall of 1877.
341. Lehi (in Arizona), 1877.
342. Papago, 1877.
343. Showlow, 1877.
344. Snowflake, fall of 1877.
345. Jenson, fall of 1877.
346. Mill, winter of 1877-1878.
347. Junction, before 1878.
348. Almy, before 1877.
349. Loa (Rabbit Valley), before 1877.
350. Mesa, January, 1878.
351. Taylor, January, 1878.
352. Forest Dale, February, 1878.
353. Pine Ward, 1878.
354. Conejos, 1878.
355. Los Cerritos, 1878.
356. Mountain Dell, February, 1878.
357. Merrill, 1878.
358. Burnham, 1878.

The colonies listed are those established in the Great West while President Brigham Young was directing Mormon land settlement. A few of them were settled after his death which occured on August 29, 1877, but those colonies were in Arizona and Brother Brigham had planned the project before his death.

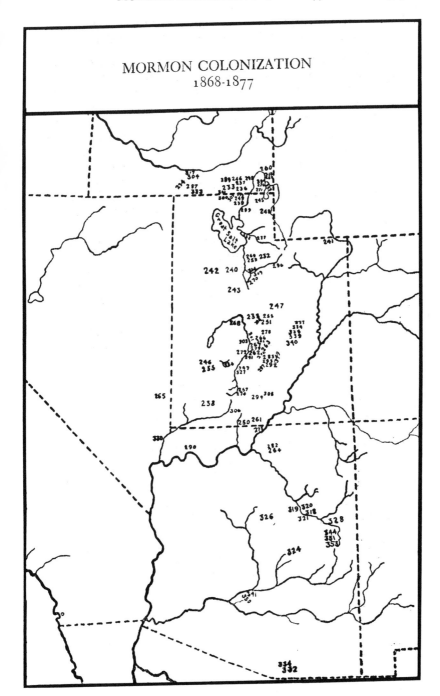

MORMON COLONIZATION
1868-1877

BIBLIOGRAPHY

I. BIBLIOGRAPHICAL NOTE AND MATERIALS MOST USEFUL IN PREPARATION OF THIS BOOK

1. *Bibliographical Note*—This book is based almost wholly upon manuscript materials found in the collection of the Church of Jesus Christ of Latter-day Saints in the Historian's Library, Salt Lake City, Utah, and in the manuscripts collected by Hubert Howe Bancroft and filed in the Bancroft Library, University of California. The writer has had access to both archives.

The manuscript collection in the archives at Salt Lake City is exceedingly voluminous. When the Mormon exiles first began their exodus to the West, Brigham Young instructed that in keeping with earlier Mormon practice a careful record must be kept of all activities and important sermons. Every pioneer company was to have an authorized camp historian who was to keep a minute record of all matters which would contribute to preserving an accurate and detailed history of the Saints. In the Great Basin each company of explorers and each group of colonizers had a regularly appointed historian who kept accurate records. Included in these records are minutes of all public meetings and copies of all important letters. The student is thus provided with a great deal of information pertaining to civil and religious life during Brigham Young's time.

The result is that at the present time the Historian's Library occupies several rooms in the Church Office Building, and a large staff is employed in compiling the records. There are in the collection the *Latter-day Saint Journal History*, the *Manuscript History of Brigham Young*, manuscript histories of all missions, wards, and stakes, complete sets of *Journal of Discourses, Millennial Star, Improvement Era, Contributors,* and all other Church publications. Also, all of the issues of *The Deseret News*, and most of the issues of *The Tribune* and other prominent Utah newspapers are in the Historian's Library. In fact, there are 500 volumes of private journals, 6,000 branch and mission record books, almost a complete file of *Congressional Records*, over 1,500 volumes of anti-Mormon books, two complete copies of everything published by the Church, and other books—in all, about 40,000 volumes compose the library of the Church.

2. *Latter-day Saint Journal History*—This record contains a daily report of the important events of the Church from its organization in 1830 to the present time. It includes transcripts from original documents of the Church, letters, diaries, exploration and other official reports, minutes of important Church meetings, and relevant newspaper reports. The collection is made up into large scrapbooks, with typewritten pages in loose leaf form. There are over one hundred volumes. They fill shelf space some six feet high by more than twenty feet long.

3. *Manuscript Histories of Stakes and Wards*—These manuscripts were second in usefulness in preparation of this book. This collection of important data includes transcripts from original Church documents, extracts taken from the *Latter-day Saint Journal History*, letters, newspaper reports, field notes of the assistant Church historian, Andrew Jenson, and other materials which present a rather full account of every settlement established by the Mormons after arriving in the Great Basin. There are approximately a hundred volumes in this collection, similar in size and composition to the manuscript history previously referred to.

4. *Manuscript History of Brigham Young*—It is the work of historians and scribes under the direction of Brigham Young who kept a contemporary record written in the first person as if Brigham had recorded it himself. The period covered is from 1844 to 1877, the time when Brigham was at the head of the Church.

5. *Letters on File in the Historian's Library*—A miscellaneous collection of letters and other original documents is alphabetically arranged in a filing case.

6. *Mission Manuscript Histories*—These volumes are similar to the manuscript histories of stakes and wards.

7. *Private Journals*—A number of extracts from private journals appear in this book.

8. *Journal of Discourses*—There are twenty-six volumes (Liverpool, 1854-1886) in this publication, containing hundreds of speeches given by President Brigham Young, his counselors, the apostles, and other Church leaders. These speeches supply an excellent historical source.

9. *The Millennial Star*—This publication was begun in England in 1840 and continued to the present time. It contains news items, instructions from Brigham Young and the other Church officials to the European Saints, items relative to doctrine and practices of the Mormons; therefore, it is of great value to the student of Mormon history.

10. *The Contributor*—This is another periodical which supplied historical data useful in the preparation of this book.

11. *Manuscripts in the Bancroft Library, University of California, Berkeley, California*—The archives at Berkeley contain approximately fifty manuscripts which deal with early Utah history and which have been used in the preparation of this volume. Because of their inaccessibility to the public in general those manuscripts will not be listed here.

12. *State of Deseret Documents—Laws and Ordinances of the State of Deseret, Compilation of 1851*—Reprint, Salt Lake City, 1919.

13. *Newspapers and Periodicals—*
Alta Californian, San Francisco, May 20, 1858.
Deseret News, Salt Lake City, 1850 to 1877.
Manti Sentinel, Manti, Utah, August 1, 1889.
New York Tribune, October 9, 1849.
Los Angeles Star, December 27, 1857.
Ogden Herald, December 27, 1919.
Tullidge, Edward W., ed., Quarterly Magazine, III (Salt Lake City, 1878).
The Utah Genealogical and Historical Magazine, XVII (Salt Lake City, January, 1926).

14. *Works Contemporary with Brigham Young—*
Bowles, Samuel, Our New West. Hartford, 1869.
Burton, Richard F., The City of the Saints and Across the Mountains to California. London, 1861.
Chandless, William, A Visit to Salt Lake City. London, 1857.
Ferris, B. G., Utah and the Mormons. New York, 1854.
Gunnison, John William, The Mormons, or Latter-day Saints, in the Valley of the Great Salt Lake. Philadelphia, 1860.
Howe, E. D., Mormonism Unveiled. Painesville, Ohio, 1834.
Hyde, John, Junior, Mormonism: Its Leaders and Designs. New York, 1857.
Kelley, William, Across the Rocky Mountains. London, 1852.
Linforth, James, Route from Liverpool to Great Salt Lake Valley. Liverpool, 1855.
Stansbury, Howard, An Expedition to the Valley of the Great Salt Lake. Philadelphia, 1855.
Stenhouse, T. B. H., Rocky Mountain Saints. New York, 1873.

15. *Unpublished Theses—*
Crook, John G., The Development of Early Trade and Industry in Utah. Thesis (M.S.)—University of Utah, 1926.
Fox, Feramorz Young, Mormon Land System. Thesis (Ph.D.)—Church Historian's Library, n.d.
Houston, Flora Belle, The Mormons in California, 1846-1857. Thesis (M.A.)—University of California, August, 1929.
Larson, Gustive O., History of the Perpetual Emigrating Fund Company. Thesis (M.A.)—University of Utah, 1926.
Malloy, William Doyle, Carson Valley, 1857-1860. Thesis (M.A.)—University of California, December, 1931.
Neff, Andrew Love, The Mormon Migration to Utah, 1830-1847. Thesis (Ph.D.)—University of California, May, 1918.
Olsen, Joseph William, Erastus Snow, Missionary and Pioneer. Thesis (M.S.)—Brigham Young University, 1935.
Romney, Thomas Cottom, The State of Deseret. Thesis (Ph.D.)—University of California, August, 1929.
Sutton, Susie, Historical Development of Utah, 1847-1850. Thesis (M.A.)
Snow, William James, The Great Basin Before the Coming of the Mormons. Thesis (Ph.D.)—University of California, December, 1923.

II. SUPPLEMENTARY READINGS IN MORMON HISTORY

1. *Special Studies—*
Allen, Edward J., *The Second United Order Among the Mormons.* New York, Columbia University Press, 1936.
Bennion, M. Lynn, *Mormonism and Education.* Salt Lake City, Deseret News Press, 1939.
Birney, Hoffman, *Zealots of Zion.* Philadelphia, Penn Publishing Company, 1931.
Cannon, Frank J., and Knapp, George L., *Brigham Young and His Mormon Empire.* Chicago, 1913.
Clemens, Samuel L., *Roughing It.* Hartford, Connecticut, 1891.
Crafts, Mrs. E. P. R., *Pioneer Days in San Bernardino Valley.* Los Angeles, 1906.
Creer, Leland Hargrave, *Utah and the Nation.* Seattle, University of Washington Press, 1929.
Egan, Howard R., *Pioneering the West.* Salt Lake City, Skelton Publishing Company, 1917.
Ellis, Charles, *Utah, 1847-1871.* Salt Lake City, 1891.
Erickson, Ephraim Edward, *The Psychological and Ethical Aspects of Morman Group Life.* Chicago, 1922.
Esshom, Frank Edward, *Pioneers and Prominent Men of Utah.* Salt Lake City, 1913.
Gardner, Hamilton, *History of Lehi.* Salt Lake City, Deseret News Press, 1913.
Geddes, Joseph A., *The United Order Among the Mormons.* Salt Lake City, Deseret News Press, 1924.
Golden, Frank A., *The Mormon Battalion.* New York, Macmillan Company, 1933.
James, George Wharton, *Utah, the Land of Blossoming Valleys.* Boston, 1922.
Lindsay, John Shanks, *The Mormons and the Theatre.* Salt Lake City, 1902.
Little, Jesse A., *From Kirtland to Salt Lake City.* Salt Lake City, Juvenile Instructor Office, 1890.
McClintock, James H., *Mormon Settlements in Arizona,* 1921.
McGavin, E. Cecil, *U. S. Soldiers Invade Utah.* Boston, Meador Publishing Company, 1937.
Raup, H. F., *San Bernardino, California: Settlement and Growth of a Pass-Site City.* Los Angeles, University of California Press, 1940.
Roberts, Brigham H., *The Mormon Battalion.* Salt Lake City, Deseret News Press, 1909.
Romney, Thomas C., *The Mormon Colonies in Mexico.* Salt Lake City, Deseret News Press, 1938.
Thomas, George, *The Development of Institutions Under Irrigation.* New York, Macmillan Company, 1914.
Tyler, Daniel, *History of the Mormon Battalion.* Salt Lake City, Juvenile Instructor Press, 1885.

Widtsoe, John A., *Priesthood and Church Government.* Salt Lake City, Deseret News Press, 1939.

Widtsoe, John A., *Principles of Irrigation Practice.* New York, Macmillan Company, 1914.

2. Biographies, Autobiographies and Journals—

Cannon, George Q., *Life of Joseph Smith.* Salt Lake City, Deseret News Press, 1907.

Clayton, William, *Journal.* Salt Lake City, Deseret News Press, 1921.

Evans, John Henry, *Charles Coulson Rich: Pioneer Builder of the West.* New York, Macmillan Company, 1936.

Evans, John Henry, *Joseph Smith, an American Prophet.* New York, Macmillan Company, 1933.

Gates, Susa Y., and Widtsoe, Leah B., *The Life Story of Brigham Young.* New York, Macmillan Company, 1930.

Hughes, Delila G., *Life of Archibald Gardner.* American Fork, Alpine Publishing Company, 1939.

Jenson, Andrew, *L. D. S. Biographical Encyclopedia.* Salt Lake City, Deseret News Press, 1901.

Little, James, *Jacob Hamblin.* Salt Lake City, Deseret News Press, 1909.

Cowley, Matthias F., *Wilford Woodruff.* Salt Lake City, Deseret News Press, 1909.

Nibley, Preston, *Brigham Young, the Man and His Works.* Salt Lake City, Deseret News Press, 1936.

Pratt, Parley P., *Autobiography.* Chicago, Law, King and Law, 1888.

Richards, Claude, *J. Golden Kimball.* Salt Lake City, Deseret News Press, 1934.

Roberts, Brigham H., *The Life of John Taylor.* Salt Lake City, George Q. Cannon & Sons Company, 1892.

Snow, Eliza R., *Biography of Lorenzo Snow.* Salt Lake City, Deseret News Press, 1884.

Werner, Robert Morris, *Brigham Young.* New York, Harcourt, 1925.

West, Franklin L., *Life of Franklin D. Richards.* Salt Lake City, Deseret News Press, 1924.

Whitney, Orson F., *Life of Heber C. Kimball.* Salt Lake City, Juvenile Instructor Office, 1888.

Young, John R., *Memoirs.* Salt Lake City, Deseret News Press, 1920.

3. Histories and Chronologies—

Alter, J. Cecil, *The History of Utah.* New York, The American Historical Society, 1932.

Bancroft, Hubert Howe, *History of Utah, 1540-1886.* Vol. XXVI, San Francisco, A. L. Bancroft and Company, 1889.

Berrett, William E., *The Restored Church.* Salt Lake City, The Deseret News Press, 1936.

Evans, John Henry, *History of Utah.* New York, Macmillan Company, 1933.

Evans, John Henry, *The Heart of Mormonism.* Salt Lake City, Deseret News Press, 1930.

Evans, John Henry, *One Hundred Years of Mormonism.* Salt Lake City, Deseret News Press, 1905.

Gottfredson, Peter, *History of Indian Depredations in Utah*. Salt Lake City, 1909.

Jenson, Andrew, *Church Chronology*. Salt Lake City, Deseret News Press. 1914.

Linn, William Alexander, *The Story of the Mormons*. New York, 1902.

Roberts, Brigham H., *A Comprehensive History of the Church*. 6 vols. Salt Lake City, Deseret News Press, 1930.

Smith, Joseph, *Documentary History of the Church*. 6 vols. Salt Lake City, Deseret News Press, 1902.

Smith, Joseph Fielding, *Essentials in Church History*. Salt Lake City, 1922.

Tullidge, Edward W., *Life of Brigham Young*. New York, 1876.

Tullidge, Edward W., *History of Utah*. Salt Lake City, Star Printing Press, 1886.

Tullidge, Edward W., *History of Salt Lake City*. Salt Lake City, Star Printing Press, 1886.

Whitney, Orson F., *Popular History of Utah*. Salt Lake City, Deseret News Press, 1916.

Whitney, Orson F., *History of Utah*. 4 vols. Salt Lake City, George Q. Cannon and Sons Company, 1892.

Young, Levi Edgar, *The Founding of Utah*. New York, Charles Scribner's Sons, 1923.

INDEX

Adams, Arza, early American Fork settler, 241.

Adams, William Henry, one of first settlers at Pleasant Grove, 244.

Allen, Daniel, murdered by Indians, 274.

Allen, Rufus, explored Colorado River in 1855, 86; president of Santa Clara Indian Mission, 322ff.

Allred, James, first settler of Spring City, 269.

Allred, James T. S., prevented Indian attack, 270; Indians worked for, 314; Las Vegas missionary, 345, 348.

Alta Californian, quoted, 87.

Alpine, founding of, 246.

American Fork, founding of, 241.

American Frontier, conditions of 2f.; process of, hypothesis of, 142.

American Indians, origin of, 311; Joseph Smith's attitude toward, 312; Brigham Young's attitude toward, 313ff.

Ames, Ira, early Utah tanner, 191.

Ammon, Chief Walker's brother, conducted supply train to Manti, 263.

Angatowata, Ute Indian, 230.

"Anti-bigamy Law" (1862), 141.

Arze-Garcia, expedition of, into Great Basin (1813), 21.

Ashley-Henry Fur Company, activities of, 23ff.

Astorian Fur Company, activities of, 22.

Babbitt, Almon W., delegate to Congress in 1849, 132.

Baker, Benjamin, quoted — asked Brigham Young for colonists for Grantsville, 257f.

Bancroft, Hubert Howe, quoted— Mormon missionary work, 14.

Basin, Mormons migration to, 13; roads and bridges built in, 80.

Battalion brought wagons over Corridor route in 1848, 73.

Battle Creek, Mormons and Indians, battle at, 243.

Beal, Samuel M., quoted—missionaries to marry Indian girls, 360.

Beatie, Hampton Sidney, established Mormon Station (Genoa), 273; quoted—lucrative trade, 274.

Beaver Valley, description of, 52; exploration of, 55.

Behunin, Isaac, first settler of Ephraim, 270.

Behunin, William, murdered by Indians, 341.

Benson, Ezra T., directed colonization of Tooele Valley, 61, 251, 256, 259; activities at Ogden of, 226.

Billings, Alfred N., president of Elk Mountain Mission, 337ff.; wounding of, 341.

Bishops, colonizing activities of, 63; duties of, 120f.; function of, in State of Deseret, 126ff.; controlled water utilization, 168.

Bolton, Herbert E., quoted—regarding Brigham Young, 8; regarding Great Basin, 10, 29; Mormons and building of railroad, 90; Mormon irrigation, 169.

Bonneville, Captain, expedition of, 27.

Book of Mormon, publication of, 2; Brigham Young's receiving of, 4.

Bountiful, founding of, 213.

Brannan, Samuel, urged Saints to go to California, 194; life of, 195.

Brandeburg, Chief Justice, left Territory of Utah, 134.

Bridger, James, Great Salt Lake discovered by, 25; opinion of Salt Lake Valley, 12, 31; property of, Indian troubles, 299; attempt to arrest, 300; surveying his land, 301; moved to Missouri, 301, 307; Brigham Young's first meeting with, 229.

Brigham City, leather industry in, 192; founding of, 291; molested by Shoshone Indians, 293; arrival of Lorenzo Snow at, 293; visit of Brigham Young at, 294; cooperation at, 295.

Bringhurst, William, president of Las
Vegas Mission, 83, 344ff.; trip to
California of, 348; quarrel with
Nathaniel V. Jones of, 351f.; dis-
fellowshiped from Church, 353.

British Northwest (Fur) Company,
activities of, 22f.

Brocchus, Justice, left Territory of
Utah, 134.

Brovitt, Captain, killed by Indians,
274.

Brown, James, trip to California in
1847, 37; Miles Goodyear's property purchased by, 219; first Mormon settler of Ogden, 220ff.; generosity of, 220f.; quoted, 195.

Brownsville (Ogden), founding of,
220ff.

Buchanan, President, "Expedition" to
Utah, 136ff; peace offered Mormons, 139.

Bullock, Thomas, quoted, 59; record-
ed allotments of land in Salt Lake
City, 152; quoted—description of
Utah Valley, 245.

Burgess, William, quoted—description of Indians at Salmon River
Mission, 253.

Burton, Richard F., quoted—description of Brigham Young in 1860, 16;
quoted—Mormon ecclesiastical government, 123f.

Cajon Pass, location of, 22.

California, possible location for Mormons' new home, 10; gold fields in,
12.

Call, Anson, early settler of Parowan,
53; Call's Landing established by,
88ff.; Fillmore founded by, 282ff.;
Harper founded by, 295; Indian
children adopted by, 316f.

Call's Landing, establishing of, 89ff.

Cannon, George Q., Mission to Hawaii and vision of, 96.

Carrington, Albert, Utah Valley
sighted by, 37; Clerk and historian,
124; constitution of State of Deseret drafted by, 128; assessor and
tax collector, 130.

Carson County, creation of, 276f.;
location of, visited by Mormon Bat-

talion members, 274; directed Mormon colonization of, 277ff.; Mormon's abandonment of, 279.

Carver, Thomas Nixon, quoted—Mormons as colonizers, 365f.

Cedar City, founding of, 200.

Cedar Valley, Johnston's army camped
in, 139.

Chalk Creek, Pratt's company wintered there in 1850, 49.

Charles III, king of Spain, 19.

Chipman, Stephen, early American
Fork settler, 241.

Chittendon, H. M., quoted—trappers
as explorers, 25.

Church Government, Latter-day Saint
system of, 118f.; efficiency of, 124.

Church of Jesus Christ of Latter-day
Saints, establishing of, 1; leaders of,
13.

Church Membership, in 1847, 13; in
1851, 14; 93.

City of Zion, plan of, 149.

Clay, Henry, Omnibus bill of, 132.

Cleveland, Grover, attitude toward
Mormons of, 141.

Colonization, people for, and extent
of plan, 13ff.; of California, 19;
purpose and methods of, 64ff.

Colony Sites, selection of, 52ff.

Colorado River, explorations of, 85,
86, 87f.; navigation of, 89; navigation project abandoned, 90.

Commerce, Illinois, site of, 5.

Congress, petitions to, 81f.

Connover, Peter W., captain of Fort
Utah militia, 235, 236.

Cooperation, in water utilization,
167f.; against the Gentiles, 180f.

Council Bluffs, Saints at, 11.

Cowdery, Oliver, Prophet's scribe, received Priesthood, 2f.; vision in Kirtland Temple, 4.

Creer, Leland Hargrove, quoted—
woman suffrage, 130.

Crickets, plague of, 221f.

Crosby, Jesse W., quoted—burning of
Fort Supply and Fort Bridger, 309f.

Cumming, Governor Alfred, second
governor of Territory of Utah, 133,
136ff.

Curtis, L. D., killed by Indians, 360.
Davis, William, first settler and bishop of Brigham City, 291.
De La Mare, Philip, sugar industry, 185.
De Smet, Father Pierre Jean, prophetic views of Great Basin of, 30f.
Deity, Brigham Young's faith in, 13.
Delaware-Cherokee Indian Mission, 319.
Deseret Iron Company, organizing and functions of, 73, 203ff.
Deseret Agricultural Manufacturing Society, establishing of, 179.
Dixie, 54; Footnote, 87.
Dominguez-Escalante Expedition, 19f.
Donner Party, route of, tragedy of, 29.
Douglas, Stephen A., presented State of Deseret memorial to Congress, 132.
Draper, founding of, 215.
Drummond, Judge William W., corruption and false accusations of, 135.
E. T. City, founding of, 258.
Edmunds Law (1882), 140.
Edmunds-Tucker Law (1887), 140.
Edwards, Edward, murdered by Indians, 341.
Egan, Howard, Corridor route traveler's guide of, 75.
Elk Mountain Mission, discussion of 337ff.; abandonment of, 342ff.
Emigration, beginning of British, 92f.; emigration 1850-1855, 103ff.; 1840-1855, statistics of, 105; 1856 statistics of 109; 1857-1860, statistics of, 115; handcart migration, 106f.; Church teams, 1861-1887, statistics of, 116ff.
Empire, Brigham Young's dream of, 13; gather Israel to, 93ff.
Ephraim, founding of, 270f.
Evans, David, first bishop of Lehi, 242f.
Evans, John Henry, quoted—Brigham Young's trip south, 15; description of Jacob Hamblin, 327.
Explorations, of Salt Lake and Tooele valley, 35ff; of Cache Valley, 36; of Utah Valley, 36f.; of northern route to California, 37f.; of southern route to California, 38f.; of Southern Exploring Company, 41ff.; of Beaver, Pauvan, and Dixie valleys, 50, 52ff.; of upper Sevier country and Weber and Provo rivers, 56ff.
Farnsworth, Philo T., early settler of Pleasant Grove, 244.
Farmington, founding of, 214.
Far West, Saints moved to, 9.
Farr, Lorin, activities of, in Weber Valley, 224ff.
Farr's Fort, erecting of, 224.
Fillmore, capital of Utah, 283; founding, naming, surveying and growth of, 284ff.; Legislature held at, 288; location of, 53.
Fillmore, Millard, Omnibus bill signed by, 132.
First Presidency, office and function of, 118f.; Brigham Young, president of, 125ff.
Fitzpatrick, Thomas, South Pass discovered by, 23.
Ford, Governor, frontier condition in Illinois described by, 3.
Fort Bridger, purpose of, 71f.; location of, 306; Mormons desired, 299ff.; purchase of, 306ff.; burning of, 309; federal army taking over of, 310.
Fort Lemhi, erecting and naming of, 358; Indians attacked, 361.
Fort Supply, purpose of, 72f.; founding of, 302ff.; sending assistance to handcart companies from, 305f.; burning of, 309.
Fort Utah, construction and description of, 231, 42.
Fox, Feramorz Young, quoted—Brigham Young's dream of an empire, 144f.; small farms, 145f.
Fox, Jesse W., surveying of: Tooele townsite, 255; Grantsville townsite, 257; Fillmore townsite, 285; Brigham City townsite, 291.
Fremont, John C., explorations of, 27f.; naming Humboldt River, official report of, 28.
Frost, Burr, blacksmithing of, 200f.

Galvez, Jose de, Visitador General of New Spain 19.

Gardner, Archibald, quoted—first sawmill in Utah, 183; early settler of Mill Creek, 214.

Gardner, Hamilton, quoted—description of Bishop David Evans, 241.

Gaunt, Matthew, first Utah manufacturer of woolen goods, 188.

Genoa, founding of, 273; surveying of, naming of, 277.

God, selected Basin for Saints, 13.

Goodyear, Miles, property of, 218f.

Goodyear Fort, location of, purchased by Mormons, 219f.

Great Basin, selected as home for Saints, 1, 10, 11, 62, 365, 66ff.; description of, 18, 124, 134, 136ff.; 29, 31; exploring of, 20ff., 22, 26ff., 34.

Great Salt Lake, discovery of, 24; exploring of, 25.

Grant, George D., Grantsville named after, 257.

Grantsville, founding of, 256ff.; naming of, 257f.

Green River Valley, location of, 299.

Guadaloupe Hidalgo, treaty of, 128, 132, 160.

Gunnison, John W., quoted—statement regarding Mormon Theo-Democracy, 128; murdering of, 240.

Haight, Hecter C., first settler of Farmington, 214.

Haight, Isaac C., quoted—description of Little Salt Lake Valley, 48; report on iron industry, 210.

Hambleton, Madison D., first settler of Mount Pleasant, 259f.

Hamblin, Jacob, Tooele settler, 258; Indian boy adopted by, 316; Santa Clara Indian missionary, 322ff.; made president of the mission, 326; description of, 326f.; narrow escape of, 327f.; conducted Gentile merchants to California, 328ff.; trips to the Moqui Indians of, 332ff.; circled Grand Canyon, 334; missionary success of, 335.

Hammurabi, irrigation practice of, 165.

Handcart Migration, Willie Company disaster, 111f.; Martin Company disaster, 111f.; summary of, 115, 116ff.

Hardy, Wiliam H., navigation of Colorado River, 90.

Harmony, Santa Clara Indian Mission at, 322.

Harrington, Leonard E., first bishop of American Fork, 341.

Harris, Secretary Broughon D., left Utah Territory, 134.

Harris, Major, opinion of Great Basin of, 31.

Harrison, President, proclamation of amnesty to polygamists of, 141.

Haskell, Thales H., Indian missionary, 324.

Hatch, Ira, Indian missionary, 323ff.; narrow escape of, 330; Muddy River Mission, 331ff.

Hennefer, William, Indian missionary, 323ff.

Hickman, William A., trading post on Green River of, 300; sheriff, probate judge, 307.

Higbee, Isaac, settler and president of Fort Utah, 230ff.

Higbee, John S., first president of Fort Utah, 230.

Hockaday, John M., Government surveyor, 301.

Holmes, Samuel Oliver, first settler of Kaysville, 214.

Holladay, John, first settler of Holladay, 214.

Homestead Act, terms of, 162.

Hooper, William, early settler of Alpine, 245.

Houston, Senator Sam, criticized Democratic administration for Utah War, 138.

Hudson Bay Company, activities of, 22f.

Hunt, James W., murdered by Indians, 340.

Hunt, Jefferson, trips from Basin to southern California, 38ff., 71f.; early settler of Fort Utah, 231, 233.

Hunter, Edward (Bishop), financial

director of Perpetual Emigrating Fund Company, 99ff.

Hunter, John D., assisted in bringing remains of George A. Smith, Jr., to Salt Lake, 334.

Huntington, Dimick B., Indian interpreter at Fort Utah, 230; Indian troubles in Pauvan Valley, 285.

Huntington, Oliver B., secretary of Elk Mountain Mission and Indian interpreter, 338ff., 341f.

Hyde, Orson, colonizing efforts of, 61; presiding in Pottawatamie country, 99; directed activities in Carson Valley, 277ff.; William B. Preston appointed to be bishop of Logan by, 297; directed colonizing of Green River Valley, 301ff.

Indian Policy, Joseph Smith's, 312; Brigham Young's 313ff.; American frontiersmen's, 313; Indian missions, 318ff.

Indian Mission, Delaware-Cherokee, 319f.; Skull Valley, 320f.; Santa Clara, 322ff.; Elk Mountain, 337ff.; Las Vegas, 344ff.; Salmon River, 357ff.

Industries, Mormon, 173ff.; early Utah, 175ff.; manufacturing, 177f., 183; sugar, 185ff.; sawmills and gristmills, 183; cotton, 187; wool, 188; agriculture, 188ff.; leather, 190ff.; iron, 194ff.; development of, at Provo, 239; at Manti, 266f.

Israel, doctrine of gathering of, 92ff.

Ives, Lieutenant J. C., explorations of the Colorado of, 86.

Jenson, Andrew, quoted—statistics on emigration, 1840 to 1855, 106.

Johnson, Aaron, early settler of Springville, 244.

Johnson, Joel H., taught Indians, 314f.

Johnson, Luke S., settler at Clover, 259.

Johnston, General Albert Sidney, at Fort Bridger, 138, 310; camp established in Cedar Valley by, death of, 139, 294.

Jones, Nathaniel V., early Utah tanner, 191; efforts to mine lead of, 349ff.; quarrel with William Bringhurst of, 351.

Judd, Zodoc K., cotton gin of, 187.

Kane, Thomas L., 55, 134; mediation of, during Utah War, 138.

Kanosh, good Indian chief, 228, 283f.

Kaysville, founding and naming of, 214f.

Kimball, Heber C., trip south, 53; counselor in First Presidency, 125f.; chief justice in State of Deseret, 130; portioning of land by, 150.

Knowleton, Quincy, early settler of Alpine, 245.

Kirtland, Ohio, 3, 365.

Lake, W. Bailey, killed by Indians, 363f.

Larson, Gustive O., quoted—handcart migration, 105, 116.

Las Vegas, settletment of, 83.

Las Vegas Mission, location and purpose of, 344; founding of, activities at, 345ff.; abandonment of, 354ff.

Laws, irrigation laws, 171f.

Lawyers, lack of, 121f.; Brigham Young's opinion of, 122.

Leavitt, Dudley, narrow escape of, 330.

Lee, John D., explorations of, 54; founding of Harmony by, 322.

Lee, William, president of Skull Valley Indian Mission, 320f.

Lehi, founding of, 242ff.

Lemon, William M., surveyed Manti, 265.

Little, Jesse C., explored Cache Valley, 36; stage route of, 80.

Logan, founding of, 297.

Lunt, Henry, quoted—iron works at Cedar City, 201.

Lyman, Amasa M., directed colonization of San Bernardino, 61, 90; Carson Valley visited by, 274.

Margetts, Richard, molasses mill of, 187.

Magrow, W. F., false charges of, 135.

Manti, founding of, 250ff.

Martin, Edward, handcart company disaster, 111ff.

Mary's Vale, described, 44.

Mattinger, Bannock Indian, 251f.

Maughan, Peter, first settler of E. T. City, 258; founder of Wellsville, 296f.

McBride, George, murdered by Indians, 361.

McBride, James, early settler of Grantsville, 362f.

McKenzie, Donald, Snake River expedition, 1819-1820, 23.

Mead, Elwood, quoted—irrigation law of 1852, 171.

Mendon, New York, home of Brigham Young, 4.

Mendon, Utah, founding of, 296.

Mercer, John, early settler of Pleasant Grove, 244.

Merrill, Marriner W., colonizing efforts of, 61.

Mill Creek, founding of, 214.

Millard County, creation of, 282; naming of, 284.

Miller, Henry W., mission to Cherokee Indians of, 319.

Miller, James, killed by Indians, 362.

Miller, William, early settler of Springville, 246f.

Milton, founding of, 259.

Missions, opening of L. D. S., 94ff.

Missionary work, world-wide program of, 68; Church's teachings regarding, 14, 70.

Missouri, attempt to build Zion in, 3ff., 365; trouble there, 4f.

Morley, Isaac, first settler of Manti, 41, 135ff.; baptized Chief Walker, 137; quoted—letter to Brigham Young, 139.

Mormons, migration of, 13; water policy of, 164; beginning of Anglo-Saxon irrigation by, 165; purpose of colonization 156; summary of colonization of, 365ff.; land policy of, 291, 345; trouble with Missourians, 5; temporary pause at Council Bluffs of, 30; secure necessities of life, 12; faith of, 366.

Mormon Battalion, service of, 11; gold discovered by, 194.

Mormon Colonization, summary of, 365ff.

Mormon Colonizer, 12, 53, 58, 70, 74.

Mormon Corridor, 71ff.; definition and purpose of 70, 72, 283; development of, 75; transportation and communication on, 80ff.; Mormon colonies along, 76f., 83; Colorado River transportation and, 85ff.

Mormon Empire, efforts to build, 68, 69ff.; 174f.

Mormon Grove, 103.

Mormon Mecca, 52, 56, 63, 71f., 78f., 90, 92.

Mormon Outpost Settlements, 71ff., 75, 367ff.

Mormon Station, founding of, 273ff.

Mormon Tabernacle, description of, 375.

Mormon Theo-Democracy, discussion of, 118ff.

Mormonism, truthfulness of, 13.

Moroni, appearances to Joseph Smith of, 2.

Mott, Israel, early settler at Mormon Station, 277.

Mount Pleasant, founding of, 269f.

Mulliner, Samuel, first Utah tanner, 190f.

Murdock, John, proselyting in Australia, 97.

Nahraguts, Indian guide, 332.

Nauvoo, naming and growth of, 5, 365; charter of, 6; trouble at, 7; preparation to leave, 10; exodus from, 11.

Navajo Indians, threatened Jacob Hamblin, 327f.; George A. Smith, Jr., murdered by, 333f.

Nebeker, John, whipping post, 125; early settler of Fort Supply, 301.

Nelson, Lowry, quoted — frontier opinion of free land, 147; City of Zion, 149, 156.

Neff, John, first gristmill in Utah, 183f., 214.

Ogden City, founding of, 223, 365; Lorin Farr, president of, 224; naming and growth of, 226f.; 23; trappers' rendezvous at, 25.

Ogden, Peter Skeen, explorations of, Ogden City named after, 23.

Old Spanish Trail, location of, 344, 283, 27.

Overland Route, trade on, 300.

Pace, James, founder of Payson, 248f

Pah-van-te, tribe of Indians, 281, 284.

Palmyra, New York, 37.

Palmyra, Utah, founding of, 249f.

Parowan, naming of, 54, 200; founding of, 199ff.

Pauvan Valley, description and location of, 52, 55, 283f.

Paxson, Frederic L., quoted—frontier opinion on free land, 147.

Payson, founding and naming of, 248f.

Perpetual Emigrating Fund Company, establishment of, 98ff.; operations of, 101ff.; dissolving of, contributions of, 70, 15, 116f., 140.

Peterson, Canute, early settler of Lehi, 240f.

Pinto Indians, industry of, 54.

Pioneer Company, westward trek, 31.

Pleasant Grove, founding of, 243.

Plural Marriage (polygamy), political issue in 1856, 136; "Anti-bigamy Law" (1862), 139; Edmunds and Edmunds-Tucker Laws, 140; Manifesto, 140f.

Powell, John W., attack on Fort Lemhi, 361.

Pratt, Addison, description of southern route to California, 39f.; mission of, 94.

Pratt, Orson, vanguard company of, 31, 33ff.; exploration of Salt Lake Valley, 34; missionary work of, 98; Perpetual Emigrating Fund and, 100f.; surveying of Salt Lake City by, 149; first Mormon irrigation, 166.

Pratt, Parley P., exploring of Utah Valley by, 37; leader of the Southern Exploring Company, 41ff.; Hispanic-American mission opened by, 96; quoted — Mormon Theo-Democracy, 126f.

Pre-emption Act, terms of, 161.

Presiding Bishopric, functions of, 119f.

Preston, William B., first bishop of Logan, 297.

Priesthood, restoration of, 2; rights of, 123.

Provo, founding and growth of, 238ff.; woolen mills, at, 188.

Provot, Etienne, attack by Indians, 24.

Pugsley, Phillip, early Utah tanner, 191f.

Quincy, Josiah, quoted—statement regarding Joseph Smith, 6.

Rancho del Chino, Hunt's party at, 73.

Reese, Enoch, early Spanish Fork land owner, 249.

Reese, John, activities at Mormon Station, 275.

Religion, potent force of, 13; cause of Mormon migration, 13.

Resurrection Camp, 50.

Reynolds, George, polygamy test case of, 139f.

Rich, Charles C., settled San Bernardino, 61, 103; chief military commander, 124.

Rigdon, Sidney, vision of degrees of glory, 4.

Richards, Franklin D., directing emigration from Europe, 107; founded Deseret Iron Company, 203ff.

Richards, Willard, counselor in First Presidency, 126; secretary of State of Deseret, 130.

Rockwell, Orrin Porter, Indian troubles, 254.

Roberts, Brigham H., quoted—Brigham Young's policy on domestic manufacturing, 179.

Rowberry, John, quoted — Indian troubles in Tooele Valley, 255; first president of Tooele, 253.

Rush Valley, settlement of, 259.

Saint George, naming of, 62; founding of, 87.

Saint Johns, founding and naming of, 259.

Saints, migration of, 10ff.

Salmon River Mission, discussion of, 357ff.; location and purpose of, 357; founding of, 358ff.; abandonment of, 362ff.

Salt Lake City, site selected, 34; laying out of, and portioning out land at, 148ff.; land office at, 162; State of Deseret organized at, 128; leather industry at, 190ff.; colonial laboratory, 366, 212; description of

(1849), 215f.; seat of government moved from Fillmore to, 288.

Salt Lake Temple, construction of, 375.

Salt Lake Theatre, erection and description of, 375; pictures of, 376.

Salt Lake Valley, bareness of, 11; crop failure in, 12; Mormons entered, 31ff.; explorations of, 34ff.

San Bernardino, location and settlement of, 73, 96, 76ff.; gathering place for Saints, 79; abandonment of, 84f.

Santa Clara Indian Mission, discussion of, 322ff.

Santa Clara Valley description of, 324; flood in, 335.

Santa Fe, road, trade, 21f.

Seagulls, crickets destroyed by, 221f.

Sessions, Perrigrine, first settler of Bountiful, 213.

Severe, Harrison, early settler of Grantsville, 256f.

Sevier River, explorations of, 56ff.

Sherwood, Henry G., surveying Salt Lake City, 149; surveying Willard and Brigham City, 290f.

Shoemaker, Theophilus, killed by Indians, 263.

Shoshone Indians, molested settlers at Brigham City, 291; Salmon River Mission attacked by, 361.

Skull Valley Indian Mission, discussion of, 319ff.

Smith, George A., 52; colonizing efforts of, 61; quoted—free land, 150; Parowan founded by, 199ff.; in Utah Valley, 239f., 248f.; quoted— build forts, 317; quoted—description of Fort Supply, 304.

Smith George A., Jr., killed by Indians, 333ff.

Smith, J. W., quoted—narrow escape from Navajo Indians, 327f.

Smith, Jedediah S., member of Ashley-Henry Co., 24; explorations of, 25f.; death of, 26.

Smith, John C. S., superintendent of Deseret Iron Company, 205.

Smith, Uncle John, first president of Salt Lake Stake, 124.

Smith, Joseph, visions of, 1ff.; published Book of Mormon, received Priesthood, organized Church, 2f., 119, 311; tarred at Hiram, 4f.; plan of City of Zion, 4, 149; built Nauvoo 5f.; literary accomplishments of, 6; persecutions of, martyrdom of, 2, 7; doctrine of gathering of, 92; Indian policy of, 312.

Smith, O. K., disastrous trip through Death Valley, 74.

Smith, Thomas S., activities at Salmon River Mission, 357ff.

Snow, Erastus, colonizing accomplishments of, 61ff.; entrance into Salt Lake Valley of, 33; mission to Scandinavia of, 96f.; quoted—immigration instructions, 103; Deseret Iron Company established by, 203ff.

Snow, Lorenzo, mission to Italy of, 94; cooperative system of, 192. 296f.; presiding at Brigham City, 292ff.; quoted—description of reception given Brigham Young, 292f.

Snow, William J., 21.

Social Hall, erection of, 374.

South Pass, discovery of, 24.

Southern Exploring Company, 41ff.

Sowiette, Chief, Indian attack prevented by, 238.

Sowiette Park, location of, 238.

Spaniards, irrigation practices of, 165.

Spanish Fork, founding and naming of, 249ff.

Spanish Missionaries, Basin visited by, 19.

Spencer, Orson, president of European Mission, 93.

Spring City, founding of, 268; Indian troubles at, 269.

Springville, founding of, 247f.

Stakes, description of, 120; functioning of first Utah stake, 124.

Stansbury, Captain Howard, quoted— Mormon-Theocracy, 127, 131f.; quoted — Mormon cooperation, 153; survey of Great Salt Lake by, 251.

State of Deseret, extent of, 71; courts

of, 127f.; founding, officers, and constitution of, 127ff.

State House, construction of, picture of, 286.

Stiles, Judge George P., corruption and false accusations of, 135.

Sugar House, naming of, 186.

Supply City, founding of, 306; burning of, 308.

Sutter's Mill, discovery of gold at, 194.

Tabernacle, description of, 375.

Tabian, Chief Walker's brother, 263.

Taylor, John, mission to France and Germany of, 95; quoted—Mormon methods of land settlement, 158f.; establishing beet sugar industry, 185; death of, 140.

Temple Block Public Works, purpose of, 176f.

Temporary High Council Abroad, 121.

Territory of Utah, creation of officials of, 132f.

Thatcher, Hezekiah, early settler of Logan, 297.

Theocracy, Utah established on principles of, 1.

Thomas, George, quoted—Mormons obtaining land titles, 163.

Timpanogos, mountain, 228; river, 230.

Tolman, Cyrus, early settler of Tooele, 251.

Tolman, Judson, early settler of Tooele, 251.

Tooele, derivation of name, 234; founding of, 251ff.

Toquer, Indian chief, 323.

Traveling High Council, functions of, 119.

Trueworthy, Thomas E., navigation of Colorado River, 94.

Tresedor, Charles M., quoted—arrival in Salt Lake of first handcart company, 110.

Tullidge, Edward W., quoted—Brigham Young, 8; quoted—bishops, 63.

Tut-se-gab-its, Santa Clara Indian Chief, 325.

Twain, Mark (Samuel L. Clemens),

quoted—description of Brigham Young, 60.

Twelve Apostles, list of, colonizing activities of, 60ff.; office and functions of, 119.

Tyler, Daniel, quoted—Saints not going to gold fields, 197.

University of Deseret, founding of, 375.

United States Government, Mormons' trouble with, 83, 134ff.

Utah, statehood of, 141.

Utah Forty-Niners, discussion of, 194ff.

Utah Territorial Legislature, land laws of, 160ff.

Utah Valley, exploration of, 36f.; description of, 228; colonizing of, 228ff., 238ff.

Utah War, 83f., 137ff.

"Valley-tan," meaning of, 193.

Vancott, John, marshall, 124.

Vasquez, Louis, bill of sale of Fort Bridger, 307.

Velasco, Lopez de, Spain's colonizing achievements, 373.

Virgin River, exploration of, 55.

Wolfskill, William, 22.

Walker, Chief, requested Sanpete Valley to be colonized, 41, 260; suffering of, 261f.; baptism of, 245; visited by Parley P. Pratt, 43; threatened to attack Mormons, 238.

Walker, J. R., trip to California of, 27.

Walker War, 207, 240, 245, 248, 267ff., 299.

Wards, description of, 120.

Washington, founding of, 187.

Water, limiting factor in land settlement, 145f., 120, 166; policy of, 164ff.

Watts, B. H., messenger from Fort Lemhi to Brigham Young, 362.

Weber Valley, settlement of, 366ff.

Wellsville, founding of, 295f.

Werner, Morris Robert, quoted—estimate of Brigham Young, 138.

Widtsoe, John A., quoted—founding of modern irrigation, 165.

Willard, founding of, 290.

Willie, Captain James G., handcart
disaster of, 111ff.
Willis, William, mission to India, 95.
Winter Quarters, Brigham Young's
letter from, 10f.
Woman Suffrage, in Utah, 129.
Woodruff, Wilford, quoted—conditions in Weber Valley, 226f.; Manifesto issued by, 141f.
Young, Brigham, birth of, joined
Church, an apostle, 4; moving of
Mormons from Missouri by, 5; a
colonizer, 8; 59f., 61f.; trouble at,
Nauvoo, the exodus, 9f.; letter from
Winter Quarters of, 10f.; crossing
plains, 11, 30ff.; requesting Saints
to remain in Basin, 12; humility and
faith of, 13; "This is the Place!"
19, 34, 68, 194ff.; explorations of,
35, 41, 53; Perpetual Emigrating
Fund Company, 14, 98ff.; methods
of land settlement of, 15, 143ff.;
199, 201, 209, 229ff.; 245f., 260,
265, 277f., 305; land policy of,
146ff.; small farms, 154; farm-village system, 156; early ideas on
irrigation of, 166; selecting sites
for: Ogden City, 222ff.; Manti,
265; Provo, 238; Fort Utah, 232;
Fillmore, 283; Fort Lemhi, 359ff.;
Mormon Empire, plan of, 68ff.,
144; descriptions and estimates of,
8, 16, 60, 141; Corridor project of,
75ff., 86ff., 93; gatherings of Israel,
94ff.; relationship to the handcart
migration, 100ff.; home industry,
173ff., 184, 187ff.; leather industry,
190f.; leather factory of, 192; building telegraph line, 84; political activities of: creating State of Deseret, 128ff.; elected governor, 130;
appointed governor of Territory of
Utah, 132; replaced by Governor
Cumming, 133, 139; report to federal government, 134; Utah War,
137; quoted—letter to Thomas L.
Kane regarding Pauvan Valley, 55;
creating Millard County, 282;
quoted—why capital at Fillmore,
286; quoted—moving of seat of
government to Salt Lake City, 288;
opinion of lawyers of, 122; outpost settlements of, 267ff., 84, 279,
354, 362; reception at Brigham
City, 292f.; sustained President of
Church, 125f.; powers of, as President of Church, 119; released President Bringhurst, 352ff.; mining
policy of, 194ff., 198ff., 203, 243,
349; iron industry, 206; quoted—
conditions at iron works in 1855,
209; Indian policy of, 311ff., 233ff.,
339f.; Indian missions created by,
319ff., 332ff., 337ff., 344ff., 357ff.;
quoted—appointing of Jacob Hamblin, 326; instructing Hamblin to
visit Moqui Indians, 332ff.; visit to
Santa Clara of, 335; to build forts,
317; quoted—battle with Indians at
Fort Utah, 236; quoted—Indian
troubles at Tooele, 254; first meeting of James Bridger and, 229; desiring Bridger's property, 299; purchasing of Fort Bridger, 306; colonies visited by, 251, 265; achievements of Brigham Young as a
colonizer, 372ff.
Young, Ewing, trip across Basin in
1821, 22.
Young, Mrs. Harriet, first impression
of Salt Lake Valley, 11.
Young, Levi Edgar, estimate of Jedediah S. Smith, 26f.; quoted—Old
Spanish Trail, 283.
Zion, attempted to build, 4; Basin
ideal place for, 93; immigration to,
99f.; hoped to build, 365.
Zion's Cooperative Mercantile Institution, establishing of, 181; reasons
for, 193.